BUNKER'S WAR

BUNKER'S WAR
The World War II Diary of Col. Paul D. Bunker

Paul D. Bunker
Edited by Col. Keith A. Barlow, U.S. Army

PRESIDIO

Grateful acknowledgment is made to the following for permission to reprint copyrighted material:

On Active Service in Peace and War, by Henry L. Stimson. Copyright © 1948 by Henry L. Stimson and McGeorge Bundy. Copyright renewed 1976 by McGeorge Bundy. By permission of HarperCollins Publishers.
Corregidor: The Saga of a Fortress, by James H. Belote. Copyright © 1967 by James H. Belote and William M. Belote. By permission of HarperCollins Publishers.
Battles Won and Lost: Great Campaigns of World War II, by Hanson W. Baldwin. Copyright © 1966, 1994 by Hanson W. Baldwin. By permission of HarperCollins Publishers.
Ten Men Escape From Tojo, by Melvin H. McCoy and S. M. Melnick. Copyright © 1944. By permission of Henry Holt and Company.
Great Mistakes of the War, by Hanson W. Baldwin. Copyright © 1950 by Hanson W. Baldwin. By permission of Curtis Brown Ltd.

Published by Presidio Press
505 B San Marin Drive, Suite 300
Novato, CA 94945-1340

Library of Congress Cataloging-in-Publication

Bunker, Paul D. (Paul Delmont), d. 1943
    Bunker's war: the World War II diary of Col. Paul D. Bunker / Paul D. Bunker; edited by Keith A. Barlow.
        p.   cm.
    Includes bibliographical references.
    ISBN 0-89141-538-6
    1. Bunker, Paul D. (Paul Delmont), d. 1943—Diaries. 2. World War, 1939–1945—Campaigns—Philippines—Corregidor Island. 3. United States. Army. Coast Artillery Regiment, 59th—History. 4. World War, 1939–1945—Personal narratives, American. 5. World War, 1939–1945—Prisoners and prisons, Japanese. 6. United States. Army—Biography. 7. Prisoners of war—Philippines—Diaries. 8. Prisoners of war—United States—Diaries. 9. Corregidor Island (Philippines)—History, Military. 10. Soldiers—United States—Diaries. I. Barlow, Keith A. (Keith Andrew), 1932-   .
II. Title.
D767.4.B86   1996
940.54'1273—dc20   95-4511
                                                                                              CIP

Printed in the United States of America

*To all those American Fighting Men and Women,
living and dead, who suffered unbelievable horrors
as prisoners of war and who maintained their integrity, courage,
and honor not only for themselves but for
their country.*

PREFACE

The Bunker diary first came to my attention in 1955, when as a cadet at West Point, I noticed a reference to it in a volume of the United States Army Historical Series: *The War in the Pacific*. Ten years later, as an instructor at the Military Academy, I happened across a dusty manuscript of yellowing rice paper. The cramped handwriting was barely legible. But the story those faded words told was interesting, and I couldn't put the book down. Within those brittled pages I found an almost unbelievable, detailed account of the siege of Corregidor and the subsequent experiences of a POW in the hands of the Japanese.

I told Tom Russell, the Rare Book Custodian at West Point, that this volume should be published for all the world to see. It shouldn't be available just for scholars to take out of it what they want; Bunker's tale should be told in his own words. Tom told me it was all mine, and with a word of encouragement said, "Go to it!" Thus, after writing Colonel Bunker's son, LTG William B. Bunker, for permission to edit the diary, and after obtaining an enlarged photostatic copy of the diary from Tom, I was ready to work. However, Uncle Sam had other plans for me, and I was off to Vietnam.

On my return trip to the States, I flew over Corregidor and was reminded of the important project that I wanted to complete, and yet, being a Regular Army Officer, I had little free time to accomplish such a task. Fortunately, however, I found myself attending the Marine Corps Command and Staff College, which graciously allowed me time to complete the editing job as fulfillment of their student requirement for a research project. In addition to my indebtedness to the Command and Staff College, I am particularly grateful to my faculty adviser, Lt. Col. C. C. Zimmerman, for having faith in the final fruition of the project and for his very able counsel. The Office of Military History unselfishly provided me with many of the documents for the diary. I am indebted to Col. Ty Wilson of the Virginia Military Institute who connected me to some excellent leads. I thank Dr. Maurice Matloff in the Office of Military History and Dr. Stanley Falk of the United States Industrial College for their professional guidance in the editorial approach to the diary.

I am also indebted to the following for their unfailing responsiveness in providing materials: Mr. Aimone of the West Point Library; and Kerry Strong of the USMC Command and Staff Library.

In addition, I am obligated to Pat Vono, who graciously assisted me in the original job of transcribing the manuscript. Thanks to Nancy Willets, Debbie Sheheen and all in Skills Unlimited for making the manuscript computerized for publication. There are others who encouraged me over the years. Most recently one of the former POWs, Monk Riggins, and his wife, Annie, encouraged me to bring the project to fruition when I had slowed down. Most of all, I owe my thanks to my wife Kay, my children Andy, Maryann, and Betsy, and my cousins Chuck and Joanne Plaehn, who during my moments of great frustration, encouraged me to complete the diary.

An Explanatory Note
Readers should be aware of the following editorial policies:

• Editorial comments are found in endnotes.

• Lost material, or parts that are illegible, mutilated, or vague and cannot be reconstructed have also been endnoted or put within brackets.

• Material intentionally deleted by Colonel Bunker is omitted.

• Some minor punctuation has been added to improve the readability of the diary; otherwise the typeset book is almost a direct transcription of Colonel Bunker's own handwriting.

• Periods of time not covered by Colonel Bunker have been reconstructed and are duly noted. It should be noted, however, that the book is not typeset line for line with the original diary.

• Part and chapter divisions are purely editorial. In the original diary, there were no divisions other than the daily divisions noted, and page numbers were in the margin. The latter were omitted.

INTRODUCTION

This diary tells the story of the last few days before the fall of Corregidor in World War II and the many long days of imprisonment for its American defenders. But more than that, it is a visit into the mind of a gallant American soldier of the Old Army. Certainly Col. Paul D. Bunker had no idea that his writings would be published for the world to read; but, as the reader will see, this is an excellent reason for their publication. Bunker's words are real, without vanity, without deceit. They are the words of a professional soldier struggling for life amid death and for dignity amid depravity.

Paul Delmont Bunker had been noticed early in life as an outstanding individual. As a cadet in Douglas MacArthur's class at West Point, he was chosen by Walter Camp as an all-American football player for two successive years, in 1901 as a tackle and in 1902 as a halfback. For some fifty years only Bunker and one other individual held that dual honor on the record books. Throughout his life, Bunker maintained his versatility and competitive spirit.

After graduation in 1903, Bunker followed the pattern of most regular officers in the peacetime army, moving frequently and attending many schools. His duty stations for his first five years of service included Fort Constitution in New Hampshire and Key West Barracks in Florida. At the latter he fell in love with and married Leila "Landon" Beehler, the daughter of a navy rear admiral. Landon bore him two sons and a daughter, Paul D. Jr., William B., and Priscilla. Paul Jr. graduated from West Point in 1932 and lost his life only six years later in an aircraft accident in Hawaii. William B. graduated from the academy in 1934 and later retired from the army as a lieutenant general. I met him in 1968, a year before he died. Priscilla married one of Bill's classmates, Thompson Brooke Maury III, who was taken prisoner on Bataan and was later killed when his prison ship was sunk by U.S. planes on 15 December 1944.

Bunker's first tour on Corregidor was with the 59th Coast Artillery Regiment in 1915. From there he was given command of the New Orleans Quartermaster Depot. However, his patriotism and sense of duty during World War I would not allow him to remain in a noncombat assignment, so he voluntarily transferred back to the coast artillery. During the war, he trained and organized the 41st Coast Artillery, which he took to combat in Europe. There he was rapidly promoted to colonel.

After the signing of the armistice, there followed a long series of assignments for Bunker. He commanded Fort Amador, Panama, until 1921; then tours along the Eastern seaboard followed rapidly: Pennsylvania, Coast Artillery School, Command and General Staff College, four years in the historical section of the

Army War College, and commands of the harbor defenses of Boston and Fort Totten.

Bunker returned to the Philippines for a second time and commanded the 59th Coast Artillery until 1937, when he returned to the States and was assigned to the organized reserves in California. In 1940, with war brewing in the Far East, Bunker volunteered to return to his beloved 59th Coast Artillery on Corregidor. He and his wife, Landon, stayed on Corregidor together until the War Department ordered all dependents evacuated. Landon departed Manila for the United States aboard a ship in the middle of May 1941. Bunker stayed on Corregidor until 6 May 1942, the day he personally lowered the Stars and Stripes on Corregidor and raised the white flag of surrender.

Before Colonel Bunker burned the American flag he had hauled down, he cut a portion of it out and sewed it under a patch on his khaki shirt. Later he was thrust into a prison hospital beside Col. Delbert Ausmus. Bunker told him about the patch, and they pulled it out and divided it. If he died, Bunker wanted Ausmus to carry his portion to the secretary of war. Ausmus agreed, and when Bunker died of starvation just two weeks after his last entry in the diary, Ausmus got Bunker's portion of the flag and the diary. He kept both pieces and the diary until his repatriation on 9 November 1945.

After his return to the States, Ausmus promptly presented the fragment of the flag to the Secretary of War, Robert P. Patterson. Today that piece of bunting from the American flag and the original diary are on loan from West Point touring the presidential libraries in tribute to Bunker and all others who fought or gave their lives in defense of Corregidor and the United States in World War II.

PRELUDE TO PART I

On 8, 9, and 10 December 1941, the Japanese effectively isolated the Philippine Islands from the United States through coordinated attacks on Pearl Harbor, Guam, and Wake. The attack on Pearl Harbor destroyed the Pacific Fleet's striking force and erased its capability to aid the Philippines. At the same time, closer to and west of the Philippines, the Japanese stormed the beaches in Malaya. On the tenth, they made their first landings in the Philippines at Aparri and Visan in northern Luzon. Within three days, they had surrounded the Philippines on three sides and had gained a foothold there. More than that, they had destroyed the U.S. offensive capability in the Pacific.

On the eighth, in bombing attacks on Clark Field and other fields in the Philippines, the Japanese destroyed 50 percent of the Far East Air Force, which "had been designed as a striking force to hit the enemy before he could reach the Philippine shores."[1] The active defense of the Philippines had rested with the U.S. aircraft, but by the afternoon of the eighth that hope was gone. This left the Asiatic Fleet as their final hope.

With the loss of the majority of U.S. aircraft, Admiral Hart, commander of the Asiatic Fleet, realized that without air cover the fleet would be vulnerable. He felt he should salvage as much of the fleet as he could for the defense of the Malay Barrier; therefore, he ordered all of the fleet south except for two damaged destroyers, a few PT boats, twenty-seven submarines, and various small craft. Thus, by 15 December, the U.S. forces in the Far East had nothing but a handful of aircraft, some submarines, and MacArthur's ground forces to prevent any further Japanese landings in the Philippines.[2]

On 12 December, the Japanese had landed unopposed at Legaspi,[3] thus giving them, in addition to an airfield, control of the straits between Luzon and Samar. In so doing, they split the Philippines and placed Manila in a vise.

In order to prevent reinforcements from Allied bases in the south and to cut the last American route of withdrawal, the Japanese landed in force on 20 December at Davao and on 24 December at Jolo Island in the southern Philippines.

Meanwhile, on 22 December 1941, the Japanese tightened the vise on MacArthur's Luzon forces by landing against light opposition at Lingayen Gulf some 100 miles north of Manila. On the twenty-third, MacArthur ordered the majority of his forces to withdraw to the Bataan Peninsula with Wainwright fighting delaying action near Lingayen until the other forces could establish defensive positions on Bataan.[4] Two days later, the pressure on U.S. forces was again heightened; the Japanese landed only sixty miles south of Manila at Siain, Atimonan, and Mauban. Christmas

Eve arrived with General Homma, commander of Japanese forces in the Philippines, establishing his 14th Army Headquarters ashore north of Manila at Bauang. "The Japanese were . . . in the Philippines to stay,"[5] and it would be just a matter of time until the Japanese seized Manila and attacked Corregidor.[6]

On Christmas Eve 1941, war had not yet substantially affected Corregidor. Her defenders had little idea that she was surrounded with no hope for relief. Occasionally the troops had observed numerous V's of Japanese aircraft flying south like migrating geese. They had responded to some twenty air-raid alarms without a single bomb being dropped. Light action had occurred on 8 and 20 December when high-flying bombers were taken under fire by the 3-inch AA batteries. Unfortunately, the planes flew too high. The first "kill" of the war came on 13 December, when the AA gunners brought down one enemy bomber out of a flight of seventeen.[7] Outside of this one action, there had been no war on Corregidor. The men were passively active, however, for they bolstered their defenses and restored their supplies and ammunition.

No bombs or shells had fallen on Corregidor. The men knew nothing of the violence about them in Bataan other than the occasional overflights made by the Japanese bombers and fighters. Now and then the distant roar of artillery could be heard coming from Bataan. The troops on Corregidor still ate regular meals, men played poker in the evenings, and the officers had their nightly cocktails.

During the morning hours of 24 December 1941, Col. Paul D. Bunker, commander of the seaward defenses of Corregidor, probably enjoyed changing into his freshly laundered uniform, as was his daily habit. He was still living up to his reputation for "spit and polish." To the enlisted men and junior officers, he appeared to walk at attention as he made his daily inspection of the various batteries under his command.[8] During the afternoon, he undoubtedly watched the interisland steamer *Mayan* evacuating President Quezon and High Commissioner Sayer with their families and staffs to Corregidor.[9]

As Christmas Eve night wore on, Bunker could have witnessed the great flames of the navy's burning fuel dump across the bay. Earlier that day, "over 1,000,000 gallons of fuel had been fired."[10] Just before midnight, Bunker undoubtedly saw MacArthur's USAFFE staff in ships, silhouetted against the fiery shore, making their way to Corregidor in "great disorder and excitement"[11] as they evacuated Bataan. Later, during the early morning hours after Bunker had retired, Admiral Rockwell and his naval district staff arrived on Corregidor accompanied by 900 men of the 4th Marine Regiment, which was now attached to the army for tactical employment.[12]

Meanwhile, MacArthur's northern Luzon force and his southern Luzon force were both attempting to withdraw into Bataan under heavy pressure from Homma's forces driving south and north in a gigantic pincers threatening Manila.[13]

MacArthur, realizing the dangerous position Manila was in, had ordered the evacuation of the city the night before Christmas. The following day, in order to prevent key installations and supplies from falling into the hands of the Japanese, U.S. forces began the systematic destruction of those facilities. All day long, Marines installed "improvised 300-pound mines"[14] around the naval base at Olongapo near Subic Bay. In the bay, they scuttled the old armored cruiser *Rochester.* At the same time, other Marines destroyed the naval base at Cavite; they blew up ammunition and even sank a disabled submarine.[15] To the north of Corregidor, the coast artillery defenses at Fort Wint in Subic Bay became untenable; consequently, MacArthur ordered its commander, Col. Napolean Boudreau, to abandon the base and turn his troops over to Wainwright on Bataan. Boudreau evacuated most of the guns that were movable. The fixed artillery that was too cumbersome he rendered inoperable. After his troops joined the forces on Bataan, he assumed command of the coast artillery base at Fort Frank in Manila Bay.[16]

Heavy traffic carrying supplies and ammunition from Manila to Bataan formed a continuous moving arc along the northern shore of Manila Bay. But, for some unknown reason, the numerous Japanese aircraft overhead failed to strafe this bumper-to-bumper traffic.

Christmas night was one of great violence. From the north, heavy artillery could be heard. From Manila and Cavite, the men on Corregidor could hear the demolitions doing their work. A burning French ship floated listlessly between Corregidor and Bataan.[17] Later in the evening, Bunker probably saw the last sea voyage of the submarine tender *Canopus* as she steamed out of the bay.[18]

On 26 December, Manila was declared an "open city." According to MacArthur, "Manila, because of the previous evacuation of our forces, no longer had any practical military value."[19] The port was still denied the Japanese as long as Corregidor, guarding the entrance to the harbor, was in U.S. hands. All day the population of Manila streamed from the city in long, slow-moving columns that wound back into the mountains where the native villages lay. That night, the blackout of Manila was over; the city was once again "ablaze with light."[20] Late on the twenty-sixth, Marines from Colonel Howard's 4th Marines "made the seven and a half mile voyage from Mariveles' docks to North Dock on 'the Rock.'"[21]

On 27 December, the remainder of the 4th Marines, some 125 officers and 1,400 men, landed on Corregidor. Colonel Bunker reinforced the 4th Marines with his own 75's and 155's.[22] By this time, the coast artillery Command and the harbor defense of Manila Bay were commanded by Maj. Gen. G. F. Moore. Under him were the following commanders and their units:

Col. Samuel L. Howard, Beach Defense Command
  4th Marines
Col. Paul D. Bunker, Seaward Defense Command
  59th Coast Artillery Regiment (U.S.) (less Battery I)
  91st Coast Artillery Regiment (Philippine Scouts) (less Batteries C and E)
  92d Coast Artillery Regiment (Philippine Scouts)
  1st Coast Artillery Regiment (Philippine army)
Col. Theodore M. Chase, Antiaircraft Defense Command
  60th Coast Artillery Regiment (U.S.)
  Battery I: 59th Coast Artillery
  Battery C: 91st Coast Artillery
  Battery E: 91st Coast Artillery[23]

Evidently, the Japanese flying over Manila on the twenty-seventh were unaware that the city was "open," because "for three hours at midday, successive waves of unopposed bombers . . . wrought great destruction on port installations and buildings."[24] And yet they still avoided bombing Corregidor. By midnight on the twenty-eighth, Corregidor, or "the Rock," as it was later called, had had twenty-eight distinct false air-raid alarms. The men had grown accustomed to their sound and had grown tired of unnecessarily diving for shelter.

Thus on the twenty-ninth, when the air alarm sounded, "most of the men paid scant attention."[25] It was not until the AA opened fire that the troops ran for shelter. Some eighty-one medium bombers and ten dive bombers attacked the island for two hours. When the last 300-pound bomb had been dropped and the last Japanese plane had flown away, the Americans and Filipinos crawled out of their tunnels and discovered that the real war had finally come to Corregidor.[26] The Japanese had finally given the tiny island a thorough lacing. Dive bombers had strafed the AA positions. The station hospital, with its huge Red Cross on the roof, was the first of many permanent structures hit that day. Nearly every one of the utility lines had been disrupted. Meanwhile, however, the battle was not all one-sided; the AA had knocked down nine medium bombers and four dive bombers. That day the defenders lost twenty-two killed in action and eighty wounded in action.[27]

Prior to this raid many of the gunners were reluctant to dig holes or provide themselves with overhead cover, but no urging was required to get them busy after the raid. "Units all over the island began digging tunnels for added safety." Before the campaign was to end, hundreds would owe "their lives to those tunnels."[28]

Because of the devastating effect of the bombing, USAFFE headquarters went underground the very next day. The spacious location in the concrete building at Topside had to be abandoned for the closer but safer confines of Malinta Tunnel. Because of no active Japanese aircraft over the Rock on the thirtieth, time was made available to inaugurate Mr. Quezon as the president of the Philippine commonwealth in a small ceremony in front of the east portal of Malinta Tunnel.[29]

Very light enemy air activity occurred on 31 December and 1 January, resulting in one "low flying fighter being shot into the sea."[30] It wasn't until 2 January, the date Manila was occupied, that the Japanese aircraft "came back in force."[31]

Japanese bombers, taking advantage of a low ceiling on the second, dropped "through the clouds letting go wherever they happened to be," and disappeared into the safety of the "clouds again."[32] This day Fort Drum received its first baptism of fire when the Japanese bombed it with a secondary effort.[33]

The heavy bombing Corregidor received on the second was but a prelude to five days of continuous air raids, which covered nearly every square foot of the island with craters or fragments. Now let us relive those ensuing days through Col. Paul D. Bunker's own words.

Notes

1. Louis Morton, *The Fall of the Philippines,* United States Army in World War II series (Washington, D.C.: Office Chief of Military History, 1953), 88.

2. Ibid., 97.

3. Douglas MacArthur, *Reminiscences* (New York: McGraw-Hill, 1964), 123.

4. James H. Belote and William M. Belote, *Corregidor: The Saga of a Fortress* (New York: Harper and Row, 1967), 38.

5. Morton, *Philippines,* 144.

6. Ibid.

7. Belote and Belote, 41.

8. Ibid., 68.

9. Morton, *Philippines,* 164.

10. Ibid.

11. Belote and Belote, 43.

12. Col. William C. Braly, "Corregidor—Name, Symbol, Tradition," *Coast Artillery Journal* 90 (July–August 1947), 6.

13. Col. Stephen M. Mellnik, "The Life and Death of the 200th Coast Artillery," *Coast Artillery Journal* 90 (March–April 1947), 5.

14. Lt. Col. Frank O. Hough, Maj. Verly E. Ludwig, and Henry I. Shaw, *Pearl Harbor to Guadalcanal,* Vol. 1 of *History of U.S. Marine Corps Operations in World War II* (1958), 168.

15. Ibid.

16. Braly, 6.

17. Lt. Col. Allison Ind, *Bataan: The Judgement Seat* (New York: Macmillan, 1944), 188.

18. Ibid., 175–78.

19. MacArthur, 126.

20. Morton, *Philippines,* 232.

21. Hough, Ludwig, and Shaw, 168.

22. Braly, 6.

23. Ibid., 4.

24. Morton, *Philippines,* 234.

25. Belote and Belote, 49.

26. Braly, 6.

27. Ibid., 6, 7.

28. Belote and Belote, 53.

29. Morton, *Philippines,* 482.

30. Belote and Belote, 53.

31. Morton, *Philippines,* 482.
32. Braly, 4.
33. Morton, *Philippines,* 482.

Wednesday? or Saturday, 3 Jan, 3rd Bombing of Corregidor!

Awoke early and went down to C1 and relieved the watch officer. Breakfast and then to G/91 for bath and shave as usual. On way back, dropped in at Crockett and, when I got to Geary they sprang the usual air alarm on us which usually occurs when that lone Jap observation plane comes over every morning,[1] thus wasting an hour. All clear at 9:46 and barely got to Regtl. HQ when the new Malinta Hill siren blew again. Bought toothpaste and shaving cream in the heap of ruins which was once our post exchange. Drove to my quarters for Kleenex and bookcase. Lunch at Wheeler. Went to C1 and, as all was quiet, went to my dugout to arrange its contents, when Wham-o! She started! this was our 2d dose of Jap bombing, composed of 4 courses across the Rock—said to be by 2 flights of 6 and 8 planes respectively, some of them the largest of the Jap bombers.

At 12:33 the alarm sounded—after we could hear the planes! the first lot of bombs dropped at 12:35, then a few AA [antiaircraft] shots, then a string of about 18 bombs close together. Could hear them swish about 5" before they hit. Planes came over again at 12:39 but could hear no bombs. I phoned C1 and (probably) Hawes said they landed "between C1 and B/60," showing he was terrified, because I later found that none landed very near us—though they sure *felt* close. Heard planes coming again at 12:50 and our AA opened fire 1½ minutes later; seemingly far off and only a few rounds (or it might have been bombs) then more AA. B/60 opened at 12:56 for about 15 rounds, then a distant battery, then B again. Then I heard the planes and Swish—Boomity—Boom! the bombs arrived at 12:58, about 18 of them and very strong, especially 1 of them. The dull drone of the planes continued, instead of fading out as usual. B/60 opened at 1:01, then another battery or two, as the drone became louder. Then the usual "Swish—Boomity—Boom" at 1:03. This was the 3d trip across. Then everything was quiet except for the sounds of the bursts of the AA shells.

A few distant AA bursts at 1:11 and B/60 (near us) opened at 1:12, with the planes barely audible in my dugout. The bombs, fewer than before, fell at 1:13. B/60 ceased fire at or before the initial whistle of the bombs—showing that they were taking cover. This was the 4th and last trip across us. All clear sounded at 2:00 P.M. Visited C1 and as I was going to my car, there was another short alarm, evidently false, which ended in a few minutes.

Got in my car for a tour of inspection, especially since we could get no communication with Cheney. Arrived at barracks at 2:35 and what a scene of devastation met the eye! Huge patches of corrugated roofing missing and scattered in painfully distorted shapes all over front and rear parades. Practically every shell window in the barracks blown out, leaving gaping square empty openings. Capt. Julian[2] met me and smilingly reported, "Colonel, I have no office now." A huge bomb had landed just across the car track in rear of his place and blew out a crater 25' deep and 40' across, cutting rails and trolley wires and shattering every window on rear face of barracks. A smaller direct hit on B/59 mechanic shop, where the mechanic had practically finished making me a filing cabinet! Our Regtl. Workshop and Topside Checker burning fiercely and, of course, no water at Topside! One could see, from the direction of the wind, that it would also burn the other buildings, including the "Spiff Bar" [the local officers' club]—as it later did. I went up into my library and found utter chaos. Glass case containing my shell collection blown to smithereens and thousands of books littering the floor everywhere, even some outside! Going downstairs I found soldiers already looting the PX like ghouls. Reported this to HD HQ [harbor defense headquarters] and stationed a sergeant off the Hyde as guard temporarily. This morning Cooper had acquired for us several of Buster's chairs and cushions. I drove with Simmonds[3] and Edison[4] on a tour, after picking up my camera and taking picture of barracks, then to Club where we waxed sentimental over the ruins of the place of happy memories for all of us. Then looked at work on C1 Bombproof which is mighty slow, because of fear on part of workmen. To Hearn and viewed damage of two direct hits on gun platform. Looks bad but may get gun working soon. Many craters near by, and road to NCO [noncommissioned officers'] Club impassable. Then to Cheney and Glassburus' AA battery. An MG [machine gun] here had a bomb burst within 20' of it, a big one, yet no man was hurt. An MG nest at Hearn had a 2' round rock land in the middle of it, yet nobody was scratched. Men at Cheney digging a tunnel and I made Steiger send a squad to barracks to prevent fire from RSO [regimental supply office] shop spreading to barracks. Chow at Hearn. Then to C1 to check up on things. Drove to my quarters for tobacco and found my quarters hit at last. In the desk I noticed fragments of the window shells ("Capiz") on dining room floor; they came from the back door transom. As I neared the front door, the dirt on the floor increased. Went out on front porch and saw that the NE bedroom window was out and standing lamp upset. No holes in porch so, on going out to front walls, found where one bomb had exploded at base of our coconut tree, about 50' from quarters and another 8' further away, across the sidewalk. Craters about 4'–6' deep. They sure had thrown debris at my quarters And to think that about 5 months

Saturday, 3 Jan 1942 (continued)
ago, Landon[5] and I really enjoying this porch and revelling in its comfort and beauty—now it is so dirty and dreary and desolate. All doors were forced open by the blast and bang hollowly in the breezes.

Before dark I drove down with Edison, who is now sporting Major's leaves, and Simmonds, who is now wearing Lt. Col.'s silver leaves. To the entrance of our proposed Bombproof for C1 and found the progress very disappointing because the Filipinos run like hell at every air alarm.

This evening, when I came on duty we couldn't get Col. Hopkins[6] at Hughes because he was down on the wharf, concerning a condenser to save water from his steam pump. Meanwhile his fort was not being well run. I bawled him out on the phone and chased him up to his station.

"Daisy May," the pet deer, is still alive. Saw her today, browsing at Hearn and eying Colin[7] speculatively.

Books I want to read:

Almanac for Moderns, by D.C. Peattie
The War of Lost Opportunities, by Gen. Hoffman
A Book of Food, by P. Morton Shand
Salsbury Tales, by Christina Stead
American Renaissance (Literary Criticism) by F.O. Matthiessen
A Study of History, by Toynbee
Death of the Heart (Novel) by Elizabeth Bowen
The Managerial Revolution, by Jas Burnham
Isabella, by Keats—Praised by Arnold
America's Growing Pains, by Geo. R. Leighton
Lucinda Matlock and Ann Rutledge, by Edgar Lee Masters
Caleb Catlum's America, by Vincent McHugh
New York (City?) Panorama, WPA Project
Technics and Civilization, by Lewis Mumford
The Culture of Cities, by Same

What a desolate sound is corrugated iron, rattling in the wind that soughs through an empty and ruined barracks!

Sunday, 4 Jan 1942

Bombing of Corregidor.

"There is no excellent beauty that hath not some strangeness in the proportion."—Bacon

Got up at 3:00 A.M. and relieved Maj. Edison as Watch Officer and he turned in, in my dugout, and slept like a log in fancied security. To avoid disturbing him, I went to breakfast first and then came back and woke him and took him with me to barracks of G/91st CA [coast artillery] where we both enjoyed our showers hugely. I also shaved and got my usual clean underwear from Chong, who seems happy. To Old. Comsy. [commissary] but it is deserted except for a rotten smell from the meat market. To Regtl. CP [regimental command post]; scrutinized grounds near huge crater back of RSO for signs of my card index drawers, but no trace was visible, dammit! Capt. Julian was working there on a decrepit Cadillac searchlight truck, trying to get it to run. Went over to my quarters to mourn over the remains and, as Edison and Simmonds had suggested to me—and as Capt. Hauck[8] had approved, I sent my chifforobe and medallion rug to Btry. Crockett for storage, forgetting to secure the 4 drawers of genealogy index cards therein! What a mess *that* will be! I also moved my shell collection to my regimental office, but didn't bring over the cabinet. Went to lunch at Wheeler at 11:45—2 short air alarms while there.

Going to C1 at 12:36 I passed B/60, evidently alerted. "They're coming in now" said they, pointing. I could hear the planes as I hit my dugout and, at 12:39, distant AA guns opened fire. Planes closer at 12:40 and still louder at 12:41 but barely audible at 12:42, and lowered in tone to a mutter at 12:45, with a few distant bursts, possibly from Drum, a 2-gun battery. Planes inaudible at 12:49 except for a staccato muttering; distant AA firing of about 10 shots at 12:51; then, more, also far away—but no bombs yet at 12:53. Drone clearer at 12:53 nearer at 12:54 when a single battery opened fire far away, but there was no appreciable change in sound of planes. At 12:55½ firing was continuing and then there were distant bombs. More firing at 12:57½ but still no change in the sound of airplane motors. At 1:00 P.M. with the planes inaudible, B/60 opened with 10 rounds, then more at 1:01. Planes coming in fast and B Btry. quiet and no bombs dropped and planes out of hearing at 1:04. Another approach without bombs. Maybe these harmless traverses are but "dry runs" for those bombers? After another dry run, under fire, the planes came in again at 1:18 to accompaniment of distant firing of increasing tempo until B/60 opened at 1:19 with about 15 rounds. Two other batteries joined in at 1:20 at faster rates. Planes nearing and B/60, quiet temporarily, fired a jag of about 15 rounds. At 1:21 I heard the first "Whish" of the first stick of bombs, and they were either small or distant. Distant AA fire at 1:22, all quiet 1:24; at 1:29 B/60 put out about 15 rounds at approaching planes—30″ quiet—resumed firing at planes audibly approaching. The "Whish!" came at about 1:30:10 and sounded close by, bad on the ear drums. These sounded closest of any I've heard (1 landed 50 yds. away, near our trail past B/60 and evidently exploded in a tree about 50′ away from the same 3″ gun which suffered a direct hit the first day. No casualties!). B Btry. now quiet but could hear their faraway bursts. I went out of dugout and found the air filled with smoke (I could detect the smell of powder) and falling dust; thought they might have fallen over toward my C1 station. Apparently small bombs.

After some distant droning, a far-off battery opened at 1:38 but the planes came in and laid their eggs at 1:41. I counted or estimated 27 of them and much farther away than the second set. Being undisturbed in their bombing, the Japs take their time; dropping their bombs and then recrossing once or twice to observe results, correct their sights, and *then* try again! Later we heard that 7 of our few remaining planes (I thought we had none) attacked these bombers and ruined 3! All quiet at 1:49. Walked to my C1 station and at 2:05, saw them drop a flock of bombs on Mariveles. At 2:27 we started to check our communications but at 2:32 we got word, "They're coming over again" and the bombs fell 2 minutes later. There was smoke drifting over us from the direction of the barracks but nobody knew its source (later known to be Bottomside dock area). At 3:11 the high invisible bombers dropped a load in Mariveles Harbor north of the drydock Dewey,[9] and Abston[10] was evidently firing at them. At 3:21 they dropped another load, probably aimed at the Dewey, but they all landed on land south of the Dewey. All clear at 3:50.

Visibility was poor. In fact, B Battery said they not only didn't see the plane they were aiming at, but couldn't even see their bursts! What a waste of ammunition.

Got out and went on a drive of inspection in my car, primarily to find the cause of the dense black smoke which was blowing over my C1 station from the northeast. Found that the Japs had devoted considerable attention to Bottomside. There is now no post power at Middleside or Stockade level. Lourdes barrio is hit — see notes in tomorrow's account.

Fired barges in Port area.

It is illuminating to note how differently people behave *now,* compared with their actions before we were bombed. Then they would flock around doors and archways and watch the planes, in spite of our warnings. How changed all that is now! Now they all stampede for the nearest cover and get as far under it as possible—especially the Filipinos. We are trying to educate our men so that, after promptly taking cover, they will, if no airplanes are heard, come out and carry on with their work. This works OK with our soldiers but not with Filipinos. They are most cowardly and jittery—seemingly not the same breed who fought us in 1898.

Reports from the north are unanimous in saying that they will not stand, but will run without firing a shot. If, in camp, a man accidentally fires a rifle, they all grab their rifles and start shooting—wildly and into the air—anywhere so long as they can fire! And those are the "heroes who are fighting so gloriously" that Pres. Quezon raves about in his eulogies. The bare facts are that the Filipino will not fight under these politically appointed Filipino officers. Under American officers they can, in time, be made into good troops, but that is the only way. That's why the Philippine army is no good compared with the Scouts.

To return to shelter during air raids: A great effect was caused by the near breakdown of our Aircraft Warning Service. In our first real bombing we had practically no warning: it was only a few seconds after the alarm that the first bombs fell—and in profusion. The planes had evidently dropped their bombs before we knew they were near. That shook the confidence of all, and now when the alarm sounds, everybody feels that the bombs will be along in a few seconds —and they act accordingly. Also, there is a great tendency to stay in the shelters until "all clear" is sounded.

Wednesday, 7 Jan 1942
No bombs today.

After breakfast I had a spit bath at my dugout. Had turned out at 4:30 to relieve Foster.[11] Welch drove to G/91 and got my clothes from Chong, who can do no more about it because now there is neither water nor electricity at Middleside. I visited Cheney and talked with Capt. Steiger because I wasn't sure of his morale, he is such a griper, but it appears as though he is OK. Went to my quarters in search of a percolator, but no luck. Then to Regtl. HQ and found it deserted because we have moved it to the HD [harbor defense] Bombproof—just vacated by HD CP in favor of the Malinta Tunnel! Good enough for us! Talked with Capt. Julian, my intrepid RSO about water—which is sure scarce! Then visited Smith and Hearn Btries. and found lax concealment discipline at Hearn: shiny dishpans visible, etc. then to C1 where Moore is improving our path camouflage which has been ruined by men building "Shantyville." Then to my dugout where we added 4 sandbags at weak points and did a modicum of fixing up.

Was astonished at McReynold's[12] poor camouflage of kitchen: shiny pots in the sun! Bawled him out for it and also Simmonds, the Bn. Comdr. Found C Battery's latrine so bad that the surrounding ground was crawling with maggots. Stirred up the Medico there. We have succeeded in prying 2 more Medicos out of the Malinta Tunnel: one is now at Btry. Crockett and will also care for Geary nearby and the other is at Hearn to cover the units in that vicinity. These, with the one at Wheeler, fix us up a bit better. But we had to fight hard to pry them loose from the clutches of a colonel the Harbor Defense surgeon, who wanted them all under him in the safe old Tunnel.

As the hours rolled by today and still no enemy bombers appeared, we all began to wonder what the surcease meant. One explanation lay in the USAFFE [U.S. Army Forces Far East] news that Formosa had been so severely bombed, yesterday, by "friendly" (to us) planes that the Jap bombers could not take off! Would that it were true, but my hunch is that they were too busy attacking our Bataan forces to bother with us. I understand that our forces in Bataan are catching hell.[13] And I worry about Brooke.[14] From about 5:00 P.M. we thought we could hear artillery firing from that direction. Too slow and regular for bombing.

Toward sunset, while Foster and Simmonds and I were taking our ease in front of my dugout, Lt. Moore III came from C1 and reported an aircraft carrier in the offing, so we all went down to have a look. I couldn't see it through our DPF but Foster, Simmonds, Edison and others could, and swore it was a carrier. It was away north past Hornos Pt. steaming south. We reported it to Harbor Defense Command Post and awaited developments—but there were none. It was totally flush deck, with no funnel sticking up and so we diagnosed it as a Jap carrier. She hung around until darkness hid her. As she was, at one time, only 39,080 yds. from our Btry. Hearn, we could have paid some attention to her, had we a pair of 16″ guns in our makeup.

We all hung around C1, hoping for developments but there was nothing doing. Finally Simmonds, Foster and I adjourned to my dugout and had a couple of snorts of my Scotch. Simmonds seems always around when there's any drinking to be done, and likes 'em plenty stiff and numerous—but is conspicuously absent when it comes to supplying any of the booze. They left at 9:30 and I turned in.

Thursday, 8 Jan 1942
2d day of no bombs.

Turned out early and relieved Edison as watch officer and let him sleep in my dugout. Breakfast at Wheeler and I sure did enjoy wheat flakes! They have improved their latrine but the seat holes are so close together that a customer is apt to wipe the wrong posterior. Had a conference of group commanders: Simmonds, G1; De Carre,[15] G3; Kohn,[16] G4; also Foster and Edison, on our plans of operation if Jap ships come within range. As we ended, Gen. Moore and his aide came in and chatted a minute. He has a bad cold.

Drove to Btry. Hearn and got a shave. Chatted with McReynolds and Verde. To Regtl. HQ in old HD "Bombproof" and saw Julian and Cooper. Inspected wreck of our cine—hit by bomb in first attack—heavy concrete balcony shattered into ground and entire building gutted. Walls intact except bulged in one place. All roof trusses evidently OK. To PX [post exchange] where Welch[17] found some motor oil and took 12 quarts Gargoyle. To bindery and salvaged typesetter's platen, 4 fonts lead type, paper cutter and stored them at my quarters. Looters there had stolen the small keg of cherry brandy, but no other signs of looting. Drove to my dugout and had Welch go to motor pool to change oil, check battery, etc. Our local crew has finished camouflaging our C1 trail, so let them go back to their digging.

That "aircraft carrier" was again visible this morning! Evidently the high command decided not to attack it. Their only excuse, in my mind, is that it actually was *not* a carrier, but 3 of my field officers swore it was last night. When we spotted it, up north past Cochinos Point—we sent a message to our inshore patrol to this effect: "Aircraft carrier in square 5343, range 39,080 yds. Comdr. Harrington at Mariveles says he has 4 P.T. boats raring to go." And what a reaction *THAT* jeering message stirred up—as we knew it would! In a short time back came: "How do you know it is a carrier? How do you know where it is? WHO SAYS THAT ABOUT HARRINGTON?" But we all knew that our gallant (?) Navy would not dare send out an attack—even against such a plum as a carrier—and they didn't. One commander of a P.T. boat is to be court-martialed because, when he found himself near 2 Jap transports, instead of attacking them, he cut down his roaring engines and sneaked away! I bet they *won't* court-martial him.

At 12:29 the air raid alarm sounded. A rumor current today is that Gen. MacArthur said, 2 days ago, "After 14 more hours, the Japs cannot attack Corregidor unopposed" I wish it were true! Maybe that ties in with the absence of bombing yesterday? "All clear" sounded at 1:15. No bombing of Corregidor or nearby.

They say that water is again available at Stockade level, so I intend going down there later this afternoon for a bath. What a discomfort this lack of water entails! Our RSO has gone to work tooth and nail to truck enough water to our mess for drinking and cooking. We are distributing empty powder cans for storing the water as they have rubber gasketted lids, but nobody gets ahead,—they live from hand-to-mouth and often have no water at all. And, the other day some dame in Malinta Tunnel was heard to exclaim in utter horror and dismay: "And they say we'll have to cut down on our baths!" The haute monde in the Tunnel have had electricity and water right along.

Got my Remington Automatic and my L.C. Smith double from the man at Btry. Wheeler who has been cleaning them. A spring in the former was broken so he took mine and gave me a better one. Verde is trying to get me a revolver: Cal .38 in a Cal .45 frame!

President Quezon's yacht "Casiana" has been hit by a bomb and sunk at her moorings. This was formerly owned by Doheny of the Teapot Dome scandal and was bought by Quezon about Nov. 1936—See my diary of that time.

Friday, 9 Jan 1942

3d day of no bombing!

Slept through to 7 A.M. Breakfast at Wheeler. Moved my good twin beds down to Btry. Crockett and put them under Hauck's charge. A barge of food is ashore at Searchlight No. 1 and everybody who has a truck is taking it for their battery messes. Found Capt. McCarthy reading a magazine and put him in command of Headquarters Btry. over Capt. Lewis, with orders to move HQ Btry. Mess to Ordnance Bombproof. Barry, the Ord. Ofcr. [ordnance officer][18] wants a "guarantee" that no tools, etc. will be touched, yet now the doors are open and anybody can take anything they wish! Arranged to hoist a new flag over Corregidor and to sequestrate the one that has been flying as a trophy for the 59th C.A. It is now tattered and torn and will be a swell regimental trophy. Edison and I inspected the Ordnance Instrument shop and warehouse, where considerable damage has been done. But no desirable property there. Post power now available at Btry. Hearn! A houseboy was pressing Fulmer's[19] trousers when I paid a visit there at noon. Came to my tent and shaved myself for a change.

Air raid alarm sounded at 3:50 and I heard from my dugout, AA firing in the far distance—possible Cabcaben. Welch improved my wash-bench installation outside my dugout. All clear without local action.

Seaward, nothing happened—in fact, nothing of importance has happened since the war began—outside of glimpsing that plane carrier yesterday. We watch assiduously but there are no naval targets for us.

Had dinner, Edison and I, with Capt. Steiger at D Battery—at Cheney and a very good dinner it was, except the rice was poorly cooked and soggy. Then Edison and I drove to G/91 and had a delightful shower-bath. They still have no "electric" there, but Chong had clean underwear and a uniform for me. Then we drove to Bottomside where the guns were and hunted for a Graener without success. Found a Parker but couldn't find its forehand. Men broke open a box of Colt's revolvers and were carrying them away wholesale in spite of the guard. Edison and I each got one. Drove to Hearn and saw the big micrometer set that Verde had. He still promises to get me that nickel plated .38. To C1 and loafed around for a while. Schenck showed up late and I left Foster in charge and went to my dugout about 8:30 after we had chased the Navy patrol out after a suspicious looking banca [dugout outrigger] out beyond Ft. Hughes.

Efird phoned that a poker game was on, so I went down to C1 for an inspection of the field and found Capt. Schenck[20] missing and Lt. Moore on duty. This is not according to the program, because there is a lot of jittery stuff to handle during the first 2 hours of darkness, until things calm down for the night. And so I stayed there until Col. Foster showed up and also Schenck. Sat in the poker game for awhile and then Col. Elmes,[21] QMC [quartermaster corps], showed up with Edison and Simmonds. So I quit the game, gave my winnings to Lt. Gibbon and took Elmes etc. to my tent for a couple of Scotches. His ideas of the Navy are exactly like ours—a bunch of false alarms. The bums stayed and kept me awake until 12:30, when they let me turn in and read myself to sleep over a *Field and Stream.*

As we were dining at Cheney, the men were unloading a truckful of dried fruits: raisins, prunes, apricots, etc. obtained free from the barge that came ashore near Searchlight No. 1. As far as I can learn, every one of my batteries has received a truckload. The boxes are labeled for Shanghai. Some of the men broke open boxes and ate the dried fruit, including apples. Now if they'll only drink a lot of water, they'll be fixed fine!

Am glad that post power now is available at Batteries Hearn, Grubbs, Cheney and Wheeler. It helps out our overworked 25 kilowatt sets.

Saturday, 10 Jan 1942
4th day of no bombs.

Slept until 7:00 and then walked down to breakfast at Btry. Wheeler but, when I found they were having "creamed beef," I left and motored to Btry. Cheney and had breakfast with Capts. Steiger, Dewey, etc. Chatted awhile and then returned to Btry. Wheeler and chinned awhile with the officers there—being apprised, from afar, of the presence of Col. Ausmus[22] by his loud ranting. Turned down Lt. Simpson's gift of a revolver holster. To C1 for my morning devotions and was caught in a most embarrassing position by an air raid alarm which, later turned out to be a mistake—thought I could hear distant firing that sounded like AA. Then to my dugout. It is raining over toward Ft. Drum and Frank. Another air alarm at 9:49. Went to C1 at 10:45. All clear at 10:48.

While we had no bombing all day, it is said that there was a dog fight over Cabcaben this morning.

Have moved HQ Btry. Mess to the old Ordnance Machine shop "Bombproof" rather than have them in the open near Btry. Wheeler. The men only eat there; at all other times they are dispersed at work.

After dinner, drove with Simmonds to G/91 and had a shower. Schenck also was there. Got clean uniform and underwear from Chong. Then to Hearn where we played poker until 10:15 and had trouble finding Derr afterwards. To C1, Foster on duty. Ft. Frank scouts report that Japs are in Naic; that they made the rounds and took half of everybody's money—tore up all U.S. money. Also are in Ternate, and many more to come tomorrow. Turned in at 10:45 after an uneventful day.

Sunday, 11 Jan 1942
Won Peso (P) 3.50.

Barber 20¢.

5th day of no bombing.

Awoke and went down to C1 about 5:15 and relieved Lt. Moore. Col. Foster came around later.

A most queer performance occurred. A plane came roaring around C1 and (Daws avers) fired a burst at No. 3 light or at least at Corregidor. At the same time, the Inshore Patrol, of all people, reminded us of a message from Capt. McNair (of the AA defense) which they had given us earlier, to the effect that 3 *friendly* planes would be around here before dawn! At about this same time the Marines around by James ravine cut loose with their cal. 50 machine guns and somebody at Mariveles did likewise—so the air was filled with red tracers! To cap the climax, Capt. Schenck phoned in a whining way, asking if friendly planes *had* to fly so *close* to his battery as to keep his men awake! What a chance he booted—to bring that plane down! And what was the matter with all of the 60th?

Later I drove with Col. Foster to Btry. Hearn to see them fire a ranging shot, a 700-lb. land projectile, and what a fiasco *that* was! They spent 40 minutes getting the projectile out! Then their secondary station at Ft. Frank lost the splash! There was so much smoke at the battery that their own observer couldn't get the range to the splash!

Asked Gen. Moore to do something about the burning oil barge near our Engr. wharf which is laying down a smoke screen over our fields of fire—but he said the fire can't be put out and is too hot to permit towing the barge away! Some more swell brain work by our brass hats who moored that barge there! Couldn't they tell which way the wind was blowing? They didn't even dare try to blow it up. Meanwhile it jeopardizes our whole defense scheme.

Sat down for a delayed breakfast and waited and waited. Finally they brought us some coffee, but just then the air alarm sounded, and we all went inside the battery until all clear sounded in about 30 minutes. We resumed breakfast and I managed to gulp a brace of hot cakes before the air alarm sounded again at 9:25, and so we again took cover, as I could see a burst or two over Cabcaben way when Abston started his battery to firing. AA on the rock opened at 10:12, but no bombs fell on Corregidor. In the plotting room at Hearn, one could just hear the AA guns as dull "booms," indistinguishable from the sound of closing our outer steel doors. All other sounds were submerged in the whine and drone of our motors, fans, and air circulation. Got bored with waiting, so had Derr drive me to C1 where Snoke was in charge. They reported that the bombing was toward Cabcaben. It seems that every time one of our pursuit planes becomes active, the Japs give the air field at Cabcaben another bombing. Went to my dugout and wrote up this log.

Inspected HQ Btry. Mess at Ordnance Bombproof. Went home and secured the little silver tray (Champion Athlete Trophy USMA 1902). Then to library—to Btries. Geary and Crockett to look around. The 7000-gallon gas tank there had been leaking, so they were trying to drain it. To Hearn and got a shave by the battery barber. Many battery barbers on Topside are from Lubang. In P.M., took a siesta in my dugout, over a picture book showing things of 1905. Nostalgic—especially Dr. Osler's dictum about chloroforming all men of 60 years or over. Late for chow. Then drove to G/91 for our usual shower-bath. Then to Hearn for our usual conclave and adjourned to Regler Fellers Club for poker. Hawes was high winner but I collected P.3.50.

Quiet evening, with Edison in charge. Turned in at 11:00. Nowadays I have Colin sleep in my dugout and, to prevent him from running around in the brush and alarming the sentries, I keep him tied up.

At 3:25 there was an air alert. Could hear plane. B/60 fired about 5 shots but nothing happened, and all clear sounded at 3:40.

For the last few evenings we could hear distant artillery firing from along about 6 P.M. to midnight—over on Bataan Peninsula. No hard fighting there now, evidently.[23]

We are all wondering: "Why have the Japs laid off us for five full days?"

Wednesday, 14 Jan 1942
Fired Hearn.
Won P4.00.
Japs Bombed Corregidor.
7th Bombing of Corregidor.
My quarters Hit.
We've now had 7 full days of no bombing—possibly explainable by the London report that yesterday 145 Jap planes bombed Singapore. I wonder what damage they did to *Naval* and other vessels, which are said to be closely packed in the harbor there. British antiaircraft artillery are credited with bringing down only 6 Jap planes. Came off watch at 7:15; wrote up log, went to Btry. Wheeler for breakfast. Shaved myself and was just starting for Hearn when I heard some bombs (2 bursts) over Cabcaben way. B/60 blew whistles as their private alert signal, following it immediately with the regulation alarm of beating the hell out of suspended projectile caps—and I took shelter in Btry. Wheeler, with Edison, and dozed until all clear was sounded at about 9:30. Later we heard that 12 Jap dive bombers bombed Cabcaben again. Drove to Btry. Hearn and saw them shoot 5 calibration shots, using the Chilean 700-lb. projectiles that we intend firing at ships attempting to land outflanking forces along the Bataan Peninsula. The technique, especially at the start, was sloppy and dilatory, and I bawled McReynolds out about it. Lt. Col. Simmonds is not a great help. But the gun shot beautifully: at a range of about 20,000 yards, the average range error was 61 yards over! This gun has always shot well. Went to Regtl. HQ, where Julian has cleaned up well, and then to my quarters where I could see no signs of further looting—and then to C1 where I talked with Col. Boudreau[24] about his G-2 service on the mainland and the alleged "bridge" at Maragondon River. Also talked with Col. Hopkins about measures to be taken at his fort (Hughes).

As I was leaving for my dugout, at 12:38, another air alarm sounded and both Capt. Hauck and I could hear the planes. Soon the AA guns opened fire and at about 12:43 the bombs fell, with their prelude of "Whish!" Since I was without my gas mask, I left and went to my dugout for it. Distant AA firing at 1:25 and their bursts but no planes, then B/60 opened (Glassburn) and planes became audible. Bursts far off: planes evidently high: Silence 1:28. A bright green "Praying Mantis" is on my corrugated iron dugout wall, just underneath my electric light and he twists his head from side to side. All clear at 2:21 P.M. no further bombs having been dropped on Corregidor.

Drove over to my quarters and found that a bomb had come through the roof and exploded in middle of my sala, or rather had penetrated the floor and exploded in the ground underneath, making a crater about 10′ deep and then blowing up. Ceilings of sala and NE bedrooms came down almost intact. Contents of room mostly in crater, covered an inch deep in gray dust. Every leg. blown off our divan table, bijuco chairs and cushions down in the crater but the wicker not much hurt. Radio busted, likewise big square blue Chinese lamp. Korean chest apparently not hit. I wanted to do salvage work but it was too depressing: dirt and dust and rubbish over everything! Didn't even have the heart to start packing my few remaining books. Will leave it until tomorrow.

Every quarters, from mine to and including the general's was hit today. Chase's quarters hit near right front bedroom and wrecked nearly as bad as mine. Next door Julian's quarters suffered a second hit and wrecked the whole building except Morehouse's bedroom and its complete set of bejico bedroom furniture. I salvaged Lt. Simmonds' 2 shotguns. Generals' quarters: Big crater west of north wing and wrecked the whole wing. Could hardly wait to get into the house. Only this morning I had asked Julian to move some of my furniture to Regtl. HQ if he had a truck—which evidently he hadn't. Drove down to G/91 with Edison and Simmonds and had our showers. Chong had left for barrio as I was late. Fresh uniform and underwear helps morale. Back to Hearn at sunset for a chat. Verde gave me a fine 1″ micrometer from Coughlin. We went to C1 where Col. Foster was in charge and, as everything was quiet, we adjourned to our Regler Fellers Club and played poker until 11:15. I won P4.00. But Capt. Schenck had a field day and won about 27¢! Visited C1 and then turned in at midnight.

I wonder if the government will reimburse us for the personal property we are losing by these Japanese bombs? Even if it does, in a monetary way, it cannot replace our sentimental losses. Some of our things have more sentimental than monetary value such as my old Kawit bolo, for example.

Later: Japs dropped their 2d loads in North Channel and that's why I heard no explosions. They say we shot down two and possibly three of the 9 planes that came over.

Transition
(3 January–15 January 1942)

For the soldiers on both Bataan and Corregidor, the period from 3 to 6 January was one of unceasing Japanese pressure. Corregidor was being bombed almost continually, and Wainwright's troops were withdrawing into Bataan, having suffered nearly 40 percent losses due to disease, capture, death, wounds, and "in rare cases,"[25] desertion. On 5 January, MacArthur placed all of his forces on half rations[26] because of the severe supply shortages.

MacArthur was given a respite on the seventh, however, and because of a lull in the bombing, he was able to reorganize his Bataan forces into two corps and a rear area service command. Wainwright commanded the Philippine I Corps in the west, and Parker commanded the Philippine II Corps in the east.

Meanwhile, near Mariveles in the rear area service command, infantry

troops were so scarce that Cmdr. Francis J. Bridget, the senior navy aviator in the Philippines, was given command of a provisional naval battalion, which was to defend Mariveles and help the army defend Bataan's
west coast.[27]

On 10 January, MacArthur paid his only visit to Bataan, and after seeing Wainwright, wired Washington on "the seriousness of the situation."[28]
That night he received a note from General Homma stating, "You are
doomed."[29] Later that evening, leaflets were dropped urging the Filipinos
to surrender. That same night the Japanese occupied Cavite unopposed.[30]

On the eleventh, there was another letup in the bombing, but on the
twelfth, even though outnumbered two to one, Homma commenced his
main assault against[31] II Corps, and until the fourteenth there was heavy
fighting on Bataan.

For some unknown reason, on the thirteenth a Japanese steamer
sailed from Naic toward the stern of Ft. Drum, since all of Drum's turrets
and fixed guns pointed out to sea. However, unknown to the Japanese,
Drum had prepared for such an eventuality just the day before, and its
newly emplaced 3-inch gun scored a direct hit on the Japanese vessel,
forcing its hasty return to Naic.[32]

In a series of bloody battles during these first two weeks of January, the
Japs continually attempted to drive a wedge in the U.S. lines. On the 14th,
in an effort to turn the U.S. flanks, they moved down the west coast of
Bataan by both land and sea.[33] On the same day, another Japanese col-
umn was attempting to "turn Parker's left flank on the slopes of Mt. Natib.
Finally on the 15th, the Japanese found an opening and drove through."[34]

Despite the severity of the action on Bataan, very little information concerning it was disseminated to Colonel Bunker on Corregidor.

Notes

1. Morton, *Philippines,* 482. Every "morning a lone photo reconnaissance plane . . . would circle Corregidor and the other fortified islands for a time and then return to base. About 12:30 the bombers would come."

2. Charles N. Branham, ed., *Register of Graduates and Former Graduates 1802–1964,* 430; hereinafter cited as *Register.* Major Harry Julian was Colonel Bunker's RSO (regimental supply officer). He later became a POW and was killed on a POW ship that was inadvertently torpedoed about two hundred miles off the southeast China coast on 24 October 1944. It is believed that only nine people survived.

3. Belote and Belote, 160. Lt. Col. Norman Simmonds was one of Bunker's subordinate commanders.

4. *Register,* 425. Maj. Dwight D. Edison, Bunker's deputy. He later became a POW and survived the torpedoed POW ship only to be killed by a Japanese guard on 23 December 1944 at San Fernando, P.I.

5. Landon is Colonel Bunker's wife; she was formerly Miss Leila Landon Beehler, the daughter of Rear Admiral Beehler, USN.

6. Maj. Calvin E. Chunn, ed., *Of Rice and Men* (Los Angeles: Veterans Publishing Co., 1946), 19, 129. Lt. Col. Armand Hopkins, CAC, was the executive officer at Ft. Hughes and the commanding officer of the 3rd Battalion, 59th Coast Artillery. Later he became a POW and was interned at Camp 1 at Cabanatuan, where he became the commander of Prison Group 1. He was repatriated in 1945.

7. Colin is Colonel Bunker's pet dog.

8. Morton, *Philippines,* 560, and Belote and Belote, 181. Capt. Herman H. Hauck, CAC. During the initial part of the siege he commanded B Battery 59th CA at Crockett. Later, he led the final counterattack of sixty men against the Japanese landing on Corregidor. He escaped from them after the surrender and hid out for a month in Cavite Province. Some Filipinos captured him, trussed him up like a pig on a pole, and turned him over to the Japanese. He later was forced to help refurbish the big guns on Corregidor; however, while so doing he effectively sabotaged them.

9. Morton, *Philippines,* 155. This floating drydock had been in Subic Bay and was moved to Manila Bay for protection.

10. Chunn, 19, 50. Capt. Aaron A. Abston CAC commanded Globe Battery, a 3″ AA unit. Later he was captured and became part of the prisoners' staff at Camp 3 at Cabanatuan.

11. Belote and Belote, 112. Col. Valentine P. Foster commanded Ft. Hughes.

12. *Register,* 432. Maj. Samuel McReynolds CAC was the headquarters and

headquarter battery commander of the harbor defenses. After being captured he died of colitis in a POW camp at Fukuoka, Japan, on 1 February 1945.

13. Gen. Jonathan Wainwright, *General Wainwright's Story,* ed. Robert Considine (New York: Doubleday, 1946), 45. General Wainwright's forces had just withdrawn to the Bataan Peninsula on 6 January, his flanks had been "crushed" south of San Fernando, and "the enemy never let up" in their withdrawal to Bataan. His original force of 28,000 had been reduced to 16,000.

14. *Register,* 438, and Chunn, 155–56. Maj. Brooke Maury 3d FA. He was Colonel Bunker's son-in-law and was married to Bunker's daughter Priscilla. During the Bataan fighting, he was the S3 of the Provisional Field Artillery Brigade. He was captured on Bataan and participated in the Death March. He was killed on the Japanese prison ship that was sunk by U.S. bombs in Subic Bay on 15 December 1944.

15. Belote and Belote, 69. Col. Octave De Carre, commander of the Philippine Scout 92d CA Regiment.

16. Ibid. Col. Joseph P. Kohn, commander of the Philippine Scout 91st CA Regiment.

17. Welch was Colonel Bunker's orderly.

18. Wainwright, 164. Col. Edwin F. Barry was the commander of the Harbor Defense Ordnance Department. He was later captured and died of streptococcus infection in his throat at Tarlac on 17 June 1942.

19. Belote and Belote, 63. Lt. Richard Fulmer was one of the more aggressive artillery observers.

20. *Register,* 431. Capt. Harry Winfield Schenck was a battery commander of the 59th CA located at Battery Wheeler. He was later captured and died of colitis in a POW camp in Fukuoka, Japan, on 21 February 1945.

21. Col. Chester H. Elmes was the post quartermaster.

22. R. Ernest Dupuy, *Men of West Point, The First 150 Years of the United States Military Academy* (New York: William Sloane, 1951), 201–2. Col. Delbert Ausmus CAC was a close friend of Bunker's. He stayed with Bunker throughout their captivity and was later repatriated. (See Introduction.)

23. *Japanese Land Operations, December 8, 1941, to June 8, 1942* (Campaign Study no. 3) (Military Intelligence Service, War Department, Washington, D.C., 1942), 13. On the contrary, since 12 January the fighting had been bitter all along the line Olongapo–Lubao.

24. Morton, *Philippines,* 485–86. Col. Napolean Boudreau CAC commanded Ft. Frank. (See Introduction.)

25. Wainwright, 48.

26. Hanson W. Baldwin, *Battles Lost and Won,* (New York: Harper and Row, 1966), 129.

27. Hough, Ludwig, and Shaw, 175.

28. MacArthur, 128.
29. Ibid., 129.
30. Belote and Belote, 82.
31. Baldwin, *Battles,* 130.
32. Ibid., 129
33. Belote and Belote, 82.
34. Louis Morton, *Strategy and Command: The First Two Years of the War in the Pacific.* Subseries of *The U.S. Army in World War II,* ed. K. R. Greenfield, (Washington, D.C.: U.S. Government Printing Office, 1962) 183.

Thursday, 15 Jan 1942
 Lost P0.50 at poker.
 1st day of no bombing.
 Woke at 7:30. After breakfast drove to Regtl. HQ and ordered inventory of all foods which we have salvaged from the QM burnt (sunk) and beached barges. MacArthur has ordered us, through Gen. Moore, to do this, possibly with the idea of making all hands turn these stores in! And yet his damn staff had days in which to salvage this stuff and did nothing! Our troops saved it from utter loss and are now to be punished! "How to raise morale!" Col. Crews furnished me with this order—and I was thunderstruck to see him on Topside, outside of Malinta Tunnel.
 Drove to my quarters but just then 9:30 A.M. an air alarm sounded, so I stayed in Btry. Wheeler until all clear, went at 10:30. Some dive (?) bombers, around 4–6 of them, and it is said we shot down 2 of them. Some machine guns fired. There was another plane flying around, in and out of clouds earlier, but no alarm was sounded for him although, later, he was said to be hostile.
 Sent Welch and 2 men to salvage the furniture in my living room, which they did, taking it to my office in the barracks. Bijuco chairs, divan table top, Korean chest. Some of the cushions were ruined by fragments. Sent him back to salvage my grass rug and have some powder cans placed there for my clothes. Simmonds, Edison and I adjourned to my dugout's azatea [porch] while I shaved and chatted till noon.
 Gen. King[1] and Edison dropped in on my dugout later. Drove to my quarters and packed Box No. 20, with professional books, filling the chinks with type, pallets and bookbinding equipment. Had to go to Ordnance Machine shop to take the book press apart. To my dugout to read Brooke's long lost song book, and sent Welch back to screw the box shut and deliver it to Btry. Cheney with my others but, at 3:40 the wailing of sirens and the banging of projectile caps (and incidentally, the drone of a motor) spoke of Jap planes in our vicinity. Probably caught Welch half through his job. Nothing happened and the alert was soon over. Drove down to look at C1-G1 Tunnel: they have installed 15 frames of 12x12 timber about 5′ apart—with 3″ roofing and have excavated some feet farther. Plan now contemplates another addition about 60′ farther down the trail. Drove to Btry. Crockett for chow and it was a gorgeous meal, even if I had had a preliminary piece of pie at HQ Btry. Mess beforehand. Drove to G/91 and had my usual shower-bath. To Hearn and chinned with McReynolds as a false air alarm sounded. Then to my dugout. Am tired tonight.
 Cloudy today, so most of us expected the Jap bombers to slip out of the clouds and strafe us, but evidently no bombs were dropped on us. The USAFFE news

bulletin of last night claimed that we had shot down 76 Jap planes from start of war up to 13 Jan. Mostly bombers and about equally divided between AA and our Air Force.

Went to C1 about sundown. Edison on watch. All quiet. Left soon for our "Club" and played poker till 11. Chipped away on a whole stack before winning a pot. Quit 50¢ loser.

Col. Foster says that the high command in Malinta Tunnel burned intentionally $2,500,000[2] of U.S. bills, "perhaps to prevent it from falling into the hands of the Japs"!!x?! Why damn their eyes, who says the Japs are going to take Corregidor? We haven't even had a chance at them yet. All we've done in the Seaward Defense, is "take it." Give us a chance to "dish it out."

Friday, 16 Jan 1942

2nd day of no bombing.

Lost P1.50 at Poker.

Slept till 8 AM. Breakfast punctuated by an air alarm, probably for our old friend (?) that morning reconnaissance plane. A few AA shots and a lot of machine gun fire sounded. No more action so, without waiting for all clear, I went to C1 and saw that everything was all quiet there. Then to dugout but left immediately via South Shore Road and visited our Searchlight No. 4 and the Monja Tunnel where they were all inside, for air alert—Simmonds and Edison among them. I having been too late to go with them in official car. Tunnel is fine but ventilation poor. Drove back to my dugout and started sanding the blistered stock of my new L.C. Smith double, but sirens sounded another air alarm at 11:30. Heard distant explosions, as of AA or bombs, at 11:35 and again at 11:43 and sporadically thereafter, but they were too faint to diagnose. At noon Morehouse[3] said 9 Jap bombers were giving Cabcaben a working over and had dropped bombs; dense smoke arising over there from a non-visible source. All clear at 12:35. Siren again at 1:06. At 1:10 we heard an all clear siren signal and simultaneously, some AA fire! Somebody evidently misplaced the decimal point. Also heard planes and some AA bursts at 1:18—but no alarm.

Sporadic air raid alarms all day, but Corregidor was not bombed. Two Jap dive bombers played around Cabcaben and Abston shot one down in flames. That makes the 15th plane his battery has shot down—more than any two other batteries.

Went down to G/91 as usual and had a shower and donned the clean clothes that Chong had ready for me. Great for morale! Back to Hearn for a while and then to C1. Played some quiet poker later and quit P1.50 loser.

MacArthur issues exhortation to troops: "No further retreat! Thousands of men and hundreds of planes are en route to help us, but must fight their way, and so will be delayed—etc."[4] (If the Navy is responsible, they'll never get here!) Rumors are persistent that instead of a 6 months' reserve of food, we have only 3 months! Brass Hats in Malinta Tunnel have a rotten mess and are complaining that our enlisted men are too well fed—even though they are on half-rations! So perhaps that is one reason for the stink they are raising because we salvaged the food from those grounded and sunken barges.

The Japs bomb the landing field near Cabcaben at least once a day in an effort to prevent our few remaining planes (about 5, they say) from using it. However our field crew, so it is said, get out with their bull-dozers every night and level off the bomb-craters so that, by morning, it is about as usable as ever. The planes, too, are now never left on the field, but are hidden away at a safe distance therefrom. What a pity our aviators didn't have sense enough to do that at the start of the war. It is humiliating to think of the number of planes of ours that the Japs destroyed through our own dumbness and inefficiency.

Everybody got a good laugh today by reading General Emmon's[5] utterance from Hawaii: "Let them come, we are ready for them!" They might well be, by this time, the war being 6 months old!

Another owlish remark was that of Admiral Yarnell,[6] as published in our USAFFE[7] bulletin: "The result in the Pacific will be determined by the preponderance of power there." Nothing less than a mighty intellect could evolve such a gem of brilliant cogitation and deduction.

Saturday, 17 Jan 1942
Lost P3.00

3rd day of no bombing of Corregidor.

Awoke at 5:00 with remnant of yesterday's diarrhoea. Relieved Col. Simmonds as watch officer and stayed on duty till 7:40, which is now about daybreak, considering our daylight saving time. At about 7:00 a Jap plane could be heard and at 7:30 a long series of sporadic explosions could also be heard—possibly this plane bombing Cabcaben and being fired upon. It later developed that our Jap friend got a surprise: as he was playing around, two of our pursuiters appeared out of nowhere, separated and one made for him. As he swerved left to escape, the other plane came in from his left and fired into him broadside-on. The Jap fell in flames. Maybe they will desist from their early morning playfulness hereafter.

Drove down to C1 Tunnel, but they had just exploded a charge. Then to see Lothrop[8] at Engrs Tunnel to talk about our C1 Tunnel. He will not change the upper exit so as to make it handier to C1 because he says it would take a topography man 2 days to line up new stakes. He will not dig laterals for us because it would take extra timbering and he is running short. He has no power plants for us, but I got permission to send Julian aboard the *La Florencita* which may have an AC set [alternating current generator] aboard and she is on the rocks near Engr. Wharf. To HQ Btry. kitchen (they have my refrigerator). Then to Regtl. HQ, picked up a 14″ powder can and delivered it to my quarters.

To C1 and learned from Col. Boudreau that the Japs have 400 men in Naic, 450 in Ternate and 400 in Maragendon. They are digging a tunnel in hill near Ternate. Phoned Gen. Moore and asked to be allowed to fire on them from Mortar Battery Koehler at Frank. He asked MacArthur who demurred for fear of hurting natives! Promised to send a plane to reconnoiter and also will ask Navy to "reconnoiter in force"—and is *that* a laugh! *Nobody* could force a Navy ship within miles of any place known to contain Japs. They've *proved* that. Moore reported back "I know how you feel, but you'll have to possess your soul in patience. The propaganda effect of our shooting up natives would be too bad." But can't make a cake without breaking eggs. This occurred about 1:30.

The engine room of *La Florencita* is flooded with oil, so after Maj. Julian swam out to her, he could see nothing. *That* cat's tail broke off short, so far as salvage goes. Am hunting for an AC generator unit.

After my usual P.M. shower at G/91 I drove to Hearn and invited them to my dugout for a Scotch. Verde accepted but was a long time appearing. Sent invitation to Capt. Schenck, but he was on duty at C1. Of course Simmonds appeared—he is never absent when free drinks are to be had. We had 2 gentlemanly Scotches and then, of course, Col. Foster appeared for *his* drinks. I refrained from further libations on the ground that I had to go to C1 and didn't want the enlisted men to smell the booze. Simmonds also refrained but, when Foster took his 2nd drink, he couldn't withstand the inward urge and poured himself out his usual Gargantuan potion.

To C1 and, finding everything quiet, adjourned to the club rooms against my decision, played poker until 11:00 with unspeakable luck. Edison dropped in, having returned from Bataan, and brought news of Brooke—that he was well—doing his stuff in the line and firing valiantly.

Report on the alleged "Philippine Army": the Infantry, catching sight of a few Japs, run back through the Artillery positions, *laughing* and shouting and, holding up their 2 first fingers to form a V, call "Victory" and continue their flight to the rear. When they retreated from Lingayen they abandoned so many of their 75mm field guns that now they have none and so the 155mm (manned by our Coast Artillerymen) have to do their own work *plus* that of the missing 75s.

It is an obvious fact that the Philippine army is worthless because the Filipinos will *not* fight under Filipino officers. And there are practically no Filipino officers who are worth a damn. The graduates of the "Philippine West Point" at Baguio are sometimes pretty fair, but the others are political appointees whose only idea is to line their pockets. They have no control over their men.

Monday, 19 Jan 1942

5th day of no bombing.

Awoke at 3:00, decided to take another wink—and awoke at 7:00. To C1 and received a message that "4 or more P-40s" were arriving at about daybreak!

Good news if they are new planes. Thought I heard at least one arrive. Shaved before breakfast, and felt better. At breakfast, somebody said that 4 of our P-40s shot down 2 Japs already this morning. Back to dugout. Cooper came in with the day's grist. Snoke wants to buy officer's car from Co-Funds! Edison showed me big map of Ternate and Maragendon. Evidently the PX has gone on a cash basis for officers and will accept no charge accounts! Guess I'll never get my money out of Phil. Trust!

Drove to Malinta Tunnel to see Gen. Moore, but he was out, watching the firing at Btry. Rock Point and so I had to do business with Cottrell. He said Gen. MacArthur would probably never let us fire at the Japs on the Batangas shore, for fear of hitting a Filipino! He also said that charge accounts for officers are OK at post exchange; will try to get me some incandescent globes for signalling purposes. Also saw Adjt. [adjutant] King about sending library books to Malinta Tunnel. Then went to Engrs and invited Lothrup to my dugout for a drink tonight. Also invited Edison and sent message to same effect to Col. Foster, but Cooper (Adjt.) was unable to locate him. Saw Col. Rutherford,[9] formerly of our 59th, for the first time in about 4 months.   •

Talked with Maj. Mitchell[10] and he promised to take a mine yawl and inspect all ships near Mariveles for small AC generating sets. This he did, and reported results as I finished dinner, incidentally giving me a good Seth Thomas Clock which strikes ships bells but, unfortunately, on an *outside* gong.

Went to G/91 with Simmonds for my usual afternoon shower and got my clean clothes from Chong, leaving him my pajamas. This morning's planes that I heard, involved a fight with 2 Jap planes; our planes shot down one Jap, but the other Jap shot down one of our too few remaining planes and machine-gunned the pilot after he bailed out, with what results I don't know.

When visiting HD Bombproof this morning, I blistered the MP there for not patrolling Topside and preventing looting, instead of sticking close to the Bombproof so as to be handy to shelter in case of an air raid.

Welch brought me a piece of pie and some ice cream from HQ Btry. Mess before my own dinner. We also stopped there for some ice cubes (from my own refrigerator) before returning to my dugout at 6:07 and greeting the waiting Lothrup—we had a couple of Scotches and talked of this and that, principally of the scandalously cowardly Navy. They now have 105 Naval officers in their "Queen" tunnel—just sitting there and doing nobody any good. Lothrup also thinks Admiral Rockwell[11] is the worst fluff of them all. Lothrup also told of Col. Casey[12] (Engineer with USAFFE) writing report on himself and Sgt. Petersen for putting out an oil fire near our Diesel tank and getting himself a DSC [Distinguished Service Cross]—also utterly ignoring the fact that 4 other people were equally praiseworthy—and that the deed was not under fire! He, Lothrup, has changed his mind again and will actually dig us two and perhaps 3 short laterals in our tunnel, to house the C1 and G1 activities.

After the party broke up, Edison going on watch, I went down to C1 for a few minutes but, as everything was quiet, I returned to my dugout. I wonder if that ship's clock is going to awaken me every time it strikes?

Late this afternoon Schenck's mechanic, with a helper, started to build me a platform, outside of my dugout, so more than 2 of us can foregather there at odd times—also so I can work out there in the open instead of here in the dugout where it is quiet but a bit stuffy. They made good progress.

Clear skies today, quite breezy. Rain squalls all around the horizon at dawn and a regular Turner sunrise. Welch and I rigged a 10' square tarpaulin as a shade over the entrance to my dugout.

Tuesday, 20 Jan 1942
Won P2.00.

6th day of no bombing!

Awoke at 6:00 and went to C1. Hawes was still on duty and Edison showed up shortly, so I sent them both to bed. Quiet night—and morning—even the morning reconnaissance plane of the Japs was missing.

Shaved before breakfast. After breakfast, organized the expedition of Sgt. Dirks to go out in a mine yawl to the U.S. C&GS [Coast and Geodetic Survey] boat *Research* to salvage a small gasoline driven DC [direct current] generator. To Regtl. HQ and phoned Bowler[13] about a promotion of Lts. Davis,[14] Schutte and Dawe. Pawed around in ruins of radio shacks and Regtl. workshop for motors with Foster.

To my quarters to see what else can be salvaged and, in P.M., Welch went back to pack towels, shirts, etc. in another powder can, but didn't do it.

Went to my dugout and supervised the building of the platform outside it. Gen. Moore came along and we chatted of this and that.

Relieved Lewis (Capt.) and Holton from duty as "No Good" and reported them to HQ. Holton is doing well at library but is no soldier.

The peril of gasoline leakage from the big tank to the left of Btry. Geary having subsided through drainage of tanks, they finally connected the post power mains into Btries. Geary and Crockett today, thus giving grateful relief to our over-worked 25-kw [kilowatt] sets in those Batteries. These 25-kw sets consist of a 4-cylinder heavy duty gasoline engine direct coupled to a 25-kw DC generator, and there is at least one of them in every big-gun battery as emergency power sources. They are proving their excellent worth, too, being very rugged and fool-proof. One is just right for feeding a 60" Seacoast searchlight.

Nothing unusual today. We go about our business but keep one eye peeled for the nearest foxhole, in case a bomber dives at us. There is always a sort of ner-vous tension among the calmest, for none of us have confidence in our Air Warn-ing Service and assume, from experience, that our only warning may well be the swish of the bombs themselves.

Drove down as usual for my shower and gassed a bit at Btry. Hearn afterward. Went to C1, gathered up Edison and Foster and adjourned to my dugout and had a couple of snorts of Scotch. Then we went to the Club House and played poker until 11:00 P.M. I won P2, but not a darn centavo after sourpuss Gibbon joined the game!

When Gen. Moore was at my tent, Moore brought me word from Foster about a drifting barge, over near Frank. Moore OK'd our shooting at it, but when I went to C1, I found that it was too close to Frank, and ricochets might hit Limbones, Island where we still have observers on duty. So I refrained from shooting.

We are all wondering why the Jap bombers have laid off us so long. The con-census of opinion seems to be that they are busy against our troops in Bataan and, more especially, against the British in Malaya.

Today we got the pleasing word that some B-17s (which are American planes) sank a Jap cruiser and a tanker "in the south" which we hope means Davao and not Dutch East Indies. We also heard of a troop of the 26th Cavalry reported "lost" who just checked in after a 100-mile raid behind the Jap lines, where they did damage, including destruction of some Jap planes![15] This, of course, was a Scout outfit, *not* Philippine army.

A lieutenant (Rose?) who was captured by the Japs is now broadcasting, telling how well the Japs treat their prisoners and that it is a mistake to oppose them. We all know how "voluntary" these sentiments of his are!

We, too are supposed to be broadcasting, but I know of nobody who has heard it. It is reported that at last we have an Army radio contact with Hawaii and are no longer dependent upon the Navy.

Wednesday, 21 Jan 1942

7th day of no bombs!

Awoke at 7:30. Shaved after breakfast. It certainly is beautiful weather now! There is a little orchid, just outside my dugout, which is just completing its blooming and the last two tiny blossoms fell off yesterday. They were almost of the same color as the hot-house specimens sold in the States! After breakfast, I sat with Simmonds, on Wheeler "parade" and enjoyed the weather—until the men started sweeping.

Drove to C1; kicked a Navy gang out of the PX where they were stealing chairs for their tunnel. Inspected beer kegs at Spiff Bar with Foster but we agreed they're no good for water. Maj. Julian is sick with a bad cold and I found him in bed. Several of the men from my HQ Btry. who work at C1 have had bad diar-rhoea and vomiting. We are getting the fly pest under better control but there are still too many.

Drove to my quarters to view the ruins, as I usually do daily. Straightened a few things around but had no heart to do much. Showed Welch the table linen and contents of chiffonier, to pack in powder can this afternoon. Then went to my dugout and passed away the time making the detailed dimension drawing of a leg of our divan table, for use in making new ones and thus repairing the table when I get the chance. It was quiet and peaceful, outside my dugout; the swish of waves down on the South Shore, a gentle rustle of leaves overhead, birds twittering and chirping—and a wild rooster with his tenor challenging crow—much higher in pitch than that of a tame rooster. Captain McCarthy came around and I told him to get busy with more camouflage over my dugout. (Lights were off in the dugout, most of the afternoon.)

With Simmonds (who came late) and Edison (who was already there) I took dinner tonight at the usual hour of 4:00 P.M. with Capt. Steiger at Btry. Cheney and it was excellent. For one thing, the rice was well cooked and not a soggy mess; the quantities also were good and the apple cobbler for dessert might well have been made from fresh apples.

Gave Simmonds and Edison a lift to G/91 for our showers and then to Hearn and watched Verde play around with his pistol that had a bent cylinder rod. At dark we adjourned to C1 and, on the way, found a squad struggling along with a camouflage net (wire) for my dugout and, for a joke, had them dump it into the entrance of Col. Foster's tent.

To C1. Schenck on duty. Everything quiet, so adjourned to the Club and played poker until 11:00 P.M. As we were playing, Foster brought in Col. Elmes and Maj. Kriwanek. Glad to see them but couldn't quit, as that would have left only 4 in the game. So I suggested that Foster take them to my dugout for the drinks that were evidently expected by all 3 of them.

Hawes was the lucky one tonight. He *couldn't* lose. I lost P1.00. I guess Simmonds was the heavy loser.

Today they put a port phone into my dugout—it was No. 3.

Thursday, 22 Jan 1942

8th day of no bombs.

Awoke at 6:00 A.M. and got up to write up this log. Can't find my pet fountain pen—the one Paul[16] gave me.

Found it again.

Usual morning routine of breakfast, etc. Spent all morning inspecting. Starting with Btry. Smith—Snoke and Davis were out. When I arrived at Hearn Gen. Moore stopped, in his car. He said that Capt. Ivey[17] had returned from Batangas shore but brought no new information. So I suppose they will continue to refuse to let us shoot at Ternate, dammit!

Men rigged a camouflage net over entrance to my dugout. My porch platform is now nicely fitted with a table and 4 chairs.

Spent some time around my Regtl. RSO storeroom, and also ran down to Btry.

Cheney and our Tunnel. They have 28 bents installed now and are gathering lagging at Taproom and Grandstand, so no work is being done on our emergency exit.

Went to my dugout about noon and dozed in my chair while Welch made and installed another shelf—over my table. Also retrieved the desk lamp from my old desk.

Turned in, at 2:00 and slept until 3:00.

Edison came along with a gift from Col. Elmes: two nice Edam cheese rounds from Argentina. Called Simmonds in and we three made a big hole in one of them—and it sure tasted good. Stowed them in C Battery ice box when we went up for dinner. Good roast pork—and I ate too much. We 3 went to G/91 in my car for our showers and then, as usual, went to Btry. Hearn and gassed until sunset.

To my dugout and wrote up this log. At 8:00 P.M. went to C1. Everything being quiet and Foster on duty, I adjourned to our Club and played poker until about 10:15 when I checked out even with the banker—after donating 25¢ to the "short change pot."

Friday, 23 Jan 1942

9th day of no bombs!

Up at 6 A.M. and went to C1. Just before dawn there was a display of tracers, way out over Hornos Pt., which developed into a fight between our PT boat, plus the Fisheries II against a Jap motorboat or two. As day broke we could see our boats circling the Jap, finally closing and pouring lead at a range of 50 yards or so. Our boats evidently sank or burned the Jap and brought in 2 prisoners well shot up. Maybe I can get further details later. We also saw another boat, probably a Jap power-banca, sneaking closely past Hornos Pt., headed West—but the Navy refused to touch it. At about this time, the usual Jap reconnaissance plane came in and went over towards Ternate.

Went to breakfast and, afterward, witnessed sort of target practice from Btry. Wheeler, of 10 rounds of *battle* or service ammunition. It went not too well: on last shot of No. 1, the gun bounced back into battery; the lanyards were not "stretched"; the Gun Commander would have fired without tripping! Primer blew out, as usual, and it looked as though made out of pot metal. Then, with Edison, went to G3 where the engineers are putting a concrete slab on an underground plotting room to make it a Bombproof—DeCarre wants to snatch it and use it as his "Night Operations" room—wrote out an endorsement disapproving it. Then we went down to see Capt. King[18] about his excessive recommendations for citations and told him to quit running hog wild. Earlier this morning, received assurance from Capt. Bull, the PX officer, that he has cut his payroll to about one-third. Then to C1 in vain effort to ask Col. Barry for one of those deluxe automatic pistols. Then to my dugout at 12:15. (Wheeler target practice from 9:12 to 9:25 A.M. Ranges started about 14,510 and decreased rapidly.)

About 2:35 P.M. while I was cleaning a revolver at my dugout, Edison told me of a report from Lt. Bliss, who is in charge of our observers at Pucot Hill, that "Japs had destroyed our radio set. Position becoming untenable," yet the message was sent via 60th "walkie-talkies" from same place near Mariveles! If such a place, practically at our rear base, is "untenable," what are our Bataan troops doing? I can't understand it. This happened between 10:30 and 11:00 this morning and it was about 7:50 A.M. when we saw that banca sneaking around Hornos Pt.

Just as I'd finished dinner I received an alarming message from Gen. Moore: "A barge with many bancas approaching Corregidor from Manila; range 25,000 yds.; many other bancas under sail at Naic. Gen. MacArthur has given us permission to crack down on them if dangerous." I snatched Simmonds and Edison away from chow and we hustled to C1. Alerted Btries. Smith and Hearn and hustled Davis to top of Malinta Hill to adjust fire. Upon further investigation it developed that a Jap barge was unloading into the bancas—probably supplies for the Japs at Naic. So we all calmed down; Simmonds finished his coffee, Edison his dinner; Welch got some ice and water and we had a couple of Scotches—but Simmonds *refrained* (!) because he was taking some medicine for the bad boil on his calf.

Got our usual shower and Colin got into a fight with 2 big dogs at G/91 and ran them both off. To Hearn and told Lt. Fulmer I am sending him to Pucot to displace Bliss, who has shown gross incompetence in allowing his party to be surprised, there at Pucot Hill. He seemed to welcome the chance. Had a glass of Bear Brand milk with Col. Barry, our HD Ordnance officer, at Hearn. Talked of the material failures at Wheeler this morning and also about the barge load of beautiful revolvers, which he dumped into the drink. No good ones left in the box he saved.

To C1, Edison on duty. All quiet, so at 8:30 I went to my dugout. The moon is getting disgustingly bright again, though it is only a few days old—a fact which I noticed on my way back to my dugout from C1.

I am toying with the idea of sleeping on a folding cot outside the dugout, in order to get better ventilation and better sleep.

Melnik,[19] at HQ told me today that things look black for our Bataan forces because the "heroic" Philippine army is deserting en masse, leaving their positions at night, sifting through the Jap lines and working their way around to Manila! And these are the scum for whom we are fighting and whom President Quezon calls "Our Heroes" and praises their bravery. The Scouts hold them in utter contempt—evidently correctly!

Saturday, 24 Jan 1942

Awoke at 6:00 and went to C1. It doesn't get light until 6:30, these days. Edison was busy trying to check on a possible submarine about 8000 yards off shore but, before it could be shot at, it disappeared. Some tracer firing, up Bagac way about midnight. They say we lost 2 of our 155mm guns up Mauban way because they had no local defense and the Japs overran them. Damn poor work by those in charge, to assign no infantry for local protection. Breech blocks destroyed, so Japs can't use them.

At dawn the usual Jap plane came over, to the South. We had been heartened by notice from HQ that our pursuit planes would be operating from 6:40 to 8:00, but this was later revoked and this Jap played around at will—a 2-motor job and *fast*. Ft. Drum finally opened fire on him, but he was circling and far away. Saw the firing from C1.

Later, after breakfast I went to my dugout and was joined by Col. Foster and Maj. Julian and we whiled away the time in idle conversation. At 11:06 the air raid siren sounded, we heard bombers overhead and Bataan opened fire. We heard the planes again, over toward Mariveles at 11:29, and the AA over there opened at 11:31. They were too high but Abston wanted a little target practice. All clear went at 12:20. I walked over to Regtl. HQ and later drove to Hearn where they had 2 more false alarms.

I talked with HD Exec [harbor defense executive] and asked why, since the Inshore Patrol say they are patrolling Manila Bay, they should not have investigated and broken up yesterday's formation of bancas off Naic. They have 2 gunboats still here plus several other armed craft that are all moored in "South Harbor" between Corregidor and Hughes while their officers and crews are hiding in the Navy Tunnel! The Exec said, "They won't do it." I replied, "Do you mean they refuse to obey orders?" And he astounded me by saying "The Inshore Patrol is not under our orders." Why that is one of the fundamental agreements in the tenets of "Joint Army and Navy Action." This part of our Navy WILL NOT FIGHT!

Stole a section of steel filing cases out of their old Radio HQ and hid it in our RSO storeroom. Spent P.M. until 3:50 at Hearn. Then had chow at Btry. Wheeler and waited in my tent for Col. Simmonds. Welch drove us to G/91 for our showers and then to Hearn for doughnuts and cocoa. Unfortunately they were the cake type of doughnut.

Rumors: (1) Heavy Bombing of Japan's air base on Hanoi Island. One silly version said 200 tons of bombs were used! (2) Dutch Air Force has caught a big Jap convoy in Straits of Macassar, scored 12 hits with 600-lb. bombs, action continuing.[20]

The Japs in Malaya, seem to be forcing the British back by the same tactics they are using here: where the British flank rests on the ocean, the Japs put a company in small boats and land in the British rear, which makes the whole British flank fall back. This could *not* work if the Japs were kept on land and denied the water. Which brings up the question, what about the vaunted British naval superiority? Can't they spare enough smaller craft to patrol the ocean shores behind their front and smear the Jap forays? Col. Clear said the British have plenty of navy crammed into Singapore Harbor. But I bet the answer is that the British navy has fled Singapore, as soon as this attack started, just as our glorious naval heroes fled to Australia as soon as fighting developed around Manila. Seems to be a lot of yellow in our Navy friends. *Try* to get one of those 105 naval officers out of the Navy Tunnel—just *try!* Why they have a quadruple "pompom" which arrived too late to catch the fleeing USS *Houston,*[21] so they brought it over here and it is to be mounted on top of Malinta Hill for antiaircraft protection. *But,* can you get the *Navy* to man it? Not by a jugful—and so it will be manned by a detail from our 60th CA (AA)!

To C1 at 7:45 and hung around there for a while but, as there was no excitement they tried, unsuccessfully, to get up a poker game. Then Foster and Cooper adjourned to my dugout and we had a couple of Scotches on the "azatea" outside in the lovely moonlight. Turned in at 10:00 P.M. and read myself to sleep over "Soldiers in the Sun."

Transition

From 15 to 25 January, there was very little enemy activity on the Rock except for an occasional aerial observer passing over, but elsewhere the Japanese were maneuvering and fighting. They successfully forced an Allied withdrawal all along the front on Bataan; they occupied the southern periphery of Manila Bay, and they staged amphibious assaults deep behind the Allied lines on Bataan.

During this period, the Rock was quiet because, on the fourteenth, Homma had ordered his 5th Air Fleet "to Burma to take on" Chennault's "Flying Tigers."[22] Only a few bombers and fighters were left behind, and these were "to support the Bataan Campaign."[23]

The Japanese, however, were very active on the ground. Besides moving troops into Ternate and Naic on the southern shore of Manila Bay, they secretly moved a battery of two 150mm howitzers into the jungle between Saphong and Ternate; their mission was to prepare to fire against the fortified islands.[24]

At the same time, on Bataan, the Japanese succeeded in getting "many men through the narrow slot on Parker's left flank"[25] and were attacking him from the west. On 16 January, I Corps was hit by fresh Japanese troops. Wainwright "now had a three-sided front and not enough men to fight even a one-sided front."[26]

On 19 January a Japanese battalion infiltrated the American lines in I Corps and set up a roadblock astride the only American line of communications.[27] For the next few days, Wainwright attempted to dislodge the enemy, "throwing all available reserves at them,"[28] but it was futile; he realized his position was untenable, and "he would have to abandon most of his artillery and retreat by trail." The Americans moved back on foot, carrying their wounded on litters or on their own bare backs.[29] On the I Corps side, General Parker was in an equally untenable position, and he, too, had to retreat.

By 22 January MacArthur realized that the present line could not be held and that he must move back to the Bagac–Orion line,[30] so the order was given for the withdrawal.[31]

The period from the twenty-third to the twenty-sixth was the most crucial of the entire Bataan campaign. MacArthur was not certain that the troops could be reorganized on the Bagac–Orion line. It was possible that the Filipino reserve troops might retreat all the way to Manila Bay. Unfortunately, MacArthur was unaware of the severe losses that the Japanese had sustained, and he overestimated the size of the enemy forces opposing him. After consulting with his staff on the twenty-fourth, he decided the outcome on Bataan was doomed; he therefore ordered the bolstering of Corregidor in hopes that it could hold out until reinforcements came in July.[32]

The withdrawal had to be accomplished by 26 January. Its purpose was to place both corps on less mountainous terrain, thus allowing the entire front to smooth without salients.[33]

The Japanese assaulted the new line time and time again only to be halted by the defending forces. By the end of the month, "General Homma had to temporarily cease major operations to await substantial reinforcements."[34]

On the night of 22–23 January the Japanese attempted an amphibious end run similar to the successful tactics being employed by Yamashita in Malaya. The landings took place at Longoskawayan Point and Quinauan Point. The Japanese amphibious attack force ran into PT 34 on a routine patrol mission. After fighting for fifteen minutes, the PT boat sank one Japanese boat and, not seeing more, continued on its way. An hour later it sank another boat, capturing prisoners and documents. Because of the darkness and their lack of adequate maps, the Japanese force became mixed up and lost.[35] A navy lookout on top of Mt. Pucot spotted the group. But before Commander Bridget with his rear area security battalion could react, the Japanese took possession of the hill. By the twenty-fourth, they were forced back to Longoskawayan Point. But they were dug in, and it would take more than the sailors to root them out.[36]

The other landing force came ashore unopposed, and a counterattack was launched by the 3d Battalion of the 1st Philippine Constabulary. However, by the time they made contact, the enemy had dug themselves in on Quinauan Point. After numerous attempts to drive the Japanese into the sea, the U.S. counterattack force commander was relieved by Colonel Pierce, who had so successfully commanded the 26th Cavalry mentioned earlier. The 21st Pursuit Squadron was ordered in. However, as of the twenty-fifth the Japanese were still entrenched on both points.

Thus from 15 through 24 January the enemy had attempted to run around the Allied flanks on Bataan, they had successfully emplaced artillery within range of the fortified islands, and they had forced the withdrawal of I and II Corps on Bataan. Corregidor had been left alone; it was indeed the "quiet rock." Bunker was craving to fire his guns at the enemy on Longoskawayan Point. Soon he would have his "first real shoot of the war."

Notes

1. Morton, *Philippines,* 364–66. Maj. Gen. Edward Postell King, Jr., was the former commander of the Luzon Force. At this time he was the artillery officer of that command. In March he assumed command of the Luzon Force and a scant three weeks later surrendered his defeated troops to the Japanese.

2. Ens. John L. Dettbarn, USN, "Gold Ballast: War Patrol of USS *Trout,*" *United States Naval Institute Proceedings,* 86, no. 1 (January 1960), 54, 113. "Nearly $3,000,000 in American currency" along with $28,000,000 in Philippine currency was burned after "the serial numbers had been recorded and radioed to the United States." Gold and silver, which were indestructible, were gotten out at a later date.

3. Wainwright, 70. Maj. Charles Morehouse was a member of MacArthur's staff.

4. Baldwin, *Battles,* 130. The following is a portion of the entire letter sent out by MacArthur on 15 January:

Help is on the way from the United States. Thousands of troops and hundreds of planes are being dispatched. The exact time of arrival of reinforcements is unknown as they will have to fight their way through Japanese attempts against them. It is imperative that our troops hold until these reinforcements arrive.

No further retreat is possible. We have more troops in Bataan than the Japanese have thrown against us; our supplies are ample; á determined defense will defeat the enemy's attack.

It is a question now of courage and determination. Men who run will merely be destroyed but men who fight will save themselves and their country.

I call upon every soldier in Bataan to fight in his assigned position, resisting every attack. This is the only road to salvation. If we fight we will win; if we retreat we will be destroyed.

5. Morton, *Strategy,* 144–45. Lt. Gen. Delos C. Emmons, an air force officer, had replaced Lt. Gen. Walter C. Short in command of the Hawaiian Department after the disaster on 7 December.

6. Comdr. Walter Karig and Lt. Welbourn Kelley, *Battle Report: Pearl Harbor to Coral Sea* (New York: Farrar and Rinehart, 1944), 201. Adm. Harry E. Yarnell had been the Commander in Chief Asiatic Fleet until 1939, when he was relieved by Adm. Thomas C. Hart. Yarnell had been known as a "forecaster—of things that were to come in the oriental waters."

7. United States Army Forces in the Far East.

8. Belote and Belote, 77, 190–91. *Register,* 409. Maj. Robert Blake Lothrup commanded the post engineers at Fort Mills and as such was the assistant engineer for fortifications of the harbor defenses at Manila Bay. After being captured by the Japanese, he was one of the few Americans they retained on Corregidor to aid in the repair of the facilities. Sometime after May 1944, he was removed from the island. On 15 October 1944, while attempting to escape from a POW ship off Palawan, P.I., he was killed by the Japanese guards.

9. Chunn, 16–18, 50. Rutherford was a good friend of Bunker's. Later he became a very able organizer of the prisoners in Cabanatuan before he was shipped off to Formosa.

10. *Register,* 373. Maj. Floyd Allan Mitchell was the executive officer for the 91st CA. He was captured and later killed by U.S. bombs sinking the prison ship *Oryoku Maru* in Subic Bay on 15 December 1944.

11. Morison, 158, 203. Rear Adm. Francis W. Rockwell was the commander of the 16th Naval District and the Philippine Coastal Frontier. He was evacuated with MacArthur and his staff on 11 March.

12. *Register,* 342. Hugh John Casey later became a brigadier general. He was evacuated with MacArthur and his staff. He later retired from service as a major general.

13. Belote and Belote, 42, 142. Col. Louis J. Bowler was General Moore's G1. Moore later offered him a berth on an evacuation submarine, but he refused, saying, "Send a nurse."

14. *Register,* 480. Lt. Thomas Walker Davis III commanded H Battery 59th CA. He was later taken prisoner. In 1945 he was repatriated.

15. The 26th Cavalry had already gained a fantastic reputation for its fighting ability. However, nowhere in its annals did it conduct the raid mentioned here. This must have been another rumor to come out of the fighting.

16. *Register,* 427. Paul D. Bunker, Jr., was Colonel Bunker's son, who was killed in an air crash in Hawaii in January 1938.

17. Belote and Belote, 82–83. Richard Gay Ivey of the 60th CA commanded a small concealed aircraft warning detachment on Pico de Loro Mountain. *Register,* 467. Later he was awarded the DSC for his activities.

18. Belote and Belote, 63. Capt. Ben E. King commanded the battery at Geary. Chunn, 154. Later he was captured and suffered heart trouble while in prison at Cabanatuan.

19. *Register,* 425. Col. Stephen M. Mellnik was General Moore's assistant supply officer, who later escaped from the Japanese prison camp on Mindanao and fought as a guerrilla. Later he finally reached Australia. In a very readable book, *Ten Men Escape from Tojo,* he recorded his prison experience.

20. Morison, 286–91. The Dutch air force was, indeed, very active and on 23 January sank a Japanese transport in the Makassar Straits. The reference here,

however, is probably a distorted reference to the U.S. naval action near Balikpa-
pan on the twenty-fourth, when a confused naval battle took place in which the
U.S. Navy sank four transports and one patrol craft.

21. Morton, *Philippines,* 46, 91. USS *Houston* was a heavy cruiser, the flag-
ship of the Asiatic Fleet. It was ordered to Iloilo on 5 December. It fought
valiantly and was finally sunk on 28 February 1942.

22. Belote and Belote, 57.

23. Ibid.

24. Ibid., 82.

25. Wainwright, 50.

26. Ibid., 51.

27. Belote and Belote, 60.

28. Wainwright, 51.

29. Ibid., 52.

30. Belote and Belote, 61.

31. Morton, *Philippines,* 261.

32. Belote and Belote, 61.

33. Wainwright, 52.

34. MacArthur, 132.

35. Morton, *Philippines,* 300–312.

36. Lt. Cmdr. T. C. Parker, USN, "The Epic of Corregidor–Bataan," *United
States Naval Institute Proceedings,* 69, no. 1 (January 1943), 15.

Sunday, 25 Jan 1942
Awoke at 6:00 and went to C1, relieving Simmonds. All quiet. Left at 7:30, shaved, and went to breakfast. Had eggs for first time since war started. Returned to dugout and, there being an "urgent" message for Edison, I returned to C1 with him. Lt. Fulmer reports Japs had landed on 3 sides of Pucot Hill and were dug in, but Marines were attacking and were bringing up a mountain gun. Japs had trench mortars and MG. Fulmer gave exact names of the points where the Japs were and suggested we blast them out. Kinalapayan Bay, Lipai Pt., etc. I sent Edison hot foot to Gen. King's to get permission to open fire. Meanwhile, I told Capt. King at Btry. Geary to be ready to fire on the SE horn of the bay, it being somewhat defiladed from us, and told Capt. McReynolds to prepare to fire on Pt. Lipai, it being fully exposed to him at 12,000 yds. range. Finally, at 10:00 A.M., Edison called up to say that the decision is: "Do nothing at present" DAMN! I retired to my front porch in disgust. What a chance thrown away! Fiddled around my dugout inwardly raving with disappointment. Edison came and said Moore is sending some of our Marines with trench mortars at 10:00 A.M. to reinforce the Marines who have the Japs surrounded. What a waste of manpower! I suppose they will gradually send *all* Marines over there and then my regiment will have to take over the beach defense again?

Drafted endorsement on Capt. Lewis' unsatisfactory efficiency report. He is very fair about it.

Later news from Fulmer indicated that the Marines were rounding up the Japs. It now appears that the items of yesterday that I recorded under "rumors" were facts—and very pleasing facts, too. The Dutch are winning universal admiration out here.

At 2:00 P.M. Btry. Geary fired 4 rounds at extreme range to test ballistics and superquick fuses. All 4 detonated on hitting the water, but the range and deflection deviations were terrific. Technique was loose and rough. Simmonds again demonstrates his inefficiency as a group commander. I saw the shoot from BC [battalion command] which was too full of bunks and footlockers, etc. An undisciplined crew. Langeler didn't even know how to handle an azimuth instrument! Drove to battery and then went to Crockett and hung around there (after Hauck gave me a cold bottle of beer) and had dinner there. Then to Hearn and chinned until 6:30. To dugout—and to C1 at 7.

Although it was hinted about Malinta Tunnel that we would do it, it was not until about 8:00 P.M., as I was leaving C1 in disgust, for my dugout, that we got orders through Gen. King, to open about 12 salvos on Langoskawayan Pt. Commander Bridget, USN, in charge over there, said he would withdraw his men and would give us the green light about 10:00–10:30. At 10:30 I managed to get him

43

on the phone and he said all clear except 2 runners! and postponed firing "15 minutes." But it was not until nearly midnight that Edison phoned up from BC Geary to go ahead. Then we embarked on our first real shoot of the war. Geary: 12″ mortars and we used 700-lb. land-attack projectiles with superquick fuses which worked beautifully.

For effectiveness, the shoot was fine. After the 4th shot Fulmer reported that we had started such big fires that he could spot no longer unless we shot 200 yards left. I ordered Edison to shift but evidently this was not done. About the 3d or 4th shot landed on a ridge in my field of view and I could see the grand explosion, and the swirling smoke of the fire. Dope came in, through radio to Hearn: "Your shells are landing where the Japs are." Last 2 shots were a 2-gun salvo but landed so far to the right I was scared for the safety of our Lt. Fulmer, who was spotting from a point on the slope of Pucot Hill. I believe the azimuth setter at the mortar made an error of 1 in laying his mortar. Comdr. Bridget was so alarmed that he called "cease firing" because he feared endangering his men, nearby. Meanwhile, we loaded two more mortars and wanted to shoot the projectiles out, but he wouldn't stand for it!

As an example of shooting a mortar, it was the worst I ever saw—as a glance at the time schedule will show. Several reports of "lanyard broken" and "primer misfire" were received. As we were firing in zone 10 (extreme range) the powder completely filled the chamber and, in one instance, could not be forced into the chamber. For speed and efficiency it was a terribly humiliating experience—even though most of the firing non-coms had been killed in the bombing of 6 Jan. Simmonds manned the improvised spotting line through 3 exchanges to Lt. Fulmer, whose "spots," being inaudible, had to be relayed by Lt. Paddock at the Navy Bn Exchange near Mariveles. Simmonds had to scream to be heard.

Bridget finally said we had inflicted enough damage and thanked us. Then Foster, Simmonds, Edison and I foregathered at my dugout and celebrated with a couple of Scotches from the dwindling stock, discussed the shoot and finally broke up at 2 A.M.

Simmonds disclaimed all responsibility for the fiasco (in firing technique) because I had placed responsibility on Bn Commanders—and he was right. It is Edison's fault.

Monday, 26 Jan 1942
12th day of no bombs.

Awoke at 7:30, washed and went to breakfast. Gathered up Simmonds and Edison preparatory to cleaning up the Geary Shoot. Could get no dope from Fulmer except that he will report over here and tell us about it. Heard unofficially that the shoot was so good we may have another tonight.

Crews alarmed me by calling for a detail of 90 men and 2 officers to handle freight at North Wharf and Middleside Barracks all day. The freight movement will last a week! I wonder if that means our Bataan forces are being so badly licked that they are about to evacuate them, too, to Corregidor? What will we do with those thousands of extra persons here on the Rock?

Told Edison my disappointment in his not insuring King's Battery to be better trained. He admitted the corn. We went to Geary and interviewed Capt. King. Told him I was relieving him from command of his battery because he had failed properly to train his battery. Decided to take newly captainized Davis out of F and give him H. Drove down to Btry. Smith and told him about it. Then to my dugout, where Edison finally brought Lt. Fulmer, who had just arrived from his adventure at Pucot Hill last night. He gave some very vivid reports of the Jap activity there. The Jap bunch there are mature and splendidly trained men who talk American—even slang—and have outsmarted us at every turn. Their camouflage uniforms are most ingenious and deceptive; they are armed with Tommy guns and each man goes his own way, scattering and hiding and thus forming lots of 1-man armies. Each carries grenades and is adept in their use. These are no conscripts, but a *corps délite!* They have been around Pucot a long time. They ran our observers off Pucot Hill by surprise and then disappeared. It would be a fine job if we killed them all—but nobody has yet gone down onto their point to see what damage our mortar fire did last night. The Marines were planning a mop-up attack for 1:00 P.M. today but, as they had been going at top speed for 3 days and nights, they were pretty well tuckered.

Went with Edison and Fulmer to HD HQ in Malinta Tunnel and sat in conference with Generals Moore and King while Fulmer told them his story and we tried to force them to let us shoot some more. Two of our mortars have projectiles rammed into them now, which must be shot out. Also asked that we be allowed to blast the Japs off the two capes which enclose Agaloma Bay. Learned that, this morning, our P-40s shot down two of the 3 fast Jap bombers that came over this morning. (Incidentally, one of our P-40s, pursued by several Japs, fled to us for protection this afternoon and several machine guns (even of the AA regiment) opened on him until they were told to stop!) You can't blame them; our planes display no "friendly" identification flares or signals—so we have to assume that all planes are enemy planes. Though they do say that we have as many as 20 P-40s now!

To C1 to tell Capt. Hauck to help out Btry. Geary by organizing two mortar sections, thus letting us fire 4-gun salvos. This will come in handy in firing deck piercing projectiles at the Japs who are said to be living in caves on the shore at Langoskawayan Pt.—by the USAFFE G3 who admits he has heard nothing from Cmdr. Bridgett! (I dropped into USAFFE HQ to give MacArthur my felicitations on his 62d birthday, but he was not there.) However, received message that he was coming to C1 to see me, so I stuck around—and he showed up and was very affable. (I had, at Malinta Tunnel, suggested to Moore that it would be a logical idea, since my job includes command of 3 regiments, that I be made a BG [brigadier general]. He seemed doubtful, though he said USAFFE had just made 5 Brigadiers! He promised to see MacArthur.

To G/91 for shower and (privilege!) use of a toilet! Afterwards to Hearn as usual and chinned with McReynolds and Verde. Bliss also showed up and looked weak as usual. Didn't say much. At dusk, went to my dugout. (Another touch of "back door trots.")

To C1, Col. Foster in charge, until 9:45, waiting for Edison to return from a conference with Gen. King about our firing against land tomorrow. No firing tonight but they want us to pave the way for attack by 57th Infantry tomorrow.

Found today, that a splinter perforated my portable typewriter case but only dented the machine.

Edison and Simmonds came to my dugout with tomorrow's firing dope, which we discussed until 11:00 P.M. and then turned in.

Tuesday, 27 Jan 1942
Wrote Landon and Bill.

Waked at 6:00 and went to C1 at 6:30 to supervise our Btry. Geary's shoot against the Japs supposed to be at Langoskawayan Pt.

I watched the firing from C1. Bursts of the HE [high explosive] (personnel) shells were plainly visible, but the deck piercing projectiles with their 0.05-second delay fuses were harder to pick up, since the smoke of their bursts did not show up, above the intervening ridge, until 10 seconds or so after their bursts. But evidently their bursts were not entirely smothered, so perhaps they were worthwhile. During our bombardment, there was active firing, probably by 155m guns in same general location—though Fulmer reported it was up around Aga-loma Bay. He later reported our shooting very accurately; "no Jap resistance yet—this Pucot Hill will probably be a hot spot—let's move to Cochinos."

We are all wishing that we could see what that Langoskawayan Point looks like, after all our shelling—and we're wondering how anybody could be left alive on it.

Drove to Cheney and had a belated breakfast as guests of Capt. Steiger, at which Edison joined us later. Went to Regtl. HQ for necessary purpose and to get letter paper. To my quarters in vain search for stamps and then to C1. At my dugout copied the critical data of our morning's firing into the table. Edison brought me message from Fulmer: "Shooting very accurate—Jap activity at Aga-loma Bay—sniping all around me—Signs of Jap push here, etc." Phoned Moore and told him I was calling Fulmer in to Bn. HQ since he had no protection—and had Edison radio him accordingly. Foster came into my dugout with report on defects at gun drill at Btry. Geary this morning: "untrained and undisciplined"— just as I had sized them up. Edison and Simmonds left, but Foster stuck around until 1:00 P.M.

This P.M. we heard from Fulmer, that Bridgett had countermanded my orders and told him to hold Pucot with his detail plus a couple of 60th men. Also that the Marines had advanced to within 200 yards of the Point and wanted us to fire on it! Suicidal for, at 14,000 yards, we can't place shots as accurately as that and, besides, the destructive radius is well over 500 yards. Very flattering request but impossible.

HD HQ is now storing TNT in ground floors of 3 east-most batteries! of Topside barracks, thus clearing the Kindley field area. Cottrell admitted this is to "take care of more troops"—that is,—they are preparing to withdraw our troops on Bataan to Corregidor! That looks BAD. They are also shipping in ammunition from Cabcaben and war reserve food from Mariveles.

This afternoon I wrote two notes, one to Bill in Nicaragua and one to Landon, telling them all is well—but I don't know if they will get out.

Last night our P-40s took off late at night and later much bombing was heard over Cavite way. It is said that some of our bombers came up from the south and bombed Cavite and Clark Field—and that the Japs broadcast "The treacherous Americans bombed an open city" meaning Manila, which they have made *not* an open city—though they bombed it when it *was*. I wish we had bombed the Jap front lines in Bataan, instead.

Simmonds, Cooper and I had shower and saw extensive bombing towards Cabcaben. To Hearn for a while and then sat on my azatea in the moonlight with a Scotch until belated Foster appeared about 9:00. Chinned until nearly 11:00 and turned in. I still wish I had a description of what Langoskawayan Pt. looks like.

Wednesday, 28 Jan 1942
14th day of no bombs.

Slept until 7:00. Shaved and went to breakfast of sour pancakes. Afterwards took my genealogy books, in stamp cabinet, to Crockett and stored them. Also told Welch to take my two cans of clothes and linen down there. Told Capt. King, who goes to Drum tonight, to get his feet under him and get back to normalcy. His Lt. Saunders is also partly nuts. Patronized the "facilities of the Post" at RHQ. Inspected library and found numerous enlisted men coming in and lifting books. Our 3 boxes of juvenile books have been broken open and scattered. Inspected Crockett, also HQ Btry. mess and looked around for wire heavy enough to lead power from Btry. Wheeler down into C1 Tunnel. Trolley feeder line will do it!

In P.M. tried to get a siesta but failed. Lt. Fulmer showed up in P.M. and voluble over his experiences in spotting for our fire yesterday. There are plenty of Japs left at Langoskawayan Pt. After the Marines had moved well down the peninsula the Japs, who had sneaked past them on both shores and taken to the trees, opened fire into the Marines' backs thus forcing them back with 3 men wounded. They had also poured 75mm and mortar fire into the place until about 1:00 P.M., and then made their attack. The Marines evidently wanted to wind it up themselves but these Japs were just too good! The 57th Inf took over in the afternoon and the Marines, who were justifiably exhausted, pulled back. This 57th had previously completed 2 jobs just like this and sent word (after we had prepared for a 30-min. shoot from 3:30 to 4 P.M.) that their attack was progressing so well that they didn't want to stop for Artillery support. However, when they had worked down to the extreme point of the peninsula, they found that there were still about 75 Japs in caves under the point—evidently they had been around here for a long time, maybe weeks. So we are to stage another shoot tomorrow morning from 7:00–7:30 and try to pulverize the very tip of the point. It will take some lucky shooting! Got this dope about 7:30 P.M. went over the firing data with Edison.

The artillery firing on Bataan seems perceptibly closer now. I hope Brooke is all right. It seems that, after the Japs bombed Cabcaben yesterday, two of our P-40s came out of concealment on that field and shot one of the Jap's bombers down in flames. The official count of planes shot down (correct or not) now stands at about 94 by AA fire and 38 by airplane action. By "AA" is meant all AA troops in P.I. [Philippine Islands], including our 59th CA.

At dinner tonight Schenck had the officers table set out in the open and it was an improvement until the sun slanted under the trees. We three had to wait for places to be vacated. Excellent roast beef. Then to G/91 for our showers and Chong was AWOL. Stopped at HQ Btry. for piece of lemon pie—then to Hearn, where Fulmer was talking to a bunch of soldiers about his experiences and, after they broke up, could talk of nothing else.

Drove to C1 and received news about firing tomorrow and made plans accordingly.

This morning saw Col. Elmes at Wheeler and also at Crockett. He promised me a new typewriter! But I doubt if I get it. I invited him up to the azatea tonight for a Scotch and so told Foster when I saw him at C1 about 8:00 P.M. All quiet there, so I returned to my dugout. Foster came along with message from HD HQ that our walkie-talkie was interfering with the AA flash net and went up to Edison's tent—then the same message came to me from Cottrell, plus a Navy report that Jap heavy bombers are up tonight—which is rather a surprise. Went to C1 to straighten it out and there finally located Edison. Trouble was caused by Fulmer playing with a couple of sets down at Hearn, trying to calibrate them. Closed him up. "And so to bed."

Thursday, 29 Jan 1942
15th day of no bombs!
They woke me at 6:30; went to C1 and supervised our 3rd shoot against Lan-

goskawayan Pt. to blast the damn Japs there preparatory to the attack of the 57th Infantry (Scouts). It was a disappointing shoot, compared with our others.

At 7:50 we sighted a warship coming in, out Hornos way. At 40,000 yards she turned broadside and made for mainland, at about Bagac. We identified her as of the Natori class—a cruiser with 5″ guns. She disappeared behind Hornos Pt. I guess we had no bombers to send against her. Meanwhile the USS *Quail*[1] was having a swell time with her 3″ guns against the Japs, but she finally quit along about 8:30 and came in. We had a big sub come in last night, carrying a mystery cargo: some say it was mechanical fuses and .50 cal ammunition. She is to go out tonight, after the moon sets.

Belated breakfast on French toast. Then to dugout. Air alarm had gone at 9:07 but, after hearing AA fire towards Mariveles, I judged that Corregidor was safe and so walked to breakfast.

This afternoon I made a drain plate for my drip coffee pot. Had Welch put my cot out on my azatea, to see if I won't sleep better. Cooper, however, changed it for a folding cot, after dinner.

Went with Foster and dined at his mess. His racing speed in his old Ford, is 15 mph. Nice, gentlemanly mess but crawling with flies. Welch came for me in my car, after changing a flat tire, and I drove to G/91 for my usual shower. Chong was there this time.

One of my old khaki uniforms is about shot—and though Woo Lee promises results, I doubt that I'll be able to get another one.

(This morning I got after Holton, to get back on the library job, and got repercussions from Chaplain Wilcox.)

Drove to Hearn and chinned awhile and then to C1. Much arty firing up on the east coast of Bataan Peninsula at 7:00 P.M.

Col. Elmes, Maj. Kriwanek and Capt. Covington showed up at C1 and we adjourned to my dugout with Foster and Simmonds and sat there in the moonlight and drank some gin and bitters, mixed up by Simmonds. Very pleasant.

After they left, I turned in on my cot in the open, hoping for better sleep but unsuccessful and slept fitfully. Wide awake by 5:30 A.M.

Later: They have been collecting bomber and fighter pilots here at Corregidor and, they say, many of them departed on board of that mysterious submarine, tonight, presumably to join our forces in the south, and pilot some of the planes which, we hear, are arriving from the States. We all hope that they soon find their way back here.

G3 Rept. of 2 Feb:* "A wounded Jap prisoner, captured at Longoskawayan Pt.,

---

*This was obviously added later.

was asked by G2-HPD: 'What effect did the large artillery shell fire have on your force?' Answer was: 'We were terrified. We could not know where the big shells or bombs were coming from; they seemed to be falling from the sky. Before I was wounded, my head was going round and round, and I did not know what to do. Some of my companions jumped off the cliff to escape the terrible fire.' It would seem that the 12″ mortar fire from Fort Mills did a bang-up good job." Memo sent Seaward Defense Cmdr. by HD Cmdr. 3 Feb 42.

P225 left at end of month.

+P6.00 won at poker.

Friday, 30 Jan 1942

Kaypayon Hill.

Rolled out at 6:00 A.M. and went to C1. Poured some more water through the coffee grounds and found the result as bad as I had expected. All quiet and day dawned without incident. Shaved and went to breakfast at Wheeler. Determined to pay a visit to Malinta Tunnel, so drove around San José Barrio now: it is just a mess of crumpled corrugated iron and ruins, and so desolate! Barrels of oil scattered along the roads. Called on Gen. Moore and asked about PX and other checks on Philippine Trust Co. With usual Army fatuosity, we seem to be doing nothing about it. Went across Tunnel to see Gen. King and he said that 57th has completely mopped up Longoskawayan Pt. NAVY reports our mortar fire "entirely ineffectual" but they (the *Quail*) saw only yesterday's firing! The 57th "thanks the Navy for their assistance," i.e. the *Quail*'s firing of yesterday!

Then saw Elmes and he gave me a new Underwood typewriter, 14″ carriage, gratis. Saw Woo Lee about a suntan uniform and put typewriter in car and delivered it to RSO [regimental supply officer] in Bombproof, as substitute for the L.C. Smith which I formerly used. Called on Sgt. Mason at Cold Stores, at Elmes' suggestion, and he gave me some Edam cheeses, salami, bologna, and big can of buttermilk, which I distributed among HQ Btry., A and D.

As I was bawling out some men for tapping our AC power lines, Simmonds, Edison, and Hauck came along, hurrying to C1 to look at a Jap ship which had just been sighted. Sure enough, there she was, a grey blur on the hazy horizon, up towards Subic. We saw her fire landward at least once, as she turned and steamed farther out to sea. Away out of our range, and at some 40,000 yards. We all hung around for a while then went about our business. See Sunday? This was about 1:00 P.M.

Visited the hospital this morning and found Maj. Julian there. Intimated that the steel desk in the Surgeon's office would look well in our C1 Tunnel.

Loafed around dugout in P.M. entertaining Foster while Welch installed a railing on my azatea. Tried in vain to get a siesta but Foster always drops around at just the right time to stop that. Read a bit in "A Teashop in Limehouse," by Burke and found I had read most of them.

Gosh, how the days slip past, with nothing to show for them! Drove down as usual for our baths, after dinner at Wheeler. Schenck has spread a tent-fly over the officer's table, which is an improvement. But the lazy KPs [kitchen police] were loafing around and none had cleaned the men's mess tables! Schenck corrected them *gently!* Drove back to Hearn and had a glass of buttermilk—then to C1 dugout. I found that my store of Philippine money has dwindled to P5.00.

Very little artillery activity today over Bataan way. Went down to C1 at about 7:00 and hung around awhile, watching Foster strut his stuff and then, as everything seemed quiet, Edison went to bed and the rest of us adjourned to "the Club" and played poker until about 11:00. Took a reading on C1 and then retired inside my dugout. Nice, clear, moonlit night.

Colin seems to have some kind of skin disease: he has scratched himself raw under his chin and on his belly. He scratches himself and bites his back interminably.

Today I reported to HD Exec that B/60 was tapping off power for enlisted men's shacks, radios, etc. He retorted they would take care of 60th and for me to care for my regiment.

They say that no Japs were taken prisoner at the fight at Longoskawayan Pt., that they committed suicide by shooting and by "jumping over the cliffs," though I didn't know that the configuration of the ground would permit the latter. But "no prisoners" seems to be official. It is said that there are many Moros in the 57th, that they hate Japs even worse than they do Tagalogs (which is saying a mouthful) and that they waded into action with their knives as their principal weapon, with the idea of getting themselves some of the Japs' tommy guns.

Later: They say we lost two P-40s today: One started out and never returned; the other one evidently ran into trouble of some sort and the pilot bailed out north of Corregidor.

Saturday, 31 Jan 1942
Lost P2 at poker (won P6.00 net this month).

17th day of no bombs.

Awoke at 6:00 and went to C1. Had a cup of good Maxwell House coffee out of my French drip coffee pot and the change was refreshing. Slowly "came the dawn" and we found that, perhaps due to aggressiveness of Comdr. Bridgett, there were 2 small Navy boats patrolling close inshore beyond Hornos Pt.[2] No fire action, so I guess it is true that the 57th mopped up all Japs at Longoskawayan Pt.

At 8:20 went to dugout, shaved, went to Wheeler for breakfast and then watched the firing of 4 rounds there for checking new settings of throttling valves. 1st shot from No. 1, with reduced setting, was perfect, but they closed the valve still more and got it too tight. Barry seems to think that notch 30 is OK, but I prefer 34 because it makes loading easier and hides the gun better.

To RHQ [regimental headquarters] for duties and then to Officer's Mess outside east entrance of Malinta Tunnel for meeting of PX Council. The PX stock
was mostly looted and it now consists mostly of the stock of the Indian and Chinese stores which were formerly concessions. Will probably go out of business in
a month or so, for lack of stock. Representative of high commissioner appeared
and vaguely intimated that little, if anything, can be done to get PX money out of
Phil. Trust. No audit or inventory was taken as of close of business this month!
Meeting dragged on and on, until the "Termites" (brass hats who live in the Tunnel) came around with their dainty lunches on their plates, wondering why we
were occupying the table "reserved for HD staff."

After the meeting adjourned at 12:30, I went to HD Finance Office and drew
my pay for *December,* leaving my Jan. pay undrawn. Got P661.20 including $10
in U.S. money. Also, luckily found out that my allotment to Landon expires
today and so signed new allotment form for new allotment of $250 beginning
tomorrow and continuing "indefinitely" thus taking care of her if I should be captured. Also important: the notice which Washington will send her will serve as a
substitute for the radio which I *can't* send her, that I am still on the map.

Drove back to my dugout and sent Welch with Colin to the Veteran Hospital
to see what could be done about alleviating his itch. To C1 and found the 2 small
Navy boats still prowling around Hornos Pt. Just at 4:00, as I was preparing to go
to chow, Moore came and told me that Gen. Moore had given Boudreau permission to fire on Ternate! I hustled to C1 and, by dint of cussing, got them to start
shooting at 5:15—lasted until 6:20.

Shot about 30 of 12″ mortar projectiles of 700 lbs. each with superquick fuses
and we watched the bursts from C1 but, as a fringe of trees obscured our view of
the barrio of Ternate, we couldn't see the damage. After about 16 shots they
shifted fire to the hill, just south, where the Japs have probably completed their
tunnel. Blasted this hill thoroughly. Meanwhile Ft. Frank opened with 155mm
shrapnel, but the bursts were way short on the trajectory and worthless—which
we phoned them. Then they shifted to HE shell. All in all, once the firing got
started, it seemed to raise hell over there, and we have hopes that at least all the
Filipinos lit out. As to the Japs, we are probably too late: they have either dug in
or, as some maintain, have gone elsewhere.

After the shoot, had belated dinner, then Cooper and I dashed down to G/91
and had showers and drove back under a gorgeous moon that was practically full.
Edison on duty tonight. Foster came to my dugout; we sent for Simmonds and
had a couple of gin and bitters. Then went to Club and played poker, at which I
lost P2. Visited C1 and then turned in at midnight.

While at Wheeler, Col. Williams[3] told me of Brooke—that he had seen him
yesterday or day before and that he was well, was doing good work and was as
happy as conditions permitted. Commisary bill, Jan = Soaps $0.60, Cigarettes
$1.50, Undershirts .52; Total $2.62 = P5.24.

Sunday, 1 Feb 1942

Slept until 7:00—to C1—shaved—breakfast—Simmonds and Edison arriving later. To RHQ where Julian has installed quite a power plant, with an Edison battery of over 100 volts. Inspected our C1 Tunnel and found them just ready to start the exit-stair slope. They agree to dig a couple of side rooms for use as dormitories or sumpin, besides our 3 small laterals for officers. After talking with these practical mining Egrs. [engineers] awhile, I drove to Engr. Tunnel at Bottomside and talked with Lothrup about continuing our main tunnel all the way through the hill and putting an offset in the exit stairs—and hope that he may do it for us, but can't be sure.

Visited Btry. Way and met Maj. Maynard (Engrs.) in charge of the Reproduction Plant. A genial Yankee from Connecticut. Some beautiful drafting being done there by Filipinos. He introduced me to his lieutenant, who promised to develop my films for me! So I'll have to finish exposing that reel now in my camera, though I wanted to reserve the last exposure to use on my quarters when the Japs finish bombing it.

Went to C1 to check in, and then to my dugout. There is furious artillery fire over Limao way—sounds like 75mm.

See Friday's account of the Jap cruiser. It appears that Lawlor[4] fired 155mm. guns at her, at 5th ranging shot scored a hit and went into "fire for effect." Results unknown, but that probably explains the Japs' hurried departure. Also, they say that Lawlor lost 2 guns a while back. He was away on reconnaissance and the Japs got in rear of his guns. Monteith, with the men, fought their way out, taking the breechblocks with them and, somehow or other "found" three more 155mm guns and so were better off than before.

Edison came down to the dugout and we worked up Capt. King's efficiency report.

Called up Col. Boudreau's at Ft. Frank and blistered his hide for his delay of 1¼ hours in starting his firing yesterday. Recommended he summarily relieve Capt. White[5] from command of his battery. Boudreau weakly replied that "with the lessons he had learned, he thought White would do better." Hell, he *couldn't* do worse! I summarily relieved Capt. King for less! Also remarked on Shumate's inefficient handling of the firing of the 155mm. But one could hardly expect much of Shumate!

The Filipino sergeant who is tunneling below C1 presented me with a live iguana—a small one—which thoroughly aroused Colin. Had him skinned, dressed and sent to HQ Btry. Mess for cooking for dinner tonight.

At 1:30 Welch took Colin to corral in an effort to get the vet to look at him and ease his itch—also, I hope, to wash the car. Couldn't find vet.

At 4:00, Edison and I went to HQ Btry. and ate fried iguana with Capt. McCarthy. It was delicious; like chicken only richer. Gave a piece to Sgt. Gavito. Then Edison and I drove to G/91 and had our showers as usual.

Played poker this evening and won P3.00.

This evening there was a regular Fourth of July exhibit of fireworks over Hornos Pt. way. We learned afterward that the Japs attempted a landing up Bagac way, with landing boats, supported by their cruiser. One of our PT boats was up there; they reported being illuminated by the cruiser's searchlight and were fired upon simultaneously (a German technique) whereupon they shot both of their torpedoes and "went a way from there."

Their 2d "fish" hit "something" and they hope it was the cruiser. Our pursuit planes were in the fray, too, but, unfortunately, not at the same time as the PT boat. One rumor has it that we destroyed 7 of the 13 landing boats! Shore forces evidently joined in the fray. The dope is that the landing attempt was repulsed, the firing kept up until along toward 1:00 A.M. There were two attempts: the first was driven off by our artillery; the second was more serious and included a large number of barges under naval escort—launched toward midnight.

Monday, 2 Feb 1942

19th day of no bombs!

Just another day in the war but this one was brightened by the first real news that indicates we may receive help, someday. This evening it seems official that a U.S. expedition suddenly attacked and conquered all of the Marshall, the Mariana, and the Caroline archipelagoes, erasing all Jap footholds, bases, etc. in those islands![6] This is very grateful news to us, for it shows us that our reinforcements are not so far away. Guam is only 6 days' sail—even by army transport and, with good bases there, our bombers could easily operate against the Japs here or even in Japan. We all hope that they shove along fast, in order not to be too late to help the British in their losing battle, down Singapore. For today the news arrived that the Japs have driven them back into Singapore itself—that the British retreated across the causeways, blew them up, and are now holding only Singapore—but the Limeys are already whimpering that the Japs can now bombard their airfields, etc. but that they will "hold out"! They sure are great at letting other people do their fighting for them!

Note that Pres. Roosevelt's latest speech guarantees that we will redeem Philippines' independence! Gratuitous, unnecessary and damn bad strategy.

Ordinary routine all day—until we were at dinner. I'd just finished when Hawes phoned me that Gen. Moore directed fire be opened from Ft. Frank: 3 salvos each, of 2 guns, 155mm at bridge in Ternate and "Tunnel" Hill. Dusted down to C1 with Edison and Simmonds and watched the shoot. Took Boudreau over half an hour to get off the first salvo! Criminal! Shooting seemed fair, but not so good as mortars.

Hustled down for our showers and then back to my dugout to wait Maj. Lothrup CE [Corps of Engineers] whom we invited in for a drink. We all had a gin and bitters before he arrived, another after he arrived. He has agreed to run our C1 Tunnel straight through the hill! Also put offset in exit stairs. Now we'll have a real Bombproof!

Col. Ausmus brought Col. Howard[7] and Lt. Col. Hamilton of 4th Marines down to C1. They stopped on their way back and we gave them a drink. But Hamilton thought he heard a plane, so they beat it. Last of all, Foster came, and he had a drink with us! It was his gin in the first place! We all sat around and gassed. Couldn't get up a poker game. Not much moonlight in early evening because of overcast sky. I slept outside, on my porch, but the moon came out very brightly, later on.

Official Score, USAFFE, up to date, of planes brought down

Downed By—	Previously	On 2 February	Total
Antiaircraft	98	2	100
Air Corps	45	0	45

This Jap bunch that dug in on Longoskawayan Pt. is now called the Tatori Group and, as we first suspected, are a *corps délite*. Reference their attempted landing near Bagac last night, USAFFE says "This morning the beaches showed disabled barges, some burning, others adrift in the sea. This constitutes another telling blow at the Tatori Group. On our right, after stopping Gen. Nara's frontal attack by the Jap 65th yesterday, aimed at driving a wedge between our forces, one of our divisions made a sudden counterattack which overran 3 lines of enemy trenches, capturing considerable equipment."

Tuesday, 3 Feb 1942
Barber 40¢.
Won P4.00.
Up at 5:00 and to C1—but Capt. Schenck stuck around to see the spects. Another sub. We amused ourselves concocting rumors about her bringing in ordles (orderlies') freight, but came the depths of depravity to which this war has lowered otherwise sensible [men], preferably is said to be coming from Australia—anyway, she ran the Jap gauntlet.

After breakfast we gathered at C1 to watch Ft. Frank fire 62-gun salvos re the alleged Ternate bridge and the "Tunnel" Hill. Although we were looking right into the sun and hence could see but poorly, it looked as though the bursts were much better placed than before, except that only one hit the hill.

Cottrell phoned to use "delayed contact" instead of automatic contact settings in the mine casemate, because the "old" system acquires shorts and leaks. He also said that our prior Ternate firings were evidently much better than at first reported, because the Japs closed the town, would let nobody near, and evacuated hastily en masse; they left a few at Sapong barrio, across the river to the east.

Prepared maps of Corregidor and Bataan for my "Forgettery Books." To my quarters for stationery and then to Regtl. HQ for secret map of PF [position-finding] stations. While there, an air alarm sounded and our AA opened up with 3″ and MG. But no bombs fell. It was evidently a lone Jap plane on propaganda bent, for it flew towards Mariveles and dropped leaflets over Bataan. This on the say-so of some Navy men who were removing a nice safe from the old USN Radio HQ. I drove back to C1 at 12:30 and did homework, in spite of Foster coming around and boring me to death by his bump-on-a-log presence.

He loves to remark, when he finds me writing, "My, but you'll have a complete history of the war, won't you?"

As I walked up for chow, Simmonds handed me an order which Cottrell had handed him, grinning and saying "Well, here's something that should please Col. Bunker." It was an order to conduct harassing fire from Btry. Frank (155mm) on Ternate, 24 shots a day, until further orders, fire to be directed at Sapong barrio near Ternate and at the Ternate bridge. The order gave permission for a special shoot at 1:10 A.M. tonight on Ternate and the "Tunnel" Hill. Great rejoicing!

After dinner we, as usual, took showers at G/91 and adjourned to Btry. Hearn for a talkfest and then moved on to C1 to make arrangements for Ft. Frank's shoot. Simmonds, Edison and I went to my dugout to calculate the azimuths of the target from C1. Then to our "Club" and tried to join—or hoped to join—the poker game—but the ill-bred boors ignored us! Left with a snappy comment on their rudeness and, returning to my dugout, completed calculation of azimuths about 12:30.

Went to C1 to watch the shoot. First shot went promptly at 1:10 and the rest went with reasonable dispatch. First 4 were superquick fuses in "personnel" HE shells, fired at Sapong; remaining 8 were deck piercing with .05 second delay fuse, fired at bridge. We saw the impacts of the 1st 4—but not so plainly as at Longoskawayan, but saw no signs of the last 8. Probably they buried themselves in the ground.

Turned in, in dugout at 2:00 A.M.

At dinner, Cooper handed me a letter from Gen. Moore, enclosing a copy of his letter to USAFFE, recommending that I be made a brigadier general, very flattering (but pleasing) letter. Maybe it has something to do with the order, today, transferring Lt. Col. Ausmus out of the 59th? However in view of my age, I doubt that it will go through. Maybe they have something else against me—that GCM[8] [general court martial] that I was framed into, way back in 1919. It's in the lap of the Gods.

One of our big subs snuck in tonight, and unloaded lots of new AA ammunition for us. At daybreak she will be lying on the bottom 2 miles away from us.[9]

Wednesday, 4 Feb 1942

I bet we are due for a severe night bombing soon! . . . Shaved—breakfast—to RSO momentarily—then to my . . . revolvers are rusting in the damp air of the dugout in spite of [here a corner of the page is missing] . . . worked on my aza-tea until 1:30 then used the last film in my roll to get a picture of Julian's quar-ters. Took the film to Major Maynard to be developed and then, as he told me he was sending some papers out on the sub tonight, I hustled back to my dugout and started typing a letter to Landon. Joe Cottrell came along and I took him down to see our Bombproof. The slob told me I am too late to catch *this* subma-rine, that she had already unloaded and would leave tonight without returning to our wharf! Cottrell also avers that it is hopeless to try to get Admiral Rock-well to do anything. He was in the Cavite bombing and has a bad case of shell-shock (?) alias "cold feet." So he just sits in his "Queen Tunnel" and smokes cigarettes and shows no sign of life. I wish there were more like Comdr. Bridgett in this Navy!

Finished my letter to Landon, it consisted of only 1 sheet, and found a 5¢ U.S. stamp for it. After chow, drove down to G/91 for usual shower and gave Chong my new uniform to launder. Am getting some work out of him now, for yesterday Welch changed the white seat covers in Gwenny [Bunker's personal car] and he now has excessively dirty ones to wash!

Then I drove down to the Queen (Navy) Tunnel and found Comdr. Hoeffel[10] at the entrance. Asked him to get my letter aboard the submarine and he agreed to do so, took it and walked to S wharf. I left and drove to Btry. Hearn for our usual evening talkfest. Got them to break out the salami I gave them some time ago, also an Edam cheese which the boy cut into thin slices!

Tonight I feel excessively tired—for some unknown reason. Went to C1 this P.M. at 5:03 to see Frank conduct harassing fire at Ternate—and they still are not good: the correction for their second salvo was applied in the wrong direction!

Gen. Moore had ordered us to change our program—to lump the 24 shots into about 4 shoots of 6 shots each. So we slated one for 5:03 P.M. and the other about 10:15 P.M. Their last shot of 5:03 P.M. shoot appeared to ricochet along the ground.

Simmonds, Foster and I adjourned to my azatea and had two gin and bitters and chewed the fat till 9:30 when they left and I turned in, outside on my azatea.

Latest dope of our Navy is that, instead of all the islands I noted a few days ago, they captured only the Gilbert and Marshall Islands—Quite a let-down.

Today paid my commissary bill of only P5.24. Got a haircut at Battery A.

Thursday, 5 Feb 1942

Up and about, as usual. A quiet day all day in all respects. Another sub came in last night, and left tonight. They say she brought no freight, but came in solely to load up with torpedoes. Hope she finds some prey—preferably in the convoy of "40 Jap war vessels and 20 or more transports" which are rumored to have been sighted off Formosa last night! And, if true, they're probably not headed for Sin-gapore, either!

Went to the Malinta Tunnel and thanked Gen. Moore for his letter of recommendation for brigadier. Talked with Gen. King about shooting up Agloloma
and he said our shells are too powerful, that our troops would have to withdraw too far. Rumor says a Jap commander, possibly at Agloloma, radioed apologies to his boss for failing in his mission of establishing a beach-head on
Bataan's west coast!

Couldn't see Braly in tunnel and get dope on Ft. Frank, but got a good engineering map of Ternate quadrangle by signing for it.

The war is slowing down, here, and so paper work is catching up with us.
Spent most of the day on my azatea at it.

We are now staging about 4 shoots per day at Sapong and targets thereabouts.

This morning I discovered a derelict barge offshore and so staged a shoot of 6
rounds from Btry. Smith at it. They used stacked powder and, although they
failed to hit the barge, the shooting was excellent and they hit all around it and
very close.

We had to postpone our noon shoot at Sapong because of rain squalls out in
the water.

They say that the sub which left last night took 100 bags of mail out.

After our shower I drove to Hearn with Simmonds. They broke out the Edam
cheese and Foster enjoyed it hugely. Then we went to my azatea, McReynolds
and I and Foster joined us and we had a gin and bitters and then played poker
until 10:45. I won P4.00. And so to bed.

Transition

25 January–6 February

The last week in January and the first week in February marked a
period of almost constant defeat for the Japanese: the U.S. lines on
Bataan refused all attacks, Corregidor projected her combat power to the
nearby shores, and the Japanese on Longoskawayan and Quinauan
Points were killed to the last man.

As we have seen, Battery Geary was finally allowed to fire on the
points. This marked the first time that an American coast artillery piece
had fired on an enemy since the end of the Civil War.[11] This firing from
Corregidor was to continue until her surrender to the Japanese.

In addition to the firing from Corregidor, ground artillery was brought up
to support the 57th Philippine Scouts, which relieved Commander Bridget's sailors, who went into reserve.[12]

By nightfall on the twenty-eighth, the Scouts had cleared two-thirds of
the point. By dawn on the thirtieth, they had cleared the peninsula enough
so that they were allowed to return to their parent unit. The mopping up

was left to the sailors supported by the minesweeper *Quail* and Bridget's "Mickey Mouse Battleships."[13]

There had been an abortive attempt by the Japanese to reinforce the units on the points on the twenty-seventh, but before they could land, they were either destroyed or driven off by a combined U.S. air, land, and sea attack of PT boats, ground artillery, and several P-40 aircraft.[14]

The U.S. forces on Quinauan Point had a much more difficult time. There the jungle was more impenetrable, and the Japanese were better dug in. The fighting was intense, and it wasn't until 5 February that the Japanese were cleared from the high ground. On 8 February, the enemy was finally destroyed after they were either blown out of their caves by shell fire from the "Mickey Mouse fleet"[15] or trapped therein by electrically detonated land mines, which sealed the caves.[16]

Additional Japanese landings of 600 men took place further north at Anyasan and Sillicum Points. These were the forces that had been sent to reinforce Longoskawayan Point. Their mission was to drive across Bataan and take Mariveles. Unfortunately for the Japanese, the plan was discovered on the body of a Japanese officer. Having been warned, USAFFE was able to react effectively. However, it would be another three weeks before these forces could be destroyed. After the Battle of the Points, "Bridget's naval battalion was . . . detached from Bataan and sent to [help] defend the beaches of Corregidor."[17] In addition, Japanese dive bombers attacked the "Mickey Mouse fleet," and it, also, was disbanded.[18]

Meanwhile, by 26 January, the U.S. forces had successfully withdrawn to the Bagac–Orion line. The Japanese struck this line in the II Corps sector on the twenty-sixth at its weakest point, but they could not penetrate. In fact, by the first week in February, the Japanese attackers were thoroughly decimated.[19]

The Japanese in Wainwright's corps area again attempted their previously successful infiltration tactics. They succeeded in passing the lead elements of the Japanese 16th Division through the I Corps lines only to be bottled up in small pockets. The fighting in this area was piecemeal, with abortive Japanese attempts to relieve their trapped units.[20]

By the end of the first week in February, Homma's troops were in serious trouble. His units were now measured by companies, not regiments.[21]

Meanwhile, the hidden Japanese artillery batteries on the southern shore of Manila Bay were preparing to bombard the fortified islands.[22] Soon Bunker would really be able to exercise his command.

Notes

1. Karig and Kelley, 157. The *Quail* was a minesweeper.

2. Ibid., 316–17. The aggressive Commander Bridget decided he needed some personal PT boats, so he took some of the 40-foot launches off the *Canopus*. He placed an artillery piece on each of them along with some machine guns. He covered the guns and engines with makeshift armor plate. These three boats were called "Uncle Sam's Mickey Mouse Battleships."

3. Chunn, 3–12. Col. Everett C. Williams was the chief of artillery for General King's Luzon Force. He later played an important part in negotiating the surrender.

4. Belote and Belote, 102. Capt. John L. Lawlor had Battery B, 92d CA (PS). His Scouts had served in support of II Corps. By March he became delirious with malaria. *Register,* 431. He later was taken prisoner, made the Death March, and was repatriated.

5. Ibid., 84. Capt. Robert J. White was the battery commander at Koehler. Later he was fatally wounded when one of his own projectiles "burst just after clearing the tube."

6. Karig and Kelley, 249–69. On 1 February U.S. naval forces conducted raids in the Marshalls and Gilberts as a show of force. The raids did not erase Japanese power from that area, nor was this a relief column for Corregidor.

7. Belote and Belote, 51. Col. Samuel L. Howard commanded the 4th Marine Regiment, which was manning the beach defenses of Corregidor.

8. General court martial. Editor is unable to obtain information on this trial. He believes the record was destroyed in a fire at the Army Records Depot in St. Louis, Missouri.

9. Dettbarn, 51–57. This was the submarine *Trout,* which had moved directly from the United States with a cargo of "3,500 rounds of mechanically fused ammunition for antiaircraft guns on the 'Rock.'" She returned to the States with a ballast of 6½ tons of gold bullion and 630 bags of silver coins. The total value of the return load was $10 million.

10. Karig and Kelley, 135. Capt. K. M. Hoeffel originally was commander of the seagoing gunboat *Asheville.* In December he was relieved and given command of the inshore patrol. Five months later, he was the senior naval officer captured on Corregidor.

11. Belote and Belote, 64.

12. Hough, Ludwig, and Shaw, 179.

13. Morton, *Philippines,* 306–8.

14. Belote and Belote, 64.

15. Morton, *Philippines,* 309–12.
16. Wainwright, 57.
17. Morison, 201.
18. Ibid.
19. Belote and Belote, 64.
20. Ibid.
21. Ibid., 6.
22. Ibid., 84.

Friday, 6 Feb 1942

First bombardment of Corregidor, Drum and Hughes.

This morning as I had finished shaving and was leaving my dugout for breakfast I heard firing and assumed that Ft. Frank was firing another problem at Ternate, but a messenger from C1 came running down and said I was wanted at C1 at once. On going there I was told that the Japs were firing on our Forts Hughes and Drum—and, sure enough, they were! I could see splashes, wide of Drum, but they came closer and closer to it and finally were peppering it in good shape. To my surprise, Drum was firing back, with its measly 3" Btry. Hoyle which, of course, got them nowhere. On being asked his authority for opening fire, Kirkpatrick[1] sputtered, "Why, some son-of-a-bitch is firing at *me*!!" I stopped his popgun efforts but later got permission and ordered him to fire 6" up into the hills back of Restinga Pt. These guns being mounted for water targets, he couldn't use his sights for firing that high, nor were his Armor piercing projectiles suitable, but he got away about 20 shots, anyway, in the direction where he thought he had seen flashes of enemy guns.

But, as the positions of the Jap artillery were right "in the sun" from us, we were practically powerless to detect them, the sun's glare on the water being too blinding.

Pretty soon we heard the sharp crack of a shell bursting close to us, and immediately a report came, of a shell bursting in front of Btry. Wheeler's parapet. Many others followed and we knew that Corregidor was under fire. At about this time General Moore phoned us from B/25, on Malinta Hill, where he was observing developments. He phoned to use the azimuths of several puffs of smoke which indicated locations of enemy batteries but, when plotted on a profile section, indicated that the Jap batteries were 33,000 yards away—which was ridiculous, for they cannot have, over there, guns of any such range. Must have been fakes. We received a lot of other useless information that meant but little and led to no positive locations of the Jap guns.

We held a 6-shot and an 18-shot practice with the 155mm guns at Frank on two points where indications led us to believe the Jap guns *might* be—one of them the "dump" which McCullough (HD G2) thought he had spotted. But we are not very sanguine of success.

At the late forenoon we staged a mortar shoot and Stinness reported a muzzle burst, which killed one man and wounded Capt. White[2] and 7 men—and wanted a boat sent for them—which, of course, could not be done in the middle of the battle. Perhaps he had not cut down enough trees around his mortar pits?

In the late afternoon, when the sun was at our backs, we staged another mortar shoot at an alleged center of activity but had great difficulty in getting the mortars to shoot when we wanted.

I had sent Welch to G/91 with my white pajamas but when I finally arrived there he was still on deck, so I got my clean underwear after all. Went to C1 for a while and then Simmonds, Foster and Edison adjourned to my azatea and we had 3 rounds of gin and bitters and I was surprised to see it was midnight when we finally broke up and turned in.

I had Welch take Colin over to the barracks with him tonight as he barks vociferously when loud explosions occur nearby.

This morning we could see gun flashes in the Mariveles sky—as of 155mm. They seemed nearer than before. As we went for our showers we saw a big high fire, towards Lamao, probably caused by this evening's trip of the Jap bombers. And still the mountains of supplies keep arriving here from the Mariveles storehouses and we have to furnish details of hundreds of men every night to handle them at Corregidor and store them! A bad symptom of our success in Bataan. As if the high commissioner is foreseeing the worst! Even 50 pursuit planes, now, would make *such* a difference! But we have no planes, no navy, and damn little prospect of any.

Gen. Moore appeared, as Simmonds and I were having *breakfast* at noon and came to my dugout with us. We chatted and he left when I went to C1 to stage our 1:00 P.M. mortar shoot.

Saturday, 7 Feb 1942
2d day of bombardment.
Lost P2.00 at poker.
Slept till 7:00 and went to C1 to be ready for "Mr. Motu's"* morning bombardment. Sky was somewhat overcast at dawn however and, since the sun's glare was then insufficiently bad in our eyes, he postponed his shooting. Simmonds and I went to breakfast and just as we finished, at 8:50, the first Jap shot was fired—and evidently hit Corregidor—over towards Topside Barracks. We walked to C1 and stayed for the rest of the shoot. The newly installed sandbags in the station seem to give the men more confidence. Fort Drum got a good lacing by very accurate fire and I saw at least two big dust clouds from there. For the first time, the Japs fired on Ft. Frank and got two hits. Much fire aimed at Corregidor—mostly in the Kindley Field area, as if they were searching our hidden

*Prisoner's nickname of Japanese men, from popular motion picture of the day that featured "Mr. Moto."

planes out. Tried to find gun flashes and time the sounds of explosion but could get no results. Fire at Drum was too accurate to show useful overs and shorts. Gen. Moore gave us a line which we took to confirm a location we had previously made and I got permission to fire 6 mortar personnel shells at it—Done, and beautiful explosions observed—but having no *good* OPs [observation posts], all we can do is to *hope* that the fire was effective. The Japs stopped working us over at about 10:30. No appreciable damage reported from Drum, except cables to AA guns cut in 3 places. No damage reported at Frank or Hughes.

Got permission, finally, to fire on Maragondon and will do so this evening at about the Jap's dinner hour. Most of the town is just out of range of our mortars at Fort Frank, but I am hoping that the ballistic corrections will add the necessary yardage.

Early this morning Daisy May, the tame doe, came down the steps into C1 and then visited Col. Simmonds et. al. in their dugout. Simmonds, Edison, and Foster slept last night in the Gugu dugout under C1 for the first time. Hawes has been sleeping in that tunnel for some time.

They say I made the headlines on the Jap radio last night. Broadcast claimed that they had captured an officer of the 59th who said Colonel Bunker was in charge of the heavy artillery, a fine chap and a gentleman, but he should give up because he is surrounded by superior forces—and thus save useless carnage!

Went to my dugout at 11:00 and shaved and wrote up this log. Received G2 dope that there are only 1500 Japs in Cavite province: 500 at Naic, 500 at Cavite, and 500 at Ternate. Another report says none at Ternate and 1000 at Maragondon! Also that the Japs have only 8 105mm guns!

Sunday, 8 Feb 1942

Paid Club bill: Cine 1.20 and Golf 0.50 = 1.70.

No bombing or bombardment today.

Awoke at 6:00 and went down to C1. Had sandwich and coffee and stuck around in preparation of an early morning shoot, which we had prepared. We were going to search a certain valley and started with 2 shots at 7:18 but Gen. Moore phoned that we'd better wait until we heard from Capt. Ivey, over in the mountains. So we stopped after 2 shots—we couldn't tell accurately where they were going anyway. HD staff couldn't decode Ivey's message, when it finally did come in. Perhaps they are trying to pin the fault on us, but evidently McCullough erred in giving Ivey the code word. Finally a message came through that gave coordinates of a Jap gun out on Sapong Pt., and we gave them to Fts. Frank and Hughes, for preparing firing data. At about this time we spied 2 power boats rapidly towing barges toward beaches beyond Hornos Pt. They looked exactly like Jap outfits and I hurriedly ascertained from the naval inshore patrol that they couldn't identify them, and that they knew only of two Navy motor boats which were working the west coast of Bataan northward from Cochinos Pt. but didn't know about any tows! So I ordered Btry. Sunset to fire when in range. Later we were told by HD HQ that the boats were friendly. Still later, while we were firing, HD kept bothering us with silly questions about the barge that one of these motor boats turned adrift early in the game, when (it appeared to us) it was fired upon from the shore. My request to have the (then) incoming Navy patrol boat go over and investigate, was ignored.

At about 8:30 Simmonds and I went to breakfast but returned at once. I turned Colin over to Welch, to take to Barracks and return after bombardment.

At 10:15 there was aerial activity over our Bataan line. Foster followed the 3 planes with our big glasses and described their movements à la Graham Macramee [a reference to the intricate lacework known as macramé]. We saw many AA bursts and some gun flashes. Tonight the report is that we shot down 2 planes, but we saw none damaged. They say that Jap dive bombers hit 3 guns of the 200th AA, but that 2 of them may be repairable. Also got message from Fulmer on Signal Hill that they had just killed a Jap sniper 150 yards from camp! That is as bad as finding one working in Mariveles in the midst of Dept. HQ!

Along about 11:00 A.M. we started firing Btry. Frank, at Ft. Frank, with Ivey spotting for us and reporting directly to us over a walkie-talkie. The shooting started wild, "way right" so I ordered a correction of 5 left, so as to bring the impacts into the water. Then ordered two successive corrections of "Rt 1°." One gun was outranging the other and both were "opened" too much. After 7 ranging shots and 10 salvos we called a halt and worked out some calibration corrections and tried 5 more 2-gun salvos and recalibrated. The next salvo was "Hit.Hit" so we hustled out 6 more salvos and got 4 more material hits. I guess *that* gun position is now no good. Then called it a day.

Col. Foster had brought Col. Anderson[3] of the 4th Marines up to see the fun, but they got tired and left about 10:30 and so missed the whole shoot—as usual.

Rest of day passed uneventfully. Japs are broadcasting that they are going to give Corregidor a real bombardment on 10 February. We are wondering why they laid off us today. Some of our wishful thinkers opine that we may have injured some of their batteries. Others say we killed their officers in Maragondon yesterday, but McCullough tonight thought that the Japs had moved out of Maragondon a few days ago.

After dinner I just managed to get to the RSO toilet in time. Then got our showers. Edison and I to Hearn for iced cocoa and Dr. gave me diarrhoea medicine. Then to my dugout with Colin. Col. Foster came and gave a partial report on the census of ammunition in Btries. Geary and Way. They have 153 and 300 "personnel" projectiles respectively and I wish there were 10 times that many. The guy that obtained them for us was *wise*. Decided not to play poker tonight. Simmonds came along, after Foster left and chinned awhile.

Edison is on watch tonight—he didn't get much sleep last night, because of boat-shore firings on east coast of Bataan last night—or, rather, early this morning.

Friday, 13 Feb 1942*

Won P5.00 at poker.

Up at 6:30 and went to C1. At 7:45 shaved and went to breakfast, then visited RSO and my quarters where I found further evidence of pillaging. Place has not been hit recently, so I gave Welch the job of packing up some more of my stuff, including heading up the barrel of glassware that I packed some weeks ago. Returned to C1 and argued with Cottrell about bringing some more powder into Btry. Geary from the roadsides. Agreed on 20 charges. Then explained my plan for "Retaliation Fire"—one 4-gun salvo 155m from Ft. Frank and 1 mortar shot from Koehler on Jap battery positions near Sapong; one 4-gun AA shrapnel burst from Ft. Frank on Restinga Ridge; one 2-gun salvo from Hamilton 155 on Restinga and one 12″ shot from Hearn on Naic. All to be fired automatically when the Japs first start firing. It should give them something to think about.

This morning about 7:30 Fort Frank fired one "Road Block" of 4 guns 155. Hung around C1 waiting for Japs to open fire, until 11:20, and then returned to my dugout. Pvt. Novardes brought me volume 1 of Worcester's "Philippines, Past and Present" which I have been looking for.

At 12:25 a Jap bombed over Mariveles way amid bursts of our AA guns. A few minutes later I thought I heard the swish of a bomb and dove into my dugout, but nothing happened; it was an air compressor popping off.

This morning, at RSO, Capt. W. Thompson showed up, after a long tour with the 21st Infantry Phillipine army, and I assigned him to C/59 with Schenck.

Everybody hung around all day, waiting for a chance to shoot our "Retaliation Fire," but the Japs wouldn't open up so, pursuant to permission from Gen. Moore, we staged it anyway at 5:00 P.M. All 3 units at Frank shot within the second but Hearn was 45″ late. Raised lots of smoke, but we could see no effect on Restinga Ridge.

Kirkpatrick was supposed to shoot at 5:00 also. We gave him the dope at 4:50 with plenty of warning before that, yet his first salvo (which I ordered to be single shots) went at 5:32. Then the Japs opened with one gun from near Ternate and Kirk still left his guns pointed in that direction, thus inviting damage! His 2 shots burst beautifully, however, in Ternate. Later he shot 2 target practice projectiles out to sea, one going 1300 yards farther than the other! There was only 4″ between these shots! I doubt that he succeeded in measuring the "slew" of the turrets.

*No entries for 9–12 February 1942.

I left with Simmonds and drove to G/91 and got my shower. Chong showed me the seat cover that Welch ruined with bluing, damnit. Back to C1 but Lothrup didn't show up. Edison did, so we had a gin and bitters. When Foster came along to spell Edison we had another.

Then we adjourned to "the Club" and played poker until 11:00. Won P5.00 for a change. Turned in. While we were playing, at about 9:40, Btry. Frank let loose with one of our "Road Block" salvos.

They say that Ivey went back to the Batangas mainland again last night to continue spotting. Edison and I talked with Thompson and decided that we'd send him to Signal Hill to work with Fulmer a day or two and let Fulmer come in. Then, when he'd acquired some experience, we'd send him out with Ivey.

General Moore says that Quezon is in mighty bad physical shape. Somebody said they saw him hobble to his car the other day and he looked bad. Somebody else said they saw him in a wheel-chair. But he has been in bad health for years.

Saturday, 14 Feb 1942

Won P1.00.

Turned out at 5:00 and relieved Edison, who proceeded to sleep until 9:30. Brewed another batch of my M.H. coffee and it was fine. Fired our customary "Road Block" at about 7:30. Then, as Capt. Steiger came on duty for his first tour, I returned to my dugout, shaved, and had breakfast. Waited in vain for my staff and Welch until 9:00 and then went in pursuit of Welch, who had been policing my dugout. To RSO for a bit and saw Julian about stovepipes for ventilating our tunnel then to my quarters and showed Welch about packing my boxes with my remaining junk.

This morning, at 6:50, the engineers blasted through our tunnel addition to the open air! Wish they had done it 2 months ago! We were all greatly pleased. Two dull booms and then 2 sharp cracks as the explosions came through, just at entrance to our homemade tunnel nearest C1. Talked with Pigg[4] and Hador about the exit below my dugout.

Set Denby to work shifting the fly over the front porch (or "azatea" to my dugout [there is no closing parenthesis in the original]. By now it was 11:30 A.M. and our guns were all set for "Retaliation Fire."

Nothing happened all day except that a Jap steamer appeared up Subic way and hung around all day and was there in the evening. Went through our usual P.M. routine of supper, bath and change of uniform. Caught a slight siesta about 2:30 on cot on my porch. We inspected our tunnel. The air improvement is remarkable since the breakthrough and the tunnel looks better every day. Have already some plans for making it *good.*

Went to C1 and organized a shoot but Gen. Moore practically said "No shooting until we hear from Ivey." Not even our road blocks! In disgust I retired to my "chateau" and wrote up this log, to the accompaniment of dull booms of artillery fire on east shore of Bataan. Sounds like 75mm.

Told Thompson to get ready to go to signal Hill tomorrow.

Loafed around C1 awhile but, as everything is quiet, went up to "the Club" and watched some shavetails play Hearts until Schenck, Dr. Bartz[5] and others appeared, when we started playing poker, won P1.00 which is just about right, because I didn't hurt anybody and yet proved that my judgement and ability were a bit above average. Everybody was delighted that Schenck, who is not only a good player but also is usually blessed with fine luck, quit a loser by P3.00.

Visited C1 as a matter of form and then turned in at 11:30.

It is rumored that the Japs in Bataan are taking away some of their troops and that now there are only about 40,000 of them up there; that they have pulled most of their artillery back to San Fernando de Pampanga, and that the landing parties along the west coast of Bataan have been completely mopped up—principally by the 57th Infantry—which regiment has sure earned a reputation for being rough cookies! They say there were some 1500 Japs up around Anayasan Bay, but they've all been cleaned out.

Maybe that has something to do with the Jap tramp steamer which has been hanging around, off shore, up that way, for the last few days.

They claim, also, that the Japs are fortifying successive positions northward along the coast, toward Subic and Lingayen and even Xigan! As Col. Simmonds would say "I wonder" what that portends? The only news we get tells us that "Help is on the way" but we assume that all our "help" is for the Limeys in Singapore. And none of us begrudge that, if we thought that the Englishman *himself* were doing some of the fighting down there!

We are hoping for great things from the Dutchman who has just been put in charge of the Allied navies.

Sunday, 15 Feb 1942[6]

Having been up late last night, I slept until 8:00 this morning; shaved and went to breakfast. Then to RSO where Julian has fixed himself up nicely for living quarters—and also for his men there. A shower-bath is in operation, also one toilet (which requires flushing with a bucket of water). Then I drove down to the Service Club, where the Air Corps has a lot of stuff stored. Made a dicker with the sergeant there: that if they would give us a 5-kw generating set, plus a 2-kw AC-DC set, we would give Bombproof storage to 350 cu. ft. of delicate airplane instruments.

Tried in vain to find the vet but he had already inspected the corral. Back to C1 and many of our officers there, chinned awhile and then went to my dugout, where I found the Engrs.' surveyors busy running a line to the revised exit of our tunnel.

Morning news: Singapore not yet fallen. Every day means a lot now. Wonder why, considering everything we've poured into that plan for a year, why the Jap planes have such an easy time of it?

This morning Colin tangled with "Head-space" again. Gave him a good dusting of flea powder and that, with the bath that Welch gave him last night, seemed to help him a lot. (Now noon . . . where does the time go? By the time we get breakfast it is 9:00 A.M. This "daylight saving time" is terrible!)

Worked at my dugout all afternoon, preparing maps of the Ternate shore for my "Forgetteries Book." At 4:00 P.M. I was just ready to leave for HQ Btry. Mess to accept Capt. McCarthy's bid to a baked ham dinner, when wham! the Japs opened fire on Corregidor. The first shell burst near the old MP booth at North Wharf, killed 1 sailor and wounded 5. Remaining shells, which kept falling on us until 7:00 P.M. scored no casualties that I heard about. Ivey turned in, at about this time, and did alleged spotting for us. First he tried to adjust Btry. Frank on the same old Point 17 in Sapong area near beach, with such inconsistent spots that we finally asked him how he knew there was a Jap Btry. there and he replied that he couldn't see it, but judged by the sound that it was there. Then we shifted to another target, formerly identified by McCullough as "Battery Ternate Side" which McCullough afterwards said contained no guns. Ivey was at 35⁰ from the target-gun line and would say, "Hit-200 over and left"—yet when we'd move "down 100, right 100" he'd report "400 right 300 short." We finally gave up about dusk. At just this time I *saw* an enemy gun flash over a thick line of trees, about 2 miles *beyond* the point Ivey was trying to range us on! My observer also saw it, and saw another after I had left my glasses, in the same spot. Got a grudging permit to fire a few rounds from Hearn as counterbattery but, by the time the battery was ready to fire, it was too dark for us to observe. So I called the shoot off, and drove to HQ Btry. for chow, only to learn that "Smith" had disposed of the last of the ham, so our dinner consisted of a stew and a piece of apple pie.

Then drove back to C1 and dismissed Welch. Loafed around for a while, chatting with the gang and went up to the Club. Started a poker game but immediately the Japs near Maragondon opened fire and landed 2 on Corregidor. We piled down to C1 and tried to spot gun flashes, but there were no more shots. So I quit at 9:30 and went home.

And so to bed, Damn the Japs!

Damn them again! They started in again about 12:10 A.M. and got us all up but we could get practically no dope on where they were. Just on a chance, we let go 2 shots from Hearn at an alleged battery position and let it go at that. Went home and turned in. I hear that the Japs fired a few more at about 2:00 A.M. but I didn't wake.

Monday, 16 Feb 1942
Won P2.00.

Slept till 8:00 A.M. then got breakfast. Drove to RSO and, while there, the Japs opened fire and kept it up till nearly 3:00 P.M. Before that—I was told, at breakfast, that Gen. Moore was at my CP and so I hustled down there and brought him up to my dugout where we sat in comfort and chatted in peace for an hour amid Sylvan beauty. Then I went to the RSO. The Japs started in shelling Corregidor, but I had to return to C1, and so Welch took me across the parade ground. Left Colin at RSO.

Was busy until 3:00 P.M. organizing and delivering fire against the unseen Jap batteries. Ivey was off the air. Shot lots of 155 from Ft. Frank, also did a search problem back of Maragondon with Hearn.

Then figured out a new point, left of Drum and fired a 2-gun mortar salvo and 6 salvos GPF. About this time, the Japanese stopped firing but I couldn't know whether this was voluntary or forced upon them.

The Japs opened fire at 4:30 P.M. and kept it up for the rest of the afternoon but nothing much fired at Corregidor, mostly at Drum. Went to C1 but could do nothing about it.

At about 5:00 I drove to G/91 for my shower, there being no shelling at the time. Found that last night a Jap shell hit those barracks and 2 fragments hit my clean uniform, cutting 2 holes in the sleeve and one in the tails. Chong's repair job was bunglesome. Sorry to have to wear a damaged shirt. Back to Hearn. Saw 6 Jap planes fly over Cabcaben and our wide bursts on them. Then drove back to C1 and had Welch take Colin back to barracks as Japs opened on Drum. Today the Japs got into Calumpan and cut the water supply to Fort Frank. Moore has given Ft. Frank carte blanche to fire on Japs over there. Frank's saltwater tank is busted but they have their distilling plant.

Went to my dugout and loafed in the dusk. Foster came and we had 2 gin and bitters and then went to C1. No excitement there so we went to "Club" and played poker until 10:45. Then turned in.

Tuesday, 17 Feb 1942

Lost P1.00.

Touch of diarrhoea at 4:00 A.M. Stayed with Julian in C1 awhile and then turned in and slept until 8:00. The Japs sent over a few shells at Corregidor at 11:45 last night and at 5:45 this morning Ft. Frank fired 75mm at Patungan barrio at infiltrating Japs.

Shaved and went to breakfast. Just as I'd finished, at 9:00 A.M. (DST) [daylight savings time] the Japs opened fire on Corregidor. With Edison and Simmonds I walked to C1 (giving Colin to Welch and sending them to safety (?) of barracks) and found that the sun glare precluded our observation.

However, we spotted enemy flashes through a slot in the trees atop a hill in Sapong area—a slot which I had previously observed, and corroborated by a Marine officer on S. Shore Road, and we calculated firing data for Btry. Hearn to shoot it up, when observation improved. Then returned to my dugout to calculate co-ordinates and firing data.

Meanwhile, the Japs ceased firing at about 11:00 but opened up again, using a 2-gun battery, among others. They concentrated, for a while, out by abandoned San Jose at Hooker Pt. (to our delight) while we waited for the visibility to improve. We fired 12 shots from Hearn at the "Slots." [These were ravines in a ridgeline.] Our first shot was in the water but our next was comfortably over and then we raked the hill in back of the ridge thoroughly, then shifted to the right-hand slot and did the same. This phase ended about 1:30. Our observers believed we had hit a Jap ammunition dump, by the puff of smoke which looked unusual. Later, we turned loose Btry. Frank (155mm) on the same area but their figures were wrong and they went wild over. We tried in vain to get them out into the water but had to stop them and make them recalculate their data. Then, upon resuming fire, we got their single burst in the water. Then we called for a delayed salvo and calibrated all guns together. Finally, we shifted the impacts inland onto the same target as before (Point 31) and blasted about ten 3-gun salvos on the "Slot" targets. Then we went to the two "targets" which had been reported to us by McCullough, our HD G2 and poked 12 3-gun salvos onto *those* points. Visibility was now very good, but of course our targets were hidden from our view by ridges, and the smoke from bursts was blown to the right by the wind, so we had to guess at the locations of the impacts.

Finished our shooting about 4:30. Had been invited by Capt. Hauck to dinner at B Btry. He has saved some pickled pigs feet for me, so Simmonds and I drove down there and had dinner. Col. Amos[7] and Capt. Munton of the Air corps were there (the former knew Paul [Bunker's son] at Barksdale Field in 1935). They worked in the Bataan shops. Made a dicker with Amos for him to give us a 5-kw AC generating set and lend us a motor generating set of about 3-kw, for use in our C1-G1 Tunnel.

Sent Chauffeur Derr to G/91 for my laundry and took a shower at Btry. Wheeler in comfort as did Simmonds. Then we took a look at our tunnel and loafed around Hearn a bit. Drove back home and loafed on my azatea until dusk, then to C1. Later, adjourned to the Club and played poker. Early in the game I had dealt to me a pat full house but that was about the last hand I held. By careful play I managed to quit only P1.00 loser.

Went home and turned in, after taking a look at C1.

We are hopeful that our shooting, today, scored heavily on the Japs on the Cavite side. We have not heard a peep out of them since Btry. Hearn lobbed those 12 690-lb. projectiles at them this morning. They sure made a fine show, and the dust clouds of their impacts were visible to our unaided eyes; we could plainly hear the bursts. But "Mr. Moto" will probably tune up, from some other battery or gun tonight.

Capt. Ivey has succeeded in getting via Looc* back to Ft. Frank but seems to have abandoned all of his enlisted men to their fate. He was almost surprised by a Jap patrol of 4 men—shot at them, and beat it.[8]

USAFFE today reports a Jap convoy of 18 or more ships nearing Lingayen, probably Jap reinforcements. Our Capt. Thompson, at Signal Hill, reports a few Jap vessels nearing Subic, one towing many barges.

Wednesday, 18 Feb 1942

Lost P7.50.

Things were quiet today until about 1:00 P.M. when the Japs opened fire on Ft. Frank and hammered it for hours. We thought we detected flashes at the same azimuth at which I caught a flash some days ago, behind a fringe of trees to left of Ternate. We alerted Hearn and fired a rolling search back along our line of sight, starting at 4:09 P.M. on this "Point 33" and winding up behind said trees. Then, when we had ended, about 4:21, the Japs had ceased firing. We then opened up fire from Btry. Frank at 4:41 and fired salvos in there until 5:20.

Major Maynard came up in time to see the 155 shoot and he brought with him the 2 quadrangles he had mounted for us, of the 1" = 1 mile map. It is pretty.

This morning I went down to G4 and saw them shoot Btry. Hanna. Also saw their dugout system for G4, which is quite elaborate. After returning to my dugout, Edison sent word that Hanna's target had drifted out into Cheney's field of fire and suggested the battery hold target practice. So, having received permission from HD, I ordered the battery to shoot. 1st shot in 8 minutes, which wasn't bad. First salvo was well bunched but away short of the target. On 2d salvo, one gun was wild to left, likewise the 3d salvo. Gunpointer couldn't see target and was ordered by Capt. Steiger to shoot anyway—which he did! Then, being given the approximate azimuth of the target, he got back on to it again.

Meanwhile the shots were still short and the range correction was totally inadequate. I made them cease firing, to iron out the errors so the last shot was much delayed. Then I went down to Btry. Cheney and held a critique there. These disappearing batteries now have no horizontal base systems, either for position finding or for spotting and are trying to spot range deviations by DPF [directional position finder]! via a percentage range correction! Very cumbersome and slow.

Promptly after we ceased firing at 5:20 the Japs crawled out of their holes and calmly and deliberately started their nuisance firing at Frank again. Maybe it was a new battery just shooting itself in on the target, but anyway, it kept up all night.

Edison thought he had a gun spotted and put down a lot of salvos from Frank, though this was after dark. Outside observers reported in, that we were right on

---

*Town on Tablas Island, 170 miles southeast of Corregidor.

the target. But yet, soon after we stopped firing, the Japs again started shooting back at Fort Frank. I caught a huge flash at Frank, just as our guns ceased firing, and learned later that a Jap shell hit and exploded four powder charges in the emplacement of No. 4 gun in Btry Frank. Four men were hurt, one seriously. They probably came to Mills—or *were* to come—on the *Neptune*.

About 8:00 P.M. we gathered at the Club and played poker. I played in my worst luck to date; lost P7.50. Held a pat full house early in the game and won only 2 more pots all evening.

The Japs continued to lob one over onto Frank about every 20 minutes.

Thursday, 19 Feb 1942
Won P2.50.

Was wakened at 4:00 A.M. by report of bad fire at Ft. Frank. Went to C1 and saw glow and flames rising behind the island. Thought that the fort's gasoline supply had been exploded by Jap shell fire. Learned later that our ration boat had been hit, the MS [munition ship] *Neptune* and that 2 machine gunners and 1 deckhand were missing but they showed up later OK. Final report: 6 soldiers and 3 civilians injured slightly. Vessel was carrying 15 drums gasoline, 500 charges 155mm powder, 20 half-charges of 14″ powder. All this, with vessel, a total loss. Ship still burning this morning and is on the rocks at Fort Frank. No known damage to the Fort. The Japs must have an OP [observation post] close to Ft. Frank for, while they hit the fort at 20-minute intervals most of the night, when the *Neptune* arrived they shortened range and poked three shots in, in rapid succession!

Very quiet up to 9:00 A.M.—to 11:40. I worked on maps at my dugout. At 1 P.M. the Japs fired 1 shot at Hughes but it landed in the water, wide. I went to C1 and soon Gen. Moore appeared. Took him to my dugout and convinced him that we should fire Btry. Woodruff (14″) at counter battery work *if* we got a good detonation of shells. Meanwhile I had warned Col. Hopkins to be prepared to shoot the problem. About this time a Jap plane came over and, as our AA opened up on it, we took cover in my dugout. Edison had joined us. We went back outside but had to duck again. Gen. Moore left at about 2:30 after saying I was to shoot when I judged best. Edison left to arrange details. Again at 2:55 I heard AA shots at a plane.

At 4:09 we had Btry. Woodruff, a 14″ disappearing gun at Ft. Hughes, open fire upon a suspected battery position over Ternate way and search along their line of sight for 8 rounds, ending at 4:28. We thought that a few of the earlier rounds failed to detonate, but the later ones certainly did, and shot up fine clouds of dust upon impact. Then we set Btry. Frank to work on the same target; started firing at 4:53 and ending at 5:10. Then we adjourned for the day and went to get our belated chow. Everybody on Topside has evening chow about 4:00–4:30 P.M., so we in C1 are usually late.

Afterwards, Simmonds and I had our showers at 59th RSO, where there are real shower heads. Sent Welch to G/91 for my clean clothes and everything worked out nicely. To Hearn, until Japs opened, about 7:00 P.M.

Then to C1 and loafed around as usual, hoping to identify gun flashes. Major Julian is trying to work out a system of sound ranging on a horizontal base system, with one station at Hooker Pt. Indeed he and his RSO detail were out at Hooker Pt. this afternoon, installing the station.

While at Hearn, talked with Fulmer, who is just back from Bataan, and he was full of talk. Wanted to give me a Jap rifle, which I didn't want. He says the Ifugaos and Ilocanos have made it so hot for the Japs up in the mountain provinces that our flag now flies over Baguio.

Played poker, in evening, and won P2.50. At 9:00 the Japs started firing again and later Frank fired at Calumpan shore.

Col. Boudreau, at Ft. Frank, sent about 15 men over to Calumpan to repair the water pipe and, while they were at work, they were fired upon by a Jap patrol of 8 men and 2 officers. Our men killed them all. Then ours were chased out by a larger bunch of Japs but managed to get back to Ft. Frank except for 2 men and 1 civilian who were left behind. Maybe they'll come back, too!

There is so much sporadic artillery activity every day that, unless I note each shot at the time, I find it impossible to keep track of it. In general, the Japs are resorting to "nuisance" firing daily, usually from a single gun. Lately they have been concentrating their attention on Ft. Frank, with a burst on other forts too.

Friday, 20 Feb 1942
Lost P6.50.
Wrote Landon.
Up at 7:30 for shave and breakfast. Just as I started to inspect our C1 Tunnel the damn Japs opened up on Ft. Frank, but I looked over the tunnel anyway. They have now started on the final leg of the main tunnel and, with the cussedness peculiar to U.S. engineers, will terminate that exit with a flight of 25 steps on a 45° slope! However, they promise to unofficially dig out 2 rooms which they term "dynamite bodegas" [wine cellars] for officers.

Left there and was about to start for the Malinta Tunnel to smoothe down Mrs. Sayre[9] about library books, when the Japs shifted fire to Corregidor. So I returned to C1 and found that the Japs have emplaced a new gun (sounds like a 15cm) in a new position—evidently much nearer Frank. The atmosphere towards Ternate was so milky that we could see nothing, so I returned to my dugout and typed a letter to Landon which I hope to get through the Navy Censor in spite of the snapshot, enclosed, of the Corregidor Club, after bombing of 6 January.

Last night a Navy submarine came in, and the *Don Estaban* left—probably for more rice! Every other night we furnish a fatigue detail of 3 officers and 150 men to do stevedoring work at our wharves.

The Jap nuisance bombardment kept up until along toward 12:30. This is a very hot day and very little breeze; it is much more comfortable at my dugout than in C1 station.

This afternoon we were going to let Btry. Woodruff shoot a problem at Ternate and sent out phone notification to that effect. But, by a strange coincidence (?) the Japs opened fire on Woodruff 5 minutes ahead of Woodruff's starting time! So we fired Hearn instead and raked far inland to extreme range. Started at 4:05 and ended with 9th shot at 4:28. Meanwhile, Woodruff suffered an injured breechblock and wanted an hour's delay, so we cut them out and put in a few salvos from Btry. Frank, instead, starting at 4:58 and ending at 5:10. Fort Frank did plenty of spasmodic firing off and on all day at various points on nearby mainland.

During our Hearn shoot, I saw a plane circling near the target as if we had flushed it off the ground. Observers said there was another plane there too. An observation plane had been flying about, near Corregidor, for an hour or more, perhaps spotting for Jap artillery.

Anyway after our shoot, there was no more firing from Jap artillery for the rest of the day and night.

The sub went out tonight just at moon set. Cooper had delivered my letter to Chief Naval Censor, who said that mail had closed, but he would try to get my letter aboard.

Had shower with Simmonds at RSO and then drove back to C1 and loafed through sunset there with the gang. Later played poker and won only 1 pot all evening and split 2. Lost P6.50. Turned in at 11:30 on my azatea.

The Japs used 100 parachute transport planes at Palembang![10] I wonder how well we could combat such an attack? Not very well, I fear.

A bunch of Marines came near C1 Tunnel "to organize this ravine" and wanted to install their MG right over the mouth of our tunnel. So they could gradually take over our tunnel, says Foster.

Arrived in Philippines just one year ago today!

Transition

6–22 February

The Japanese Battery Kondo, which was hidden in the forest of Cavite, suddenly starting firing on 6 February with its four 100mm (4-inch) guns. This fire kept up rather steadily until 22 February, when it stopped while the Japanese waited for new orders and reinforcements.[11] The shelling of the fortified islands and Corregidor had been mostly nuisance firing; thus, the troops soon lost their fear of it. Despite this, only rarely during this period was anyone hurt.[12]

Meanwhile, on Bataan, the air force was attacking Japanese shipping, and the Japanese were attempting to land. The American pilots were griping about the large number of aircraft they had lost because of accidents.[13] "In fact, none of the six P-40s was ever damaged by the numerous Japanese" raids on Cabcaben and Bataan.[14]

By the second week in February, food had become a serious problem on Bataan; each man was limited to half a pound of rice and one-half can of sardines. Any other food the men had to supply for themselves. They harvested crops, hunted monkeys, and foraged for fruit.[15]

By the middle of February all of the Japanese forces that had landed on the western coast of Bataan had been destroyed or routed. An entire enemy battalion of nine hundred men had been wiped out, with the exception of thirty-four who had been evacuated. There was no longer any danger in the rear areas.[16]

Things were going well for the United States in both I and II Corps. The Japanese had been soundly beaten all along the front. By the end of February, General Homma's Fourteenth Army "no longer existed as an effective force."[17] He had nothing left to do but withdraw and await reinforcements before he could once again attempt to drive the Allies into the sea. But it was inevitable that he would be reinforced. On the other hand, all hope for U.S. reinforcements was abandoned.[18]

On the twenty-second, General MacArthur received word that he was to be evacuated. Nevertheless, he stayed in an attempt to hold Bataan as long as possible. By the end of February, both sides were behind defensive positions on Bataan.[19] A lull settled over the area as the Americans dug in and the Japanese awaited reinforcements.[20]

Notes

1. Belote and Belote, 59. Lt. Col. Lewis S. Kirkpatrick commanded Ft. Drum. *Register,* 376. He was later captured and interned on Corregidor, where he died of pneumonia on 27 April 1943.

2. Braly, 36. Capt. Robert J. White, the battery commander, died a few months later in Bilibid prison as a result of these wounds.

3. Hough, Ludwig, and Shaw, 171. Lt. Col. Herman R. Anderson commanded the 2d Battalion, 4th Marines, consisting of eighteen officers and 324 enlisted men.

4. Belote and Belote, 188. Capt. Ronald O. Pigg was one of the engineer officers on Corregidor.

5. Chunn, 46. This was probably Maj. Wesley Bertz of the Veterinary Corps, who was later a POW at Cabanatuan.

6. MacArthur, 122. On 15 February Singapore fell. The Japanese had skillfully outmaneuvered the British under the command of Lt. Gen. Sir Arthur Percival.

7. Ind, 18. This was probably Lt. Col. W. N. ("Pinkie") Amis of the air force.

8. Braly, 36. Ivey and his detail were attacked by a Japanese patrol on 15 February. A corporal was killed and a sergeant was captured, but Ivey and two Philippine Scouts returned to Ft. Frank.

9. MacArthur, 140. Mrs. Sayre was the wife of the high commissioner. They left with the Quezons on 20 February by submarine for Australia.

10. Morton, *Strategy,* 175. On 14 February 1942 the Japanese dropped approximately seven hundred paratroopers from some one hundred transports; however, they were nearly decimated by the British and Dutch defenders. Unfortunately, amphibious Japanese forces took control.

11. Belote and Belote, 84–89.

12. Col. Stephen M. Mellnik, "How the Japs Took Corregidor," *Coast Artillery Journal,* 84 (March–April 1945), 6.

13. Ind, 288–301.

14. Mellnik, "Life and Death," 6.

15. Ibid.

16. Morton, *Philippines,* 324.

17. Ibid., 349.

18. Ibid., 352.

19. Ibid.

20. Ibid.

Saturday, 21 Feb 1942

Won P9.00. +9.50 to date.

Slept till 7:30. About daybreak a 500-ton steamer showed up, offshore. Inshore patrol identified it as "Fisheries" until we showed them their error. Schenck phoned HD HQ, who knew nothing about her. After a long delay, it developed that the boat was the *Princesa*[1] and was *expected* by our transport bunch—who had evidently notified nobody about her! She narrowly escaped being blown to pieces by our guns.

Shaved. Breakfast. Diarrhoea again. To my dugout for a while and then to C1 to await the usual morning shelling. But the only firing that occurred all day was at Fort Frank, where they shot their 75mm (1:30 P.M.) at the nearby mainland, to smoke the Japs out of Calumpan Cove, etc.

Bill Braly[2] brought to C1 the Col. Sage[3] and Lt. Cols. of the 200th AA who are over in Bataan. Edison and I met the last two when we passed through Stotsenburg in December. Brought them all down to my dugout and chinned genially until Braly dragged them unwillingly away. Then I worked with Edison trying to unravel the discrepancies in coordinates of batteries, as published by the arty engineers.

Wrote a note to Brooke which Col. Sage said he would have sent to Brooke, in which I urged Brooke to increase Priscilla's allotment. How he expected her to live and support 4 children on 415.00 a month is beyond me. Got Cooper to take the letter down.

Rutherford, who is now a full colonel, has just been relieved from USAFFE and reported back to the 59th and came to my dugout to get instructions about how to run Ft. Hughes. Glad to see him back, for he is a genial soul and was well liked in the regiment.

Loafed at my dugout waiting in vain for the Japs to start their daily nuisance firing. Took a short siesta between visits to C1.

After chow, Edison, Simmonds and I adjourned to RSO and had our showers. Julian was there, still enthused about his sound and flash ranging.* His farmer helpers allowed their lifeboat to be chewed up on the rocks! His station is on the [ship] *San José*, on which there are a couple of over-ripe corpses. After a sojourn at Hearn, we went to my dugout and had some rum and chinned awhile and then went to C1.

*An observer who calculated distance by the difference between the flash (speed of light) and the "bang" (speed of sound) when an artillery piece is fired.

After hanging around there until dark we played poker, at which I had unusual luck and won P9.00.

Report came in via Marines that there is a bigger battle than that at Macassar Straits now going on near Bali; that 2 Jap cruisers, several destroyers and many transports have been sunk; that the Allies have air support—Japs have taken TIMOR.[4] I hope every Jap craft and plane is destroyed. I betcha the Dutch were the cause of this aggressive move. They have publicly attacked the British policy of "successive withdrawals to prepared positions." Bless their hearts!

Also a good word for Walter Winchell. At least I approve of him: He recently said, "To hell with this talk about MacArthur's *heroes*—Let's send them some *help!*" Just what we've been thinking!

Sunday, 22 Feb 1942

Won P2.00.

Not a shot fired today by the Japs and the only ones we fired were some 75mm which Ft. Frank fired over toward Patungan to scare off the Japs.

The day passed uneventfully.

Dope on Rutherford was changed by Gen. Moore, who came up to my dugout to talk it over. We finally agreed to send Lt. Col. Foster over there, promoting him meanwhile, and letting Rutherford stay on the sick list here until he recovers, when he will become my Exec. in the SWD.*

Performed the usual round of duties, winding up, at 7:00 P.M. at my dugout with Simmonds and Edison, where we had a rum. As we finished, Foster (who was on duty) sent request to open fire on a banca,[5] which I gave him, Btry. Cushing to do the firing. But we lost sight of said banca and couldn't find it again, so all bets were off.

Adjourned to Regler Fellers Club and played poker until 10:30. Won P2.00. Then visited C1 and turned in, on outside porch.

This morning's blast in our tunnel sure raised me out of bed. The workmen have started on the final rise for our exit steps and have not so much more distance to go.

This morning Capt. Munton, Air corps, delivered to us a fine 6½-kw AC generating set, 4-cylinder gasoline motor for our tunnel. I wanted to store it inside the tunnel immediately but the engineers would not tolerate blocking it at all. So we protected it with sandbags. Capt. Munton was funny: he first said he was sorry he couldn't find what we wanted (a 5-kw set) and asked if a 6½-kw set would do—knowing full well that we would *prefer* it.

---

*Seaward defense: Bunker's coast artillery command. His mission was to stop enemy forces coming from the west.

A very hot day. Too hot for a siesta, even on my "porch."

Tonight Colin bamboozled me: he pretended to want to spend the night with me, and did so until retiring time, when he stole away and I saw no more of him. This evening Simmonds, Edison and I went down to Cheney and chatted with Steiger a bit just before dark. Then to Hearn and so to C1.

Fighting here in the Philippines seems to be calming down. They say the Japs are withdrawing their lines in Bataan. 16 bombers dropped eggs on airfield at Cabcaben but did little damage. The Air Corps have streamlined their work of repairing damages to landing fields: Hidden trucks, loaded with earth, rush out to craters and dump into them (almost on the fly), then along comes the bulldozer and smooths it off—and finally a roller. Takes about 15 minutes.

Monday, 23 Feb 1942

This day just like all the others. This morning Derr picked up Colin at the Corral at Middleside, where he was playing with a couple of puppies! The tramp!

Settled down with Edison at my azatea to calculate firing data. Made Welch track down my big, 7-place logarithm tables. They are a joy! Then things became much easier.

We figured out a point on a road junction near Naic and another near Maragondon for future road interdiction firing. Then we worked out a revision of our original "Road Block," [bombardment of Japanese-held roads] for use of Btry. Frank's 155mm guns.

I also decided against Col. Kohn's wishes, to proof-fire Btry. Sunset, a new battery of four 155mm. Also to let Btry. Hamilton register and calibrate its guns on Limbones Pt. Hamilton fired 15 rounds ending at 3:15. Meanwhile Btry. Sunset fired its calibration shots to left of Monja and later registered a few salvos near Limbones. Not too good work at guns!

Hoping to organize the Maragondon road block, we fired 3 shots from the 14" Btry. Woodruff but, as none seemed to detonate, we stopped.

Then we started off with Btry. Frank on the San José road block but as Stinness was still way off the target after 12 two-gun salvos, I took over the adjustment myself. Adjusted 2 guns, then the other two, then brought the two pairs together. 30 shots in all. At the end, they were raising a swell cloud of dust on the road north of Ternate. Finished at 5:12 and went to chow, leaving Maj. Mitchell to adjust his Btry. Sunset's final few salvos.

Simmonds wanted "more stew" at chow, but as there was no more, the cook fried us some tenderloin, and it was the best food I've had since war started. Although I had finished dinner, I started in again and ate two small steaks!

Julian has an amateur brewery and still running in the latrine of B/59 barracks, where his office is. This evening I checked up on my typewriter, LC Smith Super Speed, and found that the HQ clerk has it safe in a closet in the HD Bombproof.

Edison went on duty. Simmonds and I went to Hearn for a while. Then I went to my dugout and wrote up this log.

At Hearn, Fulmer showed me a copy of the Navy's report on the Longoskawayan Point operation, also partial draft of his own report.

No poker game tonight, so turned in early. Today Welch tried to air out my dugout, which has become very close and muggy. Everything in it either rusts or mildews.

Tuesday, 24 Feb 1942

Another uneventful day, with not a Jap shot fired. They say some Jap bombers plastered an empty field in Upper Bataan with phosphorous bombs. Cottrell phoned me about cooking up some supporting fires for the west Bataan coast—something which we already had in hand, in co-operation with Gen. King. Lost Motion! We went to Artillery Engineering office to see about maps and then to the Signal Corps to see about communications. Lt. Col. Schoer not much help; would give us nothing; wanted us to call all our radio equipment into his shop for calibration and change of crystals, so his precious men wouldn't have to expose themselves.

Tried to call upon Mrs. Sayre at the tunnel about our library but found that she and her husband, the high commissioner, left us on the submarine last night! Nobody seems to know whether President Quezon left or not![6] It would be a strategic error to let him get away.

Got Major Maynard of the map section to come to my dugout and we discussed azimuth errors of grids, latitudes and departures and other esoteric subjects. He is going to check my calculations. Then continued to work on firing data, etc.

Met Rutherford in the tunnel; heard later that he has been ordered to "rest" for 6 months or so! I suppose it is necessary, considering he is said to have had pneumonia, but it means that we'll get damn little good out of him—at least during this war.

Dozed over my work at my dugout, it being another hot day—but when I lay down I became wide awake.

Finally becoming bored, I went to C1 and organized a shoot at "Maggie," our new road interdiction point near Maragondon. First of all, we made Stinness put an arbitrary correction of "down 400 yards." on his 155mm guns and fire a 4-gun salvo at that point. Then changed 3 mils right, to plunk another 4-gun salvo in what I hope was the center of Maragondon—to which place the Japs are said to have removed their food supplies.

Then we went to chow at Btry. Geary and were regaled with pickled pigs feet. Also had cold canned tomatoes and ketchup—real treats. Everybody has been on "half rations" for some time but only recently has it become apparent. Flour is short, only 3 months' supply of beef left, no spices, soap is very scarce. However, nothing serious yet, merely that the food, especially in C Btry., is unappetizing.

Went to RSO for our baths as usual, and Maj. Julian let us try some of his "apple wine"—which wasn't bad at all. After this we sat around the council table at Hearn while Simmonds had his million-dollar leg dressed, where he had a boil a month ago. Then I repaired to my dugout and copied off into my Forgettery Book some "Secret" dope that Braly sent us re Fields of fire of 155mm guns.

Pres. Roosevelt made a radio speech today, but the Japs jammed it, for us, as they invariably do when stuff is on the air that they don't want us to hear. I wonder why we don't interfere with the programs which the Japs broadcast from Manila?

Rumor says that of 35 Jap ships involved near Bali, only 1 escaped. They also say that the Allied air forces ruined 11 Jap planes on the ground and some 40 in the air—and that we have air superiority over Bali and Australia—(The Japs have no air bases in Australia yet!). When the Japs bombed our base at Port Darwin, the other day, I wonder if they caught our Air Force as much asleep as it was here?[7]

At about 9:00 P.M. I went down to C1 and had Simmonds fire our new "Road Block," two 155s at San José RJ [road junction] and two at "Maggie." The shots went off instantly and made a satisfactory flash right on our cross-wires. Back to my dugout and go to bed.

Wednesday, 25 Feb 1942
Won P4.50.

Nothing unusual today. Fired a road block salvo about 3:30 from Btry. Frank, but Japs didn't fire a shot all day.

Schenck on duty tonight and didn't fire a road block. We are adopting names for our registration points: Maggie for the Maragondon RJ., Molly for that at Malini, etc.

Hawes came to my dugout, about 6:30 and we finished the 4 snorts of Scotch left in his bottle. Simmonds and Edison couldn't be found, and so lost out.

Played poker later and won P4.50. Turned in at 11:00 outside.

(21 Oct. 1942: I read in the *Japan Times Advertiser* of 8 October that at about sunset on 24 Feb. a Jap submarine bombarded some oil tanks at Santa Barbara, Calif.)[8]

Thursday, 26 Feb 1942
Lost P2.50.

Another beautiful day. Learned this A.M. that my requested additions to our

C1 tunnel are to be made, which will give us 4 sizeable laterals: G1, C1, Kitchen, Operations, plus the 2 "dynamite bodegas."

We can never finish a meal without being called to the phone.

Went to my dugout to work up firing data. While there, at 10:35 heard a plane nearby. AA guns and MG opened on it and we heard later that it was one of our planes that we shot down.

Maj. Maynard came around to show me his calculations on our azimuths, showing that we should add 0.36 to our grid azimuths to get true astronomical azimuths, or is it subtract? Yes?

Even the Artillery Engineers office is uncertain whether our position finding system is based upon true or grid north. Presumably the former. Talked to Cottrell about firing on new positions where enemy is alleged to be putting in new gun positions.

Bawled out our crew, working on small tunnel, for loud filthy language. Its excessive use is nauseating—even to a non-puritan.

There are reports of enemy cruiser and destroyer, etc. attacking Bagac.

General Moore came down to see me and said that Quezon and his party also departed on the sub the other day. Action by MacArthur on making me a BG is postponed by Mac for political reasons.

Worked hard on figuring registration points. Fired two personnel shells from Koehler's 12" mortars, one at an alleged OP and the other at an alleged battery position. Around 8:00 P.M. we fired two 2-gun 155mm salvos at "Maggie."

In evening played poker and lost P2.50. McCarthy lucky.

Friday, 27 Feb 1942

Just another day, with the Japs quiet all day.

Spent most of the day sweating out firing data.

After breakfast, inspected our C1 Tunnel. The crew expects to break through in 4 more blasts. Went to Engineering office and suggested to Pigg that he change the location of one lateral to give it more protection and he agreed. Then rode via Btry. James to C1.

Spurred McCarthy about our power project and he promptly got into a fight with Col. Parker, which I hope I smoothed out.

This afternoon we tried to fire shrapnel in the Ft. Frank 155mm guns but the fuses were so unreliable that no good came of it.

In the evening we fired our usual road interdiction salvos at "Maggie." I hear that the Japs are no longer using the beach road between Naic and Ternate, because of our shells.

Tried to get Steiger excused from overseeing his stevedores but was turned down by the general.

This afternoon *two* P-40s took off from Mariveles and circled overhead. It was grand to learn that we have *two* of them left.

Called up the general and broached my project to remove the "delay pellet" from some of our ".05 second delay" fuses and thus add to our supply of "land projectiles."

Tried to get Swain as communications officer, but they promised me Treacy instead, when he finishes a switchboard job at Hughes.

Saturday, 28 Feb 1942

Paid Welch P10.

Overcast.

Payday!

Up at 5:00 and to C1. My coffee all gone, so had to use soldier's coffee and it was terrible. After breakfast, went to G4 and talked with Kohn about his desires as to bombproofing his installations. Explored his tunnels at Hanna, where he has moved his G4 station and it is a labyrinth. Inspected our own tunnel, in which they expect to break through tomorrow.

To RSO for some colored inks and then to dugout.

Welch waited all morning at corral with Colin for the vet but he didn't come. Succeeded in phoning him and made date for 2:30 this P.M.

I have drawn no pay for Jan. nor will I draw for Feb. On hand $115 and P618 after paying Welch P10 for striker and P12 to Chong as lavandero.[9]

Worked on firing data.

In P.M. tried to fire an adjustment problem out of Btry. Frank but it fizzled completely. Picked out a point in water, shot at it, brought both guns together and then tried to shift to Ternate. At first Frank said they couldn't see splashes, so shifted point farther out. Shots at Ternate went wild. Then Foster phoned from Ft. Hughes that there was a group of 20 men working "feverishly" just short of our impact, so we tried to shift to that point and failed miserably. Foster said we scared up "Pigeons—they may be Carrier Pigeons" which gave us all a laugh. They were big white herons and fooled us into thinking they were (a) trucks fleeing along the road but they swooped up and down so our 2d guess was (b) airplanes. Foster was funny: he said he could see the men running and, after our last salvo, he reported a man slid off the top of a rice straw stack!

Became incensed with the dilatory action of Ft. Frank in getting their shots away and called the practice off. Chow at Capt. Steiger's battery. Usual bath.

Calculated firing data till bed time.

Commissary bill for Feb. = Cigarettes $2.50, Uniforms $3.34, Sox ¢27. Total of $6.11 = P12.22. Paid in cash Mar. 3d.

Sunday, 1 Mar 1942

Won P9.00.

My cake of soap has disappeared! No soap on hand. They will sell at commissary, half cake of issue soap per person! Hope some arrives!

Small inter-island boats sneak in, occasionally, and we in the 59th have to furnish a stevedore detail of 150 men and 3 officers every other night! The 60th and the beach defense people are excused! I doubt that the Navy does any of the work—(I hear Comdr. Bridgett is now at Fort Hughes. He is a ball of fire of a fighter). Capt. Snoke[10] came to me with a tale of how his stevedore detail was bossed by Col. Ward[11] last night and made to work overtime. When Steiger's outfit went down, the other night, Aikman didn't boss them and so they were alleged to have stolen 30 cases of stuff! Steiger condoned it and I bawled him out. Now the BC [battery commander] has to go with his men if more than 50% are on detail.

Acquired a Springfield .22 caliber this morning through RSO and gave it to our "gunsmith" to clean, oil and put away.

Have a helluva job on my hands, in calling and giving priorities to the requests for additional overhead cover for their base-end stations and guns, etc. Also, the chiselling 60th is now trying to run us out of our old G4 station, which they abandoned when the first bomb fell.

This morning with an extra blast, the miners finally broke surface below my dugout, with the other end of our main tunnel. They figure on being through in 10 days!

This morning Ft. Hughes fired Btry. Hooker at a boat towards Manila and, from G3 observation, missed it laterally by 3000 yards!

This afternoon, we let Foster shoot 6 rounds from Btry. Woodruff at his "Carrier Pigeon" points and all but 1 seemed to detonate. They seemed to be well bunched too. We started this shoot about 5:00, after we had had a fine ham dinner. At about this time we started a shoot with Btry. Frank, adjusting on a point in the water and then switching inland onto the Ternate Bridge. Evidently due to the scolding I gave Boudreau this morning, the firing was much faster and much better, though, as usual, the first salvo went over by about 400 yds.

Had our baths as usual. Simmonds and I had some rum and went down to C1 for a while and then played poker until 11:30. Won P9.00. Turned in.

It is such a beautiful full-moon night that it's a shame to turn in.

Monday, 2 Mar 1942

Paid P2.00 for waiter.

Uneventful day.

Today at 11:00 A.M. and also at 6:00 P.M. the word went out: "Friendly planes will be active" and about 30 minutes later in each case the Japs came in and dropped bombs near and on Ft. Frank before they could be recognized! *Some* G2 work by the Japs!

Went to our tunnel and then interviewed Col. Parker QMC and got permission to salvage the new Navy barracks on Topside, to secure barteris (novelty siding) to lag our tunnel and keep dirt out. B/60 had us stopped because they wanted to live there and Col. Parker[12] came up to see about it. Chisellers! I put Denby in charge of salvage.

No firing, either by us or the Japs, today.

A dearth of news about the big battle near Bali, though it seems that the Japs succeeded in making 3 landings in Java—and that is *bad.*

Spent most of the day in calculating firing data for registration points.

Elmes sent me up a present of 2 cakes of Palmolive soap and a can of smoking tobacco. *Some* present!

Turned in, in my dugout, because of the noise of working at the new exit of our tunnel.

This afternoon, after our shower, inspected the remnants of our post library and borrowed a couple of books. Most of the books have been issued out to organizations.

Tuesday, 3 Mar 1942

Won P2.00.

Commisary bill P12.22.

Awoke at 5:00 and went to C1 to relieve Julian, who refused to be relieved. Brewed a pot of Maxwell House coffee and, as a necessary result, became nervous. None of the 4 ships, tentatively slated for arrival this morning, actually showed up. I wonder if the Japs are not wise to our tricks and are waylaying and bombing those ships? They say that the *Don Estaban* was attacked by the Jap bombers near Lubang the other morning and that, although not hit, the Filipino crew promptly went overboard and deserted the ship. They are mostly like that. The *Uno*, now sunk on one of our beaches, is another instance of the inherently cowardly Filipinos, deserting their ship, unhurt, and letting her go on the rocks. Maj. Julian wants very much to salvage her.

After breakfast Cottrell and McCullough came up and gave us some dope, 2 days old, about a Jap gun being taken up in the mountains back of Fort Frank and, queerly, eager to let us shoot at it, even with personnel projectiles!

At about this time Capt. Ellis showed up, from Bataan, with a Lt. but I told him to come back this afternoon.

Air raid siren sounded at 10:30 but no planes heard. They say that our 4-P40s that went to Subic the other day sank an 8000-ton transport and ruined landing barges *but* one failed to come back, one crashed on landing, and "two can be repaired"! There goes all of our Air Force again. Lots of dust at Mariveles this afternoon indicated they were warming up some of our P-40s.

At 2:15 we unleashed Btry. Koehler for 10 rounds of personnel projectiles, first firing 2 into the water for a mediocre adjustment, then shifting inland. Maybe the shortest shots of each of our two salvos were on the wrong side of the mountain. We tried to predict ahead 2½ days because McCullough's dope was 2 days old!

Then we shot about 8 from Woodruff but couldn't see the burst of a single one, though we thought we heard some of them detonate.

Becoming disgusted, I changed target to Malini, just outside of Naic and those 2 appeared to fall only a short distance right of the target.

Then we went to chow and had our showers. Hawes had been sucating out a path to new entrance to our tunnel from C1 but has also made a zig-zag path to my dugout.

Denby has been salvaging siding from Navy barracks all day and I pinned Maj. Crawford's ears back for trying to stop him.

Simmonds came down to my dugout and we had a cocktail, and inspected entrance to tunnel. This entrance is almost in a dry stream bed that carries much water during rains but of course the engineers don't care if we are flooded out!

Beautiful moonlight night. Played poker—won P2.00.

Wednesday, 4 Mar 1942

Very breezy and cool today, a "dry typhoon."

Japs did no firing and the only firing we did was 20 shots from Btry. Frank, at the same target as Monday, but the folds in the hills were such that we couldn't tell what we were doing. Fort Hughes fired Btry. Hooker and, I hope, did better than before, though they were firing right into the sun and at merely a banca. Somebody was also proof-firing the 8″ gun, which has just been installed out Malinta Hill way.

It now develops that, because of a shortage of heavy dimension timbers, we may not get the 2 private rooms in my C1 Tunnel. The 2 boss miners are beginning to make alibis about it. I went to Engr. Tunnel this morning and interviewed Lothrup and he said we could have them except for that timber shortage. Also warned him of danger of run-off water flowing into our tunnel mouth.

Then went to Navy Tunnel, saw Capt. Hoeffel and arranged to get a long-arm protractor off the *Canopus*.

Had Welch reset the traps for the damn rat that is infesting my dugout. Heretofore the big ants have been stealing the trap bait, but now, on advice of a Filipino, we incase the bait in a rag. I think the rat stole my soap and that he is making a nest behind the tin lining of my dugout.

We hear that Sir Wavell, the limey, has been superseded in supreme command of armies in Far East by a Dutchman,[13] and we are overjoyed. The Dutch seem to be real fighters, compared to the "successful withdrawers" of Englishmen. Hot fighting now in Java and our Air Force seems to be doing something. Unfortunately, our USAFFE news sheet tells us very little. The Japs complain that our air raid on Subic, the other day was "dirty bridge" because it was made at night and they couldn't see our plane markings!

In evening, worked on my firing data, etc.

* * *

Thursday, 5 Mar 1942
Won P3.00.
My fuse scheme works!
Awoke at 4:30.
The Japs did no firing today but we did plenty. First we had Fort Frank comb the nearby ridges on the mainland for possible Jap observation posts and other activity. East had done some AA firing earlier in the day, at O.P.'s.

Then we set Fort Drum to work, firing 15 rounds with their 3″ Btry. Hoyle, followed by 15 rounds from 6″ Btry. Roberts against the hill-top shack where the alleged flag was flying. The shooting was beautiful to see: several of the shells landed right in the front yard of said shack.

Then we fired 2 shots from Btry. Crockett to test my modified fuses. I had asked that 2 Mark X fuses be altered by removing the "delay pellet" thus making them quicker acting. Heretofore, the projectiles with the .05-second delay action would penetrate too deeply into the ground to produce any appreciable surface effect.

These two 1070-lb. projectiles gave beautiful results, up to my wildest hopes; the explosions on impact were equal to those of the "personnel shell," both in dust thrown up and in noise made. Gen. Moore had been worried over shortage of these shells, so I took pleasure in reporting results to Cottrell.

This wound up our shooting for the day.

After dinner, Edison, Simmonds and I went to HQ Btry. Mess and had a piece of pie apiece. Probably the last of the pie, because of flour shortage. We are now on a ration which allows only 1 oz. of flour and 7 oz. bread per man per day. In evening, worked on firing data. Then adjourned to play poker. Lt. Pierce of Navy joined us and played in great luck, winning 8 pesos. I won P3.00.

Turned in, outside, at 11:30.

Friday, 6 Feb* 1942[14]
Slept soundly until close to 8:00! The damn rat untied the strings of our bait and stole it without springing the trap! No shave—direct to breakfast and then drove to Btry. Monja where I found all officers of K Battery playing poker instead of out with their searchlights!! Just what I'd expect of Gerlich![15]

Back to C1. Edison is at Kindley Field as witness on GCM.

Lots of activity around C1 now: Arty engineers gang of gugus [Filipino soldiers] are trenching a 75pr cable from manhole 43 to north addition of tunnel and are very talkative about it. Another gang, from Engrs. are running 3 heavy power

*As in diary.

leads from Wheeler transformer through woods to same place. Conductors are 0000 (4-0) and should carry the load with no appreciable drop. Hope the Japs won't blow them out!

To economize on power, drastic reductions are being made in use of lights and fans. Everybody is wondering if similar reductions will be made in the Malinta Tunnel.

By begging hard, I managed to get Gen. Moore to let me fire 4 mortar "personnel" shells from Koehler at Halag and Maragondon. Did this about 3:30, Edison not having shown up all day.

Immediately thereafter, he and Simmonds showed up. I went to my dugout to work. Soon they showed up with hot dope that 300 Japs were in Bucal—though Gen. Moore shortly before, had said he had no dope. It is a town or barrio east of Maragondon. We prepared firing data and went to chow.

At about 5:30 we fired about 10 salvos at the place, starting with a 4-gun salvo but one gun was so wild we cut that one out. Lots of dust kicked up. I gradually adjusted the battery up and left until it was in a visible barrio.

Chatted at Hearn, after our showers and then went to my dugout and worked on dope.

Strange as it seems, reports say that the Japs have or are getting air supremacy over Java. Where are all the Allied planes—retreated to Australia? If true, that bodes ill for the future. Another report says the Japs are preparing to invade India!

Why don't the Allies do a little "invading" on their own hook? Japan proper hasn't been touched once, yet.

When will our vaunted Alaskan air bases get into action: When will Russia let us use her far eastern bases!

Not a shot from the Japs today. They are said to have 2000 men over back of the Batangas hills, toward Tagaytay. They infest our south shore so that Boudreau's men can get no information. They run all Filipinos out.

Saturday, 7 Feb* 1942

Same old routine. Some AA activity near Frank and Mariveles. Saw one of our P-40s maneuvering over Mariveles—perhaps the one that we reconstructed from a wreck.

Drove to Navy Tunnel and returned the celluloid protractor, but could get no *good* one. Told Hoeffel about our old G4 and he should move his inshore patrol gangs in there. Then to Malinta Tunnel. Got Elmes to OK my getting gasoline for

*As in diary.

Gwenny. To Arty. Engr. and got coordinates of datum points. To HD but nobody there, so went outside and joined Cottrell, McCullough and Gen. Moore. Learned about Japs being in Looc and got authority to fire a few mortar "personnel" shells at them this P.M.

Inspected our old G4 station and also Btry. Grubbs, with reference to the 60th trying to take the former away from us. Grubbs looks good but no protection for power plant doors! Gave instructions to cure defect.

Back to dugout and worked on firing data until 2:30 when we staged our mortar shoot. First we put 2 shots at Marong Dalig and 2d was fine. Then 4 shots into Looc, then four into its seaport, Caluya, then 2 more back at Marong Dalig. Bet the Filipino "helpers" of the Japs thereabouts decamp promptly!

Capt. Petrie was present at dinner, from Ft. Hughes. He has a beard and mustache and looks like hell—as most men do who try that.

Doug MacArthur sent me a keg of cigars "not only because of my old affection but as a small token of my admiration for the splendid efficiency of you and your batteries" very nice and the cigars are so mild I can inhale them.

They say Batavia has fallen.[16] Damn the Japs! I wonder what the report (that United States raided *Marcos* Islands)[17] connotes? It leads to much speculation, for the possibilities are boundless.

No poker game tonight. Went down to C1 and saw Btry. Frank fire 1 "road interdiction" salvo of 4 155 shells at Bucal. The flashes appeared satisfactorily.

A Navy bloke accosted me this evening about the inshore patrol stuff which I suggested this morning to Hoeffel.

Served notice on Capt. Gerlich that, because of his poker playing during working hours yesterday, I held him to be "unsatisfactory" in "attention to duty" and "handling officers and men" and it was up to him to change that impression of mine.

Cottrell phoned about my program for using my new jazzed up fuse. 200 to go to Frank Tuesday: 150 for the 700-lb. projectiles and 50 for the 1,046-lb.

Sunday, 8 Feb* 1942
Lost P3.00.

Up at 7:00 A.M. At 7:20 a sound as of a stick of bombs—probably at Mariveles. After breakfast went to RSO and then inspected one end of our tunnel. Engineers have our power piped in and partly installed by knobwork [open electric wiring supported by knobs]. Our soldiers are hiding the beams for timbering our "bodegas."

*As in diary.

The design of cap for C1 is unsatisfactory* in that it has no airspace and leaves G1 naked! Called Braly about it, and asked that he get busy with the engineers. No firing by Japs today. We had a little Road Interdiction firing but that was all, by Btry. Frank. Hope we annoy the damn Japs, at least.

Worked mostly on firing data.

The engineers moved in on us today and started drilling 100 holes in roof of C1, preparatory to adding 2' of concrete to our roof. Noisy as hell. They are bringing up lots of steel rails for reinforcing the cap, and the rails will be welded together!

In our tunnel, the last blasts were set off today. I am hoping that they will pour the portals while they are on this C1-G1 job.

Told Julian, today, that instead of converting the RSO into a distillery, he should build a coffee roaster. He is also busy on working up the water supply for our tunnel. We talked with Sgt. Green, the plumber, and may get a gravity feed system at each end of our tunnel.

Played poker tonight and lost P3.00. McCarthy was red hot and couldn't lose. Edison staged an overdue come-back and won P9.00, which I was glad to see.

Caught a big old she-rat in the trap last night. They will run off with my soap, will they?

The weather is getting warmer, in the middle of the day, but I sleep under a quilt every night.

Supplies are worrying us. Five of the last 7 boats were sunk and no more will sail until the dark of the moon.

The Japs evidently are patrolling all passes. And our submarines are conspicuous by their absence. The damn "Sakdalistas" tipped off the Japs about our boats getting supplies from Looc and other nearby places. Japs have landed on Mindoro, they say.

Great excitement today over Friece radio report that the greatest convoy in history had landed safely in Australia, accompanied by great naval and air protection! We are hoping that possibly it may have some effect on our position.

Chaplain dropped in, tonight, and admitted that the first real shelling that we received had got his goat and he had been hiding in Crockett magazines until he had wrestled himself out of it and forced himself out. He is a good man and I like him.

Monday, 9 Mar 1942
   Barber P0.40.

---

*Not enough room under concrete cap just installed.

This morning, while we were at breakfast, the Japs opened up for the first time in weeks and fired a few shots at Hughes and Mills, but evidently hit nothing. Gen. Moore came to C1, but everything was quiet and so he left.

Engineers are working on the cap to C1 and the place is a madhouse—although they have finished drilling the holes in roof of C1.

Had a brilliant thought last night: in view of scarcity of heavy timbering for tunnel work, why not cast the beams and struts out of concrete? When I called up Lothrup this morning about it, he said I missed beating him to the punch by only 15 minutes, that he had just finished ordering the design made for such work!

Talked with Cottrell and gave him my program of altering fuses so that we will have a total of 500 made into instantaneous type (bunker type).

Razzed Bowler about delay in getting Treacy.

Caught another she-rat in the trap at 3:45 this morning, after which I slept until 8:00!

At 5:15 we staged at Frank a 28-shot bombardment of the alleged bridge at Ternate, the first 8 shots being used for adjustment on Sapong Point. Results appeared promising but of course the bridge was concealed from our view, over the ridge.

At 9:00 P.M. there was firing as of 155mm guns over Cabcaben way. 2-gun salvos and kept up for quite a while.

Talked with Bowler about promotion of Schutte and Dawe, also about getting rid of Maj. Sawtelle.[18] Arranged to send more library books to Bataan, and told him to use 3″ AA ammunition boxes.

Arranged a program for the work of altering fuses and gave it to Cottrell. Also notified Fort commanders about it.

Issued an order today to battery. commanders to start using coal stoves for cooking in their messes, against the day when there will be no gasoline for the gasoline ranges.

Also decreed that there would be no more "contributions" by our men of cigarettes to the "front line troops." Irresponsible persons have been coming around, playing on our men's sympathies for the hardships of the "front line troops" getting no cigarettes. Our men would then contribute liberally, and the cigarettes would never get to said "front line." It is a scandal the way cigarettes and other supplies are "hi-jacked" on their way from the Bataan supply bases to the front. Bowler said a half-dozen complaints came in to him today.

After dinner and bath, went to Hearn. Got a haircut. After dark returned to my dugout and did homework. I am disgusted with the silly mistakes I make in my calculations. Too rusty!

Tuesday, 10 Mar 1942
We heard that the Jap who commanded the Philippine invasion force was so

disappointed in not over-running us that he committed hari-kari in Gen. MacArthur's penthouse apartment in the Manila Hotel.[19] Fulmer brought back that rumor from Bataan a month ago and it is just now being announced by USAFFE. The new Jap commander here is said to be the one who commanded in Malaya![20] Sounds bad for us, but we'll see!

Mixed the Japs up this morning by doing some firing in the morning: 5 mortar HE, 1 each on Halag, Marong Dafig, Mary Gordon, Looc and Caluyan. While it was going on, there was an air raid at Frank and east fired some 3″ AA at the plane.

We also fired a mortar test round from the piece which had the premature burst a while back. Also a 4-gun salvo of 155mm at Halag. One mortar shell went wild.

Nothing else doing all day.

While we were playing poker tonight and had just inhaled some pie which Capt. McCarthy furnished, who should blow into the "Club" but Brooke (my son-in-law) from his post in Bataan, accompanied by one Lt. Col. Murphy, the Brigade S4. Of course that broke up the game and we sat around while Brooke told us how war is waged in Bataan. Then we adjourned to my dugout and chinned until nearly midnight when I got Pvt. Denby to pilot them to barracks where they occupied Julian's bunks, he being on watch tonight.

I turned in, on my outside cot.

Wrote a letter to Landon but found that it would have to pass the Navy Censor and so, as I had mentioned some of the scandalous poltroonery of our local Navy shining lights, I had to rewrite the letter!

Wednesday, 11 Mar 1942

When I got to breakfast this morning I found Brooke and Col. Murphy already there. After chatting awhile, I drove them to inspect the ruins of my quarters, also those of Capt. Julian. Then we drove to Bottomside because they wanted to buy some things. At the commissary they each bought a carton of cigarettes, half cake of issue soap and half carton of matches but, being supposed to get their supplies from Bataan, they couldn't buy for their pals. No razors or razor blades available anywhere. Introduced them to Gen. Moore and I slipped across and, MacArthur not being in his USAFFE office, I left word with Sutherland to thank him for his cigars and courteous note. Then Brooke and Murphy bought oodles of stationery at the PX, which has practically nothing left.

Then we went back to my dugout. I had first taken them down into our tunnel and explained all that to them. We had also spent some time at the library, where Brooke garnered a boxful of books to take back with him. I picked up a half-dozen that I wanted.

Worked on firing data with Edison and planned a shoot for the afternoon so Brooke could see what a big shell burst looks like. He went back down to Malinta Tunnel to increase his allotment to Priscilla, thank Heaven, and returned half-hour late, but I held the shoot for him. We put two mortar shells into Marong Dalig and they made a fair showing. Then we shot a few 155 salvos at No. 4—Camaudag RJ and they showed up fairly well, even if they were behind some ridges.

Then we went to chow. More chit-chat with Brooke holding an attentive audience with his accounts. Took our showers as usual and then to Hearn where they were drilling, and stayed until 6:10. I accompanied them to the wharf and put them aboard the courier boat and returned to my dugout to enjoy the sunset. Then inside and wrote up this log.

Added a postscript to Landon's letter, telling of Brooke's visit. I also enclosed a photo of the big shell crater, back of barracks of B/59 and hope it may pass the Censor. Gave letter to Cooper to deliver to the censors and this delayed him.

Thursday, 12 Mar 1942

Awoke at 1:00 A.M. and worked for an hour and then turned in.

Massello[21] was around, all day, from his post in Bataan.

Gen. Moore called a conference of regimental commanders at 11:00 and told us that MacArthur left last night for Australia, with most of his staff. He had first been ordered 3 weeks ago, without his family or staff; he fought against leaving at all but finally had to go or disobey orders. So he left on a fast PT boat last night with his family and most of his staff. It is a dangerous trip, and I hope he makes it. He'll fly from Del Monte field, in Mindanao, the rest of the way.[22]

Now to convince our men that he has not deserted, but has gone into a job where he can do something real toward helping us. It would be bad for our men's morale if they put the wrong interpretation on his leaving.

Engineers are still welding, atop C1, and are laying big pipes everywhere, to convey the concrete from their mixer, below the hill. All paths are cluttered with pipe, and the noise is very evident.

Tonight at about 9:30, Lt. Daws discovered a vessel, looked like a sailing banca, almost 5000 yards offshore near Navy Guard ship. We asked inshore patrol to investigate but they declined because they "have only machine guns"! So we got Btry. Monja into action. Meanwhile the "banca" was sailing fast away, having turned tail when first illuminated. At first, Monja couldn't see the target, and their "Case II" shots at the intersection of our 2 searchlight beams were wild. But then their observer picked up the target, they shifted to Case 3 and, at their 7th shot, they evidently destroyed the target! Will write them a letter of commendation tomorrow. Turned in on my azatea.

Friday the 13th

Won P8.00.

Usual morning routine.

Gen. Moore dropped in on us and we adjourned to my dugout to chat for a while.

At 3:00 we opened up with Btry. Frank and tried to demolish the bodega over near San Juan, but couldn't get it with 28 rounds! Lit all around it but never hit it. Battery work was better than it had been.

The Engrs. poured the concrete apron around the N entrance of our tunnel and are dismantling that part of their pipe line and placing the pipe in our tunnel, preparatory to pouring a floor in said tunnel. There will be a pipe subdrain under the center of the floor and I'm wondering if we can use it for a sewer pipe.

In evening, played poker. Had a field day and won P8.00.

Three Jap destroyers plainly visible out towards Subic, but they kept well out of our reach. What easy picking for a gritty submarine commander!

No arrivals of supply ships for a coupla weeks. Everybody is worried about gas and diesel oil. That may prove the critical factor of our defense! There is a rumor that we may receive supplies by destroyers—old ones, renovated for this purpose and coming direct from the United States. Fine idea, but where are you going to find Navy officers who have enough guts for a job like that, borrow them from the Dutch?

The Japs, by using a few light vessels, are evidently blocking all passages leading to Manila, with no interference by our forces.

The following was inspired (?) in one of our C1 details, after hearing the orders, etc. prevalent in C1, G1, and inshore patrol stations:

Test communication, message understood
Provide illumination, Modulation's good.
Hearn, a met message; Crockett, you repeat!
Ships in La Monia passage. Keep the station neat.
Get the azimuth on that ship! Follow the beam!
Someone let the coffee drip. Who's got some cream?
How 'bout giving me a ring? Fourteen calling Seven.
Nope we cannot see a thing. Azimuth three eleven.

Saturday, 14 Mar 1942
Usual morning routine.

Along about noon Ft. Hughes shot at a couple of Jap towboats and barges, using Fuger (3"0) Leach (6") and Hooker (155mm). Also our Btry. Kysor fired, all getting some much needed practice for gun pointers. Last night one of our mines near Monja exploded and this morning four more went. Cause: probably corrosion or leakage.

Gen. Moore showed up while I was at C1 but the noise and confusion of the engineering work was so great that he left immediately. Engineers started pouring cap on C1 today but the lift was so great that it didn't work very well. At least they came with a tractor and hauled away their welder current generator thus clearing our path.

Ft. Frank indulged in sporadic firing against the mainland to prevent Japs from again cutting their water supply. Evidently successful, for the pipeline is still delivering water and all of Ft. Frank's receptacles are full and have been for 2 days.

Worked up notebook on Btry. Craighill, a 4-gun mortar battery at Hughes, preparatory to using the Bunker fuses against the Batangas shore. Drew chart, etc.

We are getting a master gunner from the artillery engineer and also a communications staff sergeant, which will help.

Inspected our tunnel. The concrete apron at west entrance is OK and Denby has made some diversion dams which should prevent rain run-off from entering that mouth of the tunnel. Talked with Keevan about east portal and breaker slab, which they may omit. Shower is installed outside officer's end (west portal).

After dinner, bathed and worked on Craighill dope on my porch.

Transition

21 February–14 March

The Japanese artillery battery in the jungles of Cavite ceased firing on Corregidor about 22 February, causing a spell of near quiet to settle over the island until 15 March. There was occasional firing at the smaller islands but nothing of any consequence. Ft. Frank had had a few casualties, but none of its guns were damaged.[23] The twenty feet of concrete on the roof and the thirty-foot-deep casemate surrounding Ft. Drum[24] were only chipped and dented.[25]

While on Bataan, Homma's decimated troops completed their withdrawal by 24 February. In many ways they were in as bad shape as the Americans. They had cut their rations from 62 ounces of rice a day to 23 ounces. By the end of February, Homma's effective troop strength was reduced to 3,000 men. But because of reinforcements during the first weeks in March, this strength rose to 11,000. In addition, Homma received many more aircraft with which to bomb Corregidor.

MacArthur had delayed departure for three weeks when he first received orders to leave;[26] however, the Japanese had so isolated Manila Bay by land and sea that on 10 March he decided to delay no longer. He felt it would not be safe to wait until 15 March for the next submarine.[27]

The Belotes say in their book that MacArthur's departure gave hope to the garrison on Corregidor.[28] But as the weeks to come would show, his departure really portended the beginning of the end.

On the twelfth, Wainwright gave command of I Corps to Brig. Gen. A. M. Jones,[29] and General King took over field command in Bataan, while Admiral Rockwell was replaced by Captain Hoeffel.[30]

On the fifteenth, Wainwright visited the Rock to ask B. G. Lewis Beebe, who was controlling Bataan's food, what the supply status was for the men on Bataan. As a result of this visit he had to cut the half rations then in effect by a third in order for them to exist until 10 April.[31] Despite the shortage of food on Bataan, there was one group at this time that started eating well.

In the middle of March, the air force flight surgeon, Lt. Col. William Keppard, realized his pilots were ineffective without proper food; consequently, he approached General King on the matter and told him "there would be no more flying unless the pilots were given proper food."[32] At once, the twenty-five pilots were put on full rations with vitamin tablets for ten days. The enlisted ground crews evinced no resentment at this, and almost overnight the extra food worked a miracle on the pilots' efficiency.[33]

By the middle of March, the Kondo artillery battery in Cavite had been replaced by the Japanese 1st Heavy Artillery Regiment. It was armed with the most powerful howitzer in the Japanese arsenal, the 240mm (9.4-inch) howitzer.[34] The Japanese received ten of them. Soon the islands in Manila Bay would feel the horror of their power.

By way of a threat, General Homma's psychological operations staff sent a message to Ft. Frank stating that all of Cavite now belonged to the Japanese military and that their large howitzers were being massed there in preparation to destroy Ft. Frank, then Drum, and finally Corregidor, which would then be assaulted by "crack Japanese landing troops."[35] The Americans would receive good treatment if they surrendered before the assault.[36] Boudreau answered the offer by firing his 12-inch mortars at suspected enemy locations.

The Japanese batteries retaliated by opening up on the forts on 15 March.[37]

Notes

1. Morton, *Philippines,* 396. On 21 February, the *Princessa* was one of many interisland steamers that were resupplying Corregidor. The *Princessa* had just arrived from Cebu with seven hundred tons of food. Many of these ships failed to make the hazardous journey and were sunk by Japanese gunboats.

2. Belote and Belote, 93, 117. Col. William C. Braly was General Moore's G3. He had been largely responsible for the establishment of the roving 155mm guns in order to draw fire away from the island's fixed installations. Colonel Braly spent three years in prison and was subsequently released. On the liberation of Corregidor, his diary was found and returned to him. He has written numerous articles for service magazines and has published a book on his experiences entitled *The Hard Way Home.* Wainwright, 198. Colonel Braly, somehow, saved his violin even after capture, and this raised morale in various POW camps.

3. Mellnik, "Life and Death," 3. Col. Charles G. Sage was the commander of the 200th CA (AA) of the New Mexico National Guard. Morton, *Philippines,* 451. Later General King made him commander of the Provisional Coast Artillery Brigade (AA), which was made up of 2 AA regiments that were to fight as infantry for the Luzon Force before its surrender. Wainwright, 244. He was later taken prisoner and shipped to Manchuria with General Wainwright. In prison he composed songs to keep up the POWs' morale.

4. Morton, *Strategy,* 176. On 20 February, Timor had fallen. Karig and Kelley, 209–19. On the night of 19 February, a large naval battle between Dutch and U.S. forces on one hand and the Japanese on the other did take place off Bali; however, it was not as big a victory as is stated by Bunker. Actually it was somewhat of a fiasco, which lasted until the twentieth. In a very interesting gun and torpedo duel, at least two Japanese destroyers were sunk and another was severely damaged. The Dutch lost their destroyer *Piet Hein.* There was a minimal amount of friendly air activity in the Java area.

5. *Banca*—a Filipino native fishing boat.

6. Morison, 203. Unknown to Bunker, President Manuel Quezon and his family left the island aboard the submarine USS *Swordfish* on 20 February. It returned on the twenty-fourth for High Commissioner and Mrs. Sayre.

7. Ibid., 320. The enemy launched seventy aircraft against Port Darwin on 19 February. They succeeded in destroying twelve ships and eighteen aircraft as well as destroying the airfield.

8. This was obviously added much later.

9. *Lavendero*—laundry boy.

10. *Register,* 479. Capt. Donald Richard Snoke was in the 59th CA; he was later captured and died from wounds received on 9 January 1945, when his POW ship was bombed in the harbor at Takao, Formosa. It had departed the Philippines on 28 December 1944.

11. Ibid., 367. This was probably Lt. Col. John Taylor Ward, a quartermaster officer from Bataan who was supervising the unloading of supplies from Bataan; he was later captured, and he was subsequently killed on the Death March near Limay on 11 April 1942.

12. Ibid., 462. This was probably Lt. Col. James Young Parker of the Air Corps, who had been the executive officer at Nichols Field but was now the executive officer of the Provisional Beach Defense Battalion on Corregidor; he became a POW and was later repatriated.

13. Morton, *Philippines,* 356. Wavell had indeed been told to dissolve his headquarters on 27 February and to turn it over "to Netherlands' authorities before leaving for India."

14. For some reason, Bunker wrote "February" for the dates of 6, 7, and 8 March. He catches it on 9 March.

15. *Register,* 468. Capt. Frederick John Gerlich was commander of K Battery. He was later captured and killed on a POW ship, which was torpedoed some two hundred miles off the southeast China coast; of the 1,790 people aboard, only 9 are believed to have escaped.

16. Morton, *Strategy,* 169. Batavia fell on 2 March 1942.

17. Hough, Ludwig, and Shaw, 207. Many small airstrikes were being conducted throughout the Pacific at this time. They were designed "to harass the Japanese and provide at least one outlet for efforts to fight back at the enemy when the news from all the other fronts was gloomy."

18. *Register,* 349. This was probably Maj. Donald William Sawtelle, who was captured and later repatriated.

19. John Dean Potter, *The Life and Death of a Japanese General* (New York: New American Library of World Literature, 1962), 101. Here Bunker is speaking of General Homma. This was nothing but a rumor. However, it did portend what was to happen to Homma.

20. Ibid., 41–93. Bunker refers to Yamashita as "the tiger of Malaya." This too was another unfounded rumor.

21. *Register,* 424. William ("Wild Bill") Massello, Jr., had been a battery commander in the 60th CA (AA); here he is a battalion executive officer. During his tour on Bataan he was highly decorated, having received the DSC, -2 SS—LM and 4 PH. He was captured and later repatriated.

22. MacArthur, 142–45. At 7:15 in the evening on 11 March, General MacArthur told his wife, "It's time to go." A short time later they were aboard PT-41 accompanied by three other PT boats. As the boat made its way through

the minefields, MacArthur wrote, "Up there, in command, was my classmate, Paul Bunker. Forty years had passed. . . . I could shut my eyes and see again that blond head racing, tearing, plunging—210 pounds of irresistible power. He and many others up there were old, old friends, bound by ties of deepest comradeship."

MacArthur made it to Cagayan on Friday, 13 March. From there he caught a plane and flew to Australia, where he narrowly missed being hit by Japanese bombers. Morison, 203. Admiral Rockwell was also aboard the boat with MacArthur.

23. Belote and Belote, 89.

24. Brig. Gen. John J. Kingman, "The Genesis of Fort Drum," *Coast Artillery Journal*, 88 (July–August 1945), 24–26.

25. Belote and Belote, 89.

26. MacArthur, 141.

27. Belote and Belote, 89.

28. Ibid., 90.

29. Wainwright, 67.

30. Lt. Cmdr. T. C. Parker, "The Epic of Corregidor–Bataan," *United States Naval Institute Proceedings*, 69, no. 1 (January 1943), 16.

31. Wainwright, 68.

32. Lt. Col. William E. Dyess, *The Dyess Story* (New York: G. P. Putnam's Sons, 1944), 61.

33. Ibid., 62.

34. Col. Homer Case, "War Damage to Corregidor," *Coast Artillery Journal* (May–June 1947), 39.

35. Belote and Belote, 91.

36. Braly, 37.

37. Belote and Belote, 92.

Sunday, 15 Mar 1942
Big bombardment.

Awoke at 6:00 and puttered around and dozed until 7:30 when the Japs opened a bombardment on Corregidor, first one shot, then another, then a burst of four. The Japs opened up on all four of our fortified islands simultaneously and kept up the hot pace until about 1:30 when they slacked off for a while and then took up their shooting with renewed energy and continued so until dark.

They concentrated for hours on Ft. Frank and then on Ft. Drum, but even after they shifted to Ft. Hughes, they continued to pound Frank. For the first time, we knew that the Japs are using larger calibered guns than 150mm. One shot penetrated the armor at Btry. Roberts on our concrete battleship [Fort Drum] and burst inside the casemate filling the ship with flame, smoke and fumes. Nobody in the casemate at the time, so there were no casualties.[1] The base of the bursted projectile was about 10″ or more in diameter! We wonder if it is a gun which the Japs brought down from Fort Wint.[2]

Comparatively few Jap shots were fired at Corregidor until our Btry. Hamilton opened up on them and then they started plastering Hamilton, which is just below C1. We got numerous reports of gun flashes seen, but the morning sun was in our eyes and we could hardly see a thing. However, we used all of our armament which would bear upon the Batangas shore, and did the best we could to neutralize the enemy fire. By afternoon we received report that Btry. Craighill shells had been fitted with "Bunker" fuses in about 12 projectiles so we fired them at what we believed was the Jap battery that was plastering Drum just then. That battery quit, but another one opened on the Craighill pit and scored two hits down in the pit.

Fort Frank got a fearful working over: probably all guns of Btry. Frank (our wheel-horse, heretofore) put out also (maybe) the four AA guns; many machine-gun nests hit; water mains cut in several places, besides much other damage.

At Hughes, the damage was nominal. Equalizing pipe cut at Btry. Gillespie, but we are not using that 14″ gun anyway. The two shells that landed in Craighill B Pit only knocked off the handle on an elevation hand wheel.

But it was a severe bombardment: About noon Frank had counted over 300 shots at them and over 63 hits on that Fort. Practically every shot at Drum was a hit. It hurt me like blazes to see my friends under fire and be so powerless to help them. But our G2 service is giving us absolutely no information. It is just as if we were in a foreign country instead of an alleged friendly one.

Worked up a map, showing suspected enemy positions and General Moore (who came up to C1 for a while) promised to try to get a P-40 plane to fly tomorrow and try to verify some of our guesses. But even if it does, the damn Japs will move.

In going down for my laundry, Welch got forced off the road by a Filipino driver, PESCASSIO, driving a big Mack Truck No. 412789; smashed right rear and left front fenders and put a big dent in rear trunk. The SOB! And Gwenny had come through the whole war, so far, unscathed. Tough luck!

To my dugout to rest and figure firing data. I wonder if the bombardment will continue tomorrow? The engineers are working all night, pouring the cap to our C1 Station—the Jap firing now having ceased (8:30 P.M.).

Monday, 16 Mar 1942

Another day of bombardment by the Japs, though they waited until 9:45 before starting. But, once started they kept on briskly. Detecting a few flashes over Ternate way, we opened with our 12″ Btry. Hearn, with personnel projectiles and the Japs went to cover for a while, but began again, later, in a desultory way and we could detect no more flashes. We were going to fire Craighill too, but Col. Hopkins begged off because of poor visibility.

Didn't go to RSO this morning; used Btry. Wheeler instead. Sent Welch to U.S. Engineers shop with my car and they took the fenders off for repair. I continued work on firing data, at my dugout.

In P.M. we started firing the Btry. Koehler mortars at Looc, Caluya and Restinga ravine, but before we could finish, the Japs drove our men below with their effective counterbattery firing at that Fort.

We also opened up with Btries. Woodruff and Craighill on other points and the same thing happened.

The USAFFE people could not send up a P-40 to spot enemy batteries because there is only one P-40 left, and its speed is only about 140 miles.[3]

Gen. Moore told me that MacArthur is OK: he successfully made the boat trip to Del Monte, in Mindanao, as per schedule, but that the planes were not there to carry his party to Australia. The planes will make the trip tonight. A great load is lifted from my mind by this news.

Last night one of our big subs came in, after 11:00 P.M. and departed about 3:30. I wonder what she brought in?[4]

It is reported that the Japs made a small landing, at Cebu! That is now our supply base. I hope we don't lose it.

In evening, worked on firing data and read "Sucker's Progress."

Engineers seem to have finished pouring concrete cap on C1 so I slept outside my dugout.

Tuesday, 17 Mar 1942

Day opened beautifully but the Japs had to spoil it, at 10:18 A.M., by opening their bombardment, though it was not so heavy as usual. To retaliate, and show them that Ft. Frank is still in commission, we fired a salvo of 6 shots, using the 1046-lb. projectile with Bunker fuse, into the ravine behind Restinga Pt. where old-timer May [reference unknown to editor] has "located" a battery for us, possibly the same one that Capt. Thompson reported to us from Signal Hill. By this time the Japs shut up. Later, about sun-down, they sent a few more over at Hughes.

"On the whole," as Bairn's father would (or did) say, "the day passed quietly." The engineers have finished pouring the cap for C1! and are now busily erecting forms around G1 and, as the whole job is visible to everybody on the Cavite shore, I had McCarthy get busy and erect a camouflage net over the job.

Played poker this evening and wound up even.

Progress on our tunnel seems to have slowed down. They are now lagging the tops and sides of our 4 laterals. Denby, our handyman, has put up a shaving mirror and shelf over the gorgeous washbowl that is temporarily set up in the officer's end. The "novelty siding" which I had battened down over the 2″ cracks between the siding planks, looks well. In time, it will be a grand dugout. The shower and a 2-holer are already in place, outside the officer's end, but the portal is still just a hole in the ground.

Today we shot a few from Koehler at Buri Point, down toward Looc, where we deduced that the Japs have at least one of those cussid, 240mm guns of theirs. Kirkpatrick says that when one of them hits Ft. Drum, the whole ship rocks. They make a wicked burst. It was one of those that hit near a gun of his Btry. Roberts and came into the casemate—but not through the shield, as I was told at first.

Wednesday, 18 Mar 1942

P1.00 for cigarettes.

Over in Bataan, supplies for front line troops are handled execrably; the trucks are hi-jacked en route. On the front lines, they say, men sometimes pay as high as a peso apiece for cigarettes and if outfits don't go back and bring forward their own supplies, they get only carabao and rice to eat. Of course, here on the Rock, we have laid in our own supplies, but even so, rice is the basis of every meal.

This morning everything was going along nice and quiet when the damn Japs opened up on Ft. Drum at 11:30 and there was some of the 240mm stuff among it, too. I had been down to Engr. Tunnel and South Wharf, where I cornered Maj. Lothrup and explained to him my discovery of how to "frame" his tunnels with the 6″ channel-irons which are now in our HQ Btry. Mess. He agreed to help me get our "bodegas" blasted and built.

Then I had gone to G3, talked with Lt. Col. Miller and ordered him to improve the phone hook-up of the C1-G3 command line. Also ordered him to get busy and improve the camouflage of his station. A . . . lieutenant in the station tried to give me an argument—'nuff said, I pinned his ears back with a few choice words.

The engineers continued building forms in front of our observing slots, so as to increase the roof thickness of G1. Their lumber obstructs our field of view very much and we can hardly observe our own fire. I'll be glad when they get to hell out of that neighborhood.

They are now digging a trench down the center of our tunnel for an 8" subsoil drain and I am trying to get a sewer pipe laid in the same trench, to carry off the waste water from our washbowls, etc. Just trying to exercise a little of the jerevision [flexible foresight] that is so damnably missing in our Army.

One Maj. Rumbough[5] was in our midst all day and, after hearing him and a few others of the Bataan heroes hold forth, I am moved to assert that I've never seen a war where modesty was less a virtue than this one. The slob admitted that 3 Jap bombers routed our entire force which was supposed to defend Antimonan and the country south of Manila—that the Philippine army ran like sheep, and yet he seemed to see nothing shameful in it. Of course, this route of our troops at Antimonan was the main reason we could not hold our lines north of Bataan, and necessitated a hurried retreat.

This morning, after the Japs started firing, we opened counterbattery as soon as we could get a few hints as to where the Japs were firing from. By 1:30 P.M., we had fired Koehler 6 rounds at the Buri Pt. gun and done well. Craighill's 5 shots at the Restinga Ravine position, however, were pretty sour.

About 5:30 P.M., the Japs having remained quiet meanwhile, we fired 8 rounds of mortar shells over behind San José and Barrio Julio and especially the last looked very promising. Woodruff (14") also fired 8 rounds up into the back-country at a position which we deduced from resection of flashes—the last 4 being at another position that I "pulled out of the hat"—behind another hill at a shorter range. Woodruff showed commendable speed of fire.

Capt. Coleman, beard and all, of 57th Infantry[6] was at Hearn when we arrived, fresh from our showers, and we gassed while Simmonds took Rumbough to his boat for the return trip to Bataan.

McCarthy brought a pie to the poker party last night and I couldn't get to sleep. So I got up and planned the channel-iron method of making tunnel frames, to replace the timbers which are now scarce. This is the scheme I sold to Lothrup, this morning.

Spent the evening in my dugout, figuring firing data.

Thursday, 19 Mar 1942
Won P1.50.

Heard yesterday that MacArthur has been placed in supreme command in the Far East; Army, Air corps, even Navy! Three rousing cheers! Maybe we'll get somewhere now!

Japs fired 6 shots at Frank at about 11:00 A.M. We retaliated with one mortar shot at 6 points: Looc, Caluya, Buri, May's Btry. etc.

Rutherford, who is just out of the hospital after being away for months, enjoyed the shoot. Took him through our tunnel. He is convalescent from pneumonia and malaria and is pretty low, physically.

Japs fired no more all day but at 5:15 we gave them another working over: fired another "flower pot" from Koehler: 5 shots at 5 different targets, then fired about 16 from Craighill at Ternate and Maragondon plus about *24* at Naic, most of which went short, dammit, though we thought we could see 2 hits on the church.

Then went to chow—shower—then calculated data until 8:10 when we adjourned to play poker. Had to buy 2 stacks, but quit a slight winner. Simmonds reamed me twice, but I got back at him once in good style.

Gen. Moore dropped in, this morning, and chatted awhile, about our MPs etc. Two of mine are being tried for sleeping on post and two more for leaving post during air raids.

Engineers are repairing my car, but I doubt that they make a good job of it. There is no acetylene left on post for welding.

Friday, 20 Mar 1942

At about 11:15 we shot our flower pot from Btry. Koehler's 12″ mortars and it sounded grand. My car is back and, while the ravages of the collision are still visible, they did a surprisingly good job of it.

Today we fired a few shots from Btry. Geary's 12″ mortars, to test an experimental fuse taken from a 155mm shell, in an effort to get a projectile which would get up high enough to hit these high-flying Jap bombers, who know so well the limitations of our antiaircraft guns. If it can be made to work, it will sure jolt the Japs.

Rumor has it that the Japs caught our Air corps on the ground again. This time in Java, where we should have great air superiority. Will these damn fool aviators never learn? We lost most of our planes here that way.

Japs fired never a round all day, and we fired only as above. Engineers are delayed in pouring cap for G1 because they cut their rails 2′ too long. Draftsman's error! It will be several days of delay. They brought their electric welder back on the job and will weld our channels for us, for our tunnel "sets." All our channels are now cut.

Worked on firing data at odd moments all day. As I was inspecting our tunnel, Braly and McCullough came up with a bit of futile "secret" information about Jap guns, etc., but even they gave it a rating of only "doubtful." Took them through our tunnels and to my azatea for a chat.

After a very good dinner, which featured apple pie and Edam cheese we got our showers and then went to Btry. Hearn for a chat. Then to my azatea to read, for a change, but somebody has stolen my "Sucker's Progress." Edison told me that Lt. Bliss, whom I sent back to Pucot Hill as observer, has worked his men so hard they are getting sick. Once he made them do 6 round trips up the hill with supplies. That is too stiff, will pull him in.

No poker game tonight, so I retired to my dugout to work.

Saturday, 21 Mar 1942

Bad bombardment of Frank and Drum.

Today the damn Japs started bombarding us early, about 7:30, and kept it up furiously till along about 1:00 P.M. or so. We glimpsed a few flashes over Ternate way and west of the slots but, when Woodruff and Craighill started to shoot back, the Japs concentrated on them and the men had to take cover. But Craighill managed to get in about 8 shots.

Fort Frank was hard hit today. Early, a Jap shell hit the entrance to a tunnel, killing about 13 and injuring 27.[7] By the end of the day there were 26 soldiers dead and 43 injured. This brings Fort Frank's casualties to about 75, so far. A boat is going over from here tonight to pick up the dead and wounded. There are no burial places possible on Frank. Their mortar battery is so full of debris that it is out of commission for at least 24 hours.

At Fort Drum, our concrete battleship, a shell hit a seam of a turret and opened a crack 4″ wide and 18″ long, so you can see clear sky from within. Periscope hoods of both turrets have been shot away. The Japs are hacking away at the 2 casemate guns on the broadside and have knocked away the concrete to a depth of 8 feet! Those 2 6″ guns that side are now in commission. At least, one is and the other soon will be. No casualties at Drum today.

At Fort Hughes: one man slightly injured.

In a desperate effort to silence the Japs we fired old reliable Btry. Hearn about 6 shots at what we diagnosed as an enemy battery way back. We wound up with the gun elevated against the elevation stops, and that wasn't any too much. Of course, having no observation, we couldn't tell what execution we were doing. At any rate, about this time, the Japs stopped firing for the day. This was around 1:30.

Worked on figuring firing data for new points and checking. The engineers welded the steel in the roof of G1 all day. Had to keep scolding all day to prevent them ruining our camouflage. Spread burlap bags over the glaring concrete and told McCarthy to disguise our observation slits with black paint. Got no chance to examine our tunnel, but miners say they'll be out in 3 days. Lucas came around to see how many lights could be saved in C1-G1 when we move and to discuss location of our power plant.

In evening Simmonds and Rutherford came to my dugout and we finished the rum. Then Edison and I calculated firing data for a sunrise salvo to the Japs in the morning, but the Craighill mortars will probably be unable to reach where we want to shoot!

Turned in at 11:30. The damn moon is getting bright again! That will mean no supply ships. I wish they would send us a few submarines filled with diesel oil! The sub that came for the high commissioner robbed us of 30,000 gallons of fuel oil. What a blunder by the U.S. authorities! Why couldn't she have refueled in Australia on both legs of the trip? No fuel for our mine planter, to keep the mine-field up!

Sunday, 22 Mar 1942

O! Sprig, geddle Sprig!

Won P8.00.

Awoke at 6:00 and went to C1. Gave the Japs a matutinal salute of 2 shots from Woodruff, 2 salvos from Craighill and a turret salvo from Drum—and then quit. After breakfast I walked through our tunnel and engineers say they'll be through laying pipe today. But they are still welding steel atop G1. Had my staff working on layout of lights and phones in the tunnel.

Gen. Moore came and we chatted for a while. I suggested that we now remove the breechblocks from Btries. Greer and Crofton (2 14" guns at Ft. Frank) and store them here at Corregidor. These two guns are no good for landward firings but, if the Japs captured Ft. Frank, would be effective against every other fort. Moore said he'd think it over. When I asked him for replacements for Ft. Frank he said he didn't know where to get them.

The USAFFE Bulletin is now full of fulsome praise of Lt. Gen. "Skinny" Wainwright, now commanding here in the P.I.—though Beebe is deputy chief of staff for MacArthur still.[8]

Worked on firing data until, bored, I picked up Col. Rutherford and set out in my car, since the heavenly twins were using the regimental car. Bawled out McCarthy for not supervising the camouflage paint job on C1—and for failing to get our channels welded while the engineers' welding unit was up here. Anderson ordered it to Bottomside, dammit!

Then visited G3 and talked with DeCarre about the camouflage of his station. Then to G4 where I found Simmonds and Edison and chinned with Col. Mitchell about having all "met" [meteorological] data posted—and officers instructed in adjustment of fire. Then back to C1 where I found McCarthy wielding a brush on the paint job. To my dugout and conferred with Rutherford on the layout of the electric lights in our new tunnel. As drawn, they look excessive—very—but they use only about 2 kilowatts.

After chow, which included ice cream, we had our showers and then adjourned to Btry. Hearn (A/59) and gassed there for an hour. Figured up the scheme of the Drum turrets firing surprise salvos at night as harassing and interdiction fires. In daylight, it isn't safe to fire towards land, because the Japs immediately start counterbattery with extreme accuracy and *might* blow an obstruction into the bore of a gun which was just about to fire. Tonight he will fire one shot towards Naic, if he can reach it, otherwise at Maragondon. If Koehler's mortars are dug out of the debris, they will fire a couple of salvos, at 6:45 A.M., tomorrow, at the position of an enemy gun, as reported by Mayhew's amateur seismographic sound-locating device.

Poker game arranged by Rutherford tonight. Won freely P8.00. There is much malaria among our troops in Bataan, about 25% of our casualties—or more! They say that a plane flew in here, the other night, carrying quinine, which is very scarce.

Tuesday, 24 Mar 1942 (continued)

men.[9] While I was here at RSO the Japs dropped two sticks of bombs, but none came near us. I heard, later, that it was a formation of about 27 and that our AA fire broke up their formation and scattered the planes. Becoming bored with sitting around in RSO, I had Welch drive me to C1, where everything was quiet. All clear sounded again shortly after I went to my azatea.

Laid down on my outside cot for a rest before chow, but the Jap planes came back and the siren blew again at 4:00 P.M. but the planes seemed distant, and no bombs were dropped.

One of this morning's bombs landed near the main entrance to the C1 Tunnel but evidently did no damage except to a water cooler. Our power plant was unhurt.

Another stick landed near Btry. Monja and deposited much dirt on runway of No. 4 light and raised Cain with the 2 kitchens there. Gen. Wainwright was in Monja Btry. Tunnel when it happened which may help.

After this we had 2 more alarms before 6:00, one of them just as I was finishing chow, but nothing came of them. Couldn't find Rutherford when bathtime came, so we went without him. In order to do my bit towards saving power, I am wearing my outer uniforms 2 days instead of 1, so Chong can save his electric ironing.

At dinner I saw our "official photographer" hanging around, and he promises to send me several rolls of film for my camera! That will let me take some much wanted scenes of the devastation on this post.

While at my dugout this evening, Capt. Treacy reported to me for duty, and I promptly made him communications officer for the whole seaward defense—and told him his first job is to get the phones of C1 working. After the air alarms ceased, the gang of Filipinos were back on the job of repairing the big break in our cables near Ordnance office and will work all night.

The engineers sent an inspector to view the damage at Wheeler, but nobody had started to work on the job, so we had to start our 25-kw sets there and will run them during hours of darkness. This gives light to C1 (and my dugout) and also to our tunnel—besides 1 searchlight. Luckily, the power cables from Wheeler to C1 were not damaged.

Simmonds and Edison came down to my azatea at sunset and we chinned, and had a small cocktail apiece. Then Edison left to give fort commanders our firing schedules for tonight and tomorrow morning. I also told Cottrell to assign to Group 4 the job of handling all boat traffic and mine-field control for tonight.

Adjourned to my dugout to figure up more firing data, write up this log, and read about architecture.

Even had we been moved into our tunnel, all our phones would have gone out, because the bomb hit *before* the lines branch. It is a cinch we have much to learn about vulnerability of power and water systems. Bombs have revolutionized the safety requirements of such installations. At that, the Japs have the luck of the devil in the few bombs which miss vital points: water mains, big telephone and power cables, etc. The Ordnance storehouse which held the 3″ AA ammunition which was exploding all day, was supposed to be "bombproof"!

At 9:00 P.M. another Jap plane came over and another alarm sounded. It seemed to drop a bomb, far away,—or it might have been an AA burst that I heard. The sentry came down to my dugout, but soon left for his post. At about 10 P.M. a stick of light (or far away), bombs swished down but no sign of life from our AA outfit. At 10:06 another bomb fell, but still no AA activity. Sentry again came tearing down to my dugout. This burst was closer and louder. At 10:15 two more bombs but no swish. All clear at 10:40.[10]

Wednesday, 25 Mar 1942

At 6:40 we got away our morning salute to the Japs, with no comeback. Dawn now arrives appreciably earlier, but it was still barely daylight when we fired our assorted salvos from Koehler, Marshall, Woodruff and Craighill. Could see no flashes of bursts because of intervening hills.

After breakfast, went to RSO for a few minutes and, on the way back, across the parade ground, stopped to inspect some lazy Filipinos excavating a deep bomb crater to repair cables. Another gang was working on the broken water main near Quarters 28. As I finished, the air raid alarm sounded and Welch and I beat it for my dugout. Then I walked down to our tunnel and found Rutherford at the entrance and all laterals filled with a hodge-podge of humanity.

Two bombs dropped at 9:20, which I heard from the tunnel. As things became quiet, I went up to C1. The Japs returned in spite of our AA fire and dropped more bombs at 10:47—perhaps in the direction of Btry. Geary. Edison and I checked firing data and I wrote a letter urging a baffle wall for the main entrance to our tunnel, because the tunnel now points exactly along the Jap trajectory.

Quiet now prevailing! I returned to azatea to work on firing data but at 11:15, the damn Japs came over again and dropped some more bombs. They do this with impunity because they know we have not a single plane with which to bother them.[11]

This morning, same as yesterday, the Jap guns on the Cavite side lobbed over a few shells but at long intervals and not many.

Planes kept pestering around continuously; more bombs dropped at 12:55.

Very little work being done anywhere because the planes come back frequently and the AA guns opened on them but with very little success because the planes fly above our range, dump their eggs, and go back to a nearby field for another load.

Just as we were finishing chow another air alarm sounded and our AA fired but no bombs fell. We waited around for a while and then we had Welch drive us to RSO for a shower. As we reached there, the all clear was sounded. Welch gathered up my clothes and departed for Middleside but, before he could get there, another alarm sounded and the AA started to bark. Welch took cover in Btry. Ramsey until the fusillade was over, got my clothes and started back, when another burst of fire made him take cover in a ditch. Still no bombs—just nuisance flying. (Already the 60th is claiming 5 planes today but they, unfortunately, lie like hell.) We finished our baths and, everything appearing quiet, we drove toward C1 but just as we got to B/60 it started firing, so we took cover in Wheeler, with Simmonds in the lead—so much so that he tripped and fell on his nose and barked a knee! No bombs fell and so, after hanging around awhile, I walked down to C1 where I had finally got Mr. Strong and his Filipinos out of the tunnel to take down the forms around G1.

Off and on, after this morning's first bombing, the Jap artillery poked shells at us, continuing for a couple of hours. One killed a Filipino KP and wounded another—and the damn hospital people in the tunnel said they couldn't send an ambulance because the road outside the tunnel entrance was "blocked." Fifteen of their hundreds of "termites" could have cleared it in a few minutes. No other forts were shelled.

Today's bombing seems to have been aimed at Bottomside. We rejoice that bombs fell near both entrances to Malinta Tunnel. The bakery was hit and the Marine shops. At the burning carpenter shop a few workmen were trying to firebreak the blaze, and at the same time, several members of our "Fire Dept," proudly sporting their red arm bands, were snug in the tunnel and refused—or failed—to come out and fight the fire.

Edison came to my tent at dark and we concocted our scheme of fires for tonight and tomorrow morning. Got Schenck to turn on DC power from Wheeler. Some of our main phone lines are repaired: we can get Groups 2 and 4—also H over post phone. Guess they'll work again tonight on our cables. Engineers, repairing Wheeler transformer damage, brought up and installed inadequate new transformers—and have done nothing else.

Air raid, 1 stick of bombs, about 8:45: searchlights caught Japs but out of range. Another alarm about 10:30 P.M. Bright moonlight night. Another attack at 11:00 but our searchlights made the Japs drop their bombs in the water and beat it. Today the Navy mustered up the courage to send their gunboat *Mindanao* a few miles toward Manila, after a Jap concentration of boats. They all escaped, of course. Japs at Cavite fired. I betcha the M. crew will all get silver stars! This was the first sign of life from the Navy in months.[12]

Thursday, 26 Mar 1942

Up at 6:00. Our morning shoot went off without incident. Shaved early and so was finished at RSO before Simmonds started for breakfast. Went to C1 and looked around. All the concrete forms are now removed and again we can do a modicum of observing through our slits—just like old times. McCarthy had Flippen painting the exposed concrete surfaces, but the engineers made such a mess around our station that it is going to take a lot of work before we are properly concealed and camouflaged.

The AA claim they got one plane in last night's attacks and from 3:00 to 5:00 (depending on the speaker) in yesterday's daylight attacks. Official bulletin credits them with 4 planes on the 24th but I fear this is optimistic.

I never saw a more beautiful morning than this one: the air, at my azatea in the woods, is cool and fragrant; the sunlight sifts down through the trees and dapples the ground; a light cool breeze rustles the leaves and brings strange exotic scents of dead leaves and forest mould; birds beyond number are whistling, cooing and flitting about—and there is the thumping of Colin's heel, under my cot as he scratches a flea. One is glad to be alive, to enjoy so much beauty.

At 10:00 A.M. the air raid alarm sounds and, I suppose, the damn Japs will bomb us for the rest of the day. And all we can do is to sit and take it, for they usually fly above our maximum range. At 10:24 our AA opened and then stopped, but planes buzzed nearer; at 10:27 a swish of bombs but no explosions; they fell at west end of Corregidor, mostly in the water. At 10:46, the Japs dropped more bombs, and at 11:15, they dropped more in San Jose Bay. One AA fired, both times. At 12:12 they came again. AA fire but no bombs. At 1:05 the planes came near, but no AA and no bombs. Just nuisance threats, evidently. We can't get much work done at this rate, which is probably what the Japs are figuring on. At 1:45 a plane spotted for gun fire snappily.

Air alarms and raids continued almost without interruption. At 2:45 they bombed the vicinity of Btry. Hamilton. At 3:12 another raid. At 4:30 we took cover again and finished our chow inside the battery. Then I started for a bath, but 27 bombers came over and simultaneously, the Japs started shelling us. Colin and I took cover again. One of the shells hit a concrete NCO set, back of Btry. Wheeler, and set fire to a powder dump therein. Probably 155mm powder. Furious fusillade. Capt. Schenck's men prepared to fight the fire. During this, Welch brought the car down but, rather than have him drive to G/91 for my clean clothes, I decided to take my shower at our tunnel-mouth. Went to C1 and saw the big fires there, the work of said "27 bombers." It would appear that the Japs are turning on the heat for us: renewed activity in Bataan.

Edison is going to Bataan tonight to give dope to a bunch there (about 2 offi-cers and 4 men) who contemplate going to the Cavite side and spot the batteries for us. Another Ivey stunt—hope it works. Hope to get Edison back tomorrow morning.

Went down to entrance of our tunnel and got my shower, but the water gave out just as I finished—much to Capt Hawes' discomfiture. Col. Rutherford was resting on his cot there all by himself, so I asked him to come up to my azatea, but he stayed below. Simmonds moved his bed into the tunnel this evening.

Visited our C1 along about 8:00, just in time for another air raid! Searchlights lit up a plane, but, as usual, too late. Heard either a few bombs or AA shots. Julian on duty and I made Moorhouse come on duty with him instead of Lt. Hodgkins a green reserve lieutenant.

As soon as our all clear signal went, the Jap planes returned at 9:20 and laid their eggs toward James and Cheney Ravines. A few AA shots. Got G2 message from McCullough about Jap positions—both of which we have strafed thor-oughly. Gave the mission of hitting these two points, tomorrow morning, to Btry. Craighill and Woodruff.

That 1:45 shoot was dangerous! As soon as the plane arrived, so did the shot, so quickly that I didn't have enough time to reach my dugout, only 15 feet away, as I would have had in the case of a bomb.

They say our ice plant is out!

Friday, 27 Mar 1942

Got through my morning chores (shaving, breakfast, etc.) early and went to C1. Our morning shoot from Btries. Koehler, Woodruff and Craighill went off at 6:20 and 7:20 per schedule. Our first air alarm went at 7:55. Japs bombed Mari-veles air field heavily, 7 bombers. Dropped bombs at 9:30 over near Btry. Cheney and Monja? One caved in a MG shelter of 60th killing 2 men and setting a fire which 1st Sgt. Lefew and others extinguished. According to Burns, some of these bombs burst in the air. At 9:55 the Japs dropped more bombs, probably at Bottomside, but we couldn't tell. However, we were soon notified that "Port Power Plant will be shut down for repairs for an indefinite period." This is most serious, if it means that our refrigeration and ice plant is out of commission. Many bombs of this string were in water.

At 10:15 the Japs opened fire on Monkey Point and fired a few shells. All clear sounded about 10:30. The AA claim that they got 1 Jap plane for sure, and possi-bly some two more.

The engineering gang didn't even report for work on our tunnel this morning, but when the air alarm went, all the Marines for miles around flocked into our tunnel. One Marine major even ordered about 35 of his men up there to "rest while off duty" and "of course it will be all right?" It was *not* all right.

Gen. Moore came around and chatted. Said he would take up the Marine problem with Col. Howard.

Alarms and planes flying around with impunity off and on all day. At 2:30 P.M. Alarm sounded and bombers flew in but the overcast sky gave them no hole, so they released no bombs on this trip. But they dropped plenty on the Mariveles next trip over; they landed just west of us apparently at Cheney and Monja, and terrific cloud of dust blew out to sea. Cheney phones went out and we thought Cheney was hit but, instead, it was one of their cables that was hit, and may not be repaired for 2–3 days.

More air alarms during the rest of the day but no more fell on Corregidor. Sky, being partially overcast, was favorable for bombing and unfavorable for our AA, which couldn't see the bombers, while the latter laid their eggs through holes in the clouds.

This afternoon, Ft. Frank saw some Japs on Patungan Beach and so smoked 'em out with 100 rounds of 75mm and made a fine show.[13] Rain squalls all around us and even we received a tiny spit of rain. And hence visibility was fine towards sundown.

Capt. Treacy, my communications officer to be, was AWOL for 2 days (ever since he reported). I sent out a call through HD for him, and he reported by phone from HD Bombproof at 8:00 P.M.!

Maj. Edison not having returned from his trip to Bataan, I took his tour as tonight's watch officer, Capt. Hawes being my relief. Managed to get a shower at the mouth of our tunnel and felt much better. Stayed on watch until 12:30 A.M.

Improved my time by calculating firing data—including 3 new ones for our turrets, concerning which I checked with Capt. Madison.

Our turrets fired 6 shots, along about 10:00 P.M. at various points down Looc way. Their flash lights up the whole harbor and, queerly, seems to terminate in liquid fire pouring out of the muzzle onto the deck!

And so to bed.

Wednesday, 1 April 1942

$417.50 on hand.

Nothing unusual today, except that it was unusually quiet. There were the customary air raid alarms, but fewer than usual. While Edison and I were checking data at my azatea, a plane or two came over and dropped a few bombs but they were so distant that we could not place them.

The Japs seem to be worried over something or other. Big fires are raging over in Batangas down toward Nasugbu, and other big fires have been burning toward Tagaytay Ridge. Maybe just burning off the rice paddies?

At 2:40 a plane or two came over but they were so high that our AA fired only a few shots. No hits, no runs, no errors.

(Edison and I spent most of the morning figuring out data for Koehler on a new point, where 3 guns were observed firing, by a man of Julian's at our signal station.) Will fire around 5:00 P.M.

At 2:50 those planes came back, and dropped bombs on us that shook the ground, though they were so far away we didn't hear the swish. The 2:40 trip was evidently just one of their "dry runs," so as to adjust their bomb-sights. That's the way they worked, long ago, against the Chinese, who had *no* AA defense nor planes.

Later, they say that one load of bombs fell towards Bottomside and another small batch on Morrison Hill.

The south shore road is pretty well torn up by bombs from end to end. Many have landed near upper part of James Ravine, but mine casemate is undamaged.

We still have no post power at Wheeler and Cheney, and no water, also. The engineers and HD refuse the concrete baffle wall to protect our C1 Tunnel mouth and so I am toying with the idea of moving a torn-out concrete block from Wheeler, but doubt Capt. McCarthy's ability to handle the job.

Four destroyers (Jap. of course) left Subic, headed south, this evening. Full moon tonight which, under other circumstances, would be beautiful. But what an aid to bombing!

Our mortar shoot, this evening, was a fizzle. We saw the first burst but none of the others. And, when we put in the corrections which *should* have brought the bursts into plain sight on another ridge, we never saw them, nor could we bring them into sight. The answer is that our Army surveying field parties ran their contours in by guess and the maps are criminally inaccurate. I've heard some of the culprits brag and laugh over how they fudged in their work. We are now reaping the penalties.

Our master gunner, Humphery, reported today, and started work. I made a list of registration points where I am ahead of Edison and gave him the list to check.

Took my spit bath about sundown and then loafed around C1 for a while. Everything quiet, so I returned to my dugout.

At 9:30 they sounded the air raid alarm.

Earthquake at 10:10! Immediately thereafter the plane dropped a most peculiar bomb. No loud explosion, and Pvt. Denby says it whistled in a very unusual way.

Thursday, 2 April 1942

Awoke at 4:00 A.M. so I went down to C1 and relieved Capt. Cooper for the remainder of his watch. Brewed a batch of fine Maxwell House coffee and shared it with Capt. Gerlich and the enlisted men in the station. At daybreak the same Jap ship was blockading the water south of Fortune Island. When Capt. Davis relieved me, tardily, after 7:00 A.M. I got a needed shave, then breakfast. Drove to G3 and inspected. Camouflage is a bit better. A bomb has finally hit

Cottrell's quarters in center. Then drove down to visit Batteries Geary and Crockett. Didn't see our Chaplain. Told our band leader, Mr. Wirship to get busy and work up some music or singing among the men. Drove back to C1 and checked firing data with Edison.

Air raid alarm at 9:14 and 9:36, the Japs dropped a big stick of bombs, said to be at Kindley Field. Somebody said that a bomb hit General Moore's present outdoor quarters.

Soon Gen. Moore arrived at C1 and waited for the all clear. We talked of this and that and adjourned to my dugout porch, where we discussed citation for Fort Frank, promotion of Schutte and Dawe, and incidentally, myself. He promised to speak to Wainwright, but there is some skullduggery somewhere. Evidently Moore incensed MacArthur about Marquat's BG[14] and Mac is taking it out.

At 11:15 the Japs, dropped more bombs—perhaps at Bottomside this time—a long drawnout string of them. It is said they are dropping 155mm shells which have been converted into bombs.

Planes audible more or less continuously.

The engineers are trucking water to our tunnel today, so our concrete work should move along with reasonable speed. Our water situation is getting critical, not for lack of water, but for lack of fuel to pump the water!

We have been at war almost 4 months now and, so far as we can see, no slightest effort has been made to help us. From the first, knowing the Naval War College solution to the Philippine problem, I have secretly felt that we are slated to play the part of another Alamo. However, if anybody can help us it is MacArthur. He is our only chance. It is disturbing, however, to read that our president has appointed a *Board* of all nations to control the "strategy of the war in the pacific"—why hamper MacArthur? He says he once told Roosevelt, "If you once lose the Philippines, you'll never get them back." Now let's see what he will do! This blockage is throttling us.[15]

This afternoon we received dope (a) that but few Japs in Ternate and none in Maragondon (b) that Japs have moved out their artillery and taken it to Antimonan and Lingayen (c) that we destroyed the Ternate Bridge some time ago and it has never been repaired (d) that some Japs were running an observation post on Pico de Loro. So we fired 14 shots from Btry. Koehler at the Peak and strafed it in fine style.

So the Japs are moving artillery to Antimonan, eh? The other night Edison and I agreed that Antimonan is the logical landing place for any relief expedition for us. I wonder if, at long last, some such reinforcements are due soon? Some Navy officer is said to be offering odds of 5 to 1 that relief will appear before 5 April. I'd like to get about $500 to $2500 of that easy money.

Wrote letters (a) commending Ft. Frank (b) citing Pvts. Novardes and Stephenson and Lt. Holton (c) recommending Edison for lieutenant colonel.

Turrets fired 1 shot each at Looc and Caluya about 7:30. Just one P-40 took the air at about 4:00 P.M. and (at 10:00 P.M.). There hasn't been a Jap plane around since then!

Took a jaunt to C1 at 10:30 and then turned in.

Easter Sunday, 5 April 1942

Usual morning routine. Fried mush and salty bacon for breakfast. A couple of Jap destroyers playing around beyond Limbones. No sign last night of the Navy's vaunted convoy coming in. Two P-35 planes were expected but we didn't know if they actually came in. A seaplane of the Japs came down, beyond Hornos Pt. and was fired at, from shore. Probably sunk. Another seaplane fluttered around, possibly attempting to rescue the pilot. We don't know if he succeeded.

Last night there was excitement: a Jap cruiser showed up, seaward, blinking toward Bataan. Edison alerted Smith and Hearn, but Cruiser kept out of range. Simultaneously there was an air raid and another attempt at landing up beyond Limay, on east coast of Bataan. Corps asked us to stand by, but things calmed down, the cruiser went south, and nothing happened. Edison handled it all very well.

Shortly before noon the Japs dropped a few bombs over on Mariveles shore, perhaps up Cabcaben way.

I worked at azatea, doping out the ammunition situation at Btry. Koehler.

No bombs nor shelling of Corregidor or any of the fortified islands today but the Japs bombed in Bataan, off and on, all day. Evidently another Jap attack is being made, up there. Jap ships were offshore to the South all day—may be laying mines or just patrolling. At least one of them was a destroyer, says Simmonds, but all kept well out of range from us.

Our Air Force in Australia seems more concerned with attacking the Japs in India, for the benefit of the Sprinting Englishmen, than in paving the way to helping us. MacArthur's radio to the CIO in the USA indicates to me that he is again hearing the presidential bee buzzing about his head. If so, and he succumbs (in addition) to the blandishments of British propaganda, then there is but very little that we can hope for here in the Islands. We'll all be "sold down the river."

> Cut off from the land that bore us,
> Betrayed by the land we find,
> The brightest have gone before us,
> The Dullest are left Behind.
> Cho: So stand to your glasses steady
> They're all you have left to prize.
> Here's a cup to the dead already;
> Hurrah for the next man who dies.[16]

Sentimental but holding a grain of truth, at that.

The worst of it is that we are being "betrayed" by "the land that bore us"!

Went to C1 in evening but all was in order and Simmonds was on watch, so I left. Things probably won't start popping until after midnight.

Monday, 6 April 1942

P1.50 Shoe repair.

This morning I went over to see how Major Crawford is coming along with splinter-proofing Btry. Grubbs and found the place crawling with 60th men, machine gunners, radio men, 3d Bn. HQ men and some of our personnel section. They had the rotary converter running, a lavendero was using an electric iron and they were importing an electric refrigerator! A happy country home for the 60th chisellers who evidently had not heard that a war is on. Their standby radio set was working full blast. Ascertained from Col. Kohn that they didn't need the power for M1 and so I had Edison phone an order to shut down the rotary converter.

Got caught by air raid, first, at Hearn, but didn't wait for it to clear. The bombs were dropped at Mariveles. In fact, all of today's bombs were dropped over there.

During the forenoon the Japs started shelling us again, after letting us alone for a few days. They started with one gun, bombarding Hughes and we looked long and hard for flashes of enemy guns. Finally we opened with Btry. Hearn at a point well inland, and her first shot fell about 10,000 yards short, in the water! Raised her to maximum range and 0.40 left but couldn't see the next burst. Then down 1000 and saw burst left and short. Up 800 and 0.30 rt and lost it, though it might have been wild, in "Slots." Ceased firing in disgust and sent Simmonds to battery to find the trouble but he reported that everything was OK!

In P.M. Edison brought spots of flashes from Julian, so we fired a few shots from Craighill. The first spot was "short 1000 yards," which is impossible for a mortar. Total correction, up 1300 yards and the corrections were applied with exasperating slowness. Put in a parting salvo of 2 shots and called it a day. Schenck and Julian swear that their work was accurate and that the fault was with the mortar!

The USFIP [U.S. Forces in the Philippines] daily bulletin tonight was more nauseating than usual: MacArthur asking blessing of the minister who baptized him, and Wainwright broadcasting a sycophantic speech to the USA lauding Roosevelt and telling how "heroic" the poltroon Philippine army is and how brotherly the Filipinos are! Faugh!

Planes around again at 6:00 P.M. but no bombing here.

Spent some time in our tunnel, early this morning, supervising the activities there. It is a mess, the way the "termites" have flocked in. Gen. Moore came down for a few minutes. Gave orders to start celotex linings: kitchen water supply, electricity, etc.—also installation of baffle walls to stop shell fragments.

About sunset I went to our tunnel again to look over the situation and found Rutherford had placed the first "channel-iron" baffle too far in, on the left and had omitted the second one. One panel of celotex done on ceiling of C1. Hawes supervised scratching out a trough for base plates of the first baffle wall. Sgt. Harper, when Hawes told him to get some cement hidden, replied, "I'm on duty tonight" in a sullen tone, and I proceeded to stand him up and pin his ears back in "Old Army" style.

Edison, Simmonds, Rutherford and I chinned for a while, all of us stripped to the waist. Then I climbed the stairs to C1, conferred with Capt. Schenck on the evening's program, and repaired to my dugout.

Called Healey of the Navy censor office about the snapshot which I sent in my last letter to Landon (of the ruins of the officers' club) and he assured me that the letter went out on the sub and that the photo slipped through, though against Navy censorship regulations.

Craighill sent over 2 more shells tonight at this afternoon's registration point.

Worked till 11:00 P.M. and then read "Death Valley." Not so much artillery activity as usual on east coast of Bataan tonight.

Elmes shipped to Brooke the oats that he wanted. I hope he gets them.

Tuesday, 7 April 1942

Overslept this morning and did not wake until 8:00. After breakfast I went to RSO. (Somebody stole 6 bbl of gas from him!) They say that a *real* "dive bomber" attacked Ft. Frank this morning, dropped 2 bombs and both hit the fort, but probably did no damage. To my dugout for a sadly needed shave.

Air raid alarm at 10:00 A.M., another at 11:50.

Schutte finally got his captaincy and was at C1 this morning, wearing his new captain's bars. Am making him Assistant P [plans] and T [training] for Seaward Defense and assistant to Edison. Braly dropped around to talk about fields of fire of Btry. Sunset and other GPF* batteries.

Japs flew around freely all day, occasionally dropping a load on the North shore from Cabcaben and, presumably on our front lines.

At 2:15 the Japs opened fire on Fort Drum and, firing about 50 shots, hit it about 30 times. I was alarmed to see a fire start emitting smoke, flame and explosions. I first thought that the fire was in the sally port but it developed later that the Japs set fire to a bunch of 75mm ammunition and that is what caused the blaze, no casualties.

---

*Batteries that fired according to prearranged map coordinates (ground position fire).

At about 3:00 P.M. we let go 4 shots from Koehler at 4 different points and the Jap firing ceased—maybe because they had finished anyway.

At 3:30 two Jap bombers dropped eggs at Ft. Frank which fired furiously at them. The bombs missed. So did Fort Frank.

In the 11:50 air raid this morning, they say the AA turned back the bombers, and the 60th claim to have got one of them, but nobody saw it shot down.

They say that the Japs had 9 bombers plus 12 fighters escorting them in today's forays over our Bataan lines.

It would seem that things are going not too well in the center of our Bataan line. The last two days of our official bulletin admit that the enemy has gained some ground. I hope it doesn't mean *some* ground! We received orders today to give up 53 beds and mattresses for the Bataan hospital. I hope that doesn't mean excessive men injured in battle. It may be due to the increased malaria rate over there. This means 53 of our men will sleep on the ground, as we have not enough now to go around, since we have already been mulcted to care for the outsiders who flocked in here from Manila.

Tonight I learned that a sub will arrive and depart, so I dashed off a hurried note to Landon and had Welch take it down to Capt. Hoeffel at the Navy Tunnel. She is due in here at 9:30 and now, at 9:05, the air alarm has just sounded! Probably the Japs know she is coming in—their spy service is wonderful. But I hope nothing happens to her. Maybe she is bringing quinine, of which we have a shortage.

Engineers have finally finished pouring the floor of our tunnel and we sure are glad to get rid of them. My first channel-iron baffle is OK but, even with 3 officers watching in the tunnel, they made a botch of putting in the 2d baffle! Rutherford is sure useless! And so is McCarthy! He *still* hasn't got the muffler installed on our generating set!

The engineers finally got the post power through to Btries. Wheeler and Cheney today but I'm sure the first Jap bomb will put it out of commission again. But it is a comfort to have it on!

Went to C1 at 9:30 and looked for our sub, without success. Big fire, on one of Lubang Islands. Air raid, all clear had sounded about 9:40.

Wednesday, 8 April 1942

Up at 7:00, shaved, breakfast RSO. Air raid when I got to the tunnel at 10:00 A.M. Another Raid at 11:30 but no bombs. Japs opened on Frank at 1:25. We opened with Woodruff on points 78 and 79. Jap air raid simultaneously and bombs dropped at Mariveles. Woodruff fired 6 shots each on points 78 and 79 and Japs ceased firing on Frank.

They bombed Mariveles again at 3:15.

It appears that our Philippine army Bataan forces have crumpled and run, letting the Japs penetrate our center and roll up our right. At about 6:00 P.M. Stubbs gave us request of corps to put down fire from Hearn on east coast of Bataan from Paudau River down to Limay on 4 points, 2 shots per hour on each. We delivered 1st shot in 15 minutes and kept it up until ordered to stop. They first stopped us on Limay and we began to hope for better things. Our fire kept up most of the night: about 34 shots each from Smith and Hearn.

Our sub came in and departed successfully.[17]

Later: 18 of our Pursuit planes were supposed to arrive tonight but luckily they failed to come, because tonight the Japs over-ran our Bataan air field!

The Japs are dropping leaflets in Bataan: "Your U.S. Convoy is due in the Philippines on April 15th but you won't be alive to see it Ha! Ha!"

Transition

15 March—9 April

From 15 to 22 March the newly arrived Japanese artillery in Cavite shelled the fortified islands almost incessantly. With the exception of the disaster at Ft. Frank on 21 March, there were very few casualties on the islands.[18] Fort Hughes was never attacked by air, and it was only lightly shelled later. No one had been killed at Ft. Drum. However, one of the turrets had been cracked. Eight feet of Drum's concrete casemate had literally been whittled away, and the two 3-inch antiaircraft guns on the deck had been destroyed.[19]

The lull on Bataan, which had lasted from the middle of February, suddenly came to a close on 3 April, when Homma's newly reinforced troops, supported by a massive aerial and artillery barrage, attacked through the II Corps sector on the eastern side of Bataan. The Japanese overcame the debilitated U.S. forces, and by 4 April, the U.S. retreated. By 8 April, when Bunker was firing his road interdiction mission on Limay, organized resistance against the Japanese had almost halted.[20]

Unknown to Bunker, on the night of 6 April, a large group of people left the bowels of Malinta Tunnel for a breath of fresh night air. The Belotes in their book describe vividly what next occurred. "The Japanese lobbed two 240mm rounds . . . at the portal of Malinta Tunnel. . . . Without so much as a warning whistle the two great projectiles struck, one a dud, the other bursting squarely among the men, killing fourteen and wounding seventy."[21] The doctors worked feverishly all night long performing unbelievable tasks.

However, not all the personnel on Corregidor were heroic. Bunker describes the tunnel rats who never left the safety of Malinta Tunnel. As Baldwin states, "'tunnelitis' became an occupational disease."[22] Despite this underground attitude, there was a sense of duty in those above ground. During the first week in April, water was stockpiled in powder cans all over the island, and the beaches were fortified with splinterproof defenses.[23] Corregidor was girding herself for an all-out attack.

The air attacks against Corregidor increased steadily during this period. At 9:24 in the morning on 24 March, Corregidor heard her seventy-seventh air raid alarm. For two more days the Japanese bombs rained from the heavens. On the twenty-seventh, Capt. Arthur Huff, commander of B Battery, 20th Coast Artillery, had his crews tracking seven heavy bombers. They were at 27,000 feet; from there the bombs took more than forty seconds to fall. Because of the short range of the antiaircraft guns, the crews had to wait until the bombers were overhead unloading their bombs before they could open fire. The crews often got off eighteen rounds or so before the first bomb would impact. According to Braly in his book, "It took plenty of iron nerve to stand there turning a handwheel or wait, projectile in hand, for the order to load, with the bombs falling faster every second."[24]

The troops of the antiaircraft batteries were typical of the day-to-day heroes found on Corregidor. But it was somewhat easier for those who were eating well than for those starving on Bataan. This disparity in diet between Bataan and Corregidor came into the open during the first week in April, when a Bataan military police detail halted a supply truck destined for three antiaircraft batteries stationed on Bataan but supplied from Corregidor. The MPs were shocked to find that these batteries were eating the Corregidor allowance of one-half ration per day per man, while the men on Bataan were down to practically nothing. The news of this incident spread rapidly to the front line troops, causing Colonel Carpenter to write to General Beebe that the "Bataan troops . . . are discriminated against." He added that the "clandestine manner of getting . . . luxury items to Harbor Defense troops on Bataan . . . does not seem ethical."[25]

Certainly there was a disparity between the Bataan and the Corregidor ration; however, according to Morton, "The equal distribution of food between the 100,000 men on Bataan and the 10,000 on Corregidor could not have saved Bataan and might have led to the weakening of the harbor defenses."[26]

Because of the deterioration of the situation and of his troops, General King sent his chief of staff to Wainwright on 7 April, telling him that he (King) might have to surrender.[27] Wainwright, remembering MacArthur's final message ("There must be no thought of surrender. You must attack")[28] told King to attack.

On the eighth, I Corps attacked, but men were dropping like flies from exhaustion while moving forward. On the ninth, General King shoved the

last of his reserves into the battle, including dismounted cavalry, engineers, and antiaircraft gunners fighting as infantry.[29] The Japanese broke
through, however, and began occupying the southeastern portion of
Bataan, where they quickly emplaced their artillery.

A few hours later, Corregidor was shelled for the first time from
Japanese gun positions on Bataan, and the island was inundated with
Bataan's fleeing survivors.

Notes

1. Braly, 38. There were several burn and fume inhalation casualties in the casemate.

2. Case, 39. These were the 240mm howitzers firing from Cavite. The craters in Drum made by these shells are still visible today. They measure 18–24 inches in diameter and are 2–4 inches deep.

3. Dyess, 46, 48, 60. Actually there were seven flyable aircraft on Bataan at this time. There were two P-40s, two P-35s, an old army 0-1 biplane, a dilapidated Beechcraft, and an ancient navy amphibian, which had been repaired after it had been sunk.

4. Parker, 17. This submarine was the *Permit,* which had probably been scheduled for the MacArthur pickup. She left for Australia with approximately forty naval officers.

5. Morton, *Philippines,* 193. This was probably Maj. Ralph E. Rumbold, who was in much of the very confused action along Route 23 south of Manila toward Atimonan.

6. Ibid., map 18. 57th Infantry (PS) was the USAFFE reserve located at the southernmost tip of Bataan.

7. Case, 39. These men had been lined up in Crofton Tunnel at Ft. Frank in order to get smallpox shots. A shell had gone through the 3-foot-thick earth cover, and thirty-four were killed.

8. Wainwright, 67. Brig. Gen. Lewis Beebe reported only to MacArthur, and yet he had control over all Bataan supply matters; thus the authority Wainwright had was somewhat undermined since MacArthur was now in Australia.

9. Appears to be a page missing here, since "men" starts this first line off without a sentence before it on the preceding page. However, the pages were numbered consecutively by Bunker, and there are no missing page numbers.

10. Braly, 38. The Japanese press called the 24 March raids against Corregidor "the largest air raid carried on so far in the Philippines."

11. Dyess, 46. The air force had the two P-40s and five other assorted aircraft until the surrender of Bataan.

12. Belote and Belote, 112. Within three weeks, this same crew, after the boat was disabled, manned the mortars of Battery Craighill on Ft. Hughes.

13. Braly, 39. In the morning the observers at Ft. Frank noticed some forty-five bancas (small native boats) assembled near Patungan. Boudreau's afternoon firing destroyed all of them.

14. Morton, *Philippines,* 10, 359. Brig. Gen. William F. Marquat was MacArthur's antiaircraft officer. He was taken out by PT boat along with MacArthur and the remainder of his staff on 11 March.

15. Morton, *Command Decisions* (New York: Harcourt Brace and Company, 1959), 33. In both the Orange Plan and Rainbow 5 (two U.S. plans for the defense of the Philippines), the United States "had virtually written the Philippines off as indefensible in a war with Japan." The plans called for a six-month delay by the army in the Philippines until the navy could rescue them. But, because of the U.S. Navy's defeat at Pearl Harbor and its resultant inferiority to the Japanese navy, the plan was hopeless, and as a result, Corregidor did become another Alamo.

16. Poem writen by Bartholomew Dowling, "The Revel," commemorating those who died in a cholera epidemic in India.

17. Parker, 19. This was one of the many submarines carrying food from Cebu to Corregidor that were running the Japanese naval blockade. This one, the *Seadragon,* departed for Australia with twenty-seven naval officers and men.

18. Belote and Belote, 94.

19. Case, 39.

20. Belote and Belote, 104.

21. Baldwin, 135.

22. Karig and Kelley, 323.

23. Baldwin, 135–137.

24. Braly, 37.

25. Ibid., 39.

26. Morton, *Philippines,* 375–76.

27. Ibid., 376.

28. Wainwright, 79.

29. Ibid., 80.

Thursday, 9 April 1942

Japs fire from Bataan!

Up at 7:00 and to C1. Two Philippine army Q-boats and 2 motorboats which had been ordered to go from Mariveles to Mills north wharf, turned deserters and, threading the minefields, escaped to sea. We fired a few shots across their bows in a vain effort to stop them.

A Jap captive balloon up, near Cabcaben.[1] We are evacuating soldiers from Bataan to Corregidor! Evidently the staff is giving up Bataan. Commencing about 9:30 the Japs flew around incessantly and with impunity, bombing where they listed.

Air raid at 9:30, with bombs probably at Mariveles. We have received orders not to fire on Bataan shore until further orders! At 10:00 A.M. we were all excited by what seemed to be heavy cannonading at sea toward Fortune Island but were deflated to learn that it was caused by a Jap destroyer firing at our deserting Q-boat, which came back into our harbor. I hope they shot the skipper. The other Q-boat, evidently discouraged, also put back into harbor! Skunks!

At 10:15 a load of bombs hit in water near Searchlight No. 7. At 10:25 another load lit on south shore road near Searchlight No. 5. At 1:00 P.M. the enemy bombed Mariveles and at 3:00 P.M. dropped another load up toward the golf course. At 3:50 peculiar sounding bombs lit (perhaps) toward Bottomside and a second load in front of C1, some of them in the water. We are doing very little AA firing because the bombers are so high. As the enemy started shelling us from the Cavite side, we set Woodruff to work to search back of point 4, at base of hat-shaped hill, but had hard work to get there because the enemy shifted fire from us to Woodruff and forced us to take cover by the accuracy of their fire.

At 4 P.M. the Japs started shelling us from Bataan—a crucial point in our operations—a milestone.[2] Fire was accurately aimed at Topside, between HQ Btry. Mess and Parade ground. We set to work to spot flashes and got tentative spotting around Cabcaben, but are still prohibited from firing over there.[3]

At 4:40 bombs fell near C1, in front also to east. At 5:00 P.M., 5:55 and 6:25 still more bombs landed on us. One of them severed a 100-pr phone cable, thus messing up our communications. Another, if the Japs only knew it, landed among our mine cables and put practically the whole mine field out![4]

The 5 P.M. bombs landed just *before* Simmonds and I got to Btry. Wheeler for our dinner!

This P.M. the "Tai Ping"—loaded with bombs, exploded in Mariveles Harbor. A burning oil barge, over there, cast a bright light. Numerous small boats have been arriving all day—and try to land here:[5] some with fleeing members of the 31st or other soldiers, some with civilians. One engineering civilian, with 4 Filipinos is dashing out tonight in his auxiliary sailboat.

Shooting died down, towards sundown, and then, from many miles at sea, a Jap ship turned her searchlight on us!

We had Craighill fire 2 shots into a valley which we suspected as holding the guns that fired on Frank the other day. This went after dark.

Edison today got his promotion to lieutenant colonel—as I recommended—and, no silver leaves being available, wrapped some tin-foil around his gold ones!

We all gathered in C1 for a while and then turned in, to get some rest against tomorrow.

Our artillery in Bataan, though furiously active last night, has been quiet all day.

Our Capt. Thompson arrived on this morning's boat, and reports our forces in Bataan as routed and the defense (except on west coast) collapsed!

Friday, 10 April 1942

Up at 6:00 and shaved in semidarkness. Then to early breakfast. Told Rutherford I want him to turn in at hospital. He is a broken old man and cannot seem to recover.

Then to C1 and could plainly see the shameful things at Mariveles: truck after truck of men pouring into town and concentrating there. Our observers swore each truck had a white flag flying! Jap flags also visible. Looked later in the day, like many men marching into town from up the west coast way.[6]

Higher HQ finally said we could fire upon Bataan, but only against definitely located battery positions and, even then, no searching would be done.

Enemy fired no guns from Bataan side except a few early. From Cavite they started cannonading early, trying to hit our boats which had moved from north to south Harbors. Opened a few rounds with Craighill and they shifted their fire to Ft. Hughes and peppered it for hours. We could get no indication of where the shots were coming from, so we shot 7 shots from Koehler at random, but had no effect. At about this time Julian reported a definite location for two 2-gun batteries—and they are over 31,000 yards. from us—so far away as to be well beyond the maximum range of any of our armament! And we, "the richest nation in the world" let our 14″ guns be outranged and silenced by enemy 6″ portable guns!

Air attacks were practically continuous throughout the day. Our first alarm went at 8:30 but it was not until 9:30 that the bombs fell in front of C1, with no detonations. At 9:50 bombs fell in water southwest of Ft. Drum. Then 2 loads of leaflets were dropped—faultily because they all fluttered, out to sea over North Channel. More bombs fell, over towards Btry. Sunset. Bombs fell nearby at 9:55—a few more fell at 10:40; and at 10:53 still more. We are firing very little with our AA guns—probably because bombers are too high.

Japs laid off for siesta but were back at 2:10 with more bombs. At 3:17 they dropped a heavy load near Btry. Monja. Then, at 3:45 they started work on Ft. Hughes and plastered all the high ground. At 3:57 they repeated, taking in the low ground and starting a fire at wharf. Just as I went below for chow they hit Hughes heavily again.

Chow in our tunnel for first time, with HQ Btry. Mess. It was a swell meal of chili beans, cold ham and cold salami in vinegar. Looked over the progress made in our tunnel and it is coming along. Dined on Chet Elme's nice dining table.

Came up to my azatea, but they promptly pulled another air raid and dropped more bombs on us.

Welch is to bring Chong back with him this evening, so he can be handy; then Welch won't have to go to Middleside daily. He is also to take Rutherford to the hospital.

Lt. Gibbon got back from Bataan last night—and lucky to make his escape. He tells scandalous tales of cowardice over there, especially among the so-called Philippine army. The Scouts, contemptuous of the PA, tried to make up for their cowardice and were cut to pieces.

They say Gen. King (who fell heir to that whited sepulchre of Wainwright's) is now up north arranging terms of surrender![7]

Hung around C1 for a while and then turned in early—but could not sleep. Dugout air is close. At about 2 A.M., Lt. Moore phoned a message from Cruze— that the Japs had prepared 6 boats with machine guns and 75mm and would attempt a landing on Corregidor tomorrow.

A Lt. Strong, 31st Inf., is hanging around and wants to attach himself to us. I told him to get to hell away from us and report to Harbor Defense HQ.

Lt. Ellis also phoned me—how he got here from Bataan I don't know.

Saturday, 11 April 1942
Cigarettes P1.00.
Won P3.00.
Day dawned clear. Shaved before breakfast and went down into C1 Tunnel. Was astonished, even at the entrance, by the poor air coming out—worse below. Caused partly by use of curtains, during the night, to hide lights. Waited around entrance quite a while before breakfast was ready: cracked wheat, rice and gravy, coffee and some marvelous ice water! Walked up to C1—all quiet. One of our mine yawls went over to Monja to rescue the party that landed there yesterday. Glad we did not shoot them up. I hope it is our Pucot Hill detail.

Mariveles, this morning, is still crowded with men and trucks. Evidently the enemy is evacuating prisoners. The place is crowded.

The first bombs of the day were not dropped until 10:07, much to our surprise, and we heard no bursts. Meanwhile the Japs started cannonading our south wharf area, so we picked three registration points out of a hat, and one of them agreed with some observations of Julian's so we fired three shots from Koehler there and four at other places. The Jap fire stopped, but whether or not because of us, we don't know.[8]

More bombs for us at 11:15, also at 12:15 while I was in our tunnel inhaling some soup. Then at 12:35 they came over again and this time the post power to Btry. Wheeler evidently went out, for the light in my dugout slowly faded, came back a few minutes and then snapped out. More and closer bombs fell at 12:48.

Our C1 Tunnel is a welter of many bunks and belongings. At main entrance it is the same. Not enough space.

The 12:35 bombs evidently landed in our Post Power plant, raising hell with the diesel engine that was running, and cutting a fuel line, but not hurting the other one which was sandbagged. However, post power is out for a while—and now we are not permitted to wash our face and hands, as there is no power to push water to Topside.

As yesterday, the enemy took siesta from noon to 2:00 P.M. at which time he dropped 2 loads. At 2:18 another load dropped in front of Cheney. Still more at 5:15 and at odd intervals over the afternoon. A pair of planes came in lower than usual and many of our machine guns opened on them.

Late in afternoon a destroyer peeped out momentarily beyond Hornos Point, and we were unable to reach it. Soon 8 landing barges came around Hornos Point, making for Mariveles and we finally got Group 4 to firing at them. 6 of them beat it back, but I fear we didn't hit any of them. Sunset fired 32 rounds! Slow getting started!

Very hot in station this afternoon, so I finally gave up and went to my dugout. Edison and Simmonds came down and we had a coupla snorts out of Foster's bottle of Bourbon. A treat.

Thunder over Cavite and heat lightning over Mariveles. Wish the wet season were on.

Our baffle plates for entrances of our tunnel are coming along and we started moving desks, etc. into the C1 and G1 laterals today. The phone hookup is still not wholly crystallized.

Played poker tonight in our tunnel and won P3.00.

Returned, with Colin, to my dugout and turned in at 11:00 P.M.

Pvt. Welch brought Chong, my houseboy, up from G/91 to me, and I had Welch install him in our tunnel as mess attendant.

Sunday, 12 April 1942

A rough day all day. The Japs started at 6:00 A.M., shelling us from the Bataan side with numerous guns, probably mostly 105mm but with some 150mm mixed in. Maj. Julian and Capt. Schenck were right on the job with their flash ranging and we cut loose with Btry. Geary at a Jap concentration near Lokanin Pt. After destroying an enemy battery here, we shifted to another battery, got it and its adjacent ammunition dump and then landed a few in a bunch of tanks and set them afire. Observers said the fire was perfect and the Japs were hurriedly leaving the place.

More Japanese guns opened up and we started counter-battery with our 155mm, 6″ disappearing and all other small and medium caliber guns which would bear on the Bataan shore. Because of our inexperienced personnel it took so long to get corrections applied to the guns that the enemy had time to bring lots of fire to bear upon our guns. Our guns and emplacements are very vulnerable. Two men were killed at Btry. Kysor (an officer—Arnold? had to have his leg amputated this afternoon) and at Fort Hughes. Many of our guns suffered direct hits and other damage. The only gun of Btry. Sunset which bears on Bataan will be out of action for days.

This artillery duel kept up all day and we worked furiously to combat the accurate fire of the Japs. In the afternoon, they started shooting at us from Cavite side also, aiming at Ft. Hughes, at Kindley Field, and at our shipping.

In the morning we tried to register Btry. Craighill on the pier and boats at Mariveles, but had to give it up as a bad job, the shooting was so erratic. General Moore was in C1 at the time and was not particularly impressed with the shooting.

There were air raids and bombings throughout the day, and all on Corregidor. I don't know where they all landed but the Japs seemed to try mostly for James Ravine and the post power plant—which has been already hard hit. Some say that the plant has lost all its ammonia. There is no post power now at most of our batteries and we have to run our emergency 25-kw sets—and the staff won't give us enough gas for that! In our C1-G1 set up, we use my little 6-kw Air corps alternator.

Edison never did get his breakfast this morning, but Chong brought us all up some fine tomato soup about 1:00 P.M.

It seems official that a B-17 plane of ours flew in here this morning and then left. One aviator swore he saw two! Col. Foster averred that Cavite Navy Yard and Nichols Field were bombed this morning![9] It did seem that the Jap bombing of Corregidor was a bit less intense than yesterday, but not much. I fear for the post power plant.

Today I renewed my former recommendation: that they take some of their war reserve of aviation gasoline and use it for diluting our present low-octane gas, thus about doubling the amount on hand—instead of (as they are doing) holding back the airplane gas as sacred and then finding out, when our "Issue" gas is gone, that they can't use the sacred gas in our engines without burning them up!

Was the last man of our mess to get dinner. Tough carabao, but it tasted good. Soon I expect we'll be on preserved meats, if any. Lay down on my cot for a while. The "bodegas" are going very slowly and I now doubt that we'll ever use them. We have no drilling or blasting facilities.

I feel awfully crummy, being unable to shave. Lack of water. And how I'd enjoy a shower-bath! There being no quorum for a poker game, I returned to my dugout and read myself to sleep.

It is not going to be so good when the Japs start using against us those ten 240mm guns which, we are told, are coming down from the north.

This evening gave Welch the job of going to Crockett and retrieving my chifforobe and leather desk chair.

Monday, 13 April 1942

Won P4.00.

Up at 7:00 and smoked on my azatea, pondering and enjoying the peaceful quiet of daybreak, the fine coolness among the trees, the fresh morning smell of morning, the birds piping—and then the harsh rattle of corrugated iron, down on the south shore road, as of somebody shielding his dugout.

This was another day of artillery activity. The Japs plastered us with shells from morning to night. Schenck and Julian had our flash ranging system working almost continuously and helped immensely with our spotting of hostile batteries—of which there were many—and giving us corrections.

Battery Geary—my old 12″ mortar battery—under Captain Davis, bore the brunt of the fight, although we also fired Koehler on two new points on the Cavite side, where enemy guns were shooting up our boats in the harbor. Silenced those guns for a while, but later others started up.

The Bataan batteries, and bombs, cut out our *Don José* OP and at B25 (which received a direct hit and Lt. Bliss got a head wound) also our new Geary Station at old G4 and the nearby Hearn primary, ruining its fine new depression finder.

All lines to Harbor Defense HQ went out but they patched up two lines fairly soon.

We are still prohibited from firing road interdictions! Haven't the brass hats learned *anything?* They pulled the same boner, months ago, when we wanted to interdict the Cavite roads and thus delay the Japs. But no, they wouldn't hear of it, so, the Japs poured in and used the roads with impunity—and the termites later squawked when the Jap artillery opened up!

Nobody had sandbagged the power plant at Btry. Morrison! So a bomb fragment today put a radiator out. I hope the power plant and the rotary converter were uninjured.

After I went down to chow the Japs cannonaded us with about 50 more shots.

Only a few bombings today. We guess all the Jap bombers are being used against our forces in Cebu, for a big flight of them went south over us today without dropping any eggs on us.

Corralled my fine big desk chair today and installed it at my desk in C1. Played poker tonight and won P4.00.

Tuesday, 14 April 1942
Hot fight all day!

Another strenuous day, though not so bad, in general, as yesterday.

Later: The hell it wasn't strenuous!

3d air raid at 9:50, the first 2 having no bombs. Braly dropped in, making the rounds. Bombs again at 10:30 evidently hitting a small dump of our ammunition. This was the 5th raid and featured a very queer whiffling sound, as if a plane were hurtling down—but it wasn't. At 10:50 we had 2 more bombings, which seemed to be back of us, near B/60. At 11:40 bombs lit between Hearn and Smith. At 3:00 P.M. we had a duel between Btry. Monja and a Jap gun which had come into action west of Sisiman. We won, though the Jap had been registering on Monja Island for hours. Japs seem to think we have something important at Monja Island.

At 4:00 P.M. lots of bombs, and possibly 2 shells, fell close by C1 Station on both sides of us. At 5:20 more bombs fell. Slight lull at 1:00 P.M. and around 6:00.

This evening they started something new against us,—as soon as we lit our No. 2 Searchlight the Japs instantly shot hell out of it. No. 8 was used for safety of back area and also brought forth much Jap fire on it and on wharf area, which brought forth remonstrances from HD HQ. So, as an experiment, we put No. 1 in action for 15 seconds only—then the man snapped our light out and ran. Yet he hadn't turned the corner, 20 yards away, before the Jap's shells landed at the light, one of them ruining the light! Which proved that the Japs had their guns loaded, laid, and men at the lanyards, with orders to shoot instantly when the light showed.

Whenever we showed a light, all through the evening, the Japs cannonaded furiously.

Today we started a new roster of duty, removing Maj. Julian and Capt. Schenck from the roster, and dividing the night between Simmonds, Edison and me. I was supposed to stay on only from 6–11 but we were so busy in counter-battery against the Jap shooters that I didn't leave the station until 12:30. Turned in, in my dugout.

Monday, 20 April 1942*
Up early and about. Quiet night. With Edison sat outside the portal smoking in

*From 15–19 April 1942, Bunker made no entries.

the cool of the morning. Zimmerman gave me an advance cup of alleged coffee.

Heard that Gens. Wainwright and Moore were on their way to see us, so I had to get into uniform to meet them, my habitual costume being shorts but naked above the waist—an effort to stop my bad prickly heat, went up to C1 and met the generals and led them below to see our tunnel. Wainwright says we have food for 4 mos. and fuel for 2 mos.—swell news!

After breakfast I went to my old dugout and shaved. Air raid on but all clear went soon, with no action.

Found some ginger ale in my dugout and gave it to McCarthy for a celebration by officers tonight. Am still keeping my shaving stuff, etc. at my old dugout. Last night they fixed the approach floor to the officers' azatea ("lanai").

Last night Julian managed to fill the tank (250 gal.) for our shower and, as soon as we fix a catch basin for waste, we'll let everybody have a shower and use the waste for washing clothes, etc.

Japs had not peeped by 10:00 A.M. Air Raid alarm 10:15. At 10:25 two bombers dropped loads in water near Ft. Hughes, amid AA fire—all clear about 10:50 and another alarm at 11:00.

Six "heavy" bombers attacked Ft. Drum at 12:26 and three at 12:45 and dropped bombs, but all were misses. They must have been large, for I distinctly felt them in our tunnel.

Not a shot was fired by the Japs until we started proof-firing Btry. Grubbs at 6:30; then the Japs opened, but not heavily.

Meanwhile, after dinner, we adjourned to the lanai and, by thoroughly overhauling our piping system, got the shower-bath to working.

This evening a flash came in, saying that Tokyo this morning was under a 4-hour bombardment—maybe some other cities too—and that great damage was done in commercial districts. It cheers us up to think that maybe Nippon is at last getting a touch of her own medicine. Hope it is all true.[10]

This evening at about 10:00 the Japs suddenly sent out from Hornos Point one "Invasion Barge" towing two others. They headed toward us, passed through the rocks at Cochinos Pt. followed the Mariveles boom barrier and, unscathed, entered through our north channel and proceeded towards Manila! Scandalous! I dashed up to C1-OP and tried like hell to get Kohn's Group 4 to do something about it but they seemed unable to do so. Finally Btry. Monja got off a few shots very slowly but the shooting was very poor. Btry. Sunset also fired about 3 but they also were wild. The barges finally disappeared around the corner and that was that!

Gen. Moore called about it and I told him about the occurrence, trying to control my disgust. Previously he had phoned me to "drive" Kohn and I had written and phoned orders about immediate action for Btries. Hanna, Grubbs, etc.

Nothing left to do but turn in. (In the early evening Edison and I finished the bit of Scotch that remained in one bottle left. It was nice in the sunset.)

Tuesday, 21 April 1942

Fine batter cakes for breakfast. Then Edison and I drove towards my quarters but were stopped 100 yards away, by bomb craters which have blown hell out of the officers' road. Derr had previously brought me the training manuals which vandals had scorned to steal. Found my Christy helmet on the floor and retrieved it. Just then the air raid alarm went and I scrambled over bomb craters to Edison and Derr and we went to HD Bombproof for shelter. Stayed there awhile, cooped up with gugus, sweltering as they were cooking electrically therein, but as nothing happened, we resumed our ride to G4 where I investigated the causes of last night's miserable performance by questioning Cols. Kohn and Mitchell.

Boats were first detected by G4 in moonpath, but #3 light had no power at that time, probably because engineers were working on cable! Our No. 4 light was slow in coming around to cover target. Then, because of the notoriously execrable quality of our GPF sights, the gun pointers could not see the small targets and so Monja simply fired 2 at Hornos Pt. and then fired merely at the beam intersections with rotten results. Sunset had Scott sights but also could not see target; fired 3. Both batteries fired very slowly, at about 1' intervals! Hanna's field of fire was so far seaward that the enemy slid through before they could get going. No. 3 light couldn't follow targets far, and No. 2 was out of commission. When targets got out of No. 3, Btries. Grubbs etc. could not see them. All other guns were out of commission and roving guns couldn't see. A great fiasco! Humiliating! Hughes couldn't bear on the area. When we tried to use No. 1 light the enemy quickly fired 3-gun salvos, injuring 3 Marines. We were helpless.

A Navy patrol boat was on station where it could easily intercept the enemy but when we asked them to do so, they declined, saying they had only cal .30 machine guns! Beach Defense would not fire because Gen. didn't want to disclose its guns! So the Japs sailed calmly past, one boat towing the other two!

Returned to C1 and made arrangements for two searchlights with crews from 60th and sent Daws and Gerlich out to reconnoiter positions.

At 11:23 a string of heavy bombs fell on golf course and Geary magazines. No casualties or damage.

Capt. Ellis dropped in, with our Capt. Thompson, and chewed the fat. He doesn't know what became of Brooke. Offered to send radio to Landon.

At about 3:20, hearing of heavy truck movements at Amo River, north of Cabcaben, we lined up Geary to fire. Fired 2 rounds and then, Julian's gang being all mixed up and unable to coordinate, we ceased fire with nothing accomplished except to stir up the Japs to some vicious counterbattery. Dammit. Thus the excitability of our observers stirred up a useless tempest. The Japs continued nastily, Mitchell asked to fire Monja against a gun they'd found and we told them OK and not spare the ammunition and work up some speed. They had to stop because the cliff started caving. At 5:55 we ordered Geary to fire 2 shots at Sisiman, as we heard that is the site of the battery of Japs now firing still. Those 2 shots silenced them but some other battery started up and kept it up for quite some time.

Then we had a bad time with two portable AA searchlights which Peterson was supposed to install for us, one at the Kindley Field car station and the other near RJ 100 near Rock Point. At 10:00 P.M. neither were hooked up, although the responsible officers were notified at 2:00 P.M. so they had plenty of time in which to reconnoiter the roads.

Edison, feeling on the bum, turned in early. I stayed up and played cribbage with Hawes.

Our men are making swell progress, the last two days, in digging our bodegas—private laterals—in our tunnel.

Turned in at 11:15.

Moon is pretty bright already, which works for us and minimizes need for searchlights.

Wednesday, 22 April 1942

Edison is recovered this morning. Awoke when our fluorescent lights came on and went outside to smoke a few scags before breakfast. The Japs fired a couple at us about 1:00 last night and 6 more at about 6:00 A.M.

First air raid alarm 8:30. Restrictions on our firing relaxed by Gen. Moore so that hereafter, we may fire on all troop and truck concentrations, on all definitely located batteries. Not to fire on troop areas except when enemy battery is definitely located therein.

Japs opened fire at 10:00 A.M. from Cavite on Hamilton. At 10:45 another air raid sounded. "One bomber diving on Ft. Hughes." Koehler ordered 12 shots on Jap guns firing from Cavite side. Several short air raid alarms but managed to go to my azatea, shave and wash a bucket of dirt off my head. Craighill fired at caves in Patungan Cove, to assist Ft. Frank.

Our amateur miners are continuing to make fine progress on our bodegas. There may have been one bomb dropped near Ft. Hughes this morning early but, though there were a couple of raid alarms during the forenoon, no other bombs were dropped.

Everything was quiet until after dinner when Japs opened sniping fire with one gun. Gen. Moore said they were getting casualties at Bottomside and asked if it was a Jap "general bombardment" preceding an attack—but we told him it was a 3-gun battery.

At about this time, an observer at Ft. Frank saw some "invasion barges" moored to the rock 300 yards southwest of our old friend Longoskawayan Pt. We verified the dope and then put Geary to work. The first salvo of 3 shots hit the point. Of the next and last salvo, putting one up 200, one down 200, and the last left 300 yards and we hope we raised hell with them and spoiled their projected trip of these barges into Manila.[11]

At about this time, 7:30, the Japs opened more guns, firing at Geary and some landing just outside our tunnel. So we got mad and started our 1st dress rehearsal of our retaliation shoot: Drum 10 rounds on Cabcaben, Geary 4 shots and 6 shots at 2 targets; Craighill 10 rounds at Jap battery south of Cabcaben; our two roving guns at another Jap battery, using about 100 rounds. After this, Craighill said they saw flashes of a Jap battery and opened fire but, the Japs came down on them and they took cover. I guess they were shooting at the bursts of our 155s. By 10:30 the only firing was sporadic Jap firing against Hughes, so we buttoned everything up and turned in.

Geary is sure the good old work horse!

No new "scuttlebutt" (rumors) today. Tokyo evidently is worried over the secret base of the U.S. planes that bombed her on Saturday. So she bombed the airfields at Del Monte in Mindanao also some in China.

Thursday, 23 April 1942

We were careful to use our searchlights freely around Hornos Pt. last night, and no landing barges attempted to run by.

Usual morning routine; outside to smoke cigarettes until breakfast. To lanai for cool of morning but, of course, the air raid siren blew, which it usually does about 8:00 or so. Probably an observation plane making his daily photographs of us. By 9:00 A.M. the Japs had not fired a shot.

My old dugout is about empty now and sure smells moldy. All clear blew shortly. No sea activity except the usual 2 Jap blockade ships on the horizon: one destroyer and one mine layer.

At breakfast Gen. Moore appeared, asked about consumption of gas at our Btry. Morrison, seemed satisfied at our answers, and disappeared.

Air raid at 10:45 A.M. but nothing happened. Another air raid at 1:20 and no bombs fell. The 60th opened fire. Also the Japs put a few shells atop Morrison Hill. Planes passed over Drum, dropped 1 bomb and missed. Big string of bombs fell on Corregidor at 2:06, more at 2:18. AA fire at 2:50, bombs fell almost immediately somewhere on Topside.

After dinner we started big shoot: Monja 40 rounds at quarantine wharf, Cheney 6 rounds at Mariveles: Turrets 0. Byrens used 14 shots to register on road north of Cabcaben, No. 145 and did fine shooting. Then we started Btry. Farris on Road Bend 132 south of Cabcaben—During all this time, no Jap gun fired but, just as Farris finished his 15 rounds with a good adjustment, and we started adjusting Geary on the Jap Looc Dump, down came the Japs from a battery way back of Paligigan (causing 1 slight injury later) but the first 2 were duds.

At this time, Ft. Frank said they could see some more of those Jap landing barges off Longoskawayan Pt. so we dropped 6 shots of "personnel shells" there and hoped for the best. Then I ordered Hanna and Monja to have 1 gun loaded and laid on Hornos Pt., ready to go instantly if the enemy showed his nose around the point. We ordered 2 salvos from Koehler, to shut up the Cavite Japs, so Geary could shoot at the barges.

Then Ft. Frank reported they had chased a Jap patrol into the caves in Patungan Cove, so we let Craighill mortars fire a few shots at that point. Whereupon the Japs opened up on Ft. Hughes in retaliation. Quite a bit of firing—57 rounds of all calibers. By 8:40 things had calmed down. Half moon tonight, setting after 1:00.

The Japs have been advertising, over Cavite way, that they were going to stage their big push on this date. They have less than 4 hours to go.

After a short lull, the Japs tossed a few more over some landing in water in front of No. 4 light. Edison, after I turned in at 11:00, went up to the OP and pestered around until about 1:00.

During the night, the Japs fired one burst of about 12 and later a few more. I guess we'll have to start night harassing fire ourselves.

Later

[These three paragraphs were written after Bunker was captured.]

It is the testimony of many Americans who were patients in Bataan Hospitals Nos. 1 and 2 (and contradicted by nobody) that the Japs almost completely surrounded these hospitals with their batteries, placing them as close as possible to hospital boundaries and sometimes inside the bounds. On our part, we had strict orders not to fire into Hospital areas, although the staff was at first unable to tell us even the approximate locations of the hospital grounds and buildings. Soon, however, Col. Braly did give us the coordinates of the perimeter of hospital grounds and we passed these on to every battery commander. Later we received orders to fire upon enemy batteries if they were positively identified as being within a hospital area. In only 1 case did we do this: on a battery which we located about 25 yards within a hospital area.

Patients in the hospital agree that we landed shells within the hospital area dangerously only twice: one shell, on its way over the area, hit a tree, detonated, and killed about 14; the other one landed in the middle of a ward but was a dud and hurt nobody.

As to the date of these occurrences, testimony varies, but I judge that the 1st was on this date of 23 April Col. Atkinson, Infantry says both were about this date.

Friday, 24 April 1942

Awoke early and went to our lanai to enjoy the fresh morning air. Lt. Hudgins appeared, dirty from his hazardous tour of duty on the *Don Jose* and, to my astonishment, found enough water in the pipes for a shower-bath. And so immediately after breakfast, I grabbed my towel, went up to my old dugout, shaved and then came down hill to the lanai and started luxuriously on my own shower-bath but, just as I was washing the soap off, the first air raid sounded and, as the AA started shooting, I had to duck, naked, into our tunnel, until the planes had passed. A fresh suit of underwear made the finishing touch to a pleasant performance, and caused that "grand and glorious feeling."

Had a disappointing experience trying to adjust Farris on a road interdiction—because of bobbles in our flash ranging section through their woodenness in orienting. Had to call off the problem until the cause of trouble was found.

Received word that, in our Group 3, Col. DeCarre, Maj. Miller and Capt. White are taking such a defeatist attitude as to be subversive! I am expected to line them up, avoiding drastic measures by higher authority.

Periodic air raids all morning but no action. At 10:35 two bombers dove at Fort Hughes, dropped one bomb—which missed.

About 3:00 P.M. the Japs started desultory shelling of Corregidor which got rapidly heavier. At first we had no rover batteries working—when we tried to open with Geary they started firing 240s at it. Then we tried in vain to start Craighill, and the enemy came down on that. So all we had left was the Drum turrets, so we got Kirk busy and he did yeoman service in silencing 3 Jap guns—probably 240mm. While doing this, Japs started firing on him from Cavite, so we started Koehler to working that bunch over, and they stopped as soon as Koehler opened fire.

Meanwhile, Btries. Byrne and Rose started shooting at enemy batteries and Monja silenced a Jap battery before landslides stopped them. All in all, it was a hot duel. At about 5:15 a big one came under the overhang of Btry. Crockett and perhaps entered the powder room. A man appeared at our tunnel, closely followed by Lt. Crandall and another man, almost hysterical, saying the "battery is blown to hell" but knew nothing of what had happened. We couldn't get any word from Crockett in any way. First reports were alarming—that "the powder was afire and guns ruined, many casualties." Efird started in official car with fire extinguishers for Crockett. Phoned Gen. Moore. Later reports were less alarming: that the fire started in the office and spread and may endanger the powder.

Final dope: Powder did not burn, but office and storeroom did. 1 staff sergeant killed, several injured. Capt. Fox MD badly hurt. Rauck was at Bottomside when it all happened. At Bottomside, the guards were running everybody into the tunnel "because Crockett is going to blow up." The Marines, just below Crockett, did their share in spreading wild reports broadcast.

Evidently our shooting from the Drum turrets was right on the Jap big guns that were shelling Crockett, for they shut up—and not a bit too soon, for their airplane spotting was superb. They set fire to our dump of AA 75mm ammunition just south of Crockett, and the bursts of this stuff kept up for quite a while after shelling stopped.

Rest of evening was quiet and nothing occurred.[12] I was very tired and turned in at 10:30; Edison went up to the OP.

Saturday, 25 April 1942

Awoke when the power from Wheeler ceased and our own AC came on at about 6:30. Crandall appeared, still shaken from the Crockett cannonade. I got my camera and Pvt. Derr and drove him down to Btry. Geary, whence we walked to Btry. Crockett and viewed the wreckage there. No. 1 gun and emplacement was completely wrecked and ruined. Elevation arm broken off and recoil cylinder punctured by 240mm shots. Many came through openings and ruined shot hoists and even penetrated into powder room but without igniting the powder. No. 2 can probably be used but there are no means of supplying guns with projectiles. Took one picture but the sun was too low for success. All is a desolate scene of devastation around the battery.

Back to C1 and had breakfast, then to lanai for air raid alarm sounded but nothing happened. All clear at about 8:50 followed by another alarm from 9:25 to 9:35, no bombs. Coupla more alarms by 12:40. Ordered rover guns to open on 250 Japs near San José, Bataan. Also cooked up shoot for Btry. Geary at enemy dump. 1:15 bombs fell on Ft. Hughes. Geary was firing at enemy dump and a roving gun was firing at San José barrio. The Hughes bombs fell on the east margin. Before this, another string of bombs lit on Fort Hughes. 1:25 Japs firing on Corregidor from Cavite; shells landing near Btry. Hamilton and Geary.

At 2:15 ordered Col. Foster to fire Woodruff at the Jap gun, in Cavite, that was firing at Geary. During the last salvo from Geary a Jap shell landed in the middle of the pit, seriously injuring one man. At 2:40 spotted 3 enemy guns just south of the dump and told Mitchell to cut loose on it with a roving gun.

By 3:00 P.M. the Japs ceased firing, at least temporarily. Col. Foster had not yet opened fire on the Cavite gun, and he never did open, though it was one of his own observers who reported the flashes of the gun. Later I practically forced him to fire Craighill at a battery in Babuyan Valley but he was so slow that he got away only three shots before the Japs lowered the boom on him.

Along after dark the Japs lobbed over a dozen near our target range and, sad to relate, caught Sgt. Shumiack, our mess sergeant, injuring him but only scaring his 3 mess boys to death. Capt McCarthy went out, saw him, and said he was perhaps not seriously hurt. We first heard he was killed.

It is quite muggy in the tunnel now, with so many men habitually in it. Must devise ways of running them outside.

Our barricade for our outside stove is almost complete. The baffles to the officers' addition are all filled with earth and . . .

Burns is moving his gun tonight to a position in front of HD HQ. Farris is due to move tomorrow to a position unknown.

Japs put over a few at 10:00 P.M. They seem to resort to this harassing sort of fire about every even-numbered hour. So we had Drum put 2 into Cabcaben and 2 in the No. 151 area as retaliation fire.

Sergeant Shumiack died of his injuries. A great loss!

Later: A couple of the shells in the 10:00 P.M. attack fell at the west entrance of the Malinta Tunnel, where men had evidently congregated to smoke and chat before turning in for the night. Reports of the casualties vary, but it seems that at least 13 were killed outright, several more dying of their wounds later, and some 25 injured.

Tuesday, 28 April 1942

Awoke at 5:30 and so up and around. After breakfast, much truck traffic through Cabcaben observed and so we put Byrne to work on interdicting it. He adjusted quickly and did good work, starting a fire there. Then he went to west after the Arno River bridge, south of Cabcaben, "You can see timbers flying." Btry. Rose also started up. After we ceased firing the traffic started again, so we also began again. We suspended fire the first time because a Jap plane came over to spot who was firing at them. This was all before 10:00 A.M.

Surprise, before breakfast, to have a call from Braly, reference roving guns. Gen. Moore dropped in during breakfast for a call.

While Byrne was starting the ball, I went up to my dugout and got a shave, and brought my toilet articles below. Welch cleaned out the rest of my plunder from my dugout, so that now it is well cleared out.

Found, to my disgust that a fairly new carton of Chesterfields has mildewed in my desk, so I wrapped my reserve supply in waxed paper.

Enemy opened fire from Bataan at 10:50. At 10:55 one dive bomber attacked Ft. Hughes, released 1 bomb and missed. All clear at 11:30. 12:10 Byrne adjusted on Jap battery. Japs reopened fire on Corregidor from another battery at Gorda Pt. and we sicked Monja on them—also Cheney. At 1:10 the Japs opened a 3-gun salvo from another battery. Cheney started firing at 1:10, short 400 yards and right about .20°. The Jap 3-gun salvo landed near Byrne's roving gun in front of HD HQ. Cheney fired 9 rounds into the Sisiman Battery and Way gave them a good working over and got very fine training. Byrne lost 1 man killed and others injured by a shell of that 3-gun salvo. At about this time a heavy truck movement was seen heading south through New Cabcaben and we put Rose onto it: right 900, over 300. Hard time getting him on. At 2:05 the Jap observation balloon went up, portending fire from 240mm guns, which did not occur. Everything quieted down about 3:30. Then the Japs started shelling Ft. Frank from a gun near Caputatan near Maragondon and shot 60–70 shells at Koehler. After the usual delay, we got Craighill shooting at 7:00 P.M. and also told Rose to sink the APO, the P.I. government revenue cutter anchored near Cabcaben. The Japs at Caputatan ceased fire as soon as Craighill opened on them. Rose got 4 direct hits on the APO and started a fire aboard that burned nicely at 9:30, so I guess the Japs won't get any good out of her! Of the 59 shots fired at Frank by the Japs, 13 were hits, but there was no damage or casualties. Way got off 21 shots and did well.

At about 9:30 I was starved. This rice diet fills you up *temporarily* but it doesn't stick to your ribs. So I went to the kitchen and retrieved a piece of my Edam cheese.

Wednesday, 29 April 1942

The birthday of Landon—and also the Japanese emperor!

They awakened me by turning on the alternating current lights. Went to lanai to enjoy the freshness of morning for a while, then to C1. Aussie broadcast says Corregidor had its 250th air raid. Inspected C1 entrance to our tunnel and found camouflage lacking, so told McCarthy to get busy with camouflage. At 7:25 our 1st air raid and at 7:30 the Japs bombed Hughes and the south harbor. At the same time the Jap observation balloon went up near Cabcaben. The APO is still burning and the fire has worked its way aft; the ship is now listing badly. At this same time the Japs opened with one gun against Corregidor. They sure are starting early. We all predicted they would take this way of celebrating the emperor's birthday and it will probably be plenty before the day is over.[13]

Broke out my French-Drip coffee pot and the remnants of a can of Maxwell House and brewed us a pot of it. A fine treat but not so good as if it were fresh.

At 7:51 more bombs arrived: they sounded distant, but our observer said that they landed on Topside, much smoke near Cheney. By 8:04 one of our ammunition dumps was exploding and several Jap guns were firing at Mills, mostly light calibers. Many of them started landing close to us, in our tunnel and they felt fairly heavy too. At 8:20 Ft. Hughes was being shelled from Bataan, and by 8:25 the Japs were firing 240mm at our Btries. Geary and Crockett: we ordered our stereotyped retaliation shoot but, at this time, most of our batteries were under fire, so we were slow in getting started.

Edison and I lost out on having batter cakes for breakfast because the Jap shells hit too close to our outdoor stoves, where the cakes were being made and all the cooks beat it into the tunnel; no damage, however.

At about 9:00 A.M. there was a *temporary* lull. Planes overhead at 9:15; heavy string of bombs at 9:16, *close* to us—can smell dust in tunnel though the bombs hit near Btry. Monja—*Heavy!* By 9:30 our turrets had fired 20 1660# shells at various Bataan points. At 9:37 more bombs, some hitting in water near Ft. Hughes. Ft. Frank under fire from direction of Ternate, about cal. 105mm. All clear 10:08. Geary had finished 10 shots and Way had finished 12 on enemy OPs. Another raid, with all clear at 11:00 A.M.; no bombs; only planes. 2 gasoline fires at Kindley Field; smoke 3000' high. Things calmed down for awhile around

11:30 A.M. 12:30 Bombers dove on Drum and bombs missed; then attacked Drum again with 4 planes, missed both times. (At Spot 7, one man killed by bombs and Lt. Erhart wounded.) Planes also flew over Hughes and either bombs or shells hit. Things again calmed down along about 1:00 P.M.—Japs' siesta?

Looks as though B-Pit Geary is permanently out: power plant blown up; many hits on mortars and emplacements; pit full of debris, etc.

A big bomb, 500 lbs. or over, hit the tube of one gun of Btry. Marshall about 3′ from the turret, *but did not explode.* It smashed, scattering powder all over the deck, but did no damage to the gun! Gen. Wainwright sent word to fire like hell or words to them effects. We used Monja as range finder to identify alleged battery for major caliber guns. It was a failure: F4 observer failed to identify!

A shell caved in the power plant of No. 8 light on Malinta Hill, and set fire to gasoline. First report: 8–9 killed; others injured, including 60th CA men.

Heavy truck traffic being reported between Naic and Maragondon, we put 1 shot from Wilson in Naic and 6 from Koehler at various points, 3:00 P.M.

Air raid 3:00 P.M. bombs immediately, heavy and plentiful. Perhaps near B/60. At 3:19 our AA opened and immediately many heavy bombs fell nearby, shaking us up a bit. They fell near Crockett and a fragment entered C1. More AA fire and another long stick of bombs at 3:21. A plane dropped 1 bomb at Bottomside at 4:00. And Japs were firing about 2 guns at us. A dump was exploding near Crockett trail—but Japs were quiet.

Pie for dinner. Byrne shot some more and a Jap battery shot at us a bit. I read a bit in Sherwood's "Petrified Forest."

At about 11:00 P.M. two Navy flying boats flew into south harbor, landing at 11:20 and leaving at midnight. They unloaded 1500 pounds of 31-second time fuses for our AA, plus some medicine. They took on a load of passengers but who they were, we don't know. Some of us think they were aviators, especially Navy aviators, and all of us hope it was Admiral Rockwell. The operation was skillfully and quickly performed. Bright full moon added hazard to the work, as did the noise of their motors.[14]

Rest of the evening and night was quiet.

Transition

9 April–7 May

The period beginning with the fall of Bataan and ending with the surrender of Corregidor has become known to historians as the "last twenty-seven days."[15] These were days of death and debilitation for the defenders and destruction for the defenses.

Except for an occasional airplane and scrounging from disabled ships, the 11,000 defenders[16] were resupplied only by submarine and a rare interisland steamer. Because of this, the troops had been on half rations since 5 January. By the end of April, the first signs of malnutrition had appeared.[17] To add to the discomfort of the troops, by 30 April they were limited to one canteen of water per man per day. This being the dry season, and most of the pumps having been destroyed by enemy fire, the supply of water was becoming critical. It was only possible to pump water into the reservoirs on one day during the entire month of April. Thus the men were starving and slowly drying up.

In addition, the defenders of Corregidor were already showing the strain of long, sleepless nights, the incessant pounding by bombs and artillery, and the presence of death everywhere. One or two troops suffered from battle fatigue. A few even went insane, as did one who had to watch his friend's head fly by. Oddly enough, the Corregidor surgeon saw only six or eight mental cases throughout the siege. The surgeon felt the low rate of mental sickness was due to the fact there was no place to send the men for rest. There on the island the war was always present, "and once the initial adjustment was made, there were no new adjustments to be made."[18]

Adjustments were also necessary to keep Bunker's artillery effective on the islands after the intense shelling and bombing of April. For during that time, the real destroyer, both mental and material, had been Japanese artillery.[19] The Japanese had ideal conditions for their artillery. They could see accurately over all the islands with their observation balloon (Peeping Tom)[20] and their observation planes.[21] In addition, they could move their guns freely at any time. Thus, they were able to keep their battery positions hidden, while the locations of all U.S. batteries were known.[22] Truly, the Japanese had ideal artillery conditions.

The Japanese divided Corregidor up into zones corresponding roughly to the beach defense sectors and assigned a specific zone to each battery.[23] In this way they guaranteed full coverage of the island.[24] In addition, they plotted each battery on Corregidor as the center of a two-hundred-yard square, and then they put everything they had into that square. The batteries were fired on in succession and were gradually eliminated during April.[25]

During April, with more than 400 pieces of Japanese artillery firing at the fortified islands,[26] the U.S. artillery losses were heavy. Two of Battery Rock Point's 155s, four of Battery Sunset's 155s, four of Battery James' 3-inch antiaircraft guns, and two of Battery Hamilton's 155s were destroyed early in the month. In fact, by 14 April, all the 155mm and 3-inch batteries on Corregidor's north shore had been destroyed or were out of action.[27]

The following week, Battery Morrison's 6-inch guns were out completely, and its crew (C/91) was moved to Battery Grubbs,[28] which by the eighteenth also had to be abandoned because of damaged guns.[29] Also on the eighteenth, a 240mm Japanese shell penetrated the magazines of Battery Geary. The resultant explosion picked up one of the ten-ton mortars and threw it one hundred yards through the air.[30] The explosion was so powerful that two- and three-ton chunks of concrete were tossed some 300 yards away.[31]

On the other hand, not all was bleak. The roving 155 guns had been brought on-line and, after firing twenty rounds, were shifted to new locations. Numerous antiaircraft guns were salvaged,[32] and with parts from Battery Crofton, they were still firing at the end of the third week in April.[33] Battery Way's four 12-inch mortars, which had not been used in years, were reconditioned and put into action by the twenty-eighth.[34]

On 29 April alone, Corregidor felt the impact of 10,000 Japanese shells.[35] But despite this pounding, roving Battery Rose set the Japanese ship *Apo* afire by pumping four rounds into her that same day.[36]

By nightfall of the twenty-ninth the Rock had withstood its 260th aerial bombardment.[37] This, along with the intense shelling, changed the topography of the island. Corregidor's north shore road was literally thrown into the bay.[38] The thick foliage covering the island was stripped away by the heavy projectiles.[39] Caves that had been dug in the sides of cliffs collapsed. On one occasion in April, forty-two Filipino gunners at Battery James were sealed in and smothered in an unreinforced cave when an overhanging cliff collapsed and sealed the entrance.[40]

By 30 April, Bunker's heavy artillery was being destroyed faster than he could get it restored,[41] and the beach defense forces' casualties were escalating.

Elsewhere others were suffering casualties but in a different way. After the fall of Bataan on the ninth, the infamous "Death March" took place. It is likely that between 600 and 650 U.S. troops and from 5,000 to 10,000 Filipinos died or were killed during the three-week march from Bataan to Camp O'Donnell.[42]

Meanwhile, the siege of Corregidor was in its last week. Because of the intense shell fire, the critical nature of the siege of Corregidor, and the rigors of the initial period of captivity, Bunker was unable to maintain his diary during the first three weeks in May.[43]

Notes

1. *Handbook of Japanese Military Forces,* TM-E-30-F80 (15 September 1944), 47. This was the observation balloon out of a Japanese balloon company. It worked in conjunction with an artillery intelligence regiment, which had sound and flash, survey, sound detector, and plotting units.

2. Braly, 40. This was a Japanese 75mm, which had set up near the beach at Cabcaben. Evidently unknown to Bunker, Kysor destroyed it with 155mm fire.

3. Morton, 536. They were prohibited from firing because General Wainwright feared that U.S. shells might hit hospitals, civilians, or U.S. troops on the peninsula.

4. Ibid., 537. These were the cables that controlled the moored mines in the bay. Fortunately, the Japanese were unaware of this.

5. Belote and Belote, 106. Some "2,300 soldiers, sailors, and civilians, Filipino, and American, managed to flee . . . Bataan." Small groups of noncombatant service units totaling 500 men came without authorization. Approximately 1,800 others came by themselves, some in small boats, rafts, or even swimming. Very few were trained soldiers despite the fact they were assigned to beach defenses. General Moore intimated that most were dead wood.

6. Stanley L. Falk, *Bataan: The March of Death* (New York: Norton, 1962), 77. These troops with the white flags were the survivors of Bataan who had just surrendered and were about to embark on the infamous "Death March." They came in groups to gather at the Mariveles and Cabcaben airstrips.

7. Ibid., 72. King had gone out to contact forty-six Japanese on the ninth.

8. Belote and Belote, 121. Unknown to Bunker, much of his counterbattery fire was very accurate. Postwar tabulation by one of the Japanese artillery commanders records a total of twenty-five 240mm and 150mm pieces as damaged during the siege of Corregidor.

9. Wainwright, 88. According to Wainwright, a dozen B-17s raided Davao and Nichols Field near Manila. However, he stated this was done on 10 April. Parker, 19. Parker states that this was in fact on the twelfth but that only one aircraft hit Nichols.

10. Morton, *Strategy,* 269–73. This was true. Lt. Col. James H. Doolittle had attacked Tokyo with his B-25 bombers on 18 April. Actually there was little damage, but the enemy could no longer think they were impregnable.

11. Belote and Belote, 115. On the nights of 14, 16, and 17 April, Homma had slipped the majority of his landing barges into the bay past the island fortresses under the cover of darkness and artillery fire.

12. Braly, 41. After dark on the twenty-fourth an all-volunteer crew from the 59th and 60th CA boarded the U.S. engineer launch *Night Hawk* and "made a

reconnaissance up the east coast of Bataan looking for any concentration of troops or landing craft. Off Lamao they contacted a small Japanese boat with two men, whom they took prisoner. Later they had a fire fight with a larger launch. They killed most of the enemy crew, but the two prisoners they had captured earlier attempted to escape and had to be killed. The *Night Hawk* got back to Corregidor at 5 A.M."

13. Hough, Ludwig, and Shaw, 189. The emperor's birthday marked the beginning of constant bombardment both day and night until the surrender.

14. Braly, 43. These aircraft brought in hospital supplies and 740 mechanical fuses for the 3″ AA guns. They took out "fifty selected passengers (including about 38 American nurses)." Morison, 205. One of these aircraft was wrecked in Mindanao, and the passengers were captured; the other made it to Australia.

15. Wainwright, 86.

16. Ibid.

17. Morton, *Philippines,* 544.

18. Ibid., 545.

19. Case, 39.

20. Morton, *Philippines,* 537.

21. Col. C. L. Irwin, "Corregidor in Action," *Coast Artillery Journal,* 86 (January–February 1943), 11.

22. Morton, 537.

23. Ibid.

24. Ibid.

25. Irwin, 11.

26. Braly, 42.

27. Baldwin, 139–40.

28. Braly, p. 41.

29. Case, 39.

30. Ibid., 39–40.

31. Ibid.

32. Baldwin, 140.

33. Case, 39.

34. Braly, 42.

35. Hough, Ludwig, and Shaw, 187.

36. Braly, 42.

37. Morton, *Philippines,* 539.

38. Baldwin, 141.

39. Hough, Ludwig, and Shaw, 187.

40. Belote and Belote, 114.

41. McCoy and Mellnik, 11.

42. Falk, 197–98.

43. The first three weeks in May have been reconstructed.

Transition: The Siege and Fall of Corregidor

The final siege of Corregidor took place during the first week in May. It began with a heavy artillery bombardment that continued for six days; it ended with the surrender of the Rock and all U.S. forces in the Philippines.

The Japanese prepared carefully for their amphibious assault on the island. During the first two days in May, the Japanese 4th Division conducted amphibious rehearsals along the coast of Bataan.[1] During that week they constructed thousands of bamboo ladders with which to scale Corregidor's cliffs.[2] They gathered their amphibious shipping, which Bunker had vainly tried to halt. They gathered their artillery and continued their intense bombardment of the island.

The shelling continued without letup, and on the second, Battery Geary was once again blown apart,[3] thus ending her firing days. This same day the coast artillery mine planter *Harrison* was hit by repeated bombing attacks, which set her afire, and ultimately, she sank into the oily bay.[4]

On or about the second, Wainwright heard that a submarine was in the area, preparing to return to Australia[5] for more torpedoes. He arranged for it to come to Corregidor.[6] The submarine, the *Spearfish,* was the last sub to evacuate personnel from the island. On the third, under the cover of darkness, she slipped through the dark waters between Cavite and Corregidor. She loaded up with passengers and quickly departed. Most of the passengers were nurses, but there were also several staff officers, including Wainwright's G3, who had very bad ulcers.[7] Others were Colonel Hoyle, the former commander of the 45th Infantry on Bataan; Colonel Jenks, the finance officer; Colonel Hill, the inspector general; and Colonel Savage, the air officer.[8] In addition, there were six naval officers, one navy nurse, and a reserve naval officer's wife.[9] Captain Miehler, the chief nurse on Corregidor, had been scheduled to go, but she refused to leave as long as there was a single patient in the hospital.[10]

On 4 May, the enemy greatly stepped up artillery activity, pounding everything within the bay. During the morning hours, enemy artillery in Cavite ranged in on the minesweeper *Tanager,* and within a few minutes she was on the bottom of Manila Bay.[11] Within one five-hour period later in the day, General Moore and General Wainwright calculated, one 500-pound, 240mm projectile hit Corregidor every five seconds. This amounted to some 1,800,000 pounds of steel exploding on the island during the five hours.[12]

The rapidly deteriorating situation on Corregidor prompted General Marshall in Washington to ask Wainwright for an estimate of the situation. After spelling out the details of enemy bombardment, General Wainwright said: "In my opinion the enemy is capable of making an assault on Corregidor at any time. The success or failure of such assault will depend entirely on the steadfastness of beach defense troops. Considering the present level of morale, I estimate that we have something less than an even chance to beat off an assault. I have given you, in accordance with your request, a very frank and honest opinion on the situation as I see it."[13]

By 5 May, Corregidor had suffered one thousand casualties.[14] More were to occur because of the ever-increasing artillery fire and aerial bombardment, which caused a cloud of dust to hang over the entire island. Most of the permanent installations had been destroyed. Most of the antiaircraft batteries were quiet; only Batteries Flint and Chicago had one operable gun apiece.[15]

Planes now swooped low overhead because of the quiet antiaircraft guns. At 12:30 P.M. on the fifth, Bunker commenced counterbattery fire with everything he had left. This barrage destroyed three Japanese ammunition dumps and silenced several enemy batteries.[16] At 2:47 P.M. Bunker certainly heard the threehundredth air raid alarm announcing an attack on Fort Hughes. The enemy aircraft, being able to swoop low, were very accurate.[17] Their bombs filled Craighill's* pits with debris and wounded many of the crew.[18]

By 6:30 all the fortified islands were receiving a terrific pounding. Seeing a full moon overhead on the evening of the fifth, General Moore exclaimed to Colonel Braly, "Damn that full moon! They'll probably come tonight."[19] At 8:00 P.M., the Japanese shifted their fire to the beaches all along the north shore of the island, driving many of the defenders inland.[20] By 9:00 P.M. the enemy artillery fires had failed to slack off as usual after dark, and instead the fire had grown more intense. Noticing this, Colonel Howard ordered his men on alert. At 9:30 some of Colonel Chase's 60th CA sound locators heard the well-known sound of Japanese invasion barges starting up near Limay. At 10:30, Colonel Howard received word that a landing was imminent.[21] A few minutes before 11:00 P.M. on the fifth, the bombardment grew to its highest peak along the tail and north shore of the island. Then, at 11:00, it suddenly shifted to Malinta Hill.[22]

*Name of one of the batteries.

At 11:10 P.M., troops at Cavalry Point noticing the barges approaching shouted, "Here they come!"[23] At 11:15, Wainwright received the word about the landing.[24] The enemy could be seen falling "like dominoes" in the barges as the heavy automatic weapons fire poured from the beach defenses. One Japanese unit landed on the left flank but was "virtually annihilated" because they had landed below "low, precipitous cliffs from which twenty-five pound fragmental bombs"[25] were falling. Prior to the attack, the troops overlooking these beaches had gerry-rigged metal chutes over the cliffs so that they could utilize the aerial bombs stored at Kindley Field.[26] Only 30 percent of the Japanese in this initial wave reached shore. Most of these came ashore at North Point, where many of the defenders had moved inland to escape the initial bombardment.[27] "Shortly after the initial landing, Bunker sent the 59th CA personnel manning . . . Cheney, Wheeler, Crockett, and Geary to" Colonel Howard as beach defense reserve.[28]

Despite heavy losses, the Japanese had gotten a firm hold along the north side of Kindley Field. On the west, a determined group of the 803d Engineers continued to hold ground.[29] However, by midnight, the Japanese "had succeeded in knocking out most of the resistance along the landing beaches"[30] with the exception of a few isolated pockets, which continued to hold out.

The second wave of Japanese barges started in about this time, but they too suffered heavy casualties. The pocket of U.S. troops, commanded by Army Lt. Ray G. Lawrence's on the tail of the island, spotted this second group and opened up on the enemy. Later, he said that he doubted if any ever reached shore. At daylight he counted over twenty half-sunken craft; four others, containing at least sixty dead Japanese soldiers each, drifted slowly out to sea. "Hundreds of bodies [clad] in orange . . . life jackets floated in the water, giving sharks and barracudas a feast."[31] The initial wave had consisted of 2,000 Japanese; of those, 800 made it to shore. The second wave totaled 10,000 men, of whom over 4,000 were lost.[32]

Meanwhile, on Water Tank Hill, the remnants of the initial Japanese landing force "held all but the forward slope"[33] A stalemate had been reached. They could go no further without reinforcement from Bataan. One of the periodic rolling barrages employed by the Japanese between Bottomside and Water Tank Hill nearly decimated two attacking companies of the 4th Battalion, 4th Marines. One of these companies, C-59th CA, was commanded by Capt. Harry Schenk. Many of his men were killed, "including the battery executive officer, Captain Arthur D. Thompson." The survivors of the barrage remaining in C Battery, and Captain

Hauck's B Battery, moved into position from which to launch a counter-attack.[34] The Japanese on the hill under the command of Colonel Sato could do nothing but beat off these disorganized counterattacks while waiting for scheduled reinforcing waves, which were to come at dawn. "As the sun rose, the enemy was still there; the battle had yet to reach its climax."[35]

At 4:00 A.M. on 6 May Wainwright received a final message from Roosevelt. It read:

> During recent weeks we have been following with growing admiration the day-by-day accounts of your heroic stand against the mounting intensity of bombardment by enemy planes and heavy siege guns.
>
> In spite of all the handicaps of complete isolation, lack of food and ammunition you have given the world a shining example of patriotic fortitude and self-sacrifice.
>
> The American people ask no finer example of tenacity, resourcefulness, and steadfast courage. The calm determination of your personal leadership in a desperate situation sets a standard of duty for our soldiers throughout the world. In every camp and on every naval vessel soldiers, sailors, and Marines are inspired by the gallant struggle of their comrades in the Philippines. The workmen in our shipyards and munitions plants redouble their efforts because of your example.
>
> You and your devoted followers have become the living symbols of our war aims and the guarantee of victory.
>
> Franklin D. Roosevelt[36]

Certainly Bunker's prediction of another Alamo was coming true.

At 4:40 A.M. on the sixth, the reinforcing craft were spotted by observers Topside. Probably under Bunker's cool, calculating direction, the heavy 14-inch artillery on Drum, the one remaining heavy mortar at Way, the single 155 at Battery Stockade, and roving Battery Wright all took these barges under fire. The enemy craft took heaving pounding, but not quite as bad as the two initial waves had suffered. The batteries were so enthusiastic that Bunker had to tell Battery Way to cease fire when its firing had shifted to the Japanese beachhead at North Point, which was in close proximity to Lieutenant Lawrence and his men.[37]

For the remainder of the sixth, Bunker had Battery Way fire almost continuously at Bataan or on the landing barges. The Japanese counterbattery fire was fantastic and caused many casualties among the gunners, but as soon as one crew was knocked out, a replacement crew would rush out and man the mortar.[38] At midmorning, Major Massello, commanding at Way, ordered the communications ripped out so that he wouldn't be given the order to surrender. At about 11 o'clock, he was severely wounded "with a major leg wound and an arm almost severed."[39] Casualties were now at about 70 percent at Way. There was a temporary halt in the firing of the mortar because of their leader's wound. When the crew tried to resume fire, they found parts frozen on it;[40] nevertheless, according to Massello," it had lasted long enough to be the last big gun . . . to fire on the enemy. It quit just one hour before the surrender."[41]

By this time, Homma's surviving reinforcements had reached the Water Tank Hill. Howard then committed his reserve 4th Battalion under Maj. Joe Williams, USMC; it consisted of four ragged companies, Q, R, S, T,[42] each of which was truly an interservice team. "Coast Guard, Navy, Naval Reserve, Insular Force, U.S. Army, Philippine Army, Philippine Scouts and Philippine Constabulary; the whole trained, led and inspired by the tradition and *esprit* of the Marines."[43] Q Company under the command of Capt. Paul C. Moore, U.S.A., was in the lead, followed by companies R, S, and T. Captain Hauck's Battery B now followed this as the battalion reserve.[44] All they could do with heavy supporting weapons was to launch a frontal assault. "The men advanced courageously, firing as they went . . . scoring a gain of . . . [about] three hundred yards on the left flank."[45] Gallantry was commonplace that day. But despite the many forays against the forces on Water Tank Hill, Major Williams failed to dislodge the enemy. Hauck was later committed against the left flank of enemy on the hill. Before 10 o'clock[46] they forced the enemy from the north ridge and the west end of the airstrip "into the open."

Around 10 o'clock in the morning, Colonel Howard called Wainwright and said the Japanese "were landing more tanks."[47] Unfortunately, all barriers to tanks had long since been destroyed, and the defenses had no antitank weapons.[48] "It was the terror . . . vested in the tank that was the deciding factor"[49] for Wainwright. He thought of the havoc it could wreak if it were let loose in one of the tunnels. What would happen to the thousand litter patients who lined the tunnels in Malinta Hill?[50] What would be the fate of 150 nurses? Wainwright knew the answer. He could ponder no longer. He called in General Beebe and General Moore and issued them orders.[51]

At 10:30, Wainwright had Beebe broadcast the surrender message to Homma. At the same time, he had General Moore give the order to destroy all weapons and to fly white flags over all positions. Upon receiving this word, "Colonel Howard put his head in his hands and wept. 'My

God,' he exclaimed, 'and I had to be the first Marine officer ever to surrender a regiment.'"[52] General Wainwright issued orders to Colonel Bunker telling him to personally raise the surrender flag at noon.[53] Colonel Bunker, sitting by his phone in the bombproofed C1, which had never been hit, said, "No, . . . I can't believe it."[54] Then he said in his low voice, "I guess it had to come."[55] He then ordered all batteries to destroy their equipment.[56]

After the surrender announcement, the *Quail,* the only remaining naval boat in Philippine waters, was scuttled rather than letting the gallant little boat fall into Japanese hands.[57]

Precisely at 12:00, despite enemy shelling, Bunker and Edison marched to the island's flagpole.[58] Both of them stood ramrod stiff as taps was blown by a bugler. They lowered and burned the colors, "which had been shot down and replaced twice . . . during the siege,"[59] saving one small piece of it, which Bunker had until he died. With Edison's help they ran up a white bed sheet. Observers stood around and wept.[60] Even after the white flags fluttered all around the island, the Japanese still pounded it with artillery. A few men refused to surrender and fought till their death, and others in isolated pockets fought till their ammunition was dissipated. Finally, at 5:00 P.M., Lieutenant Lawrence surrendered his men on the north of the island.[61]

It wasn't until 4:00 P.M. that a Japanese boat arrived for Wainwright to take him to Homma.[62] And it was midnight before he returned to the Rock for the last time. Most of the night he had attempted to negotiate with the burly six-foot Homma. At midnight, on the island, Wainwright, realizing the futility of delay, drew up the surrender document surrendering not just Corregidor but all the U.S. forces in the Philippines to Homma.[63]

On the seventh the Japanese artillery continued to pound portions of the island, but there was no American resistance. During the afternoon, the Japanese landed unopposed on Frank and Drum. "The Gallant defense of the Philippines had ended."[64] "The Rock" had suffered the heaviest artillery bombardment ever known in the Far East.[65] The long years of prison were about to begin.

Notes

1. Belote and Belote, 134.
2. Wainwright, 114.
3. Ibid., 92.
4. Braly, 42.
5. Wainwright, 108.
6. Ibid.
7. Ibid., 108.
8. Belote and Belote, 142.
9. Parker, 21.
10. Wainwright, 109.
11. Morison, 206.
12. Wainwright, 110–12.
13. Ibid., 113.
14. Belote and Belote, 143.
15. Ibid., 139.
16. Ibid., 143.
17. Belote and Belote, 143.
18. Braly, 43.
19. Belote and Belote, 141.
20. Wainwright, 115.
21. Belote and Belote, 144.
22. Ibid., 146.
23. Ibid.
24. Wainwright, 115.
25. Belote and Belote, 147.
26. Ibid.
27. Ibid., 148.
28. Braly, 43.
29. Belote and Belote, 148.
30. Ibid.
31. Ibid., 150–51.
32. Braly, 43.
33. Belote and Belote, 155.
34. Braly, 43.
35. Belote and Belote, 157.
36. Wainwright, 117–18.
37. Belote and Belote, 158–60.

38. Ibid., 160.
39. Ibid., 161.
40. Ibid.
41. Case, 40.
42. Belote and Belote, 162–65.
43. Baldwin, 142.
44. Belote and Belote, 167.
45. Ibid., 165.
46. Ibid., 167.
47. Baldwin, 147.
48. Ibid., 148.
49. Wainwright, 119.
50. Ibid., 119.
51. Ibid., 119, 120.
52. Schultz, 289.
53. Wainwright, 123.
54. Belote and Belote, 171.
55. Ibid.
56. Ibid.
57. Morison, 206.
58. Belote and Belote, 172.
59. Braly, 44.
60. Belote and Belote, 172.
61. Ibid., 175.
62. Wainwright, 127.
63. Belote and Belote, 175.
64. Braly, 44.
65. Baldwin, 138.

PRELUDE TO PART II

On 8 May, the Japanese started ferrying U.S. troops from Ft. Hughes to "the Rock."[1] By late that afternoon, the island's captive population had swollen to 16,000. For two weeks, those Americans were to remain there as Homma's hostages under deplorable conditions until all of the surrender terms were met.[2]

Hostages were held to ensure that Wainwright did not repeat General King's surrender on Bataan. King "had refused to surrender the Rock and southern garrisons on the grounds that General Wainwright was Chief in Command and that only Wainwright could act for the others."[3] Now Wainwright was attempting to do the same, only this time, the enraged Homma would guarantee total surrender with his hostages. By not accepting a partial surrender of the Rock, and by continuing bombardment of the island, he could in effect legally massacre the 16,000 captives.

Through this threat of massacre, Homma forced Wainwright "to broadcast . . . to General Sharp on Mindanao . . . appealing to him to lay down his arms."[4]

On 9 May, Wainwright's surrender message reached General Sharp's subordinate commanders,[5] whose forces still controlled Mindanao and the other islands in the south. On the eleventh, Sharp was the last general officer to surrender his command.[6] However, it was not until 9 June, that his last subordinate units surrendered. There were two Filipino battalions and numerous groups of guerrillas, which never did surrender.[7]

Earlier, on 7 May, while still negotiating the surrender, General Wainwright and his staff passed through the prisoner holding area on Corregidor and left the island for the last time. But despite the mental and physical depression of the mass of captives, they rose to attention as he passed, causing tears to well up in his eyes. He was consciously aware of their cramped quarters, which lacked adequate protection from the sun, and he noticed their tragic lack of water and food.[8]

Initially, the prisoners had been allowed almost complete freedom of the island. However, in order to increase the threat to his captives, Homma had massed them into the old 92d garage area, which was located in a small depression east of Malinta Tunnel along the south shore.[9] The area was extremely small, measuring only about 100 yards square with one side in the bay.[10]

Shade did not exist except in the shadows of two blasted, roofless hangars, one of which had been set aside for the Filipino prisoners, who were segregated from the Americans. "The other hanger was reserved for five hundred of the U.S. officers."[11] These officers, including Bunker, were forced to fend for themselves on the open, scorching concrete. Painful

"Guam blisters" developed on their skin, which was exposed to the incandescent tropical sun. Most of the men built makeshift lean-to's out of canvas or pieces of roofing material.[12]

There was no water except for what a single spigot provided, from which individuals took over twelve hours to fill a canteen because of the large numbers of prisoners crowding around the only source of water.[13] There was no food available during the first week except what the prisoners had carried on their own person. Later, they received a daily issue[14] consisting of a "mess kit of rice and a tin of sardines."[15]

Initially the Japanese refused to let the prisoners cool off in the bay, but when the Japanese saw the shallow waters were horribly polluted, they quickly gave permission for swimming.

No latrine facilities existed initially in the prison area; and with a breakdown in the normal chain of command and without the resultant supervision they should have had, the area became unbearably dirty.[16] Only 10 to 15 percent of the prisoners tried to rectify the situation, "and the prisoners worked from the first day to restore order."[17]

The Japanese, in contrast, organized burial details from the prisoners. Their job was to gather all the Japanese corpses and pile them in massive funeral pyres on Kindley Field or on Bataan. Each Japanese corpse, however, had to have one of its hands cut off for later cremation so that the ashes could be sent to the deceased's family.[18] American and Filipino bodies were hastily put into shallow graves dug out of the hard ground near where each body lay. Within two days, all of the burial work was completed.[19]

The Japanese did not commit many atrocities on Corregidor compared to the great number on Bataan during the Death March, just ending about this time. The nurses were hungry and overworked, caring for their 1,000 patients, but not one nurse was molested. There was one terrible incident, which occurred when one captain was executed "for being anti-Japanese."[20]

Some men were more fortunate than the captain, for they escaped. The crew of the *Quail* left Ft. Hughes on the sixth in a 36-foot motor launch and sailed to Australia at a slow speed of five knots. One of the Air Corps captains on Corregidor swam to Bataan, joined another escapee, and ultimately made it to Australia in an even smaller boat. Captain Hauck managed to escape for a month before he was turned over to the Japanese by sycophantic Filipinos.[21]

Lt. Edgar Whitcomb and another lieutenant managed to slip away from one of the numerous prisoner details. They hid out until dark and also swam to Bataan, where after a week they secured a small outrigger, which was soon wrecked in a squall off the coast of Luzon. Swimming ashore, they joined two enlisted escapees and found another outrigger. But Whitcomb balked at sailing during daylight hours, so he left the group. As it turned out, he made a good decision, for he and only a few others were ever to escape successfully from the Rock.[22]

For those who failed to escape, the Rock was a deplorable place. However, after two weeks the leadership within the POWs came to the fore and latrines were dug. Some semblance of order started to take over their daily lives. Bunker's keen attention to detail brings this to light in the pages to follow.

Notes

1. Belote and Belote, 178.
2. Dyess, 115.
3. Ibid., 115.
4. Belote and Belote, 178.
5. Brig. Gen. John Hugh McGee, *Rice and Salt* (San Antonio, Texas: Naylor, 1962), 59.
6. Dyess, 116–17.
7. Morton, *Philippines,* 582.
8. Wainwright, 141.
9. Belote and Belote, 178.
10. McCoy and Mellnik, 20.
11. Belote and Belote, 179.
12. Ibid.
13. McCoy and Mellnik, 12.
14. Dyess, 116.
15. McCoy and Mellnik, 21.
16. Belote and Belote, 179.
17. McCoy and Mellnik, 21.
18. Ibid.
19. Belote and Belote, 179.
20. Ibid., 180.
21. Ibid., 180–81.
22. Ibid., 181.

Transition: Captured by the Japanese

A few days after Bunker was captured, he was questioned by the Japanese about defenses. Angrily they took him to his old command post that he had destroyed. They interrogated him concerning the reason for the destruction. Bunker shrugged his shoulders, smiled, and said something in Spanish. The enemy staff did not bother him again. Another time he demonstrated the same fighting spirit that had made him a two-time "all-American." On this occasion a Japanese guard at night saw Bunker's gold watch chain hanging from his pocket. The guard grabbed it. In turn Bunker seized the guard's arm, cursed him, and took him outside, saying he would turn him in to his superiors. Naturally the guard did not understand Bunker. The guard was terrified by this imposing, powerful American. He broke free of Bunker's grip and slunk away like a punished boy dragging his rifle behind him![1]

Sunday, 17 May 1942

Awoke about 2:00 A.M. and intended standing in line for water but Mr. Green[2] said our cans are full. At dawn went down to beach for plunge but water was full of Filipino feces. Before breakfast Menzie sent for me in a hurry—but it was about nothing, so I returned to bakay for breakfast of rice and coffee and 2 flapjacks. Then walked out, inspecting latrines, which are in better shape than before, managed a tiny hard movement, the 1st in 3 days.

To bata to help supervise furnishing work details. We now have Col. Englehart[3] helping us.

Last night they marched Lt. Thompson AC in here bound and with a pistol in his back. Offense unknown. Later, they took him elsewhere, yet today they ask us to produce him.[4]

It is very hot and the flies are so thick we almost breathe them. To Julian's Co. at 12:30 for cup of hot water. Am so weak I feel giddy when walking around camp in the sun. Am wearing the same uniform which I wore into this camp on May 8th and it sure is ripe.

In evening, after chow, went in swimming as usual at sundown and found it refreshing.

One day follows another without change. A brassy hot sky and a crushing sun, with two faint breezes. Heat, heat and still more heat.

Monday, 18 May 1942

Early morning swim. Washed my clothes in the sea at noon. Nothing new happened, Victory Parade in Manila, so they say. Of course rumors are rife. Received 40 more convalescents from hospital for McCarthy's Co. Tonight they shot Jo-Jo, the Battery A dog and everybody wondered about the shooting. Nobody knows what has become of Lt. Thompson A.C.: some say he has been shot.

A soldier reported today that our C1 Tunnel is not destroyed, that 12 Japs are living in it. Since the Japs are scrapping our big guns, I am going to try for an audience with the Jap CO, with a view to letting the 59th move to Topside to do this work. Maybe I can save some of my records in C1 Tunnel.

Another swim at sundown—Felt rotten and got 2 aspirins from Rutherford. Verde came around tonight, feeling fine.

Tuesday, 19 May 1942

Flies get busy at early dawn, before sun-up. Breakfast of rice and coffee. To latrine without success. To HQ and soldier gave me a big cup of hot tea. Am so weak that my knees wobble when I walk in the sun.

Col. Menzie collapsed onto a stretcher and they took him away about 11:30 A.M. Rigged a paulin over openings in roof office. Hawes, men kicking about digging latrines 2 nights in a row. Schenck doing good work in digging latrines. Dysentery does not seem to be increasing excessively.

Hung around HQ till noon and then to our shack, no rations issued for the last 2 days. Filipinos stole food, so they have gone hungry for 48 hrs., usual swim in evening. Edison's bowels now OK. Wright[5] is sick: bloody feces and vomiting. Our neighbors reconstructed their shack this evening.

Our only surcease starts about 7 P.M. when darkness makes the flies go to roost.

Wild rumors: Allies win in New Guinea; Allies spearhead reaches Berlin; Hitler government flees to Spain. Roosevelt authorizes PI to make a separate peace. Congress appropriates 20 million to repatriate us through Geneva.[6]

Meanwhile, Gen. Moore still in tunnel. I got Pvt. Derr detailed as chauffeur, among 5, this afternoon, to his delight. Couldn't get Pvt. Welch on.

Wednesday, 20 May 1942

1.00 haircut.

Wind storm last night bothered us a bit—but no rain. However there was a better breeze than usual this morning. So I loitered at our shack after breakfast until 9:00 or so. To latrine twice, the second trip being very successful. Dentist painted my mouth. To HQ and hung around there most of day. Rode Capt. Strong about latrines at end of camp. Schenck is doing well with his latrines—but couldn't help me out with extra toilet paper this morning.

Through Bonham, put Capt. Gallup[7] in charge of renovating the roofs of big garage, to make it safe and more weatherproof.

We sent out work details of about 3000 men this morning. The new barracks for Japs on hill overlooking our camp is getting siding. They say 8 *days* rations will be brought to camp today—which is impossible—but they may have to do us 8 days.

Corporal Anderson repeated his kindness of yesterday and brought me a big cup of hot tea. A lifesaver if there ever was one.

They sent out a detail of *2000* men to rustle rations but part came back by truck and there is said to have been much pilfering. About sundown they started issuing to Groups—2 days rations each and also put remainder of food under cover. I donated my dinner to the others. We also filled out a questionnaire—'officers'—for the Japanese.

Rumors of a big naval battle north of Australia, in which Allies badly defeated Japanese navy.

The flies—the flies—the flies! I have a bad cold and had to don very heavy sweater upon turning in tonight.

Got some cooking utensils for Capt. McCarthy's outfit. Badly needed. Tonight there was lots of lightning but our hopes for rain were in vain. I am still trying to get to Topside to see my stuff. No razor blades, no matches. Filipinos at wharf are selling mangoes and papayas to U.S. people for P1.00 each! Barbers charge P1.00 instead of 40¢ for a haircut.

I've got a rotten cold. Doctoring it with aspirin.

After feverish activity for days in building a barracks for our guard on the bluff overlooking our camp, last night the work order was cancelled, which causes us to hope that we may be moved out soon.

Thursday, 21 May 1942

Another day. Coffee and some rice for breakfast. Relieved Col. Teague SC[8] summarily for inefficient handling of casual officers group and put Col. Foster in charge. Took up cases of 2 thieves No. 477 with Elmes and No. 7354 with Col. Ward who is down and out in his CP. Cpl. Anderson repeated his production of a cup of hot tea. Fine.

Got another broadside of whimpers from Maj. Pyzick USMC,[9] an interpreter and I went around and showed it to all group masters and urged them to strain every nerve to perform miracles if necessary to comply with Japanese demands for work details, exemplary behavior, non-stealing of food, etc.

Rest of day per routine. At gate, at evening, saw men on work details bringing in food, etc.

In evening was invited by Japs as their guests at amateur entertainment. Had tea, milk, cake and some doughy Jap patties. Tried to get Edison and Julian to come and perform for one of the splendid prizes of food—but they arrived too late. Returned to sultry camp after dark and loafed naked (like the others) until bedtime about 8:30. Much lightning but no rain.

Cooper brings in rumors from Jap sergeant that, after 3 nights in camp we will move to Manila!

Am last night on Corregidor.

Friday, 22 May 1942

This morning our shack was surprisingly clear of flies, so I hung around there for a long time. Only 2 packs of cigarettes left. This day was more or less like those preceding it: hot and breathless in this sheltered cove, probably the worst possible place for a Concentration Camp. Everybody broiling in the sun. Colin hates to walk on the concrete, it is so hot to his feet. They still have stopped all work upon the guard barracks up on the overlooking hill, which strengthens our belief that we will move soon.

The highlights of each day are the swims at dawn and dusk—in spite of the floating dung from Filipinos. A slow nightmare of glaring heat and myriads of flies that give us no rest except at night. Hurriedly turning out work details of hundreds of men to fill the insatiable demands of the Japanese—many of whom present their demands at the Sentry Gate instead of coming to Camp HQ where we have been trying to centralize their work. As I walk about the Camp, inspecting the festering latrines, etc. I stagger with weakness, and yet I can hardly force myself to eat. Our food supplies are rapidly shrinking and the Japanese evidently expect us to live upon practically nothing. The 2-days ration, issued last night, were practically nothing.

However we are better off than the Filipinos, who have been deprived of all rations for practically 3 days, as a punishment for their stealing of food when their ration detail returned. The white troops escaped because a Capt. Wood, at the tail of our column, succeeded in concealing the fact that some of our men had pilfered from the cases.

The hospital continues to kick patients out and send them to "duty" which they are physically incapable of performing—and they have been sending all these men to my group. I shudder to think what will happen to those men if we have to move. I have protested to Col. Cooper[10] that these men arrive about dusk, too late to find a place to sleep, and oftentime unfed, but he continues to do it.

At about 9:00 P.M., just as we were turning in, came an urgent call for all group masters and vice masters to report to Camp HQ at once so Edison and I dressed and went. Then the heavens opened and the rain poured down for hours, flooding the garage and grounds and drenching everybody. Got a good drink of water by holding a canteen cup under one of the cataracts for a few minutes.

Maj. Pyzick, the Med, soon appeared and, by aid of a flashlight on the floor, gave us the dope: all hands are to move out of Camp at 9:00 A.M. tomorrow, before which the entire camp must be dismantled and cleaned up, latrines filled! A total of 130 specialists, wire men, etc. to be found and left behind. The group masters went into a huddle to arrange details—the last group to leave being responsible for filling latrines. Pyzick said OK for groups to leave at 20' intervals, but next morning he swore he never said it, and insisted everybody be ready to march at 9:00 an obvious impossibility.

We sent warning orders to our units because all of this necessitated a very early chow. So, as Edison and I walked back to our shack, about midnight, the whole camp was aglow with smoky cooking fires. Upon arriving at our shack (the rain having stopped by this time) we found our side of the shack drowned out. Our neighbors had a roof composed partly of a shelter-half on our side. When this caught a lot of rain and bellied down, the bastards pushed up on it and emptied the whole works into our shack, most of it into my clothing roll where it not only ruined my stuff with mud and water, but also added about 20 pounds to its weight.

Donned my heavy Army sweater and curled up on my blanket in an effort to get a little sleep before dawn. Edison was chilled to the bone. The blokes on the east side of our shack had avoided the deluge, but they had neglected to pull our stuff out of the mud and water.

All of this is another example of Japanese hazing. They could either have given us more warning of the move, or arranged to move us day *after* tomorrow, or moved out the Filipinos first. But no, they have to move *everybody* at a moment's notice.

Superimposed on our requirements was the order that all groups be *immediately* equalized in strength—as if that would increase any boat's capacity. We arranged that my small Group 3 would be increased, tomorrow, by attaching to me 2 full companies from Groups 1, 2 and 4 plus bringing me up to the average strength of about 830. (Instead of having 10,000 prisoners in Camp, there appears to be about 6800 Americans plus about 700 officers and some 4,000 Filipinos.)

Departure from 92d Garage Area.

Saturday, 23 May 1942

Dawn in a dismal camp full of mud puddles and everybody wet. We fed after a fashion and then started dismantling the improvised shelters that composed the Camp. Men going by with poor crumpled sheets of corrugated iron on their heads, to stack them along the pipeline; others with wooden poles, etc. Gradually a space just inside the sentry gate was cleared so the first group could form.

In our shack we weeded out our belongings, for the Japs had warned us to make our bundles as light as possible. I discarded my black bag and most of its contents, including my diary for 1941 (with a wrench). Lt. Simpson[11] thought he could manage it and put most of my discards in one of his 2 bags (but later had to discard and abandon them). Edison gave to Simpson his fine Val pack and put its contents into a blanket roll. I thought my clothing roll was not too heavy for me to tote—but I was to learn better, later on.

Group 1 moved out the gate promptly at 9:00 A.M. The Japs called me over to HQ to demand why my group was not reorganized at new equalized strength, and Pyzick would not listen to my explanation: that the strengths of my added units were unknown, etc. Group 2 moved out and then, through Edison's efficient work, we started my Group 3 out. Just then Colin disappeared, after another dog, and I had to pull out without him. This was for the best as subsequent events proved.

There were many patients in our sick bay in the garage, but all of the doctors on duty there simply packed up and abandoned them! Ausmus' group improvised litters and evacuated some 6 or so to Malinta Tunnel but the Jap sentry there repulsed them and made them double-time to rejoin the column. However, at the far end, some Navy doctor got them admitted to our Malinta hospital. But no thanks to the doctor who first abandoned them.

We took the shortcut up the hill, and I was winded at the top. We kept well up behind the tail of the 2d group with frequent rests, so we got along all right until we reached Queen Tunnel when the Jap sentries became abusive because we were not tightly closed up and by threatened clubbings, made us double-time under our loads. We were all herded like ants onto the stonepiles which lined the beach east of the south wharf and made to sit there in the broiling sun, to await the transports which did not arrive until some hours later. Meanwhile I draped my towel over my takes [private parts] and kept as quiet as possible. The wharf was well filled with 50-lb. bags of flour (gift of Red Cross) and other foods—a part of the stream being shipped out by the Japanese.

At last the order came for all "casual officers" to move out onto the wharf where they boarded launches, some of which were extremely tippy, and were transported out to the waiting ships. Then came Group 2, then Group 1 and then my Group 3. By this time the Japs were loading 2 or 3 transports[12] simultaneously and so the groups became split among various ships and, as usual, things got hopelessly balled up. The Japs have a faculty for it. Edison finally came aboard and we also had McCarthy. Upon arriving aboard our ship I didn't realize that the officers were supposed to stay on upper deck forward, so I obeyed indications of a Jap and led the way aft and down the after hatch. Here I found myself in a close, non-ventilated sort of a pen, with wide shelves across the after part. 2 wind sails above led a breeze below but only for the benefit of some of the crew. I crawled in past a couple of sailors and stretched out on the boards, but the close foul air made me giddy so I struggled up on deck and never dared go below again. Two soldiers made room for me near the after winches, giving me a musette bag for a back rest and tried hard and unselfishly to make me comfortable.

The loading of our ship was soon finished but the prisoners kept coming around Malinta Hill from our old camp all day long and, maybe, far into the night. Anyway our ship stayed immovable while the day waned and night came on. Conditions being unbearable below, the deck became a solid mass of men. They even climbed up on the booms and made their beds there. I dozed and dozed. When it rained, I stripped rather than try to keep dry by going below. Finally a soldier lent me a sopping blanket. I spread it over some prickly steel cables and, curling up, managed to get a little sleep. A wonder I didn't catch pneumonia.

All night long there was a long line of men with dysentery waiting their turn at the "heads." They slept where and when they could. Hardly room to move on deck.

We had a medical detachment of 20 doctors, etc. who were in line all day, near the pier to accompany our troops but, when it came their turn to go aboard, the Japs chased them away and back to Malinta Hospital! Onboard our ship the Jap order was issued: "Take off all Red Cross brassards. No medical personnel is supposed to be aboard." Why? Just another case of punishment?

Notes

1. John M. Wright, Jr., *Captured on Corregidor: Diary of American POW in World War II* (Jefferson, North Carolina: McFarland & Company, 1989), 8, 9.

2. Chunn, 55. This was probably Warrant Officer Green, who was in administrative charge of rations on Corregidor for Bunker. Later he was interned at Cabanatuan with Colonel Rutherford.

3. *Register,* 360. Lt. Col. Edward Carl Engelhart had been the assistant G2 of the Philippine Island Department and USAFFE. During the siege and subsequent imprisonment, he was wounded six times. Chunn, 109. Speaking Japanese fluently, he was made one of the prisoners' interpreters; he, too, ended up in Cabanatuan.

4. Chunn, 156. This was probably an Air Corps officer named Lieutenant Thompson, who was later interned at Cabanatuan. He was punished there for not stopping a fellow prisoner from escaping.

5. This was John M. Wright, Jr., who in 1945 got freedom and subsequently retired as a lieutenant general in 1972.

6. Again, Bunker classifies rumors correctly; all of these were wild.

7. Chunn, 167. This was probably Capt. Brewster Gallup, who was also interned at Cabanatuan.

8. Wainwright, 61. Colonel "Tiger" Teague of the Signal Corps had been Wainwright's signal officer on Corregidor. He later joined Wainwright in a prison camp in Manchuria.

9. Chunn, 56. Maj. Frank B. Pyzick, USMC, was later put into prison at Cabanatuan, where he along with a few others was awarded "a diploma and cigarettes for their 'cooperation with the Japanese'!"

10. Wainwright, 101, 109. This was Corregidor's surgeon.

11. *Register,* 488. This was Lt. Harry Thompson Simpson, Jr., who had been one of Bunker's lieutenants in the 59th CA. He was repatriated at the end of the war.

12. McCoy and Mellnik, 22. There were actually three of these merchant ships, which originally had been designed for only twelve passengers. Now there were nearly 4,000 prisoners crowded into each of them.

Sunday, 24 May 1942

To Parinaqua, Bilibid and Pasay.

Along toward dawn the ship got under way and headed toward Manila. I gazed on Corregidor with mixed feelings. Most of us said we wanted to never see those desolate ruins again. Our crowded deck crawled with life. There was hot drinking water available and Pvt. Robinson made me some tea and another soldier gave me some Vienna sausages.

The ship was slow. Another freighter, with 2 AA guns forward, passed us and steamed toward Pier 7. We sheered right, toward Parinaqua¹ and anchored. Meanwhile, with all deck space jammed, crazy Pyzick said the Japs wanted us to form in order of Groups and debark in that order! A manifest impossibility. Now they brought "invasion boats" (landing boats) alongside, and our men tumbled aboard via a gangway and a Jacob's ladder on port side forward and another Jacob's ladder on starboard side aft. These boats ride with bow out of water and are quite fast. The scow bow lets down to form a ramp.

On nearing shore, near the Parinaqua beach, we were all forced overboard into water chest-deep, and waded shore with our stuff on our backs. We still didn't know our destination. We formed on the beach, but groups were so mixed up that we could only form in a column of fours, regardless of Groups. As we landed, we could see long columns of our predecessors moving south along the beach to the main road. The whole bunch was, unfortunately, guarded by cavalry not infantry.

After a short time, 1000 or so of us were counted off and moved out to the highway, the extension to Dewey Boulevard and sat down there until the gang ahead of us moved out in the broiling heat for it must have been nearly noon by now. I shouldered my clothing roll and started, and my burden did not seem excessive at this time. The tar on the pavement stuck to our shoes which were, of course, wet on our feet, making blisters.

Gen. Moore luckily was landed on dry land with all of his baggage and was transported with said baggage to our destination.

As we marched along we could see Filipino curiosity seekers being kept back by Jap sentries. Many grinned at us, but whether in derision or otherwise we could not tell. Downtown, more people lined the streets, but were very quiet.

My load, water soaked as it was, kept getting heavier and heavier, and then Pvt. della Marva and Julian relieved me of it and carried it for me for some hundreds of yards. Three soldiers also took turns at it—and I offered one of them, a husky-looking man, P20 if he would carry it the rest of the way. He refused the offer but spoke cheerily of getting the bundle to our destination. I shouldered the load again and toted it to our first stop, which was probably near the Admiral Hotel. Here some of us got drinks of water. I interviewed the Jap officer in charge of our bunch, pointing to my white stubble of beard and motioning that I wanted to be picked up in the Red Cross truck that was patrolling the column. He roughly repulsed me, barking "Sit down."

Our stop was for only a few minutes and then we started again. I knew now that I could never carry that clothing roll much farther, so I just left it where I'd dropped it and had no time to remove anything from it. So I stepped off, bereft of every single article of worldly goods except what I had on my person!

Even so, lightened, I found the going tougher and tougher. As far as you could see, ahead, the prisoners were plodding along, with no sign of a stop for rest. We marched to the Elks Club, turned right in front of the Bay View, then slanted left past City Hall to Post Office, over the bridge and onto either Rizal or Quezon Blvd. all this without a rest. I was staggering by this time, and soon fell down in a daze. The Jap guards came and prodded me up and on a bit, but I couldn't make it. They gave me a gallon bottle, empty, and a gas mask case and urged me on. After standing their persecution all I could, I turned on them, tore open my shirt and, with a melodramatic gesture, indicated them to go ahead and shoot and be damned to them. Then they put me through some sort of test (I was dazed and forget what it was) to see if I meant what I said, and then they did a queer thing. They made me kneel and raise my hands over my head and lean backward. Then they made me lie down on the strip of ground in the middle of the boulevard and brought *ice* and put it on my head and chest. They hailed one truck which passed us up. At one time I thought the guards were leading me off into a back street to shoot me, as they are said to have done with 3 officers in Bataan on their march to San Fernando—when they fell out. But instead, they were very kind, and kept ice on my head and solar plexus. (How I enjoyed gnawing hunks off the ice and swallowing them!) Later, they led me across to the sidewalk and I lay there for a long time until the sentry stopped a light pick-up truck and loaded me into it. As I lay there, before starting off, a rock rattled into the truck and hit me on the rebound! I wondered if this was a sample of the feeling the Filipinos have for us now.

The truck took me to the old Bilibid Prison, which had been the destination of the Corregidor prisoners all the time, and here they helped me into Bldg. 13 where I found Gen. Moore and his aide, Brown,[2] also Simpson and Verde of the 59th. Everybody was most kind. They laid me on Brown's immaculate bed and took my dripping clothes off, and I rested a space and told my story to Moore, who held my hand!

Col. Short, the HD artillery engineer was in a very bad way and was to be moved to "Pasay Hospital" immediately.[3] Gen Moore and staff were also to go there and he said something about taking me there as a member of his staff. Dentist Cornbloom took the bull by the horns and ordered Col. G. W. Hirsch[4] and me into the same truck with Short and, after the usual backing and filling, we started off, three of us on stretchers in the bottom of a truck, and drove out to the Pasay Elementary School, which was being operated as a small hospital by the Navy medicos who had been run out of Santa Scholastica after their Cavite Hospital had been bombed out.

Now I first made the acquaintance of Pvt. Jackson Newheart, whom Gen. Moore had detailed as my orderly! He rode the truck with me and made me stiff bay rum en route! On arriving at the hospital, my face and eyes being covered all the time, they had to tilt us nearly out of our stretchers to get us around a sharp corner. They put Col. Hirsch and me into Room 2 by ourselves and here we stayed as long as we remained here. No, they put Col. Short in the same room with us, but he was in a coma. Poor fellow: he always had a fussy appetite, had been eating very little, and the march from Parinaqua had been too much for him and he collapsed at the end of the march. They gave him a saline and dextrose infusion during the night but said he probably couldn't last. His hands looked like a bird's claws.

They shoved my stretcher in a corner of the room and Pvt. Jackson did what he could to make me comfortable. Many of the Navy personnel did their marvelous best likewise. One Major A.J. Day of the 61st Division showed up and it developed that he is a nephew of the Day whom I had with me at New Orleans during the World War I. He got busy with a bang when I told him, in answer to his question, that I had not eaten since morning—and barely then—and I hoped there would be some fruit available. When he produced a Del Monte can of "fruits for salads" I was pleased as punch. "Eat it slowly" said Jackson. Then he fed me a can of hot onion soup, which was delicious. They may have also given me some other good food, I dunno—but, not knowing the conditions, I asked if I could have a drop of milk, for I had been craving it for weeks—and durned if they didn't give me a whole can of it to drink—and it was the best drink I *ever* had.

There was a store of clothing on hand, so they undressed me and gave me a clean pair of drawers and an undershirt, and I slept in those habitually thereafter. Jackson rustled around to their clothing stocks and outfitted me with another suit of khaki, several drawers, shirts, socks, handkerchiefs, bath and face towels, etc. so that now I am in good shape, from that viewpoint. They even got me a mattress, thin to be sure, but still a mattress.

Overcome by curiosity, I got 2 men to support me while I walked to the office on the other side of our compound and weighed myself on their portable scales. I knew I had lost a lot of weight but I was thunderstruck to see that I weighed only 176 pounds! And my training weight, as a cadet, was 186. That shows I've lost about 44 pounds or so, since the war began!

* * *

Monday, 25 May 1942

Now follows about a week during which I stayed in this Pasay Hospital under the fine care of the Navy party which was operating it. Col. Hirsch OD and I continued to have Room 2 to ourselves—that is after poor Col. Short died at about 11 this morning.[5] So far as I know, he never regained consciousness. An Army chaplain conducted services over his body and his brother officers attended, Gen. Moore, Cottrell, etc.

Mosquitos are bad here and Hirsch had no mosquito bar, so last night they moved our stretchers close together and spread one bar over the both of us, and it worked well. My bar was a loan from the Navy personnel and I later bought a double bar for P6.00 when I had to give it back. Meanwhile Col. Hirsch and Pvt. Jackson bought single bars and had to pay P10 apiece.

After my sumptuous feed of last night I was rudely jolted awake to realities by the morning meal, which consisted of a messpan full of rice (polished) swimming in a watery decoction of a few tiny onions. Little did I realize that I should have been especially thankful for the onions, for many was the day to follow when the menu would be rice and, nothing but rice. The prospect looks mighty bleak: a solid rice diet until the end of the war! If rice only built a little bit of muscle or pep, it wouldn't be so bad, but to be confronted with an endless vista of nauseous rice!

This Pasay school is on "Park Ave." near where you turn off the Pasay road to go to Ft. McKinley. It is built in a hollow square, and an interior veranda lines the inside about 5′ wide. The central patio is wholly enclosed and hence quite breezeless. The shell windows are nailed shut, but there are openings under the eaves, closed by barbed wire, so there is a modicum of air. Filipino prisoners occupied our side for some weeks, and the bed bugs are plentiful. I left a clean teacup on the floor one night and in the morning there were 5 husky bedbugs in it!

There is a shower in the middle of the patio which we are permitted to use for an hour morning, noon, and night. I had to pass it up for the first few days, and Jackson washed me off. He took very good care of Hirsch and me but he is fresh for a soldier and I find it hard to believe him when he says he won P5000 one night from some Colonels at Corregidor.

All hands concur in advising me not to get well too fast, so I have Jackson help me about.

Mr. Gooding does some outside buying through a Jap comprador and sells to us at a profit of 10%. This goes to pay for wastage, and to get foods for men who have no money. It also buys a vegetable occasionally to go into a soup, with our rice. We even had a bit of carabao gristle for one meal, but that was a rare treat.

All except patients are lined up in the patio in bunches three times a day and counted. This is called "bango." Patients are counted in their rooms.

There is a piano in the next room. One officer plays well on it, but when the Jap guards hammer on it by the hour, the effect is not so restful.

Tech. Sgt. Paulk, Air corps, touched me for P10 so he could lay in a stock of food (?). I doubt that I get it back. He sure got punishment from the Japs for trying to pass himself off as a mining engineer. They told him to identify a display of rocks, at Jai Alai and, when he failed, mauled him well and put him in a solitary dungeon in Ft. Santiago on bread and water for days.

Saturday, 30 May 1942

Today the whole outfit at Pasay moved to Bilibid Prison. The usual confusion which accompanies our moves under Jap control was present. We packed up right after breakfast but it was afternoon before we left and so our galley gang fixed up some rice—with a repulsive thin onion soup to go with it and we partook of that. I was astounded to see the huge wardrobe trunks, steamer trunks, footlockers, overgrown suitcases, etc. that the Navy personnel of the hospital had with them. Of course they were lucky in having been able to keep these belongings from the start—having always moved by truck and never by marching.

I bandaged my foot in a towel, to make it look as bad as possible and all of us sat around on the front lawn and front porch while the three trucks loaded and pulled out for Bilibid, and repeated the operation. Then they returned again and all of us piled aboard the last truck—patients and all, and drove to Bilibid. Saw no damage in the city except one burned place on south shore of the Pasig. Drove through Bilibid to a new 2-story building in back and there unloaded. En route we saw 2 barrows carabao meat, which raised our hopes and not in vain, as we later found out.

Hirsch and I stayed outside, hoping to be put with the hospital but, instead, they ran all of us into the east half of 2d floor with all other colonels of Army and captains of Navy. Many had already settled their beds on the concrete floor, so I settled where I could and Jackson rigged a place for my mosquito bar, etc. under a scaffold. Held our usual "bango" or muster.

For chow there was, of course, the inevitable rice—but also a soup containing lots of petahay and vegetables. Col. Howard, 4th Marines, was his usual hoggish self by scooping out 4 helpings of these and the last men in line got nothing but clear soup. They say he is always that way.

This building has been seriously damaged by the Japanese tearing out all iron work. Bars have even been torn from the windows, thus breaking them out and leaving them open to driving rains. The roof also leaks at seams in the concrete.

After we turned in, a heavy rain came up and, seeping from an adjacent E1, flooded our floor. I escaped in time, rolled up my bedding and retired to a high spot where I sat up with Chet Elmes most of the night. Some few, lucky ones had cots but I had none until the next morning when a Tech. Sgt., Air Corps, gave me one—partial payment, I guess, for the P10 he touched me for while we were at Pasay.

Here I met the Vet. Col. Worthington who, in Bataan, sold 6 cartons of ciga rettes for P500! And he had the nerve to tell me about Besson[6] and Sainte[7] (CE) selling his mess cocoa to Filipinos at excessive prices!

Here I also began to hear about the Army doctors from Bataan, who had been in charge of a sort of hospital here in Bilibid and their unethical behavior. They would refuse to treat their patients unless paid for it; they sold government drugs and medicines at excessive prices, and demanded food, also, as payment for drugs or services. Capt. Waid, 60th CA, a California reserve officer, had bad pneumonia but they diagnosed it as malaria; paid no attention to him. I talked with a civilian who vouched for this as he alone helped him. One little captain worked like a dog but he was the only medical doctor or attendant who did. That is general estimate. His name was Blum[8] and he worked ceaselessly.

As we were waiting at Pasay, to leave for Bilibid, a chorus of young voices came from a nearby house, with piano accompaniment, in a series of American songs such as school children sing. They may have done it for our benefit or it may have been a regular session of this Pasay school. The newspapers say the elementary schools will open on June 1st which may be one reason why we are moving out.

Sunday, 31 May 1942

It was mostly a draggly looking bunch that turned out this morning. I dreaded the job, but even with my infected foot I had to patronize the long roofed-over straddle trench. Breakfast was a treat because there was a weak soup with a crumb or two of carabao, with our rice. Again Col. Howard dipped in twice after Hilton had dished him out his ration! They told me this morning that they are transferring Col. Hirsch and me over to the hospital and sure enough, about noon some Navy medical corps men came over after us. I piled all my stuff onto my cot and moved that way. They met us at SOQ (sick officers quarters) and put Hirsch and me in the best place—at one end near the open door. We were the only full colonels in this gang of sick officers, fortunately. We have much better air circulation than the other patients do. It is simply grand to have a real washbowl and water closet available. In general our place looks like this of reinforced concrete with barred windows reaching to the floor. The lowest third is boarded shut but each of the upper two thirds is composed of a flap door, hinged at the top, usually shoved open but can be shut in typhoons. It is said to be the best building in the prison. The Navy gangs are working hard to put it in the best shape.

This morning I went on the warpath about my foot. The Navy doctor has been perfunctorily slapping another Band Aid on it every day and it has been getting steadily worse—now being well infected. So I demanded a bread poultice or something like that. Capt. Davis prescribed hot water soaking and I went to the old dispensary with that idea. The darn doctor tried to put me off with an echthyol dressing but I made them give me a good soaking before we moved over to the hospital. Wall of this dispensary is composed of Naval officers' trunks.

It was grand to get into the hospital, being the most comfortable looking set up we've seen yet. Jackson fixed some portable catch-alls on the wire netting partition at the head of our beds, rigged our mosquito bars and we were all set.

Monday, 1 June 1942

We got very short rations this morning: ⅓ of a 5 gallon can of rice and ¼ can of onion soup for 25 people! Subsequent events prove that this mess practically never has anything but straight polished rice—and for the first 2–3 days, very little of that. We are living, so Ausmus declares, on less than the regular ration of the Jap soldier—and I believe him. Already I can see that this damn rice is putting fat on my belly—but no pep in me or strength in my muscles. Shaved my 3-weeks beard and it was hell!

Today Ausmus checked in, a very sick man with pneumonia. He has no cot, only a blanket. The Pharmacist's mate rustled him a mattress and Ausmus lay on my bed and Hirsch's until they could convert Jackson's hammock bed into a boarded bedstead. Jackson had lashed the hammock into a low frame for his last night's bed and slept there.

Today Mr. Gooding, who has been put in charge, took Jackson away from Hirsch and me with profuse apologies and will use him in his office.

Capt. Waid died today. I believe his death was principally attributable to the neglect of our Army medicos and this opinion is based upon common report from men who were near him and tried to help him. There was a heavy shower this afternoon and it was a treat to go out in it, for the benefit of my prickly heat.

Tuesday, 2 June 1942

Another uneventful day. In the evening Gen. Moore and others of their group came over to say goodbye because they have been told to be ready, after midnight, to move out at 10 minutes notice. We hear that 5 colonels from this group will join us here in the hospital.

Wednesday, 3 June 1942

This morning Gen. Moore plus Army colonels and Navy captains left—possibly going to Tarlac or Camp Ord by bus all the way. Cols. Crews, Atkinson[9] and 3 others checked in this afternoon and people were moved out of our cage into the next building to make room for them, Hirsch and I undisturbed. I am getting "Guam blisters" now—but not so bad as Crews is.

This morning we saw 45 Jap bombers flying in a generally south direction. A pursuit pilot did some good stunts over towards waterfront. There are about 500 prisoners here; most of them to form work parties for the Japs at various points. We hear that about 30 Army nurses from Corregidor are coming here but most of us hope it isn't so. We get absolutely no news of the outside world here and even the soup additives to our rice are said to be clandestine: the Japs expect us to live on about a pound of straight rice a day and nothing else. What a hell of a prospect. This noon, however, we got a cup full of alleged soup.

Jackson made us a cribbage board today and Hirsch and I started playing the game with his very aged deck of cards. He wallops me almost continuously.

We all contributed pesos to start a "store"—I gave P10. They got their first stock in tonight but deliveries were to elsewhere and not to us.

Thursday, 4 June 1942

Today our alleged store opened, but it was slow tedious work to pass up the line and get waited on. And the prices! Here is my order: 3 duck eggs 24¢, 2 corned beef, small $1.80, 3 evaporated milk 2.80, 1 bean soup, Campbell's 65¢, 1 catsup 70¢. Jackson is now working for Gooding and can't be bothered with me anymore.

Most of the patients have cut out wooden clogs for themselves and go around in merely shorts or underwear.

My prickly heat has developed into Guam blisters—pustules the size of a pea which pop out on your hide, usually, in clusters. Crews has them bad on his legs. Ausmus says that Capt. Petries' body was covered with them, and yet he could get no medical attention and had to go to Cabanatuan with the rest.

Friday/Saturday, 5–6 June 1942

Nothing unusual. Straight rice for three or four straight days and our purchases at our "store" are the only things that let us relieve the deadly monotony of diet.

We have a "bango" (muster) at about 6:45–7:00 A.M. Then a corps man goes over to the kitchen and comes back with a 5-gallon oil can full of rice. At breakfast this is usually "luboo" or very wet, soupy rice. For other meals it is drier—but almost invariably the polished kind. I am trying to take shower-baths morning and evening. We pass the mornings aimlessly. Toward noon there is another bango and another cup of rice. Our third dose of rice arrives at any time in the late afternoon, with the third bango about 6:00 or 6:30. The only timepiece is our small hospital clock, almost a pocket Ben. The salt-water ruined my Ingersoll and everybody else had their watches stolen by the Japanese. So time means very little to us. There is nothing to do and very little to read. I have Barrow's *History of the Philippines,* but it is boring and I wish for some of my own lost books. What a lot of work I could do on my OPUS on the Bunker genealogy if—and to think of my 40 years work in that subject destroyed! Why *didn't* I send everything back with Landon.

I acquired a Gem razor and a few blades at the Pasay Hospital and, in order to make them last, I am shaving only every other morning. It is practically impossible to buy *anything*—which seems queer to us. The Japs wink at our buying a few articles of food through their selected middleman (and probably get their rake off) but they pretend it is not being done, and we carefully conceal food and all other extraneous articles during the bango inspections. Evidently it would be fantastic to hope to buy a pair of shoes or any article of clothing.

The Japanese have renamed Dewey Blvd. and call it "Heiwa" Blvd. "Heiwa" means "Peace" in Japanese.

Sunday, 7 June 1942

Today we beat the rice game a bit: for the noon meal Hirsch and I opened our can of pork and beans and added it to our rice. And for the evening meal somebody donated a bucket of boiled mongo beans. These were the highlights of an otherwise eventless day.

They have started to build a mess shack, just across the road against the wall, but work has stopped for 2 days because of changing guards checking and transferring tools.

Our store is lagging—to be sure, they let me buy 3 more duck eggs and another can of milk, but they have never got any bananas and very few mangos, dammit. And we do need fruit so badly! The "groups" of enlisted men apply for their full quota and then, as some of them don't eat mangos, one man gets many. I heard one soldier say he got 8 out of the last lot, when we only got one apiece.

Tonight another stock for our store arrived, but it was mostly delivered elsewhere, though Jackson staggered in with some candy. I slept for a while and then joined Weisblat and others outside, after rousing Ausmus out of a nightmare, Ausmus is recovering from his pneumonia.

Monday, 8 June 1942

Paid a soldier P1.00 for laundry work well done. My foot not so well this morning; more pus seepage, but my skin blisters seem to be improving. Got my shower and sunbathed the foot. Brow-beat Hirsch into making us a drink of hot cocoa—and it was fine.

Our lone fly trap doesn't catch many, but we now have some fly swatters, the damn flies are still a great pest in spite of the improvement of closing up several open latrines. But they are nothing when compared to those at Corregidor Camp.

Tuesday, 9 June 1942

This morning there was a heavy rain just after bango and I went out in it—for the benefit of my prickly heat—and incidentally fixed a new flooring for our shower-bath. Played Hirsch a cribbage game but my lousy luck is getting boring, so I quit in disgust. We placed a new order with our alleged store. Much carpenter activity on our mess shack. Sun came out about 11:00.

This evening I got a treat by opening a can of corn beef and eating most of it raw as is.

A noisy evening, too much conversation by everybody, inside and out of the room. Damn office kept chattering until 1:00 A.M.!

Wednesday, 10 June 1942

For breakfast: mixed the rest of the corn beef with my rice and made out very well. Had soup at all 3 meals! Hirsch mixed us up a very good cup of cocoa. Passed away the time by again starting an inventory of my property which is "lost through enemy action." While I was doing this, Hirsch et als. used my table for bridge. Tonight at some unknown time I awoke and was going to the rear where Mr. Gooding beckoned me to his office and gave me a thimbleful of whisky!

Thursday, 11 June 1942

Today a big order of boodle[10] was brought in and everything was cluttered up in our bedroom all P.M. Also they installed a big new cupboard. Soup at all meals. Ate parts of two (spoiled) gratis mangos, plus an egg, 1 good mango and a cup of cocoa. Beat Hirsch at morning and noon cribbage sessions, he won at night. I stayed up til midnight reading an amateurish novel—"The Ready Blade." Talked long with Cornbloom re: cameras.

Friday, 12 June 1942

Lots of wild "scuttle-butt" floating around today: that our Alaska air bases are working, 24 hours a day, at bombing Japan and supplying our Chinese bases; that the Japs are being pushed off the Burma Road and along the Malay Peninsula toward Singapore; that the Japs lost over 20 vessels in a battle in the Sulu Sea; that we've landed 180,000 troops in Mindanao; that Lloyds of London is offering 40–1 that the European part of the war will be over in 15 days; that 40–50 Jap ships have been sunk by our subs while leaving Manila Bay! If only one of them were true![11]

Friday (continued)

Blanket P4.00.

This morning they moved Hirsch and several others over to the next building, which they call the "convalescent ward." It was partially prepared for the use of the 30 Corregidor nurses who, rumor persists, are coming. They also say a total of 600 patients and all are coming from there.

After each meal, now, Hirsch puts drops in my eyes, and then we play crib-bage—best 2 out of 3.

Today they resumed work on our galley and got the roof-trusses installed and some corrugated iron on hand. Old shower out of business. I got a shower in convalescent ward but couldn't get foot dressed until P.M. Bought an OD blanket for P4.00 and gave Guthrie back the one he had donated. Also changed my bed location and rigged up a rising and falling tackle for my mosquito bar.

The bearded boy, after 3 tries, boiled an egg for me.

Saturday, 13 June 1942

Rained hard at 1:00 A.M. but what awoke me was the gabble of . . . Weisblatt, the UP man. Had to lower window on my side. Found that the blanket which I bought yesterday is so filthy I couldn't use it until washed and, though I paid only P4.00 for the whole blanket, it will cost me P1.50 to have it washed!

Another day of prison routine: shower, shave, losing at cribbage. They are clearing everybody out of the big building beyond the wall where we stayed first. Among those who left suddenly was the officer in charge of the mess! Feverish work all day on our new galley, showers, etc. Our evening rice came from the new galley but it was poorly cooked, soggy, and short of quantity. However, as everybody seems to have "outside" food, the lack was unnoticed.

Bought a box of 50 cigars for P4. Also, just about "lights out," I mixed a couple of raw duck eggs with some milk and sugar and found the result not at all bad. Read "Mr. Tutt Comes Home."

Sunday, 14 June 1942

Rained last night and day dawned overcast. Finished Mr. Tutt before reveille. The big sailor is troubled with urinary incontinence a common trait of beri-beri. Most of our patients are that way.

Rumor hath it that the generals and colonels went, not to Camp Ord at Tarlac but to the San Miguel Sugar Estates.[12]

Our 200 men did not leave as slated and again tonight they all cluttered up the store. Continued rainy and overcast all day and I played cribbage (losing) and worked on inventory of my stuff.

Monday, 15 June 1942

Bright and sunny today. Today the Japs ordered all spoons turned in! How the hell are we expected to eat? Shaved and expended one of my precious blades. Shower in our new bathhouse. Cut a spoon out of a tin can. But they returned our spoons after making us sign up for them. Today had soup at all meals except noon. The soup is the dividend from our store—as far as the Japs are concerned we feed on straight rice—that is all they furnish us! This afternoon we had violin and guitar music.

We were also inspected by the general in charge of all prisons, etc., the immediate superior of Capt. Kashimoto, who is in charge of the prisons about Manila. They say Kashimoto twice represented Japan at the Olympics in judo wrestling, that he is high class Japanese and talks English well. Changed my P500 bill.

Tuesday, 16 June 1942

Overcast dawn. Bitterness and contempt of MacArthur seems to be universal among the officers in this Camp—also contempt for his staff. We try hard to be optimistic and think that our tour of this dog's life will be a short one but, if Mac's staff is now blundering as it did at Corregidor, then our prospects (and those of the U.S. and England in the Far East) are dismal indeed. And every day is so precious to me; I haven't so many of them left, at my age, and I begrudge every one that continues my separation from Landon. I wonder if she ever received those handkerchiefs that I sent her from the Little Home Shop, last December?

My only amusement is to endure almost continuous defeat by all comers at cribbage; and to continue compiling the list of my "property destroyed by enemy action." I find this especially difficult as regards my books: I had so many that I can't remember them all.

Tonight another boodle order is coming in, and we are hoping to get plenty of mangoes plus bananas and pineapples.

Paid P1.50 for having my blanket washed, but it was a good job and worth it. The soldier said he had to use 3 bars of soap.

Later

They tell some horrible tales of what happened to our forces when Bataan fell. Our men were force-marched to San Fernando. Some say it took 5 days and others say as high as nine days.[13] In the march north many of the officers and men were so weakened by prior starvation that they could not keep up with the column. One Colonel O'Donnel, 2 M.C. was having a hard time and two other officers were helping him. The Jap guard beat up the two officers and made them rejoin the column. The colonel could then not keep up—and so, it is, said, the Jap guard shot him in the head. It is said that this same Jap guard similarly murdered a total of 16 Americans before the march was ended. One of them is said to have been Col. Burnett of 71st Infantry who had led a battalion out of Baguio over into the Cagayan Valley and then south. Major Barber,[14] field artillery is responsible for telling me about Burnett.

One Burgess is said to have seen Col. O'Donnel murdered.

Wednesday, 17 June 1942

Bright and sunny day. Regular routine of bango—rice—cribbage (losing) shave (every other day) shower-bath. Boodle turns out to be no fruit except a mango apiece! However, the comprador brought in two sets of lighter flints plus some spares—one for Hirsch and one for me. Because Major Say[15] was so good to me at Pasay, I *gave* him one flint and swapped another for two eggs! Had a signal honor paid me by Mr. Gooding: he invited me to his office, posted Jackson as guard at the door, and gave me a good stiff drink of rye! and said that I'm the only one, outside his two assistants, who is ever so honored.

The medico chiefs called us into conference about all colonels vacating hospital quarters and joining the pool of hoi polloi eligible to be shipped out. My foot is still draining and infection started this morning on the other foot, so I am not crazy about cutting loose from medical service. Later, they told us that on Saturday, all colonels would be segregated in the middle of the next building and would proceed together by truck at some unknown date and be delivered at "a house" in Tarlac—which I disbelieve.

Major Crawford 60 CA[16] is now developing jaundice on top of his fever and feels bad.

This P.M. I let Mr. Hansen have P400 in addition to the 100 I already advanced him—so the store could pay in advance for its stuff. We got a mango apiece this morning plus the flints for cigarette lighter that Hirsch and I have been waiting a week for. Good to get the old lighter going again, because the problem of getting a light for our scags is getting serious. We are prohibited matches and so we lay in wait for anyone who already has a light—perhaps obtained from the fire outside.

Had delivery of sugar (we were almost out) and 5 eggs! In the evening Hirsch cooked up another batch of cocoa and it went swell!

Working parties bring back news: Japs are loading men and tanks here for service in Mindanao. (If so, the battle in the Sulu Sea evidently didn't go so well for the U.S., else how could the Japs dare to ship troops through there?) Also, who will the Japs fight in Mindanao? Moros? or Americanos?; A Filipino told one of our work party "Plenty good-news—can't tell you more." A letter from Manila received here, quotes KGEI [U.S. radio station, San Francisco] as saying about 2 weeks ago, that London Lloyd's is offering 4 to 1 odds that Germany will quit before the end of this month—that a Russian column is now on German soil, that 1000 planes continue to bomb Germany daily, that Ruhr is empty, Krupp works ruined, also 4 German coastal cities.[17]

Thursday, 18 June 1942

My right toes were badly off this morning. The salve which the gutter pup of a corps man applied yesterday badly "scalded" all my toes. So mentally consigning the whole bunch to hell. I applied some of Col. Hirsch's expensive foot powder and sat in the sun watching a pair of Jap pursuiters dog-fighting above Nichols Field, meanwhile inhaling a cup of tea which I brewed from my once-used tea ball. It was not too good.

A long uneventful day. I have about finished compiling my list of property and time hangs heavy.

They say now that, while we were in Concentration Camp at Corregidor there was a heat wave that broke all records—even last summer's! So perhaps we were justified in "camp misery" in thinking that it was really hot.

Friday, 19 June 1942

We were awakened before daylight by the noise of much air activity. One early riser said there were many 1 and 2 motored planes some high and some low; they came from about east and headed over northwest. Significance unknown. This morning Mr. Hansen gave me back 400 of my P500. Later got another P50 and lent it to Hirsch. Very hot and breathless this afternoon so I tried for a siesta and dreamed I landed in Nantucket and an eye peered at me through a hole in a screen and said Nantucket would continue deserted until the UP took it over. Hirsch mixed up our usual cocoa in evening and we enjoyed it as usual. I beat him at cribbage today consistently.

Today people commenced pouring in, many trucks at dusk. I heard a baby crying; they say a woman and her baby (white) are over in one of the other buildings. How inhumane. The Japs drove everybody indoors while the newcomers were arriving, to prevent greetings. One Lt. Col. Hutson, Infantry was brought in on a stretcher and put into Ausmus' bunk. Crews also moved over into Ward 3. Hutson is very wasted and has some kind of bandage on his belly. There is now only 1 watercloset for 2 buildings.

Completed my inventory of my property destroyed by enemy action and found it totals in value over $8800!

Saturday, 20 June 1942

This morning early, Dr. Ericcson softly bade us 8 colonels hie us to Bldg. No. 2 where Dr. McCracken would have a space cleared for us. I went over for an early look and placed my stool in front of a barred window which reached to the floor. Roitzer had already staked out a place alongside: Crews and Ausmus were already bustling into places across the room. This is a building like the one we just left, but with a tin roof. It seems filled with (a) civilian employees (including old negro John the Corregidor barber and Mr. Cook, P.I. Revenue and Customs Agent) (b) enlisted men of the Army and Navy (c) officers of the Army and Navy including mustangs and many Navy warrant and petty officers. The atmosphere is nauseating; it reeks of hoggishness and selfishness. You can't put a thing down anywhere and take your eyes off it for 5 minutes without it being stolen. Today I left half of my soap box and a half-used cake of soap, plus a dirty old face towel in the shower and in 10 minutes, it was gone! Navy hospital record ceases today—"Infected left foot. War edema."

I took down my mosquito bar and piled all my stuff on my cot. Made a complete rectangle of my net frame and put it in new quarters. Then spent the rest of morning digging in. At best, however, this hole is terrible compared with what we have just left.

Last night they brought in a bunch of bed patients, and others from Hospital No. 1 in Bataan. Lt. Col. Hutson was one of them. His hip was shattered by a bullet last January: he has had 2 operations and now an X-ray shows that, because of the position in which he has been lying the ball is 2 inches away from the socket and the intervening space is filled with cartilage. The white woman is a girl from Washington State who married a Filipino. He returned to settle his father's estate and the war caught them. She was in a Filipino Concentration Camp and then in our Bataan Hosp. No. 1. Here she was raped by a Jap guard— and only a perfunctory investigation was made by the Japs. She has two small children with her. There is another tiny baby over there, a mere handful, but whether hers or belonging to one of the 3 Filipinos, I didn't know.

I braced open the lowest third of the wooden window shutters and had a fine cool breeze most of the afternoon. The bangoes now are terrific: they hold us out in the sun while they scour the grounds. This evening's performance took 55 minutes.

The 3 classes of prisoners get separate cans of rice—36 now feed out of our 5-gallon can, with the (numerous) hogs running to the head of the line and ladling out more than their share. The dozen enlisted men get as full a can as does our 36! I saw one gob wolf down a whole mess tin of rice, then hurry for seconds and pile up his mess pan again! He tilted up the soup can, saw there were 3 pieces of meat in it, and spooned all these into his own pan! Sights such as these are common among the primitives with whom we are now living!

I am using Hirsch's foot-powder exclusively now, and both feet are now improving.

Sunday, 21 June 1942

Landon and I were married 34 years ago—and this has been the damnedest year of all! This morning I took a shave and a shower and felt better. Asked Dr. Dartin to ship us on up to Tarlac. All of us colonels are anxious to get away from this mess. Another long bango at 7:00 A.M. but the one at 1:00 P.M. lasted only 15 minutes. These Jap guards change about every week and it takes each new group several days to catch up. Our noon soup had welcome cabbage in it.

Ausmus was unusually profane this morning in discussing skulduggery about food buying. Me, I wonder how one bloke across from me, got 48 eggs when I can only buy 5. Hirsch and I played cribbage and I got a chance to read a few "Great Sea Stories" while he played bridge this afternoon.

It is now a major operation to get things from the store. Somebody runs as soon as bango is dismissed, and gets there ahead of us. But I got 3 cans of evaporated milk tonight—by standing in line a long time at the cost of P2.88! Hirsch made up some fine cocoa, which we enjoyed hugely as usual. Then there being nothing to do (there is no good light for reading) we turned in.

A stiff poker game is continuously in progress among the Navy—can't tell if they are officers or warrant officers. Losses, "payable after the war" so judging by the contestants, there is going to be *some* welching on them!

Monday, 22 June 1942

Those damnable civil employees who sleep just beyond me, woke us all at early dawn with their loud-mouthed obscenities as they prepared and drank their early "coffee." It is native coffee and resembles real coffee like black resembles white. If the adjectives "Goddamn" and "_ucking" were abolished their talk would be cut in half in quantity and improved 1000% in quality. It was nice and cool under the trees in early morning and so, after I'd had my shower, Hirsch and I played cribbage there. At night we used the last of our cocoa while we played cribbage under the after light. His luck continues to be unbelievable.

Today the women and children prisoners left in a truck, destination unknown. Men promptly flocked into the vacated quarters to use the toilet and basin. The slobs even wash their dishes there and plug up the drains. Rained a bit last nite and also this afternoon. Borrowed a fly swatter for use at my bunk.

Tuesday, 23 June 1942

Shave and shower. Supplies are running low. Burke and Say got bananas yesterday from working parties but nothing in store but milk and cocoa. Rice ran short for breakfast, principally because of the hoggishness of those at the head of the line. I've suggested to McCracken (who is *not* a Navy doctor) ways of improving things but he has no gumption. The day passed as usual.

Wednesday, 24 June 1942

Lucked out ahead of Hirsch at cribbage, 3 out of 5! Deck sluicing in Bldg. 3 delayed shower-bath which I took finally at main shower and washed my shorts. Couldn't find "Oxford Book of Verse." Mongo bean soup with our noon rice. The news this morning confirmed by Capt. Riviera, that the Japs are releasing all Filipino soldiers[18] (including Scouts) this I diagnose as *bad*—i.e. that the Japs have the situation so well in hand that they can afford to ignore the Gugus. And yet this hardly agrees with the report that the Japs shipped out 2200 soldiers last night. I wish we could get a bit of authentic news! The Japs have even ceased giving us copies of old newspapers.

The work parties brought back the dope last night that the U.S. had just dropped leaflets in Manila, warning all Filipinos to vacate the port area by July 1st.

Last night the comprador had, just outside the prison gate, some 6000 duck eggs but the Jap guards would not let them be brought in! Not satisfied with their percentage of the profits, we guess. Meanwhile we have no eggs! Borrowed "Home Book of Verse" 3900 pp. compiled by Burton E. Stevenson—quite poor! Turned in and, as usual, it seemed a long time before the lights were doused and the talk died down. The stiff Navy game of poker continues at the big table under a special light, with another more modest Army game of 5 just beside it. The civilians, at the other end of the building play a sort of pinochle. Man for man, they are more disgustingly foul-mouthed than anybody else.

Later

Dr. Cornbloom tells a good story of him and "Ace" Faulkner, returning to Bataan from Manila where they had picked up a new Harley-Davidson motorcycle—one of 100 new ones there for the Army but never claimed. On the way back to Bataan, Faulkner upset in the road. An auto full of Filipinos was right behind him and had to stop. They yelled at him and finally zipped around him, still screaming epithets and curses. At that, the driver of the auto in which Cornbloom was riding, one de la Cruz, opened fire with his Garand rifle at the fleeing auto driven by the Filipinos. "What are you firing for?" asked Cornbloom. "They're Sakdalistas (traitors)" said Cruz. "How do you know?" asked Cornbloom. "Anybody that calls an American lieutenant a son-of-a-bitch is a Sakdalista" retorted de la Cruz. I agree with him. The Sakdalistas present a big problem to the Filipinos now and will be even more so after the war is over.

Colonel Duckworth, U.S.A. Medical Department is the subject of much bitter condemnation. While at Corregidor he used to loaf on the back porch of the hospital but when, one morning, they pointed out a bomb crater nearby, he promptly left for Bataan where he is said to have commanded Base Hospital No. 1. When Bataan fell, Japs came through the hospital and sold food to the patients but Duckworth ordered it all confiscated—and used it in his Officer's Mess! Col. Brezina, who was a patient in that hospital at the time, says that, while the patients had poor food, the doctors fed high! This seems to agree with other accounts of these doctors refusing to treat soldiers at Bilibid, later, except for payment, either in food or in kind. What a bunch of skunks they seem to have been!

Some of the Navy doctors seem to be disliked, also, as self-seekers. Capt. Davis who left with Gen. Moore for Tarlac is contemptuously dubbed a "Coffee Cooler" and they tell with glee how Capt. Loman, in some faulty political move, gypped himself out of escaping to Australia as fleet surgeon!

Other reports of Duckworth put him in a much more favorable light and I am glad of it. When the Japs overran the areas of the hospital, Gillespie, in command of one of them, was supinely inactive and hence occurred the rape of one of the American women patients (the one noted hereafter at Bilibid). But Duckworth hustled out on the road, flagged down a Jap general in an armored car, and succeeded in having a guard posted over his hospital and, consequently, everybody was protected.

Thursday, 25 June 1942

Shave and shower, etc. Another bright, sunny day. Hirsch got scuttlebutt from Adamson University that Jap-U.S. hostilities are being waged indecisively down South, that we have 1,500,000 men in Ireland! that all this dope about our successes and Germany weakening is false—that Germany had just taken Sevastopol! We were also informed that we may move to Tarlac on Saturday at 7:00 A.M. My luck at cribbage against Hirsch improved today.

Friday, 26 June 1942

Heavy showers came up about 9:00 P.M. last night and several men, who had started to bunk outside, came tearing in carrying their bedding. Rain lasted about an hour and then the night cleared off. Day before yesterday Jackson Newhart, my ex-orderly, suddenly went nuts, starting, so the corpsmen say, with what was like a heat prostration followed, when he regained consciousness, by a crying spell and pleas to "keep the bombers off him." Last night I looked in on him after bango: his hands were bound, also his feet and they evidently had trouble with him last night. While I watched he started mouthing and groaning and making noise indicative of having swallowed his tongue. He also started fighting as well as he could, lashing out with his feet—evidently in terror. It was very depressing.

I coughed unceasingly until about 12:30 this morning and arose and went to our old place for a shot of codeine cough medicine—but they had used it all up!

Awoke early this morning and went about the usual routine. After a shower and bango, Hirsch beat me two games of cribbage with most astoundingly rotten luck on my part, and on his part, good luck which astounded even him. In the 2nd game, I was over 30 holes ahead of him at one time! However, it was pleasant, out under the trees in front of our place.

This morning an elderly prisoner named May introduced himself to me and said he was the one who got this diary of mine from the soldiers who were rifling my abandoned clothing roll and gave it to Col. Kirkpatrick and Capt. Madison to give to me. I was mighty glad to learn who had done this kind act, and thanked him to the best of my ability. He hails from Weymouth, Mass. and has been in the P.I. since 1898! He is very interesting to talk to. He was at Ft. Frank when Corregidor surrendered and his testimony fills in some of the important blanks.

He says that the big explosion which occurred at Frank on the P.M. of May 6th was caused by the burning of loose powder which had been thrown into the gully and ignited (thereby violating orders): that Kirkpatrick thoroughly demolished the turret guns at Drum by putting a sandbag in each muzzle and then firing a projectile from each, thus strewing his deck with wire from the gun windings; possibly because of these thorough destructions, the Japs treated all these prisoners from Frank with special cruelty; they took them to Nasugbu (down the coast) and worked them 36 hours without food or water, 20 minutes rest and 1 hour work, carrying coral rock to repair and extend the mole. They even took their hats away—in that broiling sun! Many of the men naturally suffered heat prostration; some had lips cracked wide open, some tried to drink the sea-water! After 36 hours some officer showed up and slightly ameliorated conditions. Good old Kirk came front and center, almost got into trouble for standing up for his men and having them work under their own officers. "We're not licked" he said to them, "nobody captured Drum or Frank. The Japs never overran us. So you're not licked now. Hold up your heads and strut your stuff." A swell guy and a fine soldier.

The clerk came around and told me that we colonels will have breakfast tomorrow morning at 4:30 and be ready to leave at 5:30. These same orders apply to a big gang that is leaving for Cabanatuan. But we are still hoping that we will go by special truck, we 8 colonels, direct to our destination Tarlac. However, a truck driver who took another "taisa" (colonel) from Camp O'Donnell there, says all Colonels are going to Camp Ord, about 5 kilometers from Tarlac—with no trees, but on a hill. Much excitement in our building: some are packing, but I restricted my preparations to a shave and a shower. Gave my table to old John, the negro barber. Returned Dr. George's cribbage board and caught a glimpse of the wonderful store of fine foods that filled his footlocker to overflowing—among them was a fresh pineapple! Rumors have been rife that our Navy doctors were living on the fat of the land—and this glimpse proves it, for if a low-ranker like George is so well fixed, just imagine how well off the higher rankers are! Shaved after bango, to be fit upon arrival at Tarlac tomorrow.

This evening I stopped by to see Jackson: he was rational (nearly) and freed of his bonds. He finally recognized me and said, "I don't know that I should say it, but Colonel, you're very old; take care of yourself; don't let the 59th lose their leader." Very decent of him. I bucked him up as well as I could, and left. Said goodbye to doctors and other friends that I could find.

Saturday, 27 June 1942

The youngsters were full of talk until late last night, and loud talk at that. Evidently excited about going to Cabanatuan. We taisas tried to get to sleep early but there wasn't much chance. This morning somebody woke us at 4:00 and soon our rice appeared. Meanwhile we were taking down our mosquito nets and packing our food and few belongings furiously. Great hurry and excitement. Nobody knew what time it was, and Gooding kept yelling for hurry. In spite of my efforts, I was slow in getting packed up. The men carried my stuff out to the head truck of the waiting column (we were to lead the convoy) but just as I got out there the word came out "Colonels are *not* going" and the men were bringing our stuff back!

So, bitterly disappointed, we all crawled back to our holes and heard the big gang depart for Cabanatuan—presumably by train. The room is now cleared of all but us and 15 civil employees, so we proceeded to spread out a bit while we can, before the Corregidor bunch comes in—if they ever do. This spreading out helped our morale greatly, as did also the departure of the rabble element in our room. 3 of the warrant officers used to double up on the rice issue!

Spent most of the morning hunting for Gooding, to insure us colonels getting rice from some source and finally arranged through his clerk, that the civilians shall draw our rice. All 3 meals today were of straight rice. Our sugar is now exhausted and the rice is hard to cram down. Spent most of the afternoon sewing the rips in my cot to the accompaniment of a hard rain which started about 2:30 and evidently prevented the "inspection by the high command" which was slated for 3:00 P.M. Rain stopped by chow time and, by then, I had my cot made down and mosquito bar hung, and all prepared for an indefinite stay.

A young man from northwest Penn. gave me a scag for a light. Beat Fouks cribbage.

Sunday, 28 June 1942

Back into the routine. Shave, shower, and washed clothes. Nothing but straight rice to eat, except a cup of alleged soup at noon. Store still closed and they say it is because of a squabble between the concessionaire and the guard over the graft. Today 1 American and 1 Filipino died of dysentery. They moved some of the Filipinos out of Bldg. 16 next to us.

Japs have now decreed that there shall be only 1 fire, outside the galley, and it is crowded by men cooking mongo beans, coffee, etc. in all sorts of cans. It is hard to find room in which to boil an egg—if we had the egg.

The pimples still persist strongly on my arms and body and my foot is not well. No cigarettes, though a few dhobies can be bought by paying a peso for a pack of 30 which formerly cost 12 centavos.

Today my Eversharp pencil lead gave out; I chiselled this one from Pharmacist Mate Dunn (?) Can't buy lead refills—or anything else. The Japs change the guard here daily; there are seven different gangs, and today's is the 5th. All of them must be greased before any supplies, even sugar, can come in!

Monday, 29 June 1942

Just another day of the usual routine. Our store has been closed for a week and we are practically destitute of outside supplies. It is so hard for me to cram down our ration of straight rice, that today, I gave most of mine away. As I went to bathe, this forenoon, the cooks were disposing of the carabao bones, which had been boiled clean of flesh but not of gristle, during the process of preparing the last 3 issues of "soup"—and were throwing them into the garbage cans. This presented a too-great temptation to some of the men and, over the splashing of my shower, I could hear the frenzied yells of the cooks: "Put those back! You'll get dysentery" oft repeated. I wonder how that situation compares with the treatment we are probably giving to Jap prisoners—or especially the Japs who are interned in the States?

This P.M. one Pvt. McMahan QMC came in and talked to Col. Brezina and gave some first-hand dope about the notorious march of our captured troops from Mariveles to Camp O'Donnell, which, for his unit, took 4 days with one meal (of rice) en route. He saw several of our men who, because they could not keep up with the marching column, were bayonetted where they fell exhausted. The Japs didn't shoot them, to save ammunition. Filipinos would take off, across the fields, in an effort to escape, and these men were shot down. McMahan said there was hardly a hundred yards that wasn't marked by a dead American or Filipino. At Camp O'Donnell the conditions were unspeakable: our men died like flies from dysentery and were buried ten in a hole. Death rate of Americans got to be a peak of 78 in one day and, he says, a total of 1200 died plus innumerable Filipinos. Everybody was finally evacuated to Cabanatuan, where they are now segregated: Army, Navy, Marine Corps and a separate camp for Filipinos. He also says that the report about Col. McDonald or McConnell being shot,[19] on that march, is a lie, because this colonel is now with other colonels at Tarlac—and I wish to hell we were there also!

Today I got hold of Cronin's "The Keys of the Kingdom," a story of a Catholic priest's 17 years in China: Excellently written and so good that I stayed up late to finish it. I think Landon praised the book to me but I had no time to read it—not then.

This evening, Hirsch and I beat Fouks and "Nick" cribbage and I called Fouks for counting out of turn. Both of them merely bellow the net value of their hands and throw them in.

This morning they cleared Building No. 3 of sick officers and crammed 'em all into 4, where we used to be, by using double deck platforms for beds. Gosh but we are now feeling lucky, since we have so much room.

Tuesday, 30 June 1942

Day opened bright and sunny, with a very short bango and prompt breakfast of very watery rice. This let me get early shave and shower, after which I had my latest pustules scraped open and smeared with alcohol. There was a long waiting line at the dispensary.

I have a rotten head cold and also a cough which is very troublesome at night. Have also developed a pain about where my spleen should be—and that worries me a bit. Rowitzer woke me up a couple of times last night with his snoring. Since my cigarettes have played out I have been rationing myself cruelly on cigars, and have only 6 left. So this morning I broke down and paid P1.50 for 2 packs of dhobies—their war price being only 32 centavos! The profiteering everywhere is scandalous. Mr. Hanson gave me another pack, to be replaced when I got 'em. Hanson, says that he has now seen all seven sets of guards and hopes to get in a P1400 order tonight, but that it will consist solely of sugar and eggs—no cigarettes. I made tentative arrangements to get some sugar tonight through a Filipino. Later, I went over to his Bldg. (No. 16) and there found Riviera and Maj. McFarland eating grand: jelly, cocoa, candy, sausages, etc. Their "boy" (born in Detroit) gave me about a pound of brown sugar and promised to buy me some more when he goes on work detail tomorrow. But he came to our place later, where Hirsch and I were winning at crib and came under the domination of loud-mouthed Fouks.

I am now diluting the canned milk before putting it on my rice, in an effort to make it go farther. Soup tonight was hot water with a few green leaves in it.

We were debating what our wives are eating for breakfast and we decided that melons should be just about at their prime now. The bare idea of one of those fine Los Angeles markets is sumpin to live for!

Rain came down just about bedtime. The addition of sugar to our evening rice was a grand treat, so much so that I have no trouble in cramming the rice down.

Wednesday, 1 July 1942

Moved again! This time they ordered us 9 colonels and the 15 civilians to go over into No. 16 where there are the Filipinos who serve the Jap guards, and various other people. They showed me a wooden platform raised 4 inches off the concrete floor (to keep us dry when rains beat in and leak through the roof) 35' long—and this is to carry 9 of us—less than 4' apiece. Luckily, Dr. Vanderboget was willing to place his bed off the platform between 2 pillars—and Col. Brezina, to escape a leak in the roof, moved his bed off the head of the platform nearer to the toilet. That made it much more comfortable and we all got busy pitching our camp.

Mr. Gooding came by and said there's no definite dope as to *when* we leave but that he has been assured we'll go to Tarlac to join the other colonels.

This new place of ours is right near the wall, the new latrine, only, separating us. It seems a much hotter place than the one we just left and profuse sweating prevented my siesta underneath my fly net. The flies, also, are much thicker than in our last place. All of us, including the civilians are fed up with these frequent moves, and want to go to our permanent destination and dig in for the duration. We are still wondering if our families have been notified that we are prisoners? I have given up hope of ever being permitted to write to Landon.

As another example of hazing: At our 1:00 P.M. bango, a Jap buck private among our guards yelled to the Doctors and said "Hot?"—from his shady place in the central guard house. Replies were various, so, still grinning broadly, the Jap made signs for a fat doctor to put everybody through calisthenics—and this in the broiling sun! The usual Bosn's Mate then put the gang through a few easy exercises. Officers and sick always fall out during these exercises—which have become customary at morning and evening. Then the Jap yelled because the Mate dismissed the class instead of calling it to attention, presenting it to the Jap, and getting *his* order to dismiss it! The insulting leer of the Jap private when jeering at "you officer" was in marked contrast to the elaborate courtesy he shows to his own officers.

It is amusing to see how our adherence to the Geneva Convention will prevent us from retaliating upon the Japs when they become *our* prisoners of war. They adhere to none of the rules—perhaps Japan is not a signatory. If they did our lot would not be bad.

Robbery is forbidden by the rules, but there is hardly a watch left among our forces. Col. Crews was robbed of money by Japanese officers—and many others tell the same tale. To protest is simply to invite a false report and death. You can understand the Jap soldier's viewpoint—it is his only chance to get a watch which would otherwise be forever out of his reach. But that is no excuse for their taking blankets and filled canteens away from us.

This afternoon arrived 3 truckloads of sick from the Camarines road gang, about 32 men. They were in a pitiable state: many had to be carried on stretchers, others could barely walk. One poor wreck managed to plod along with six-inch steps by aid of a cane, he had practically nothing with him, evidently having thrown away everything in an effort to lighten his load. This Camarines gang was the "work party" of 300 men which was sent from Camp O'Donnell about 22 May via Bilibid to the Pasay Hospital, from which they were cleared just before I got there. They were even then in shocking condition; 18 of them were held in the hospital and replaced by 18 healthier men and the bunch sent on down to Camarines Porte to work there on the road connecting with Manila. Soon a detachment of 34 of them were sent back to the Pasay Hospital; later another bunch of about 20 sick came back and said that 33 had already died from dysentery, etc. This bunch that arrived today say that 36 more have died! What barbarity! And to make things worse, when they left O'Donnell they were told *not* to bring medicines or doctors along because ample facilities would be furnished at their destination—whereas actually, there were neither medicines, supplies, nor doctors! I wonder what the softies in the States would say if they knew?

After evening bango we taisas met and organized our group, and, by lot made Col. Brezina our treasurer—our agent in buying from the store. A modicum of stock came in, tonight, after a dearth of 12 days or so. It included bananas for the first time!

Hirsch and I lost 5–4 in cribbage to Fouks and Monroe. The main light in this building is right near my bed, dammit. And flies are very prevalent!

Thursday, 2 July 1942

Made up our orders for the store. Last night Germina and Echata delivered to us the 2 packages of sugar we'd paid for, so now we have a full jar. I hope that too much sugar in one's diet has no bad effect. They say a big order of boodle will be delivered on 4 July. Burke and Besson had bananas this morning which they got from a working party.

After "lugao" (rice gruel) I bathed, shaved and killed 107 flies. Place is all agog over the prospect of a big detachment arriving from Corregidor—but then, that has been imminent for a month. Some say there will be 500 patients, 90 nurses, etc. plus the "work details" of some 1500! The latter will be sent to Cabanatuan as promptly as possible.

Around 2:30 or so the Corregidor bunch started pouring in: first some Americans on foot then many Filipinos heavily laden (plenty of loot, I bet) together with trucks of sick and baggage. About 30 Filipino nurses and other Filipinos came in 2 trucks and were housed in No. 3 nearby. Among them was "Big Tit Mary," a notorious whore! A total of 1303 people came in, of all classes. I saw Colonel McCullough carried by in a stretcher and Crews dashed after him, reporting later that he is in a very bad way: prostate and utter lack of bowel control.

A typically shameful occurrence took place this evening: Mr. Gooding, in obedience to orders of Capt. Kusimotu, told one of the interpreters that *everybody* must keep out of quarters of the Filipino nurses. The interpreter then slapped and beat Gooding shamefully. Gooding stood up straight and took it all with no word or movement. To defend himself would have meant death and the Jap interpreter is said to have been trying to make Mr. Gooding

Thursday, 2 July 1942 (continued)

hit back—but he succeeded in keeping control of himself, thus earning the admiration of the many spectators. The two of them then went to HQ and everybody hopes that Capt. Kosimotu will turn the heat on the interpreter but we really can't expect it. Compare what I've already written of Capt. Thompson's run in with an interpreter at Malinta Hospital, and what happened: Thompson has not been seen since!

Ausmus and I beat Fouks and Monroe at cribbage. At about 10:00 P.M., after we all had turned in, official notice was served on the civilians that 13 of them (all but John, Joe Wheeler and Mr. Wolfe) would leave at about 5:00 tomorrow morning for Cabanatuan, with a big bunch of the Corregidor men who just arrived this afternoon. Consequently none of us gets much sleep tonight.

We taisa's drew our first order of boodle this afternoon. Mine consisted of a canteen-cup of sugar, 1 sardines, 2 bananas, 1 native cocoa = P0.78 against which I had deposited P5.00 with Col. Brezina.

Friday, 3 July 1942

No bango yesterday due to new arrivals. Wakened, after night of fitful naps, by our out-going civilians at 4:30, going out to board their trucks for the railroad station, followed by many truckloads of American soldiers. Capts. Burke and Bessin gave me coffee. It seems that only about 400 Americans left instead of the 600 they expected. Morning bango at 7:30 was correspondingly slow. We are now drawing our rice with the gang living in the other part of our building. Tonight I bought from the fat Tagalog ten duck eggs for a peso, while members of the work party were selling them for 25 centavos apiece! I immediately ate the 2 red ones (signifying they had already been boiled).

A Marine truck driver from Camp Ord came in to talk to me, remembering me from Corregidor. He told me about camps at Cabanatuan and Bangbang but was not cheerful about Tarlac. He gave me a box of matches and 2½ packs of cigarettes. I relayed the dope to our other colonels and we had a round table discussion of this and that, after I'd beaten Hirsch at cribbage!

Explored grounds for friends from Corregidor: besides McCullough, there are Minsker[20] (busted leg at Btry. Crockett), White (ruined by mortar premature at Ft. Frank), Dr. Fox[21] (also blown apart at Crockett). Couldn't find Maj. Julian, so I guess he returned with the bunch for Cabanatuan this morning. Dr. Heimbach who was at Btry. Hearn, walked about with me. Learned that Edison and Simmonds had been sent back to the Rock from Ord for questioning and were still there, counting and shipping out ammunition. Stinness also ordered back—if for questioning about the destruction of powder at Frank, I fear for his safety.

Because of wood shortage (?) the Japs have forbidden all but 1 cooking fire outside the galley. You should have seen Ausmus and Crews scrambling for the wood left behind by the departing civilians!

Saturday, 4 July 1942

Awoke early and took my cough outside, to let my companions sleep undisturbed, and to watch the dawn. Boiled my remaining eight eggs. After the A.M. bango, shaved, bathed and washed undershirt and hanky. Then had my new crop of "Guam Blisters" scraped and sterilized.

The Japs have made great capital, recently, about releasing Filipino prisoners.

Actually they are releasing only those who can produce guardians or guarantors outside. Yesterday they released 7 sick or wounded and today nine. Also, one of the "boys" in our building was evidently let go, one of ten additional released today.

Mr. Hanson asked me for P400 to help finance a P2400 shipment of boodle expected tonight but I cut him down to P100. In return, he gave me the dope that we Colonels may not go to Tarlac but, instead, to some place in Manila—and that the Tarlac bunch may join us! He hinted that the news may have come from Kusimotu himself. This might indicate improved conditions—or the opposite. Thoughts of our taking over the Bay View arise unbidden—or maybe joining Gen. Wainwright at the University Club. The Japs have been examining our old civilians today and they envision early freedom.

Evidently our expected boodle failed to arrive tonight. I couldn't sleep, for thinking about Landon, her welfare, and what a fool I've made of myself, and one of some Filipinos just outside the door gave me the remnants of a bottle of gin—about 1 inch at the bottom of the bottle.

This afternoon Kusimotu was around and I tried unsuccessfully to meet him. Mr. Gooding is still out of action after his working over by the Japs. A copy of Manila *Tribune* (Jap Operated) says "Twin Axis Drives are succeeding; the British being driven far and fast toward Alexandria."[22] Why *won't* the British do some real fighting for themselves?

Sunday, 5 July 1942

Raining at reveille so we held bango inside the building. 400 Filipinos were supposed to leave this morning for O'Donnell or some other place up north but they didn't go.

While I was beating Hirsch at cribbage, we watched the eating of the five Filipinos who cook for the Jap enlisted men, and it made us envious! They had butter, plenty of sugar, and a soup that was thick with vegetables and, perhaps, meat! We got straight soupy rice. A hell of a note when officers—or even privates—are fed on a scale so far below the servants of enlisted men!

A corps man in the dispensary, while sterilizing my pimples, was very contemptuous of the stoicism of the Jap soldier; he said two passed out in the dentist chairs during usual dental work, and that many squall over the least pain in dressing wounds or infections.

This morning I gathered the taisas around me and divided up that gin, with a camp spoon. There was about 1¾ spoonfuls apiece and we said, "How!" It was bum gin, but it helped a bit, I fancy. This morning, I took a chance on ruining it and washed my topee—the London one—the only headgear I have. Seems to have improved its looks. Jackson, my ex-orderly, is now running around loose, evidently sane. Col. Vanderborten seems to be recovering from malaria.

Yesterday a lot of hospital equipment was brought in from Corregidor! The Japs searched the Corregidor baggage and took out a lot of cans of food, turning these over to our store. I warned Capt. Sartin against letting this food go to anybody except very sick patients, but it seemed to make no impression—and we all believe it will go to the Navy officers and petty officers. Indeed, shortly afterward, I saw Gregorio, the cook and boy for Maj. McFarland and Capt. Riviera, flourishing a big can of corn-beef hash from that lot. These two officers are detailed as assistants to help Mr. Gooding with bangos etc.

This evening I gave the fat Filipino another peso for 10 more duck eggs—already boiled—this time, and they're not so good—I prefer the raw ones.

Today the decree came out abolishing the noon bango. There are supposed to be, now 1830 prisoners here in Bilibid. A bunch of sick and wounded, 70–100, Filipinos freed today.

Monday, 6 July 1942

This morning several truckloads of Filipino Scouts left, probably for the 9:00 A.M. train for Camp O'Donnell. Probably this is the gang of 400 mentioned earlier. Went over to "sick officers' quarters" and talked to my acquaintances there—as I am trying to make at least a daily habit. Yesterday P.M. I took half a rice cake, with a bit of sugar over to Minsker. This morning I had a long talk with Col. Duckworth, MD who commanded Bataan Hospital No. 1. Interesting talk, while he smoked real Camel cigarettes and used government matches—which we haven't seen for months. His dealings with Jap authorities were remarkable in that they conformed to precedent among civilized nations who signed the Geneva Convention. He is a "guest" here and may go to O'Donnell to straighten out that cesspool of disease. Riviera said that several thousand Filipinos died there, the record being 792 in one day—which I doubt. But it is acknowledged that the death rate there was terrific, both for Americans and Gugu troops.

Our noon rice had corned beef in it, not more than enough to taste, but probably enough to appreciably affect our metabolism, so I crammed down a full ration and added an egg.

Another American died yesterday at 5:05 just before bango. They die here about 1 a day, mostly from dysentery plus malaria. Quinine is very scarce and expensive. Spent another peso for 10 raw eggs. Burke treated me to his "concoction": mongo beans with a sauce of soy sauce, tomatoes, etc. that was like a breath of civilization—the first really zestful flavor that I've tasted for months.

Tuesday, 7 July 1942

This starts our third month of captivity and we are no nearer getting paid than we were two months ago. Sam McCullough is destitute and wrote a long letter about it, to the Jap authorities—but everybody just laughs, saying it is futile to even broach the matter to the Japs. This morning our Corregidor Chinese took over the kitchen and we hope that the rice will be decently cooked, at least. Yesterday there arrived for the mess 2 big tunas and 2 dressed pigs plus vegetables, so it would seem that the new Jap head of prisons is losing no time making good. But it has disadvantages because the guards seem to think our proposed enlarged menu renders our store unnecessary. Hence, last night no food cans in, only about 60 cartons of cigarettes and misellaneous articles such as shoe polish, etc.

The sole of one of my chinelas [Philippine slippers] came loose this morning, but a sailor sewed it up with copper wire, so I hope they may last another month. Had a busy morning, shower, washing underwear, and getting pustules scraped out. At noon we had a soup smelling vividly of fish, but the rice (Chinese cooked) was much better than usual.

Tuesday, 7 July 1942 (continued)

Col. Brezina collected our orders and we hope to get smokes tonight. I spent much of the afternoon reading *Reader's Digest* for May 1940! When the smokes were alloted, we each could get only 1 pack of cigarettes and 10 cigars! So I was lucky when Geronimo coaxed a Jap guard to go out and get me 8 packs of cigarettes for P1.95, giving me five paper bills of 1¢ each in change for my P2.00. Wish I could get some good white paper cigarettes instead of this brown paper kind.

Capt. Robt. White is a most pitiful sight; his thigh is no bigger than my wrist; I don't see how he can live.

Wednesday, 8 July 1942

This morning we were told that 5 more colonels are to move from the old "hospital" to our room, and I don't see where they are going to crowd them in. Wooden double-deckers are being built for them. Saw McCullough and others in SOQ this morning. Dr. Fox says bones refuse to knit because no calcium in diet. Shaved, bathed and laundered this morning. Thief stole Besson's toilet articles through window last nite. Broke out our new shoe polish and all hands polished up their shoes. I fear that mine, after that salt-water soaking at Paranaque, will not last long. That blasted interpreter is learning to drive the motorcycle and makes a hell of a racket perpetually.

In P.M. that young gutterpup, Robt. Derek, started a quarrel with Weisblatt, then extending to others. I tried to shut his vile viperone mouth and then asked Dr. Erickson to remove him. As I was explaining to a Jimmy Lego, Derek said "Tell the truth" and I took a poke at him, having shamefully lost my temper. Also, to my horror, I *missed* laying him out.

Kusimotu inspected this P.M. and told us (1) we'll all leave for Tarlac in a few days, and can lay in food before leaving, (2) that we are *not* Prisoners of War but, when we are "legally" placed in that class, we'll be paid specified amounts, (3) that Tarlac chow is better than what we're now getting and the Jap in charge at Tarlac is "a good man."

My cough is no better and I cough too much at night to get good rest.

Thursday, 9 July 1942

Was sleeping soundly when bango went this morning, after fitful sleep during early part of night. Col. Brezina made up our consolidated list of purchases, but Kusimotu said cut it down—in spite of the fact that most of it could be got at one grocery store. This P.M. we were told that we'll leave here for Tarlac "day after tomorrow." Read "Reader's Digest Reader." Geronimo gave me a new pinochle deck of cards, and I've been trying to remember the rules.

Today 6 more colonels joined us: Wood[23] (F.A.) Stickney and Mielenz[24] (CE.) Cooper (MD) and Menzie (A.G.) and stowed themselves in wooden double-deckers in middle of room. We are all steamed up a bit over leaving this lousy dump. Lynch (JAG) is also with us. Wood, ex HPD G2 has been at University Club, incommunicado, for 8 days. He's the G2 concerning whom we've heard so many bum reports on his efficiency, but he's a Jap language student and knows the language.

Col. Stickney has just come from Corregidor where he had the freedom of the post, except at night, and his revelations of the skulduggery of the I.M. and especially the Army Transport Service, are illuminating if not nauseating. He says that Col. Ward, boss of ATS, had two boxes of special revolvers (ivory handled, and nickel plated, etc.) hidden away to sell later. Also that the barge of booze from the Army-Navy Club did not sink, but the booze was stolen and hidden away in the ATS Tunnel. Also that, in I.M. laterals, choice foods such as fruit and fruit juices were stacked away by the thousand cases, hidden by a thin veneer of cans of corned beef hash! In "dry stores" were thousands of cases of such foods as tomatoes; sadly needed by troops. I wonder if there'll ever be a day of reckoning?

Friday, 10 July 1942

Day opened rainy, drizzled all forenoon. Played pinochle with the soldier who helped carry me into this place after Parinaqua march. Our order of boodle came in and the bastids charged me P5.50 for the Gillette razor! And P1.09 for a small can of corned beef! Took my last shave with the old Gun razor. Had to pay out P10.76 for purchases! Capt. Robt. J. White, CA Res. of Minneapolis died at 12:50. Staphylococcus infection of leg, etc. He was hurt by premature at Btry. Koehler. He was brave and cheerful to the end. I saw him put into the rough board box which was his coffin. Dr. Erickson came to me and said White wanted his wristwatch to get to his wife. It had no crystal. About the only thing he had. Poor devil. I'll write his widow when I can.

Straight rice noon and night. Capt. Schutte appeared and told Ausmus and me about Cabanatuan, which he has just left with a work party of 150 men, to live at Pasay School. 150 more were to follow. All under the Jap navy, which guarantees better treatment than being under the army. For instance even at Cabanatuan they get soup with *every* meal. Every other prison camp gets better diet than does this hospital station! Perhaps somebody is getting graft? This place is a hotbed of profiteering—and the enlisted men on the work details live like kings. So do the Doctors and the prison overseers (Gooding, Maj. MacFarland, etc.) and interpreters. A scandal.

We were told this afternoon to be ready to leave at 8:00 A.M. tomorrow on the 9:30 train. How overjoyed we all are to leave this scene of graft and special privilege! Did some packing tonight, preparatory to tomorrow's move.

Notes

1. Parinaqua was a suburb south of Manila.
2. Wainwright, 124. Maj. Burton Robert Brown was the aide to General Moore. *Register,* 467. Later in 1945 he was repatriated. During the siege he had been slightly wounded.
3. Belote and Belote, 183. Lt. Col. William B. Short had been General Moore's artillery engineer.
4. *Register,* 340. George Walter Hirsch had been the commanding officer of the Philippine Island Ordnance Department. He lived through the prison ordeal and subsequently retired from the army in 1954.
5. Belote and Belote, 183. Colonel Short's death is the only known death resulting directly from the march through Manila by the Corregidor prisoners.
6. *Register*, 463. Lt. Col. Robert Besson had been the commanding officer of the 1st Battalion, 21st Infantry (PA) on Luzon in 1941. Morton, *Philippines,* 176. He had been captured on 26 December when his unit had been prematurely cut off. Fortunately he endured the hardships of prison camp and was repatriated in 1945.
7. *Register,* 415. Lt. Col. Frederick Gilman Saint had been the commanding officer of the 14th Engineers, Philippine Scouts. He died on 24 January 1945 from wounds he had received when the POW ship *Enoura Maru* was bombed in the harbor at Takao, Formosa. The ship had been carrying the survivors of the POW ship *Oryoku Maru,* which had been bombed in Subic Bay on 15 December 1944. Chunn, 18, 59, 173. He had been interned at Cabanatuan and was leader of Group 3 there. After the group system was abolished, Lieutenant Colonel Saint became the camp engineering officer responsible for police, latrines, drainage, etc.
8. Chunn, 48. Capt. Sam Blum was a Medical Corps officer who was a ward officer in the hospital at Cabanatuan.
9. Ibid., 18. Lt. Col. John J. Atkinson later left Bunker and became a group leader at Camp 1 in Cabanatuan. He was known there for his great sense of humor. Later, the Japanese relieved him of his job, replacing him with Colonel Bunker's son-in-law, Maj. T. Brooke Maury. The Japanese enjoyed placing junior officers over senior officers.
10. Boodle: candy, or good things to eat.
11. Col. Trevor Nevitt Dupuy, *Chronological Military History of World War II* (New York: Franklin Watts, 1965), 33. The only thing true about this rumor was that there was a U.S. naval victory during June, but this was the Battle of Mid-

way from 3–6 June when the Japanese lost their naval supremacy in the Central Pacific.

12. Wainwright, 157. All the general officers with Wainwright, including General Moore, had indeed been sent to Tarlac. Wainwright arrived there on 9 June after having been kept under guard in the University Club in Manila up to that time.

13. Falk, 194. The "Death March" lasted over a three to four-week period during which the majority of men arrived at O'Donnell; however, small groups continued to arrive for some time thereafter.

14. Chunn, 59. This was Maj. Louis Barber of the artillery, who became an assistant engineer in the Cabanatuan prison camp.

15. Ibid., 18, 107, 149, 157. Maj. Howard J. Say had been "a one-time enlisted man at Nichols Field who had left the army and gone to work in the Philippines." Later, after being commissioned and captured, he was made a group leader at Cabanatuan.

16. Ibid., 59. Maj. George Harold Crawford had been with the 60th CA on Corregidor. He was moved from the hospital to Cabanatuan, where he recovered from his illness and where he helped build the facilities of the camp. He was later killed aboard the prison ship *Oryoku Maru* when it was bombed in Subic Bay on 15 December 1944.

17. Again Bunker cites many of the prison camp's rumors; however, once again none of them were true.

18. Falk, 118. This was a common rumor only.

19. Ibid., 106. This is probably Col. Stuart Clarence MacDonald, who made the "Death March" along the Pilar–Bagac road. He carried a pass for his fellow prisoners and himself, thus keeping them free from being molested by the numerous Japanese guards along the way. Their own group traveled almost without any guards.

20. Belote and Belote, 128, 129. Lt. Harry C. Minsker had been the pit officer at Battery Geary, which was situated in the same area as Crockett.

21. Ibid., 119, 120. Capt. Lester I. Fox had been the doctor in charge of the battalion aid station at Battery Crockett. During the heavy bombardment on 24 April, he had been tending men in the aid station when a shell broke through the roof, "breaking his leg." Despite his wounds he organized the men to put out the fires while he was hopping around on one leg. Later in the day he lost an eye, received additional multiple body wounds, lost part of his right elbow, and fractured several ribs.

22. Dupuy, *Chronology*, 32. Rommel had driven the British back to El Alamein, where he was subsequently halted.

23. Wainwright, 102, 107, 158, 244, 249. Col. Stuart Wood was the assistant

G2 for the Headquarters Philippine Department. He had been aboard the PBY that crashed in Mindanao after evacuating selected staff officers and nurses from Corregidor on the evening of 3 May. *Register,* 393. Colonel Wood lived through the war and stayed on active duty in the army until 1957.

24. Belote and Belote, *Corregidor* (New York: Harper & Row, 1967), 78. Col. Lloyd E. Mielenz was one of General Moore's engineer officers on Corregidor. He survived the imprisonment and finally retired in 1954.

Saturday, 11 July 1942
To TARLAC:
Of course the early birds, such as Crows, were up long before daylight, noisily striking camp and thus made the rest of us turn out in self defense and do our own packing. We skipped bango and Brezina procured the rice for us at the kitchen. We were all ready at 8:00 A.M. and Gooding conducted us, 14 Colonels, to the central round house, cleared us, and then to the main gate-house, where a detail had already piled our baggage. This was loaded onto a truck and, after hanging around for an hour, we piled in, on top, and drove (preceded by Kusi-motu in a Buick, to the railroad station where we had to manhandle our own baggage to the sidewalk while they got a hand truck). Heavy rain started; we moved baggage inside and down a long platform to the end of a freight train, where we loaded it into a boxcar and piled in with it. This was the "passenger car" evidently that they'd promised us. Kusimotu[1] and his interpreter saw us off and said our 5 guards were to be *helpful*. We started at a good clip at about 9:40 but the trip was very rough and jerky. At some station at 12:30, we all bought food from clamorous vendors. Cooper got me some bananas and I brought a woman down on eggs from the standard price of 10¢ each to two for my 10¢ piece. But she squared things by giving me one egg that was tiny. At Angeles I beat them down to 6 eggs for 50¢ and enjoyed eating all six!

It rained, more or less, all day. It was fine to see country which had not been devastated by bomb and shell. Everything was beautifully green. Rice planting and ploughing is in progress, though it seems there are many fewer people than usual at work. Every bridge over rivers had been demolished, many trusses down in the water, but all repaired by the Japs and now in use. Stops became more frequent and longer and the jerk at starting was terrific. Col. Wood talks Japanese, so that helped make us solid with the guards.

We arrived at Tarlac about 4:30; waited 30′ for the usual confused arrangements, to get fixed up; our car being 500 yards from the station. Finally we lugged our baggage aft and through another freight car and into a waiting truck, piling in on top of it; and were whisked to a barracks building on a knoll about a kilometer west of Tarlac, where we found the rest of the generals and colonels housed.

They made us line up in two ranks for a lecture, via interpreter, by the corporal (Jap) who seems to be the deus ex machina of the "camp." Then a talk by Gen. Wainwright.[2] Then they made us open up all our baggage and packages and inspected for flashlights, long knives and medicines! Asked me about my package of private papers but did not take them. Luckily, they didn't notice this ragged diary.

Then we dragged our stuff into a small room, crowded with steel doubledeck bedsteads, with wooden slats lengthwise for springs, and here we settled down temporarily for me, because Stickney, Cooper and I were told that because of our seniority, we would be moved to the upper floor tomorrow and given a separate single bed apiece.

Supper was soon served in the Japs' mess hall, and while a small portion of boiled sweet potatoes and 2 small fried rice cakes were on each plate that the K.P.s put at each officer's place, there was the usual dry rice, with no milk or sugar, and whole was a dry pill, hard to cram down. The mess room was crowded and Stickney and I were given places at the last table. We were supposed to contribute P4.00 a month to the Mess Fund to include January 1st which amounts to P24 for us new arrivals.

We had another bango at 8:20 P.M. I was put in charge of a squad of 6 other colonels and must answer for them. If one escapes, I'll be shot! Each of us was given a laundry number (mine is 114). Laundry of a few articles is done as a part of our mess facilities.

After bango, everybody must stay inside the building—crammed together and dodging the horde of winged ants that are just now a pest. Lights out at 9:55, but I was already in bed.

On the train trip today, we saw widespread evidence that the Japs are milking the Philippines dry of every movable article of value. In the Manila yards we even saw the two Spanish bronze cannon which, as Spanish War trophies, formerly graced the entrance to Harbor Defense HQ Bldg. on Topside, Corregidor. Other cars were loaded with scrap iron. Our train was all empty going out for freight for Manila. Northern lumber mills are shipping their products to Manila. I'll bet that the Japs have taken all the marra from the Manila Chinese furniture makers, too!

Sunday, 12 July 1942

Slept well on my slat bed last night, in spite of Rowitzer's snoring, because I did less coughing than usual. Bango at 6:40 but breakfast doesn't come until about 8:30 because the Japs won't turn on the electric light and let the cooks get to work early. This morning they were to have turned on the light at 2:00 A.M. so we could have the treat of *coffee* and *doughnuts* for breakfast—but they failed, so we had it for lunch instead. For breakfast we had a good lugao with milk and a little sugar.

Hung around for a long time, waiting for them to move me upstairs, which they finally did and I found my new conditions a great improvement: more room, better ventilation, lighter, airier, and better in every way. Upstairs is one big room, about 48′ x 300′ with plenty of shell windows 5½′ wide protected by 6′ eaves. Bunks are a single for General and a few colonels; double-decked for others, arranged in a row about 3′ from each outside wall, with plenty of room down the center for the rough tables where men are playing games all day long. The scenery is pretty, being gently rolling with plenty of greenery. No trees on this hill-top which makes up our camp, but plenty visible in the distance, and of all shades of green, with no hint of the burnt up scenery of the dry season. A few rice paddies can be seen, and cane fields too, but most vistas remind one of brushy or wooded pasture lands back home. I heard some birds singing this morning, making me wish for my bird books—and freedom to identify them.

Finally managed to get through with change of abode, and shaved with my new Gillette razor, after which I stropped the blade on Hirsch's machine. Water is not plentiful here; we catch rain water, but otherwise it comes only from the stand pipe in Tarlac and the Japs turn it on only sparingly. Formerly it was carted by wheelbarrow from the bottom of the hill! In order to wash, one must buy a wash basin for P1.25 from our alleged post exchange, which is prohibited from selling food of any description! Sorry we did not bring sugar with us for, although this is a sugar producing country, the Japs won't let us buy any, the mess bought a 160 lb. sack but, when delivered here, there was only about 18 kgm. left in the bag!

A Lt. Ugi commands this camp under a Lt. Col. Ot, but the lieutenant seldom appears, and the lieutenant colonel less frequently, so the corporal is practically boss. Besides everybody here is seemingly scared to death and afraid to ask for things, and so timidity is partly the reason for the unattractive situation of supply and privileges.

Tonight we had a thick stew of rice with plenty of meat in it—the best chow I've had since we used to eat at Corregidor. This afternoon I walked a mile in the sun for exercise and I could feel it in my left leg afterwards. Gentle rains pattered down intermittently all day, each one quickly making our exercise ground muddy. Passed the time by playing pinochle with Col. Lilly.[3] "Quiet" theoretically begins at 9:00 P.M. and lights out at 10:00. The Tarlac power plant is perhaps running short of fuel, for the Japs have recently started shutting it down at midnight. Ted Chase[4] has the bed next to me on one side and Gen. Drake[5] on the other.

Monday, 13 July 1942

Nothing unusual today. Showers. Showed the Jap corporal a trick with paper pellets and he returned the compliment by showing me one. For exercise did a tour of the Bear Walk in A.M. and a few more in P.M. and felt it in my left leg. Helped transplant some radish plants with a pair of amateur gardeners in front of barracks until driven inside by rain. Dr. Glatly[6] says my pustules are staphylococcus infections and he will annoint me tonight for them. Lilly and I continue our pinochle war. Hirsch beat me 4–1 cribbage. Got a shower while the water was on. Also sewed laundry numbers into some of my clothes. Mongo beans and eggplant in noon soup. We really feed lots better here than we did at Bilibid, thanks to a good mess officer, Col. Rogers. Frye seems to run the mess hall.

Dope on Camp O'Donnell: Out of 9500 American prisoners there, 1299 died before the Americans were evacuated to Cabanatuan including 35 officers. Only 3 Corregidor officers died: Major Ball,[7] 92d CA, Lt. Carle, 92d CA, both of whom had gone up to Olongapo—and 1 other. Latest reports from O'Donnell indicate that about 13000 Filipinos died out of 35000 by the time Col Sage,[8] 200th CA, left there on June 6th. Sage is now here: he is the one Edison and I tried to call on at Stotsenburg.

Lilly gave me the dope that must accompany my claim for property lost by enemy action, and I've sure got a big job still left in compiling all the necessary figures and dates. Spent much time in making a string braid, round, from abaca (Manila Hemp) fibres.

Night is very quiet in this camp. Looking out my window only about 3 lights are visible: one in our latrine, one in a native bahai to the southeast and a flashing traffic light in Tarlac—but no house lights of Tarlac. The frogs or crickets keep up a steady drone which does not pulsate as in the States. Plenty of bats, small and medium size, flitting about. In daylight, the scenery is beautiful. To the east is a wide plain stretching away to the rarely visible mountains which fringe the Sugar buildings and the roofs of part of Camp Ord—inmates unknown. To the west is the most beautiful of all, gently rolling with intervening trees and groves, with Zambales mountains in the distance. Weather not too hot.

Tuesday, 14 July 1942

Last night I had to take my cough down to our toilet and smoke 2 scags before I could stop and get asleep again. No lights made the trip precarious. Matches are scarce, which makes for bother. Day opened sunny. Dr. Glatly scraped open my pustules at about 5:00 P.M. and put ointment on them. Told me I must do my own laundry, dammit! Didn't finish breakfast until 9:00 A.M. Poor calisthenics at reveille, which I deadbeated. A slice of banana in rice for breakfast.

Water very low today. Did my 6 rounds of the Bear Walk and was groggy afterwards and couldn't elevate my left arm. Very hot and breezeless at mid-day but at 4:00 P.M. a grand rain fell, so I went out and bathed in it, in spite of Glatly's fresh coat of ointment. A meandering pond came into being in the swale to the east of us. But at our Camp, the run off is excellent. Our post exchange order of yesterday came in, this P.M., also wood and rations. I am pained to notice that I am getting a "rice belly" dammit!

After chow tonight we gathered in the mess hall and got our PX orders. They charged me 75¢ for a spool of thread! No long white cigarettes. I brewed me a cup of excellent cocoa.

About 3:00 P.M. a heavy rain came up and continued well into the night. Got me a swell shower-bath, and forgot my soapdish and soap, but it was returned to me!

Wednesday, 15 July 1942

Awoke last night half frozen and was glad I had a blanket—and that the urinal was near. I don't like that symptom. Played pinochle with Lilly. Clear and cool this morning. Besides the Bridge nuts, most of our table spaces are filled by officers furiously writing on Spanish and other dope.

One officer told me last night that he *saw* 4 Americans shot by Japs on the march from Bataan to Camp O'Donnell. One soldier with dysentery went aside and let down his trousers to relieve himself; a Jap guard kicked him in the shins. The soldier went ahead a few yards and again started to relieve himself, whereupon the Jap sentry raised his rifle, fired twice, and the soldier died. In the same march, after robbing the Americans of all valuables they could find, the Jap officers proclaimed that anybody who failed to turn in all money, watches, and jewelry would be shot—whereupon everybody coughed up all they had—because the said Japs had already proved that they knew all the "secret" hiding places. Col. Dennis P. Murphy is authority.

Paced off our Bear Walk and find it to be almost exactly a furlong long. So, protected by my sun helmet, I made 8 round trips or 2 miles and then sewed pleats in both sides of my drawers, to supersede the safety pins I had been using. Shrinking bellies are so common around here that they have posted a fixed price of P1.00 for taking up shorts, trousers, or drawers. I sewed mine with Manila hemp fiber. Water was on for a short time this afternoon and I managed a shower-bath. They have a custom here of elaborately engraving their canteens, names, arms of USAFFE, the verse about the "Bastards of Bataan" etc. Guess I'll have mine done, including the 59th CA arms.

Tonight when the lights came on we had a plague of gnats, thousands of them flew in our unscreened windows and bombarded us furiously, making life miserable. Many crickets also. There were none of either last night. A comfort to turn in, under a mosquito bar. Sultry evening.

Thursday, 16 July 1942

We hold reveille just before sunrise at 6:30. Then took mild calisthenics—then waited around a couple of hours for breakfast. We have about 15 generals here, 110 colonels and aides, and about 30 enlisted. The men's quarters, a nipa [made from Nipa palm] shack, leaked yesterday, so today they moved my gang of colonels upstairs (increasing congestion) and moved some of the men into that room. Lilly beat me 2–1 at pinochle. My cough is better and I slept through the night. I wonder how Landon is? I hope she stays clear of her bronchitis.

In P.M. I walked my 2 miles with a bit of jog trot thrown in—just in time to avoid a fine shower which gave me a bath and cooled the air. Played pinochle with Stickney at night and, strangely, there was not a single gnat.

Some of us are running out of Philippine money. I was asked to remind my group to see the mess officer about their deposits of P24 for the period ending January 1st. Some (Stickney, Mielenz, Brezina) have U.S. money, but that is no good now.

Friday, 17 July 1942

Rain started at reveille, preventing calisthenics. Rained all morning. Cold. My new khaki shorts were delivered at exorbitant price of P4.50 of which I suppose our Jap corporal gets half. They fit snug, so I suppose my increasing (?) waist will make them too tight soon. Copied out some Jap words and phrases to learn—they are very hard to remember. Ate some "cocoanut bar" yesterday and learned, this morning, that it is a powerful laxative. And it attracts ants. Rained pretty steadily all day, preventing my exercise. Cold too, and the brass hats appeared in leather jerkins.

In evening, a hurry call for Capt. Loman MD USN and all other doctors revealed that one Col. Edwin Barry, C.A.C. who was our HD ordnance officer was critically ill. Throat swollen and closing off his breath. No electric lights and couldn't get them turned on! They say Loman operated anyway and put a tube in Barry's throat but it was too late to save him, and he died at 10:30 P.M. Streptococcus throat, Glatly says. If so, why didn't they do something about it before? I understand.

Read Major Atkinson's translation of Spengler's "Decline of the West."

Friday, 17 July 1942 (continued)

There is a province hospital at Tarlac. Why not have taken him there? Or why the tardy diagnosis? Why not early preventive measures?

Later in the night, one of the Jap guards, known as "Whiskey Pete," came stomping and yelling through quarters, wanting to stand watch over Barry's body or something. He has put on several drunken shows: one included lunging with a bayonet at a couple of colonels.

A cold wind blew over our bunks from east windows; blankets were comfortable.

Saturday, 18 July 1942

Day opened rainy and kept it up. Our outside latrine, undermined, caved in, this A.M. and "interred" an officer. Trouble arose over Col. Barry's coffin: our agent reported to the Japs that there was no coffin, and no lumber to make one out of. The Jap answer was: "make one in not more than an hour." So we tore down a partition in our lavatory and made the box out of that. Later all hands lined up on the sidewalks of barracks and gave the Hand Salute as six ragged Filipinos carried the remains to the truck—Japs got angry and refused our request to have officer pall-bearers! The Jap Colonel Ito showed up for the funeral, but there were no services of any kind here. Full Catholic services were held at the grave; Braly and 5 others being present. Tarlac priest officiated. As the truck passed in front of us, I could see the rough box coffin. On it, in a pitiful effort toward the amenities, was a beer bottle of water, containing a lonely pink flower, a sort of ground orchid, which is now blooming along our fences. It was all dis-spiriting, to see how sordid a military funeral can be and, how ignominiously a U.S. officer can pass out. The body was buried in an alleged military cemetery nearby. Lights very dim all evenin' too dim for reading or even card playing. Started reading a "Pocket book," all apart, a Perry Mason mystery, "The Case of the Lucky Legs." Howls again from guard house indicated our guards are drunk again. Rained hard all day and evening.

Sunday, 19 July 1942

Rained and blew all night; cold. Had to close windows. 2 pigs delivered this morning. Singing at breakfast: hymns and "God Bless America." Doughnuts and coffee. I must economize on this paper: no more available. No more "cocoa bar" for me. Some nice greens for dinner, but they gave everybody diarrhea, we being unused to them. Cold and rainy all day and same bum lights at night. Col. Cooper gave me a pinochle deck, new, for teaching him the game! Gratefully received.

Monday, 20 July 1942

Rain stopped this morning. Water scarce, being trucked in. Usual routine; shave, sewing laundry numbers in clothes and taking tucks in drawers. Walked my two miles in P.M., with a bit of "Scouts' Pace" at end—between rains which gave me a good shower. Bought washbasin from our store at cost of P2.60! Electric lights good and bright at night—for their wattage—but too dim for comfort. Had pork in our gravy at noon, but 2 small shoats don't go far with 160 men or so, especially when the Jap guards take a big ham for themselves.

Tuesday, 21 July 1942

Day dawned clear, so everybody was out all morning doing their washing. The officers seem to prefer to do their own laundry of underwear rather than let the mess attendants do it and lose their clothes. Every officer is assigned a number; mine is 114, an easy one to "embroider" into my clothes. Walked 1½ mi. before rain started in P.M. I think this walking is good for me. Since our big latrine caved in, we have to use a straddle trench in the open. Gen. King and I met there this P.M. He explained to me that Wainwright had already asked, orally and by offi-

cial letter that the Japs start paying U.S. troops that are prisoners, but Jap Col.
Ito replies the matter is "under consideration." No single suggestion which has
been made to Ito has been accepted! One, based upon a remark by Col. Sage as
to the better conditions at Camp O'Donnell, resulted in refusal and, if Gen. King
had not interceded, was to result in Col. Sage being ordered back to O'Donnell!

Japs refuse to allow food to be bought except for general consumption in the
mess. This is another unwarranted punishment in violation of the Hague Convention which decrees that a store shall be started for prisoners, at which food
and other articles may be bought. And the Japs feed us on low grade food. I saw
the rice that came in this P.M. It looked like floor sweepings: full of dust and dirt,
caked together and almost moldy. One sack looked more like oats than rice. The
eggplants were rotten and had to be thrown away. Our kitchen force deserves
great credit for producing palatable results. It all seems but further examples of
the very efficient hazing process.

Wednesday, 22 July 1942

Awoke before reveille and, after visiting our "head" awaited reveille and did
calisthenics in my chinelas (which are always wet). Morning was sunny, so I got
through my shave and 2-mile walk in the sun, with bath later and brought in my
laundry to dry. Lucky, for it started to rain to beat hell about noon. Started reading "Berlin Diary" by Shirer. Gen. Moore held meeting of 15 Corregidor officers
on Gen. Wainwright's proposed organization of officers Mil. Order of the Blaz-
ing Star (or Sun) Punk because (1) Filipino officers are eligible and outnumber
us and will run the whole, (2) Enlisted men excluded, hence it will languish for
lack of patronage, (3) One object is to write truth about the Philippine Campaign—and my experience in the historical section of the war college proves that
such is impossible—for political reasons. 10 rice cakes for dinner tonight. Beat
Hirsch soundly at cribbage 4–1.

Thursday, 23 July 1942

Broke tooth.

Bright and sunny all morning which was appreciated by all. Found my topee
badly waterlogged, so put it out in sun. Last night had accident to my left rear
upper molar: couldn't tell whether the tooth broke or the filling came out—a big
hole there. This morning Dr. Glatly said it was a filling (to my relief). He put
me on the list of officers to go to Tarlac to see the Filipino dentist there. No dental equipment here. Japs have taken all dental supplies of the Tarlac dentist and
he can get no more amalgam. So when Glatly says we may not be able to get
permission, inside of a month, to visit Tarlac—it seems to make little difference.
We are trying to get permission to send a truckload of dental patients from here
to Camp O'Donnell, where it is said a completely equipped dental clinic now

is. Dry rice with a spoonful of white grease for lunch. Did my 2 miles this morning and my feet and ankles now show no sign of swelling (edema). Lights went out tonight.

Friday, 25 July 1942

Up before reveille and saw sunrise. Bright, sunny morning. Walked 2 laps when Ito arrived and we all had to stand by our bunks. He brought a volley ball and net but no carabao. Nothing else unusual today except the mess for the first time sold sugar: about a pint cupful for 7¢.

The so-called "scorched earth" policy is sometimes a fake. For example: within 3 months of their capture of Java including its "destroyed" oil wells, the Japs were delivering oil from those wells to Olongapo! A Jap major of engineers explained that this was made possible by the capacity of the Dutch and English well owners who merely "capped" their wells instead of destroying them. Thus our business tycoons force us into war and then knife us in the back. (The British claimed it would take 6 months to repair the wells.) At sunset, the eastern sky was a beautiful study in many soft shades of gray, with the mountains dimly visible along the horizon (with Landon 6000 miles beyond!) and the light green fields striped across with dark green lines of trees and copses. In the west, the sunlit clouds were edged with brightest silver. Mt. Aryat stands up darkly in the southeast.

Saturday, 25 July 1942

Day clear with a hot sun but our being sited on this knoll insures our catching the slight cool breeze that makes the inside of our big dormitory airy and comfortable. Did my usual 2 miles this A.M. Our new volleyball net is up, but only about 4 persons were using it this morning. Laundered a filthy hanky and a suit of underwear and they were dry by mid afternoon. Finished "Berlin Diary" a terrible indictment of Hitler and the Nazis—and world politics in general. Our 14 holer installed yesterday in a new site, less muddy. Struck with the skinniness of Ted Chase's legs; he was on the Bear Path for a few turns this morning. But most of our gang look very bony. Later in the afternoon—but in too hot a sun, officers had a volleyball game—also the enlisted men. Am getting a good tan, sunburn on upper legs from this mornings trek. Wish I dared open up a can of my corned beef! But they threaten to make us turn in all the food we've brought with us!

Another sample of Jap "Co-prosperity": After we left Corregidor, the Japs started a whorehouse in the quarters formerly used by the keeper of the P.O. Treasury vault in Ramsey ravine. Our U.S. engineers had to alter it into an 8-room place. The Japs then collected 7 Filipino tarts in Manila, promising them prices of P5, and P15 for enlisted men, NCOs & officers respectively. Our Maj Lothrop (Bob) C.E. was told this by Tawakita, S4 of the Jap battalion now garrisoning Corregidor, who was in charge of said cat-house. He charged each girl P50 for her passage to Corregidor, then established actual prices of P1.50, P2.00 and P3 of which he took half! His house manager also probably got his rake-off which means that, on the lowest tariff, a girl got perhaps 35¢ gold a throw! And there they are stuck because how can they leave the Rock?

Sunday, 26 July 1942
No calisthenics on Sunday morning. Doughnuts and coffee for breakfast: Doughnuts very sour, and those on my plate were so skinny that I almost quit in disgust. After shave I joined the volleyball game and enjoyed it until I quit because of the sun. Better exercise than walking. Rained hard for a few minutes last night, but the last 4 days have been practically clear. The usual Sunday morning hymns at breakfast, winding up with "God Bless America"—And looking at the poor devils singing it so fervently and feelingly cannot but bring a lump in your throat to think of their condition and what has happened to them, and yet see that, in spite of all, their faith is in America. At supper, had greens, but most of us ate sparingly, lest—

Monday, 27 July 1942
Correct! Widespread diarrhea, though less than on previous issue of greens. I trotted once during the night and once at reveille, thus missing calisthenics. Too hot for volleyball this A.M. So I did my 2 miles instead. More greens at noon and results at 4:00 P.M. Water scarce again. Made cocoa for breakfast. Short volleyball session at 4:00—Braided string. They took Gen. Stevens[9] to O'Donnell yesterday in an attempt to save his life. He has been a famous character in Mindanao for many years and I hope he lives, if only to get his experiences on paper.
The Zambales mountains are especially beautiful this afternoon: wisps of clouds outlining many successive ridges, like scattered forest fires—with high-piled silvery heaps of clouds above, shining in the setting sun.
No more of these yere "con congo" greens for me. They slaughtered the lame spindly heifer this afternoon.

Tuesday, 28 July 1942
Just another day nearer the end—whatever that may be. 2-mile walk—shave—fine beef stew for noon and clear bouillon at night. Finished a can of milk and got a ration of sugar. Volleyball in P.M. Shower just at lunchtime so couldn't get my bath. Same old routine.

Wednesday, 29 July 1942
Sergeant finished engraving my canteen and cup today with 59th coat of arms and song. A beauty. Cost P2.00. Bright sunny day. Wasted all day waiting around, in uniform, for an inspection that didn't come off, hence no washing. First songfest tonight while I played cribbage.

Thursday/Friday, 30–31 July 1942

Day dawned drizzly and rained all day—Same for Friday. Heifer arrived Friday and the beef stew for Saturday noon was grand with our usual rice. Rained steadily.

Saturday, 1 Aug 1942

Cleared off this morning. We have wasted 3 days standing by in uniforms for the inspection of a Japanese "general." This P.M. it turned out to be a Lt. Oora, who is relieving Uji in charge of this camp. We all stood at attention as the two clumped through the room; then gathered at one end while they threw the usual bull—Uji apologizing for not being on the job because he was, both busy and sick—Oora saying he will do his best for us—And we know how much joy to take in that. Got in some volleyball and a sort of bath. There is rarely enough pressure to work the shower-baths. Lent Hirsch P20 more, making P70 in all.

Last night they sent around to find out how much money (both U.S. and pesos) we have with us! Everybody wondering what the Jap Corporal wants with that—whether to know when his graft and squeeze will play out—or which of various other nefarious schemes he has in view. I reported P200 and $40, which included Hirsch's loan.

Cut off sleeves of another khaki shirt and sewed the hems fancifully with abaca.

Sunday, 2 Aug 1942

For breakfast we gorged ourselves on batter cakes, so much so that I omitted our lunch of rice with a spoonful of grease added. Today, also, we stuck around, dressed in our miserable best, waiting for this "general" who has been overdue for 5 days. Finally Col. Oti showed up and said his goodbye speech, politely regretting he had been unable to grant all our wishes, and echoing all the other Japs in telling us to take care of our health—they all stress that. Later he called all general officers outside for their special farewell and threw a figurative bomb-shell by saying that *all* of us will probably be moved—but that he couldn't say where nor when!!! Immediately the rumor-mongers got busy and had us en route to Tokyo, Baguio, Manila, and dozens of other places. At about 3:00 P.M. they said the "general" was not coming today, so I got exercise at volleyball. Col. Marshall, a sensitive soul, quit because of "too many coaches." They say he's like that. Put my sheet to soak today after scrubbing it on one side, also finished sewing my spare short-sleeve shirt.

Monday, 3 Aug 1942

Clear and breezy so, in spite of waiting around in uniform, I washed my sheet and spread it on grass in sun. The only clothes lines we have are rusty barbed wire. The new Jap lieutenant says he'll try to fix things so we can pursue our hobbies! One bloke avers that his hobby is eating steaks. How I'd like to get back to Corregidor and salvage my Genealogy and other data! If it hasn't all been burned. Again we stood in readiness all for the general who never came.

Tuesday, 4 Aug 1942

The long-awaited general arrived this morning at 8:00 with about a dozen followers. We formed in ranks on the sidewalk and gave him a hand salute at Wainwright's command. He simply walked past. Then we stood at our bunks and gave another salute. The Jap party again walked past. He made no attempt to ascertain where things could be improved, and, when Col. Hoffman[10] reported lack of meat in our diet, he said (the liar) that *he* hadn't had meat for *3* weeks! Yet our guard, this noon, had plenty of corned beef, and tonight had fish in addition to their rice! And this is more or less habitual.

We had a mess of the notorious "greens" at noon, with the usual epidemic of diarrhea afterwards. I made the *mistake* of thinking vinegar would prevent it—but not so!

Wednesday, 5 Aug 1942

Clear and bright at dawn, but at 3:00 P.M. it rained heavily, just after I caught a shower-bath, after having quit the volleyball game in disgust, because Col. Hughes was missing every point and I was getting no exercise. Walked 2 laps in my Parinaque shoes and they started to make me a blister, so I quit. Col. Sage, in charge of quarters, had to wait at head of stairs all day for Oora! No meat delivered today and only some moldy and wormy rice yesterday! Chow outlook is poor. A new cribbage tournament starts today and I have been after Col. Pilet[11] but can't corner him. Feeling pretty low today. Tired at night.

Thursday, 6 Aug 1942

Pilet easily beat me 3 straight games, the 1st being a white wash, in the opening round of the crib tournament. Looking out my window, about a mile off to the northeast I can see autos and calesas [light carriages] moving along the main highway—free and untrammeled! Gosh I wish I were in Gwenny, tooling along that road, equally free—and with Landon and no Japs near! Chow not coming in and prospects look bad. The damned cat was on the prowl again last night and upset my clogs making a lot of racket, so I arose and "secured" my cocoa candy. Our beef escaped on delivery here tonight but was later recaptured in the rain and butchered. Songfest in Mess Hall.

Friday, 7 Aug 1942

Overcast day. Last night Oora received a telegram to prepare to move us to Japan or Formosa about the 12th of this month! Hell and dammit! Today our boys are as excited as school children and airing all sorts of freak views upon our prospects as regards food and everything else. Many are even starting to pack up. I wonder how old Magpie James will pack his curiosity shop? There are also rumors again that the Japs are going to pay us—but we've heard all that before. Personally, I dread this move: the boat trip will be terrible, and we'll have no chance for rescue, but will be stuck there for the duration of the war. Also it kills all chances for me to salvage any of my property at Corregidor, alas! Dreamed of Landon and Priscilla last nite. The stewed beef at noon, though scanty, was grand. Seconds on broth. Also broth at night. Am compiling data on Jap language, but it is hard to remember any of it because it has no ties to any other language: everything is pure memory. Mostly rainy today. No exercise.

Saturday, 8 Aug 1942

Rained steadily all nite but stopped about 10:00 A.M. About 500 yards in front of our barracks Atao is busily preparing his rice paddies for planting; the carabao plods through the mud dragging the plough and harrow. Snipe shooting soon, maybe. Braly honed a razor blade for me. Hope it works. (It did.) Rain started again at 11:00; rained hard all P.M. and harder all night.

Sunday, 9 Aug 1942

Wet reveille in rain; we are now almost surrounded by ponds in the surrounding low lands; almost in every direction you look you see stretches of water amid lawn-like flats or over the wooded knolls to the west. Talked with Col. Stansell,[12] Signal corps this morning: he is in hospital with foot trouble. He feels that Brooke saved his life on the famous march from Bataan to O'Donnell: Brooke acquired 2 pieces of candy: divided one among several people and made Stansell eat the other, keeping none for himself. I'm prouder than ever of the kid.

Blister has returned on my foot, so tried to doctor it this morning, hoping to cure it before our impending move occurs. This A.M. a Jap doctor took blood smears of all of us, to test for malaria. Barked my hand in the dark last night, returning from the rear. Shaved and bathed in the rain.

No flour, so for breakfast we had straight lugao and poor coffee, but for lunch got a dab of scrambled duck egg with our rice and grease. Then a feces exam for cholera, etc. which caused vast amusement for all. Jap soldier with barked shin says he is leaving with us in 2 days. Whiskey Pete avers we are going to Taiwan (Formosa).

For dinner, we each had a fried bangos (mild fish) that was delicious. Everybody delighted over the treat. But they cost our mess P50—3 days allowance!

The expected blow has fallen, with respect to our move to Formosa! The Japs are being just as nasty—not to say cruel—as usual: We catch the 8:00 A.M. train Wednesday and that is OK. But we march to the station and *carry our* own *loads*.

We came here with 3 pieces of baggage and as usual, leave with what we can carry on our backs—which isn't much, in our condition. Upon arrival in Manila we march from the station to the boat, being in Manila only an hour. Carry our baggage here, also! Something was said about the Japs having bull carts here tomorrow night, to take our baggage to the station and leave it unguarded all night! We are all wildly hoping that this difficulty may be straightened out, for it will make all the difference in the world to us. The boat trip is going to be hell, as we who came from Corregidor on one of their alleged "transports" can aver. Crammed into the hold upon long board shelves, with no air and one primitive latrine for the whole gang! We are hoping that the trip can be made in not more than 4 days. I wonder if they will permit us on deck for the last look at Corregidor? How different it will be from my previous goodbye look at the fort, from the deck of the *Black Hawk* in 1937!

Monday, 10 Aug 1942

Still raining to beat hell; steadily, with plenty of lightning. We all pray that it clears off before we move, as most of us have no protection from the rain, also, most of our stuff is damp and will get moldy. My undersized clogs are a nuisance but they save my shoes from the wet concrete at the wash stands. My barked hand is infected and my blistered foot is unhealed. Lent Col. Foster one of my barrack bags. Gosh, but I'll feel bad to steam out of Manila Bay—it will be a final goodbye to my $9000 worth of personal property and a separation from memories shared with Landon. Even now it is depressing enough, God knows.

At 3:30 we received word that we shall leave here at *7:30 tomorrow morning!* and they want our parole for the trip. What a skillfully executed bit of persecution!

Notes

1. Wainwright, 156. Lieutenant Kusimoto "had been a discus thrower on the 1932 Japanese Olympic team which had competed in Los Angeles." Wainwright thought that he was a decent individual, particularly after, at risk to himself, Kusimoto sent Wainwright cigarettes on two occasions.

2. Ibid., 157. Wainwright and most of his staff had arrived at Tarlac on 9 June.

3. Ibid., 58, 244. Col. Edmund J. Lilly had commanded the 57th Regiment of Scouts, which partook in the bitter hand-to-hand fighting between the Anyasan and Salaiim Rivers on Bataan.

4. Belote and Belote, 44, 74, 97, 128. Col. Theodore M. Chase had been the commander of the 60th CA, Antiaircraft, on Corregidor, where he was wounded. *Register,* 317. He lived through the imprisonment and retired in 1947.

5. *Register,* 323. Brig. Gen. Charles Chisholm Drake was chief quartermaster for USAFFE. He lived through the imprisonment and retired in 1946.

6. Wainwright, 194. Col. Harold Glattley was the camp doctor.

7. *Register,* 429. Maj. William Harris Ball had been the commander of a battalion of 155 guns in the 92nd CA. He died of dysentery on 20 May.

8. Ibid., 244. Col. Gordon Sage commanded the 200th CA Regiment and survived the "Death March" to O'Donnell.

9. Wainwright, 94, 164. Brig. Gen. Luther R. Stevens had an abscess on his liver and suffered a slight heart attack. Falk, 103, 144, 169–70, 173. He had been one of General Jones's subordinate commanders in the I Corps area.

10. Ibid., 158, 167, 244, 249. Col. Robert Hoffman was the camp translator along with Colonel Wood. *Register,* 341. He had been the G3 of the Philippine Island Division. He had endured the "Death March." He endured prison and retired from the army in 1947.

11. Ibid., 141, 144. Col. N. C. Pillet had been Wainwright's assistant chief of staff G1.

12. Ibid., 14, 25, 40. Col. Joshua Stansell had been the Philippine Division's signal officer, whom Wainwright took as his own signal officer. *Register,* 340. He had endured the "Death March." He was later repatriated and retired in 1947.

Tuesday, 11 Aug 1942

Reveille at 3:30 and soon it started raining heavily, a fine prospect for our day's move, but it cleared just in time for our march to the station. No electric lights, which made it difficult for us to pack up. Had another roll call at 5:40 and then rested until about 6:30, having had our breakfast just after reveille. Lined up for exit march and missed my monogram towel—which distressed me but it was later returned to me by a staff sergeant. On our march to the Tarlac Depot I travelled easily, being burdened only with my blanket roll, but I was astounded to see the food and stuff that others were toting. Gen. Brougher[1] had to ask Gen. Pierce[2] to take one of his bundles after begging Filipino bystanders to carry for him. Our Oora went with men and also our guards. Crammed us into passenger coaches. Our truck was delayed but just managed to get all of our baggage to the train in time. On the trip to Manila, I never saw such a feverish buying of food—and such avid eating. Some of our officers, like Cordero[3] and Crews, ate steadily the whole way. James chiselled effectively and ate and talked, continuously. We passed through several rain squalls, stopping at many stations. Knee-deep in Japs everywhere. At first the country was badly flooded by our recent rains, but farther south the planting of rice was going famously, red-skirted women, etc. Everything beautifully green.

At Manila, the Japs gave us, through the car windows, a small loaf of bread apiece, the first bread I'd seen since Corregidor. Gave half of my loaf to a soldier who had none. We lined up in the yard and boarded a dozen trucks, 18 per truck. Generals in a bus. Our soldiers loaded our baggage on our trucks and we drove through Manila to Pier 7 where we hung around for several hours before boarding the Nagaro Maru and being crammed into a bunk room, the space around the forward hatch, down 1 deck. A shelf, about 13' wide had been built, against side of ship, chest high, thus doubling the sleeping capacity. Here we bunked in, with about 2 lineal feet per man—and no place at all for many, including our enlisted men. Rest of hold similarly filled with Jap soldiers returning to Japan, presumably on furlough. Bestial arrangements: the usual benjo or straddle trough on well deck forward; Tea tub and kitchen on after deck. We stayed moored to Pier 7 all night and it was so hot below decks that we all sweated profusely all night. On deck, in evening, after a surprisingly good meal of good rice with fish, agar, etc. we watched the lights on the Lunota and thought of bygone days, not many signs of gaity, only about 3 of the air conditioned rooms of the Manila Hotel lighted. Passing the Escolta at about 12:30 this noon we all remarked how empty and lifeless it was. Very little traffic, few shoppers anywhere in the city. Most Chinese stores closed. Japanese civilians everywhere—even engineers on the trains.

Our messing arrangements are queer: each 15 officers gets a pail of rice plus a cover tray in 3 compartments each holding an allotment of preserved fish or whatnot, also a rice paddle and a ladle. Food is apportioned out into each person's mess pan and they eat, then wash their dishes. Our enlisted details bring and remove the buckets. Tonight we ate huddled on our deck.

Wednesday, 12 Aug 1942

No punishment at all to get up early this morning and get out of our Black Hole and into the cooler morning air. Roll call on well deck and then our food was served there but, just as we started to eat, by improvised squads, the ship left the pier and the Japs chased us below decks, thus ruining chances of some officers to get food at all. Our boat anchored outside breakwater and we came on deck and loafed around in the sun, waiting for rest of our convoy until about 4:00 P.M. when we 4 ships, with 1 destroyer as escort, started. The Japs again sent us below decks, perhaps so we couldn't see Corregidor or Bataan and kept us there, cooped up in the sweltering heat, until 8:00 P.M., when it was almost dark and we were well outside Manila Bay. So I missed a last look at Corregidor. We had our dinner below decks. We are all agreeably surprised at the quality of our food, it is so much better than any prison chow that we've had so far. The rice is excellent in quality, often has barley in it, and is well cooked. There is always something on the side: boiled potatoes, tiny dried fish, queer pickled vegetables, boiled fish, etc. A great improvement. Although ostensibly forbidden, some of us slept on deck tonight—and on succeeding nights. Nice and cool on deck. We were supposed to go below at 11:00 P.M. Just after dark, our destroyer peeled off and went back; we hit up our speed to the limit and, I believe, parted from the other ships of the convoy. We sailed without lights and zigzagged busily! A "boat drill" was called for: it consisted of everybody grabbing a cheap Kapok life preserver and going on deck and then being chased below deck again with no assignments to life rafts. Only 1 life boat aboard! Many of us have no preservers! Efforts were made, but failed to give preservers to all. I figure that, if we were ever torpedoed, some 500 men would be trying to fight their way up the single narrow companionway! And when, this eve, they partly closed the hatch, and started zigzagging, it was unanimously our wish that no U.S. submarine found us.[4] A scary feeling. We stayed out on deck until late, watching Luzon fade and then turned in. There was a bit more air in the hold tonight and sleeping was better, though the boards are hard in spite of the straw mats spread thereon. The first night, I didn't use my blanket, thinking the mats sufficient. But they were not, so I tore down my blanket roll and used it, and got better rest.

Thursday, 13 Aug 1942

At sea en route from Manila to Formosa; sunny and hot all day. No smoking on deck, no air below decks, so everybody vacillated all day long, going below for a sweltering smoke then coming on deck and hunting around for a shady spot in which to keep cool. For chow, we lined up in squads of 15, on well deck. Washing our dishes aft later with the mess boys. The Japs onboard seem quite friendly. Several have helped me with my Jap lessons. Almost impossible to bathe or shave, our only sources of fresh water being two large wooden tanks filled with faucets, and they are usually crowded with Japs. We continued zigzagging.

Friday, 14 Aug 1942

Same as yesterday, hot as hell. Gen. Wainwright today placed me "in command" of all colonels, etc., which is a dirty trick, for they are the most selfish, undisciplined bunch I ever saw. Col. Peck,[5] National Guard, is very bitter and truculent. Richards[6] is the group glutton. Nothing today was outside the usual routine. Started to sleep on deck tonight with my topee for a pillow, it being unbearably hot below. 2 Japs scrouged [crowded] in on me but I came back later and scrouged in on *them* and had a good night's sleep in spite of cramped space and hard hatch cover. Raised a lighthouse tonight.

Saturday, 15 Aug 1942

A hell of a day. Arrived Tacau[7] at daylight, prepared to debark right after breakfast! But we loafed around doing nothing but standing check roll calls, based on a set of the forms that we have been making out frequently. A fat Jap interpreter officiated and as he read our names, we returned below decks and he gave each sheet to the desk of the new guard. Finally we were told to be ready to debark at 1:00 P.M. I decreed that we would go alphabetically—lucky, because they again used the forms for checking us: 1:00 P.M. came and we formed 14 generals and 28 colonels on deck in the hot sun (generals under cover). But no boat showed up and we waited until after 2:00 before a Diesel tug and 2 motor barges came alongside. Generals *and* Navy got aboard tug and shoved off. Then they loaded 52 colonels on a barge and we followed. The other barge went to portside and loaded our baggage from the hold instead of taking ⅓ on each successive trip. The Jap logistics never work out according to plan. We steamed a mile up the harbor and piled aboard a small coaster of the usual China coast type, yclept [called] *Otaru-Maru* and filed into the after hold. Selected our bunks and visualized plenty of room, but then came 26 enlisted men with their own baggage plus what was left on deck of *Nagara!* Fortier[8] and Hirsch made a reapportionment of Berths, stowing all away. We are evidently under Navy control since our Navy personnel has handled our generals. They plus 3 enlisted men, are stowed in the "passenger cabin" just aft of us. Our other colonels are in the forward hold.

Our hold is small, of course, and hotter than hell. Thank goodness there is an awning overhead, but not a breath of air came down the hatch to ease the sweltering heat below, nor was anybody allowed on deck. The Jap guard is evidently scared to death of us and kept us covered with rifles—bayonets fixed, too! For chow they let us send 3 men for the rice pail, etc.—for 25 minutes—When it was returned, they sent chow for 25 more and, when *that* pail was returned, they sent the 3rd and final supply for 28 men.

About sundown, the gloating interpreter announced we could go on deck for 40 minutes. Many cheers and we all scrambled up the companionway into the heavenly fresh air on deck. A wonderful cool breeze. What joy to all of us and we regretted when time was up and we had to go below again. But meanwhile the hold had aired and was much cooler. It had been easily 20° hotter than on deck. Now they allowed us to wash our dishes and go to toilet, but only 2 at a time. This boat is so old and shot that there are no electric lights. We had one kerosene lantern hanging from center beam of the hatch. A ghost ship: no steam up and all gear out of repair. We wonder if this ship *can* move—or if we'll move by train.

Sunday, 16 Aug 1942

Turned in early and slept well last night until 4:15 this morning, when Chase and I had an early cigarette together. Went on deck for drink of water and we were still at anchor. Tried to go to sleep again, but the restless ones were getting up noisily and talking, so gave it up. As we were finishing our breakfast of rice plus squash soup, we weighed anchor and started out of harbor, so our KPs were delayed in getting chow for Groups B and C. At 9:00 A.M. they let us on deck again for an hour and it was a treat. We are steaming south at 8 knots with a mountainous mainland about 5 miles to our left. Passed a fair-sized island to starboard at 8:30. To appease the habitual knockers, I arranged for B Group to get noon chow first. In the afternoon they did much photographing and even drove us up on deck for it. An artist did sketches of a few of the generals. After chow in P.M. they let us stay on deck until 7:00 P.M. Nice and cool, fresh breeze on port bow. Porthole open, helped. Turned in, in our kennels as usual, and the boards are still hard. No chow but rice and insipid squash stew all day. In late P.M. turned eastward around south end of Formosa and headed north. Cut down our speed at night.

Monday, 17 Aug 1942

Steamed slowly into our port at sunrise, past a mole with lighthouse on outer end into a long narrow harbor, and anchored for hours while they kept us below in the heat. Finally, they gave us rice and a few cans of native corned beef chips for the noon meal. Boat now tied up to a concrete wharf. Cliff in background lined with natives: children of all ages, men, women with colorful silk parasols. (Similar crowds lined our 4 km. march especially at the crossroads.)

Jap interpreter first said that those who had not breakfasted would eat on dock, but instantly changed and said all would stay aboard until all were fed. Having already packed my blanket roll I finished rice and went on deck with all the others. It was now about noon and hot. We all trooped ashore and put on our packs (some of us were refused, for no reason) and were then lined up on the dock. Generals and Navy leading. Soon we marched inside a fine big warehouse, partly filled with rice, and were checked into the usual alphabetical order. Much ado by the local guards, who were patently scared to death of us; kept aiming their bayonetted rifles at us, from all doors, etc. Many officers including a barking colonel. Finally they got us arranged to suit them, so we started the march, along the wharf and winding up the bluff. Nearby were cantonment buildings and elaborate installations, revetted banks along the waterfront and a mile or so to the right, a big radio station. No town or stores; evidently a purely military plant, and very extensive. We climbed 100' or so to the plateau over a pebbly road, to a treeless grassy plain, with clumps of houses scattered along the road: a sort of cafe at one turn of our road. All the boys in some sort of uniform, maybe ragged, but still a uniform, and this regardless of the boy's age. A few persons with a wide green stripe across mouth from ear to ear and another down center of forehead and nose. Native wild Formosans? Among all the successive crowds that thronged our path, all of us noted the absolute lack of a single happy-looking face! After the 1st kilometer, at an abominably slow pace, they led us off the road into the grass and gave us an unneeded rest. Then we renewed the march in the hot sun. The excess tarvia was so sticky in the road that it nearly pulled our shoes off. Around a bend near the sea, overlooking an alluvial flat valley, then we arrived at our destination—presumably the Presbyterian Mission which had evidently been taken over by the Jap army. A small parade ground, grassy, crisscrossed by paths and a road paved by round beach stones; several trees including a row of small banyans in front of our barracks, which is a long 2-story wood building stained dark, black tile roof; many wide windows; interior redolent of camphor wood. With much backing and filling and confusion we were lined up, issued wooden clogs and our shoes were taken away. Then, lined up in the sun, we stripped while the Jap G2 inspectors frisked us and our clothes for papers, cutlery, lighters, matches. They did not take money. They gave claim checks for things taken. A long time in the sun. When we first arrived however, our boss Lt. made us salute, in unison, the colonel in charge of "all prison camps" (a sourpuss who barked and yelled at everybody) and then the major (with many campaign ribbons) in charge of this camp. The latter made us a long speech in Japanese, mostly telling us that U.S. and England are licked, our Navy sunk and no planes left. They didn't have time to inspect the luggage we carried with us, nor did they deliver the bundles which we had put on the truck, hence none of us had so much as a spoon to eat with. They put 28 of us under Aldrich, in a room upstairs, where 28 beds of Jap style were made on floor matting, with a big roll of bedding for each. Walls lined with cupboards for storage. All very neat and clean. Porches on front and rear, upstairs and down. A well-built building with concrete pier foundations. Two arcades lead aft from main building to 2 smaller buildings: the one at the east end is the "medical," the centre one, of 2 wings, is our latrine (Jap style) with 4 laundry fountains in the central arcade-like space.

As an exception, we were given bath privileges at the laundry tubs, and how everybody did enjoy it! It was like a flock of birds fluttering and chirping about, inconvenient though the water receptacles were. After 5:00 P.M. we sent 4 officers for chow, which consisted of some soup (not too bad) and 3 slices of good bread per person, plus a bucket of hot water. The buckets were new, so the water tasted agreeably of camphor wood. Then they lined us up and showed us how to perform the ceremony of bowing to the emperor's palace. Then we returned to our rooms and, at 8:00 P.M. we rigged the big mosquito bars—4 for the whole room, 1 for each section of 7 men. Just then the Jap OD came and held roll call. Then we all turned in, but the racket of the wooden clogs on the porch floors and the concrete walks, as many officers clumped their noisy way to the latrine, all night long, interfered with sleep. Fairly new moon. High hills seem to run along a mile or two from the coast, perhaps 3000 feet high or more, with clouds usually veiling their summits, with, today, heavy rain squalls underneath—although they tell us that the local wet season has passed. So far, I can't see much difference in climate between here and Manila except that wet clothes seem to dry out at night. Before breaking ranks, on arrival, they made us all sign an oath that we would attempt no escape and would not "damage property."

Tuesday—Camp w/o baggage Karinfoe or Karenko.

Tuesday, 18 Aug 1942

Aroused by the clatter of wooden shoes "geta" [wooden clogs], washed as well as we could and, after roll call, we all bowed "respectfully" at a white, lettered stake in front of us. As we bowed, most of us could be heard muttering imprecations. Then, as seems to be usual here, we sent for our chow which again included bread and no rice. Chow here is bum compared with what we got on the *Nagara,* but the bread, which we got for only 2 meals, was hailed with joy. Our usual meal here is rice and an insipid vegetable soup.

In the afternoon they lined us up, outside, and subjected us to the humiliation of being photographed while cow-towing[9] to the emperor's palace. Then they changed our squad and room assignments. I am now in II section with Ted Chase, Alex Campbell,[10] Cordero, Callahan, Carter, Brezina, and Collier[11] in an 8-man room. Berry[12] is section leader, across the hall, with Bowler and Braly and, in another 3-man room are Bonham and the 2 Browns. We moved our belongings down from upstairs (including bedding) and found steel cots awaiting us. On each was a straw mattress, bulging high in the middle. Meanwhile, some of the musette bags and other truck baggage arrived and so, for the evening meal many at least had their spoons and a modicum of toilet paper ("chicigami"). But the clatter of wooden clogs was about as bad, tonight, as ever.

3500 non-effectives swamped Corregidor when Bataan fell but our AA couldn't get back.

Floor scrub.

Wednesday, 19 Aug 1942

Today was a busy one, what with roll calls and baggage arrivals. First came a lot of stuff that was in the hold of the *Otaru;* it was arranged on the parade ground and we filed along the rows until we came to our bundle, there we stopped without touching it until all were settled. When we all opened up and spread our stuff out for inspection. It was my footlocker that showed up and it sure had a lot of stuff to spread out. And after all, when he came, he took my other pair of shoes but let me keep a table knife and some aspirin tablets. So I crammed the works back in the box. At first the interpreter told me to carry the locker back myself, a tough job, but soon ordered out 2 of our enlisted men to do it. Then I got busy arranging my stuff in the closets and cupboards. All 3 meals today were of the same insipid combination of good unsalted rice and flat squash soup. No, for 1 meal the soup had good onions in it, and we received also 2 tiny pieces of excellent cucumber! Later in the day they brought to our porch the papers, cutlery, etc which they took from us, the first day. I reported there with my coupon; they returned to me the chain on which I carried my cigaret lighter— but kept the lighter. They also kept my rusty old scout knife but returned all ordinary pen knives! They also brought up the remainder of the "truck" baggage—my bedding roll was all I had there—and, much to my delight, found that they had not even looked inside it—or they must inevitably have copped this diary! I also found the spoon which I mislaid at the boat. Still later, my 3rd and last piece of baggage showed up—my bedding roll, containing a Navy hammock, a sheet, my thin mattress, and my Gold Medal cot! I let them store this as they didn't want us to use any but Jap bedding. So now I have all my possessions and had a good time arranging them in my 3-section cupboard. In our new quarters (Room 6) we have a big mosquito bar for each side of the room, thus covering 4 of us. Campbell tied it up as usual by snitching a bar from upstairs, which complicated things when a Jap brought us a new one. Carter arranged a nice system of toggles to facilitate rigging our mosquito bar ("kacho"). We now form for evening bango just outside our door in the hall. Upon the approach of the Jap OD our squad leader bows, has us call off, and reports (so many) present. Tonight they gave us our receipts for our bedding rolls. Many of us are having trouble staying in bed because of our bulging mattresses. They have ordered that everybody stay off their beds between 6:30 A.M. and 8:00 P.M. except from 1:00–3:00

P.M. This gripes some of the customers intensely. This afternoon Alex Campbell and I took the Japs' advice and in our cumbersome clogs, started to walk round the parade. Immediately a sentry told me to go in and don a shirt, although officially we were told that we could walk and sunbathe stripped to the waist! So I put on my shirt. When we neared Barracks B, the interpreter told us we were off limits, though we were within the red lines on the chart! Promptly upon getting my blanket roll I shaved off my 4-day beard and had a hell of a time doing it, but it gave my morale a lift.

Thursday, 20 Aug 1942

Up as usual and adored the emperor, with Berry's calisthenics afterwards. Then I whirled in on my long-deferred laundry, using up the first cake of laundry soap that I bought at Bilibid. Brezina's scrubbing brush was helpful. The hot sun dried my 4 hankies before I'd finished scrubbing my khaki uniform, but the big "B" towel dried slowly. Right after lunch they made us colonels scrub our room floor. I remonstrated with the Interpreter, saying it is soldiers' work. He got mad and said "That is American custom. This is Japan. Colonels keep clean with their own hands. Only generals are allowed attendants. You obey *my* orders." So we whirled in, having previously done the windows and side walls, and scrubbed the floors, which were quite clean, with the footsquare sections of cloth that the Japs call "mops." Probably to pay me off for my obstreperousness, they made us scrub the hall walls and the barber shop but they made our enlisted men scrub the floor. At this time, also, they moved 2 new officers from the General's room into our room, Colonels Balsam[13] and Boatwright,[14] so we had to crowd our bunks closer together and rearrange our cupboard space. For dinner, there were a few small fragments of vertebrae as soup bones; but their effect was unnoticeable. At evening bango they standardized the procedure for the ceremony. Afterwards they called in all wirecutters and cutting-pliers and had us identify some untagged knives and lighters but returned none.

Friday, 21 Aug 1942

This morning they took a long time to standardize bango, so not much time for exercise. After breakfast they lined our shoes up in front of barracks and let us select and keep one pair. I'm up against it, because my easier pair is so bad that I chafed a sore on my left toe on the march here from the boat. To sick call with the worst batch of Guam blisters I've ever had. My hand is still in bad shape, but my treatment helps more than medicine! Washed a hanky.

Later: Japs claim 200 U.S. Marines landed on Medin de (Solomon de) at dawn yesterday, and after 40-hour fight were repulsed by handful of Japs plus air force. Marines came in 2 submarines via rubber boats.—Jap *Times Weekly,* 17 Sept 1942[15]

Friday, 21 Aug 1942 (continued)
"Masonic diploma."
We discovered the sack of sugar belonging to the old Officers' Mess that we shipped with us, has been practically all stolen by our enlisted men, a choice pack of scoundrels. We managed to save about 18 pounds from them. Gen. Jones asked what to do with it: I suggested issuing it, so he gave it to me to issue. While I was at sick call Brezina measured it and found 36 cupfuls which, divided among 125 officers (I ignored the thieving enlisted men) made about 1.72 spoonfuls apiece. I figured out the amounts for each squad; we got 5 cupfuls for our 16 men. Put it in my glass jar. Our noon meal consisted solely of rice and tara? so we all used a heaping spoonful. Started enjoying our siesta from 1:00–3:00 but I got up and washed my underwear and cleaned tar off my shoes. Flies are getting troublesome, so I asked Glatly to get us some fly swatters. Pretty hot day. Had to turn our shoes in after evening bango—the Japs are so scared that we will try to escape! Where would we go? Swapped a face towel to Collier for a belt.

Saturday, 22 Aug 1942
Up and about as usual. Got into a row with Boatwright about his blankets and was slapped down by Berry. We drew our shoes again after exercise. Yesterday, while walking with Campbell we found a huge land snail perhaps a Helicostyla species and then I started trying to get the beast boiled, not only to kill it but also to see if it is edible. But it is impossible to do it: there are but 2 small stoves in the kitchen and the Japs tell our cooks when to start the fires and when to put them out. Hence we can't have tea nor hot water to drink—only lukewarm water, and only 1 pailful for us 16 men. I asked one Jap about it and he was highly amused; he gestured that I should throw it away—the shell, I'm talking about. And so I fear I must lose this fine shell, which may be rare in collections, although I picked up several damaged specimens on the lawn. Three of them each contained an immature shell about an inch long, perhaps of the same species. They seem to be out in the grass, and not on or under the trees.

Col. Young is gravely ill with, perhaps, cerebral malaria, fever 105°, and a Jap *corporal* at sick call was telling Col. Glatly how the case must be treated! Our doctors are under the orders of sloppily dressed members of the Japanese medical corps, mostly enlisted men. Mebby it will be an improvement, though our doctors object to being restricted in the amounts of our own medicines which can be used. My Guam blisters (tropical ulcers) were much worse this morning and caused comment from even the hard-boiled attendants. Loman opened them with scissors, having no scalpels, and smeared them with alcohol.

In P.M., great excitement over an inspection by "the chief of the general staff." We were to turn out at 3:30 but, at 3:10, the interpreter began screaming for us to hurry up and turn out. We did so, and rehearsed the ceremony as run by commands given in Japanese only, finally acquiring a fair proficiency, after which we stood in the sun until the inspector arrived, promptly upon schedule, at 4:15. Good looking chap, of a saturnine countenance, a chaplin mustache, and unusually well-fitting clothes. He made a short speech, and tonight dissensions are rampant over the interpreter's translation: was it accurate or not? Our 2 experts give inconsistent reports: one says that he said that *in case* of enemy action we would get the same chance as they have; the other language expert omits this but otherwise agrees with the remainder of the speech: that Japan is a God-fearing nation, but also a nation of soldiers: so long as we obeyed regulations we would be cared for, but if we disobeyed we would be strictly finished. We returned to our rooms at 4:30 and the inspector came through the barracks for a hasty look and departed. We had been hoping that he was from Tokyo and it might improve our conditions—but we later concluded he is only the chief of the general staff of the Formosa set-up.

Yesterday, insignia were dished out to us, of two kinds, made of white cotton cloth: one kind was 3″ x 6″, marked with the officer's name, etc. Each officer had to sew it onto the right breast of his shirt, blocking the pocket on that side. The other kind is a 5″ square, pinned to the left sleeve, worn by squad leaders, assistant squad leaders, a property officer in each squad, also one for the OD. Our vigilant guards wear plain white.

Sunday, 23 Aug 1942

This morning, Ted Chase and I went on duty as food carriers for our squad and we also had to wear special insignia on our left sleeve. Looks like reminiscent of chic sale. Right after exercise we took our hot water ("oyu") bucket and walked over to the alleged kitchen, procured our ½ pail of water, brought them to our rooms, apportioned them out to the officers that filed past us. Then we served ourselves all our own breakfasts. Washed the rice paddle and soup ladle here: took the buckets back to the kitchen, washed them and left them. The men at the kitchen, they load up the buckets for each squad and have them all lined up ready for the food carriers at 6:40, 11:45 and 5:45. At noon we saw bundles of scallions that looked grand. There were bundles of other vegetables also. Our "soup" is filled with queer vegetables.

Every night, 9 of our officers and 9 of our NCOs are put on "vigilant guard" in our lower hall; each pair goes on duty for an hour between 9:00 P.M. and 6:00 A.M. Principal duty: to check out and in, each person who goes to the latrine. A nuisance. I take my first tour from 2:00–3:00 A.M. tomorrow morning.

There is also an American OD serving from noon to noon, with a special armband, with 2 NCO assistants, to serve as helpers to the Japanese OD. He is selected from each squad in turn.

My tropical ulcers are somewhat fewer; my hand is drying up; my ankles are badly swollen, and my blistered toe is still bad. I wonder if Landon is still having trouble with her feet? There is a nice siesta from 1:00–3:00, with the aid of one fly swatter. Did my laundry this morning, scoured my canteen, sunned my hand.

We have started using the food which we brought with us: yesterday I opened a can of milk in partnership with Col. Pat Callahan, who has the bunk next to mine, 3 spoonfuls apiece for our rice. We dilute it with 5 spoonfuls of water and that suffices for 1 meal. The can holds 26 spoonfuls, hence enough for 4 meals. One man cannot use a can up before it sours. Now Callahan will open a can of sardines. Campbell opened a can last night and it went well among the three of us. In this way we get the maximum benefit from our food and relieve the deadly monotony of the food the Japs furnish us. Sunday services, amateur style, on the "lawn" this morning; well attended. Hirsch and I played pinochle after dinner and missed a swell sunset. . . .

Monday, 24 Aug 1942

Last night I was on vigilant guard with Pvt. Ferguson from 2:00–3:00 A.M. One of the vegetables at our supper evidently had a strong effect on the kidneys, for an average of 28 men went to the latrine hourly from 9:00 P.M. to 6:00 A.M. Mosquitoes very thick in the hall. Glad I wore my long trousers. Pvt. Fuhrman came down whimpering with a belly ache, so I roused the OD (Penrose), and Dr. Glatly who gave him a hypo. Probably ate too much of food he stole from the mess. My tropical ulcers are a mess: my undershirt is saturated with pus where it has stuck to the sores when I sleep. Am washing my underwear and changing it daily—but the Japs won't let us out in the sun without shirts.

Today 20 officers moved downstairs; and rumor has it that some English officers are coming here. Bad news, if true, because I believe the Japs hate them worse than us. Rumor also says we will be paid "next month" or on the 1st—but how can we use the money? We hope that a store may be started in our compound, though it is said we will be allowed to buy on credit "downtown." Probably the local market facilities are poor, for the Japs say that the poor few pork bones we had in our soup the other day was "all they could get."

The officers are so bitter against our enlisted men for their insolent thieving, and scoundrelly behavior that they strongly oppose a "General Mess" such as we had at Tarlac. There are a few good men but, as a whole, we are fed up on the skunks. They were selected, firstly, by the staff.

Tuesday, 25 Aug 1942

Unshipped our big mosquito bar ("kacho") in record time; our toggle system works fine. My sore back was stuck to my undershirt by pus, so after breakfast I hurried out to the fount and washed out my suit of underwear and also wiped off my torso, since the Japs are very stingy in their allowance of baths. At 5:30 this morning Col. Ed. H. Johnson was caught smoking a pipe by the Jap OD and at bango this morning the OD warned us that it jeopardized smoking privileges for all of us. This bastid Johnson commanded 31st Inf. Phil. army.

Concentrated on the job of preventing my perspiring, as I think that has much to do with these tropical ulcers. Meanwhile, after lunch, the Japs held a conference of squad leaders, and at 3:00 P.M. Col. Berry tried to pass the dope on to us, but his deafness evidently caused him to miss some important points. Gist of dope seems to be that we can hope for no canned meats nor eggs; a chicken costs 5 yen! They want us to start a piggery and hennery over the hill and out of sight behind the Jap officer quarters, they to "eat some of the product"—and we know from experience what *that* means! We are allowed to put in purchase orders for only bananas, tea, and cigarettes tonight and only a small amount of those. Natives are evidently getting their sugar on ration cards, so we probably won't get any! The enlisted men's status is confused: they say we must contribute 5 yen apiece: part to support the enlisted men and part to buy feed for the chickens and other hogs on our stock Farm! Also, each 3 officers may have an orderly—but our room wants nothing to do with them at any price. Of course, we would have to pay the men extra for orderly services, over the 5 yen! Nobody knows what their duties will be or what they can do for us. This assessment, to be taken from us, will be 2% of the pay they will give us—This pay is said to be about 300 yen for a colonel and 500 yen for lieutenant general. It is all quite confused still, and the full horrid details will come out later. Evidently it is out of the question to hope to buy a steer and butcher it for beef.

Wednesday, 26 Aug 1942

Learned to my sorrow that our smoking hours do *not* commence at reveille, as I supposed, but not until after morning bango, hence it cuts me out of an important ½ hr's smoking. Today we filled out another blank form, indicating that the Japs are going to either notify Landon of my whereabouts—or let me write a censored letter to her. It is said we will be allowed to write only 6 letters a year! Today we were told we will be allowed to run a post exchange store, and our Pat Callahan will be in charge; Jack Vance,[16] bookkeeper. This is a good sign and we are hoping for the best. It looks as though our farm is certain and that, although they acknowledge that the Geneva Convention forbids working officers, yet "Everybody in Japan works" and so we will be made to do at least some of the farm work. They also said that "Many officers of a foreign nation will arrive soon." British or Anzacs, we assume, and we'd rather they stayed away instead of overloading these local and meagre facilities. Thank heaven, a native came yesterday and partly emptied one of our latrines, so we colonels won't have to do *that* job!

Wednesday, 26 Aug 1942 (continued)

Slui ho = PX.

Today also, our orderly system started working, when one of them brought our noon chow to us. I was at the hospital, awaiting the pleasure of a Jap medical lieutenant (who really wanted to see only the bed patients) and if it hadn't been for Callahan getting my chow for me, I'd have been out of luck. As it was, I got short-changed on the porkish soup, and got no scallions. Boatwright got 3 instead of the allowance of *one.* They took one away from him and put it with my chow, and Callahan put the 2d there too, to make up for the shortage of soup. Boatwright returned; demanded "Where is that extra onion?" and, when Callahan explained he reached over, grabbed the scallion off my plate and munched it down. There is a surprisingly large amount of such selfishness prevalent among this crowd of "officers and gentlemen." Our Jap lieutenant says we expect too many luxuries—that they get meat only once a week and fish only twice a month—which I doubt. Much resentment again manifested against Col. Chas. S. Lawrence[17] QMC for bootlicking the Japs by saying (apropos the Formosa tea which we received tonight) "Fine tea; very cheap." (82 sen for 1 oz. paper pkg.) This morning he even reported, in *Japanese,* the number of men present. He is a menace, as regards prices!

Thursday, 27 Aug 1942

Today our 2 orderlies, Pvt. Hill and Pfc. Kondasiewicz 53d Inf. started working bringing our chow and mopping up our floor. Our Jap lieutenant has a new officer assistant whom he brought around with him to see us. Lawrence came into our room and I got a showdown on the 5 yen chicken and he said it was a lie. My back is still raw with tropical ulcers but they say it is improving. Started puttering around in one of the flowerless plots back of our barracks, next to Brezin's, where he transplanted some Gerbera (?) plants. A few drops of rain fell this P.M. We receive one small green banana with our noon rice. Somebody stole one of my braided cords. Evening bango delayed by failure of electric lights. This afternoon's sprinkle turned into a rain by 8:00 P.M. which continued lightly all night. The Japs are now cutting down on our rice ration and it is pretty skimpy. Everybody growls but our generals are too scared to kick. Gen. King is leader of Section 1 (generals) and he is such a milk and water appeaser that he is useless to us. Nice and cool for sleeping tonight. Had tea morning and afternoon. Good, better than Lipton's.

Friday, 28 Aug 1942

Bad night: whether because of the tea or whatnot, most of us were running to the latrine all night. No new ulcers but my back is still raw and sticky with pus. Loman, USN Medic, works it over every morning at 10:00. This morning had much-needed haircut by Lejeune. Then, after noon chow, borrowed Brezina's mattock and hoed my garden plot, smoothing it as best I could preparatory to setting out some plants beside the shrub fragments that Brezina stuck in there for me. It is quite prevalent now for everybody to hit the hay at 1:00 P.M. for a while—up to 3:00 P.M. The walkers are also active, now that we have our shoes all day, because it seems to help keep down the swelling of our ankles. Am trying in vain to get my shoes and chinelas resoled.

Set out an edging of geraniums this P.M. in my flower plot and one of the Jap guards helped me with the digging and planting. Today we made out another copy of the same blank form as yesterday. Tomorrow we'll make out the final or "record" copy. The Japs tell us to make them out carefully "because they will accompany us to the U.S."

Saturday, 29 Aug 1942

This morning was "clean-up" day, so the whole gang turned to. Collier and I took out our table and scrubbed it with sand. Picked trash up on lawns and then scratched a line on the ground for our bango position, and then set a brick in the ground to mark Col. Berry's proper position and another for Gen. King. In P.M. I made me a pen knife out of half a razor blade. Also collected 3 more Helicostyla shells and also a few empty tin cans for starting papaya seedlings in my garden. Japs weighed all of us this afternoon. At today's conference today; the Jap lieutenant volunteered "news" about the Solomon Is. Battle: that U.S. lost 11 transports, 10 cruisers, 10 destroyers, 1 carrier and 1 hurt; in all about 40 ships, whereas the Japs say they lost 1 destroyer and had a carrier damaged;[18] also that the U.S. remnants fled. This is about the only "scuttle butt" rumor we've heard since arrival here. Made out final draft of those forms that we hope will lead to our writing a letter to our families. Our post exchange negotiations seem to be progressing favorably: tobacco coming today or tomorrow. This morning our lieutenant told us that Capt. MacMillan, USN, ex-governor of Guam, is due here today (from Japan?). Sure enough he blew in, amidst much scampering at about 10:00 P.M. From Kobe, Japan. Our cigarets and cigars came in this eve and I got 100 cigarettes in tiny packages of 10. Look like Virginia tobacco and taste like Piedmonts. Thank heaven my cigarette holder fits them, or I'd get only a puff from each "scag," they are so short. But they supplied us 150% of what we ordered. Tonight we got some real beef in our soup—and it was fine!

Sunday, 30 Aug 1942

A fine night for sleeping. Saw MacMillan; he hoped Landon got home safely. Will talk with him later, but he evidently has very little recent dope, other than that U.S. troops are in Iran, and the Japs are disappointed in their Navy's showing. Got busy this morning on my routine chores, including preparing some cans for my seedlings. Bananas, due yesterday, still missing, so we all razz Callahan, the PX officer. Our Jap lieutenant asked me how I felt when we are required to bow to the emperor's palace. He knows lots of English. He judged me to be German because of my square head! Finished my braided 4-strand rope of abaca.

Monday, 31 Aug 1942

Pay day.

Tried out our chirigama: it is tricky, but can be used. Am still doctoring my tropical ulcers. Ulcers which, they say, are drying up somewhat. In afternoon we all lined up according to our prison numbers and drew pay, in Formosa yen, for this month since the 17th, the day we arrived here. We colonels were credited with Y150, of which they deposited in the postal bank Y120, giving me Y30. Of this they deducted Y1.00 for the wooden clogs which they lent us, and Y1.50 as pay for the enlisted men, a total of Y3.10, giving us a net of Y26.90. Then Jack Vance came in and collected Y15.00 apiece from us as a deposit on our PX bills. This leaves us the munificent sum of Y11.90 or less than $3.00 as our spending money for the month!

The chow is getting skimpier and skimpier; very little rice tonight and only a ladleful of very weak vegetable soup. It is getting alarming. This P.M. cleaned up a few defective snail shells, finished preparing my seedling cans, and made a razor-blade knife for Callahan.

This pay business turns out to be a mess: the Japs pretend they pay us Y310 a month but, hereafter they will actually *give* us only Y20 per month; they retain the remainder—which means that we'll never see this retained "remainder." The enlisted men get no pay—each will receive only about Y3.00 from the officers' contributions of 1% of our pay. Furthermore, cigarettes being "luxuries," our soldiers are prohibited from buying them. The supply situation here is also punk: most of the things our PX wants to buy are either non-existent or are under government monopoly and hence, unobtainable unless the Japs resurrect the army store they formerly had here.

Tuesday, 1 Sept 1942

Fine cool night for sleeping, last night. Used my Army blanket. Ration this morning still further diminished and the outlook is so bad that even our milksop pacifier, Gen. King, told Lawrence to report to our Jap lieutenant that our rations have been reduced ¼ to ⅓. Our guess is that the supplies are simply not on hand; that the Japs themselves are short of food—and other supplies. This guess was verified by a talk which Col. Hoffman held this evening with our real camp commander who has been absent, ill with dengue fever. This was not big "baggy pants" who has been senior for some time, but the be-ribboned chap who made our "welcoming" speech when we arrived. He said (1) that when we spend our Y30.00 we can draw more up to our full: that the Y30.00 limit is simply to prevent soldiers from stealing all our pay at one time, (2) that food is scarce, even for the Japs; that they must keep Chinese rice in China to feed the Chinese who have gone over to the Japs; he asked if our ration was OK at which Hoffman hemmed and hawed and said we'd like a chance to buy food. (3) That there is an artist in town whom we might hire to paint our portraits, that the town also has a wood carver whose work we might want to buy and take back to the States with us. This was brought us by Jack Vance, and gave us all a big lift. In the afternoon we were all given a hypo for dysentery.

Wednesday, 2 Sept 1942

A rotten night: to latrine at 10:20 and then couldn't sleep. Guess it was the dysentery shot that did the damage. Total of 5 trips to urinals. Am getting discouraged over my ulcers not healing. Washed out my pus-marked undershirt this morning as usual. Glatly told me I didn't need the vitamin B1 pills which will be bought for Y1.50, because of limited supply. Meat . . . this afternoon Berry came in and tried to rush us into voting for or against the "stock farm." I refuse to be stampeded into buying a pig in a poke; there are too many undecided factors: (1) where do the enlisted men head in? (2) if we *volunteer* for work on this farm, will we forfeit our rights under the Geneva Convention and render us liable to forced labor under a sentry on *any* work which suits the Jap's fancy? (3) The utility of buying 10 milk cows is denied by many—how about pasturage and feed? Who will milk and care for them? The project includes buying 200 small chickens and 50 shoats plus a few milk goats. An ambitious project, considering none of us is a farmer and knows nothing of the local conditions surrounding such ventures, such as pests, etc. And besides, Berry is deaf and probably, as usual, he didn't "get" half of what was said in the conference. Usually, our understanding of matters as reported out of conference by him, differs from that of other groups.

Today I took up the waistband on a pair of my drawers by about 4 inches. This noon some bananas arrived, but only enough to give 4 to each officer. The 35 surplus were given to the enlisted men and Squad 5 happily donated 1 apiece for them, a precedent which our sourpuss squad refused to follow. They went well, in diluted canned milk, on the scanty rice. Again they told us that we may soon be allowed to go into the town which, instead of being a big city, is now reported to be simply the center of a farming community.

To show how rumors start: Doane[19] comes around saying that the Japs told Gen. King that there is a "large" box on the way for each of us. King denies it. It appears that MacMillan's orderly saw, in a Jap paper, a statement that the U.S. has shipped or has requested permission to ship a Red Cross box to each war prisoner. What an uplift (Balsam was almost opening his box) and what a letdown!

Thursday—Mokuyo-bi, 3 Sept 1942

Some skimpy rations continue, with no improvement in sight. We rec'd 5 fly swatters and they are greatly appreciated. The remainder of our tea order came in this P.M. This afternoon, also, an alleged fire drill was held. A joke. The idea of the Japs was more to prevent our escape than to put out any fire. We were ringed about by soldiers with fixed bayonets pointed at us, in middle of parade ground. Much running about by the Japs at alarm "Hi Joe cashew!" Then a party of our soldiers ran out the gate and up the boundary lane, returning with a prehistoric hand pump on cart wheels, with some lengths of paper-thin hose, some bill hooks, etc. They all played around with several short lengths of hose for a half hour or so, then turned the water on from a hydrant near the fence. A piddly stream resulted; the final length of hose spurted water from a dozen places! After a delay, the 2d line of hose gave similar results, and a 3d line not much better. They didn't dare try the pump at all! Today they told us what will happen to us if we are sentenced to the "detention" pen: no eats but rice and water: you take nothing with you except toilet paper; no mosquito bar; can't lie or sit down from 6:30 A.M. until 8:00 P.M. No smoking of course! Rather rugged punishment! I hope I don't get it!

Tonight we had a couple of tiny pieces of beef in our stew. Also a delivery of 1 lb. salt for 3 sen: Our PX also had a fourth late delivery of shaving brushes, cigarette cases and general tawdry junk but too late to sell.

Friday—Kinyo-bi, 4 Sept 1942

"Another day, another yen." This P.M. they gave our squad leaders a lesson in Japanese numbers and orders and Berry and Braly relayed it to us at 4:00 P.M. I remade my hilly mattress and levelled it a bit, improving it, I hope. I got the job of conducting calisthenics this morning and rec'd compliments on it. Guess I must give up hope of getting more paper like this. Tired out at bedtime tonight.

Saturday—Doyo-bi, 5 Sept 1942

Last night we held our roll call by Japanese commands and will so continue at all formations. Callahan led our calisthenics this morning. We again held a general police of building and grounds. Then I laid out markers and lines for the assembly of the first 4 squads, both ranks. Just before lunch we were issued 85 small cubes of sugar for a month's supply. Ground up 2 cubes in 3 spoonfuls of milk and this helped the rice immensely. Soup was punk as usual. Gen. King reported to Baggy Pants that 2 buckets of rice were thrown out. Some good looking fish came into camp today in spite of "fish are out of season," but we got none. Night chow was hard to cram down. This afternoon I transplanted a row of Sultanas from Richards' bed into my flower bed and it was backbreaking work. Did my laundry before siesta, so it was a day full of waist-bending exercises for me. Went to bed tired. Doctor says we are on rations insufficient to keep up our strength, by at least 1000 calories. Nobody has any pep.

Sunday—Nitiyo-bi, 6 Sept 1942

Had 2 good nights sleep since I remade my mattress; got up only once last night at 3:20. The Jap medical corporal came round and joyfully announced that we now have 6 malaria cases. I worked in the hot sun rectifying my error in our assembly lines, putting them 54″ apart instead of 40″. This was at churchtime and the timid Jap lieutenant asked me if I wasn't a Protestant! He also said they could find no Jap instruction books here in Karenkou and had written to Taiwan for them. I have had 2 days' doses of our precious Sulphoanamine and my sores are healing up as if by magic—scabs flying right and left. Felt faint from exercise in the sun. I have opened up another can of milk and, until it is gone, I'll use 3 spoonfuls, plus one cube of sugar, on my rice for each meal. This noon, 2 bananas per officer came in, 50 kg. in all, but they say that about 150 kg. went to the small batch of Jap guards! And we are helpless! Last night I dreamed of Landon!; in part of it she appeared with one arm full of sliced whole-wheat bread, the other arm full of rye bread. She was nibbling on the whole wheat and smiling at me roguishly. Anyway, I'm glad to learn that the Japs have finally reported to the USA that we are prisoners of war, and not left our relatives in suspense. Baggy Pants told us this yesterday or day before. I thought this might be a good chance for me to dally with a clarinet—an instrument which I've always looked at with awe—or even a saxophone—but he tells me there is neither in town! Gee but this Karenkou must be a punk barrio!

Monday—Getuyo-bi, 7 Sept 1942

Slept under a blanket last night. Usual routine all day. In late P.M. finished assembly lines for 1st four squads and front of Wood's 5th Squad. Soup thick with vegetables, *thanks to Braly inspecting the kitchen.* This work of laying out and digging out the assembly lines in this gravelly ground will, I hope, tend to keep down "rice belly." Very hot in the sun, but comfortable in the shade. Gen. Jones again saw the Jap soldiers throw away a whole bucket of rice—which we so sadly need. Our enlisted men feverishly cleaned the small barracks across the parade. Tonite my gang went on vigilant guard again: Brown waked me at 11:00 and I waked Callahan at 10:50 by mistake because I couldn't read Brezina's watch. 41 people went to rear during my tour. Turned in and slept.

Tuesday—Kayo-bi, 8 Sept 1942

Carter half-heartedly led the calisthenics, but what can one expect of that grouch? He spent today on his bed wrapped in a spread. Aired our bedding on upper railings this morning. My sores are practically well now, thanks to that Sulphoanalimide: scabs practically all gone but I'm covered with the livid marks from them. They checked our bowls this morning. We are supposed to have four apiece and they all have names. Most of us are short one, and it complicates dishing out food. Big flag at gate today, so maybe those long-expected 91 British, Dutch, etc. prisoners will really appear tonight. Many new and repaired eye glasses came in last night and today.

This noon the soup was redolent of tuna fish, but the food situation in general is desperate. The Japs seem deliberately attempting to starve us. Today is the first time we've had a trace of fish. I've carefully enumerated, above, every time we have had a trace of meat. Otherwise we have had straight unsalted rice and boiled vegetables. Not a protein in the whole lot and we are getting weaker daily. Our 7 cases of recurrent malaria are said to be caused by that. I wonder how this will hit the free-eating Dutchmen?

They say the yen was pegged at 14¢ gold and we should use that figure. One of their brands of cigars is listed as Y32 for 25! I'd like to see one! All tobacco is of course a government monopoly and prices determined accordingly. The cigarettes are so short you can hardly light them without burning your nose; unless you keep puffing furiously at them they go out, and if you do work at them hard, then they last only a few puffs. The taste is OK but they are juicy in a holder. Altogether, you can't blame the Japs for their avidity over American cigarettes. Had a good siesta, after Balsam stopped coughing. Missed our shower-bath. We are now getting into the habit of rigging up our mosquito bar promptly after 8:00 P.M. roll call and turning in which makes a fearfully long night. God! the utter uselessness of this existence!

Wednesday—Suiyo-bi, 9 Sept 1942

Five months since the fall of Bataan. The 87 British and about 6 Dutch arrived after 10:00 last night wakening me momentarily. We had all been ordered to be abed by 9:00 P.M. "and stay there" but it was not strictly enforced. My first sight of the newcomers was at reveille roll call. They are all in queer looking shorts. They have been 3 weeks en route from Shanghai, including a week in coolie huts on a bit of sandy desert to the east of Takau. This was ostensibly because this camp was not prepared to receive them! They got their searched musette bags this afternoon. The news they bring is at least 3 weeks old: Germans' drive progressing in Russia (bad news indeed): somewhat stabilized in Egypt; confused reports about an American front in France; ¼ to ½ million Yanks in Australia; Solomon Island in U.S. hands except 1; in Naval fighting our Navy has more than held its own; that Japan has lost 75% of her destroyers and carriers, etc. If Russia only holds out, the news is good. T1 [. . . follows these letters as though he has lost train of thought.]

The food is getting me down, as it is most everybody else. Lawrence learned from the Jap lieutenant that our food would not improve until we submitted to and accepted the Jap farm plan! He thereby incurred the wrath of his section and many others. Most of us are quite irascible these days. This afternoon I laid out the skeleton markings for our last four squads. The sun continues very hot but it is cool in the shade, with usually a gentle breeze wafting through. In evening, at Squad meeting on Berry's call, we voted for the revised farm plan as proposed by the Japs: is—a pig farm only; buying young, middle and mature stock; swill to be collected from other camps and delivered at our main gate, we to tote it to the pens; no bayonets or sentries. The timid lieutenant is said to be a college-trained farmer, so we *should* have expert advice available. "Lights out" caught me reading "The Longhorn Feud," a bum western but the 3d book I've been able to get.

Thursday—Mokuyo-bi, 10 Sept 1942

Another day of dull routine. The Japs are now building around a building to our right rear and we all wonder what it is for. I fear it may be this newly threatened detention or punishment pen. But it is anybody's guess.

There is a new sidelight on our status as regards rations: the Japs have 7 kinds of prison camps: working camps and non-working camps. The inmates of the working camps receive the full ration of the Jap soldier; those in the other camps receive only the rations of civilians. Ours is a non-working camp and consequently we get only civilian rations. So it may be their way of helping us eke out these rations by our own money and a modicum of work—a "token payment" so to speak. Our boys are still seething over "work or no work" and there are heated arguments. Meanwhile we continue on skimpy rations, though today we got camotes in our rice for one or two meals.

Tonight Baggy Pants, inspecting our room, said "very good" when dismissed. I clapped Browne on the back and said "Ah ha! Did you hear that very good?" Razzing him a bit. After roll call, Baggy Pants came back and wanted to know if there had been any "scolding." We couldn't be sure what he was driving at. Maybe he thought I was mocking him.

Friday—Kinyo-bi, 11 Sept 1942

Rain.

Rained hard before reveille, slackened enough to make us fall in outside, and then gradually started in again so that we were quite wet by the time Baggy Pants came along for the roll call. Continued to mist, drizzle, and rain all day, so I omitted laundry work. Callahan and I are starting a pinochle feud. In the trial flight today I beat him 4 out of 5. We start keeping record tomorrow. Started a 4-strand square braid with crown knots but it is very slow.

The newcomers sure had a hard trip coming here from Singapore. There they were living well and practically running their own camp in an old barracks. After loading some 470 of them on this small dilapidated tramp steamer, they lay at anchor in the harbor about 3 days: then steamed slowly to Saigon and lay at anchor in that sweaty place for 3 more days. They then came slowly to Formosa and had that week's camp I mentioned above. Then by train part way here but they sandwiched in a 5-hour boat trip to bridge a railroad gap. On the steamer, each man was given bunk space 18″ by 4′, not enough to sleep in. Had to bathe and shave in tea because no water available. Only 25% allowed on deck at a time for an hour at a time, later increased to 50%. No smoking *except* on deck. Everybody in a pool of sweat. A Jap bridge-building unit was aboard also. All but about 93 of these Limeys were evidently dropped off at Takau. The bunch here seem quite peppy and are already hounding the Japanese about food.

Weather got steadily worse all day. After 9:00 P.M. a near typhoon hit us, making us close all windows—cold. Back porch swept by rain all night. Japs very busy with the British, teaching them counting, etc.

Saturday—Doyo-bi, 12 Sept 1942

Stormy still at reveille so we held bango inside. Weather moderated gradually during the morning so that by 1:00 P.M. our squad went to shower-bath in clear weather. Snail . . . I picked a fine snail off a tree, about 4″ long and, at 3:30 managed to coax the cook to pour hot water on him. Took him home and with Brezinas advice, cleaned him, added salt and ate most of him. Tasteless; not like Helixaspersa. It is too difficult to boil them, under our restrictions, so I won't try adding them to our diet. But I got a good shell out of it. Today's pinochle score: I won, 3–2 games.

Sunday—Nitiyo-bi, 13 Sept 1942

Rained and showered off and on all day. Yet I managed to do my laundry before lunch though it didn't all dry. Worthington and Pugh[20] gathered a big bucketful of snails and asked me about preparing them. So I went over to kitchen at 1:15 and helped clean them and boil them. Sgt. spoiled the broth with too much salt but the smaller snails were not bad when we gathered upstairs and sampled them. All but 5 of Squad 5 partook. Rodman also brought me some, too, because I got some forceps from the hospital to extract the snails from the shells. I saved some for my evening rice. Callahan beat me 5 games of pinochle. My average is now .333 = 3 won 7 lost. Almost finished my watch job braid. I now have several perfect snail shells of good size. Also fixed up Callahan with some. The rain has washed out all traces of my assembly lines, except the brick markers, so I'll have to do them over.

Monday—Getuyo-bi, 14 Sept 1942

The British have brought diphtheria with them: one is sick, 4 are quarantined in the Smithy and hell is popping! At Singapore they had 24 cases and 4 deaths. Since the Japs evidently knew this, why didn't they quarantine the whole bunch elsewhere instead of bringing the disease among us? Last night they asked who wanted breathing masks—a piece of cloth covering the nose and mouth and fastening behind the ears with loops. This morning they issued masks to everybody with stringent rules to wear them for at least 7 days! Must wear them at all times except when eating, washing face, etc. A big jar of permanganate outside hospital—we must gargle before every meal. No Limey soldiers allowed in kitchen; we are to keep away from the British and each other, etc. Queer: they got us all these masks at short notice, but yet they are unable to get us such common items as bananas! Or even tobacco! Turned in 7 yen to Vance to help cover the cost of the smokes *promised* us for today. Berry, our deaf squad leader, says that the dope is now official: that our allowance of 20 measly yen must cover all of our purchases for a month of all "luxury items." *But* what do the Japs class as Luxuries?? Such items as tobacco, sugar, *all* food items, tea, fresh fruits, toilet articles! It is sure going to be a rugged existence! Not even allowed to spend our own money! And we all know what will happen to that part of our money which the Japs have "deposited to our credit." So it amounts to our living on coolie rations plus such part of $2.80 a month as they choose to let us spend. They effectually prevent us from spending by simply not bringing in the stuff we want to buy! They are now extending the bamboo fence along the south boundary, and putting 3 strands of barbed wire on top of it. Finished my watch job and it looks good. Now for a watch! Tonight they finally delivered the "house slippers" for which they charged us 60 sen when we were paid. They are Jap chinelas, with the strap between the big and 2d toe: made of strips of cellophane and proudly announced *"all of the same size!"* Mine reach from my toes only to my arch and keep only the ball of my foot off the floor. *Good* for breaking down arches! The Japs have taken no action on our tobacco requisition dated 7 Sept and tonight the Jap lieutenant was so angry because Bonham had broken a dish that Si Crews, our OD, didn't dare give him the request. I put in a letter, requesting emergency dental treatment for my broken filling, and have heard nothing from it! Oft these Japs move fast when they *want* to. They are now clearing away the shrubbery and weeds along our back fence, having already felled one big tree. Evidently clearing a truck trail along the river bank. Much material piled out there; none loose inside the fence!

Tuesday—Kayo-bi, 15 Sept 1942

This morning we were weighed again, on the same defective scales. I weighed 76.5 bg = 172.9 lbs.—an all-time low for me! I didn't spot my weight at our first weighing, about 2 weeks ago, so I don't know how much I've lost *here,* but I now weigh about 5 pounds less than when, exhausted, I hit Pasay Hospital. The only ones who show gain in weight are our Enlisted Men—and they take turns working in our kitchen. Our whole squad of 16 officers shows an average loss of 3 pounds which, considering that we had previously been on starvation rations for 5 months, is alarming. But I doubt it will have any effect on getting for us more or better food. This morning I put out an assembly marker for Sir Percival's[21] British squad. Had our semi-weekly shower-bath this afternoon. After Col. Bonham finished.

Fish! . . . The first squad has finally eaten all of the extra food which they brought with them from Tarlac and even ole fluff Col. Cooper MC admits that his squad has eaten their last can. I still have 3 cans each of corned Willy and milk that I brought from Bilibid with me. But everybody is so jealous of anybody who has extra food that I hesitate to eat it. Tonight our soup had a few specks of fish in it—the fish flavor was even quite rank—but very grateful to us. Baggy Pants evidently left us last night for parts unknown. The timid lieutenant (hereafter called "White Rabbit") accepted our tobacco request and all day we hoped in *vain* for delivery. He refused our request for toilet articles, saying "One request at a time is enough." Many are running short of smokes now. Finished installing markers for the leaders of our 8 squads.

Wednesday—Suiyo-bi, 16 Sept 1942
Bawled out a Limey early this morning for making excessive chatter with his clogs. Our rice ration increased slightly today; not temporarily, we hope. Acquired a piece of bamboo near our rear fence and will use it to make a shelf and stops for my dishes. Our urine pit is overflowing but the Jap OD says that is all right! About 30 Japs in ranks at the guard house at 1:00 P.M. Seems they are changing our guard on us.

The governor of HongKong[22] arrived last night with one other officer. He wouldn't sign the oath to not try to escape, so they locked him up in the guard house instead of giving him the big separate room upstairs. This morning I saw a big rangy civilian in his shirt sleeves, being escorted from the guard house to our building by the Jap OD ringed about by 6 soldiers with fixed bayonets! A most ludicrous spectacle. He has been in prison for 6 weeks, I hear.

This morning at 9:00 I met with Brigadier Curtis, who commanded all the big guns at Singapore—the job corresponding to mine at Corregidor and we exchanged experiences which were much alike in many ways. He had five 15″ guns (ex-Navy) and the armament, like ours, was emplaced primarily for defense against *naval* action, and not against land attacks. They also had only armor piercing ammunition. Their air force pulled out and left them flat, and with no trace of observation for their guns.

The Japs moved many truckloads of cement into the fenced building that we thought might be the punishment cells. Perhaps they will build a wall between us and the river, also screening us from the school on the far bank. Much singing takes place in that school, also very complicated calisthenics.

The Jap culture is queer in one respect, the stress that is laid upon a Jap's ferocity. Soldiers of all grades utter the simplest commands in blood-curdling yells and howls, as though they were frantic with rage and hate and were suffering extreme torture. And, worse, they are inculcating this technique into the school children of all ages. Over across the river, for example, the children will be singing along calmly when suddenly their music stops and instead, sharp short yawps of hateful noises come in unison from them. Like the snarling yells of "Ga-a-ah" which the soldiers bark as they bayonet the straw dummies. A nation is being trained to animal ferocity, presumably for war purposes.

Worthington et als gathered and cooked more snails today but, having learned all I had to tell them, omitted me from the party. I whittled on bamboo strips in the shade on the parade ground. Meat? . . . Tonight, mirabile dictu, our soup had flecks of meat in it, but *not* a single globule of oil on its surface—so it was mostly fake. But the flavor was good, even though no nourishment existed.

We evidently changed guards today. The new gang is better dressed, more snappy and howls, grunts and yells with much more bestial ferocity than the old gang did. One of their sentries is relieved hourly just outside our window and the barking wakes us all up. They inspected our room at 8:30 while I was still up, reading. Checking for smokers!

Thursday—Mokuyo-bi, 17 Sept 1942

Did chores early. Sunned our bedding on parade ground. Callahan is about frantic over non-delivery of our tobacco: reduced to borrowing. He swapped a suit of pajamas to Cordero for 30 Jap cigarettes! I have about exhausted my supply of abaco fibres and must soon cease plaiting cords. By borrowing James' pliers I got 5 small brass brads.

Commencing with breakfast, our rice ration increased to the old amount, a level-ful vegetable bowl. We attribute it to our new guard who, Campbell guesses, are regulars, continued to re-read De Maupassant.

At morning wash-up, Frye said that his homecoming speech would be brief commencing with "Dearie, I've made a few mistakes" and ending impressively with "Take over the command"—to which I had to retort—"Take over command of what?" I was thinking of my own circumstances: What could Landon "take over"?

We are getting grim amusement from the Japs' latest "suggestion": for everybody to make out their *wills!* We wonder if this is a result of their observations on our decreasing weights and their evident success in starving us to death. Today they also lifted the ban on sunbathing shirtless—they now permit it, back of the other end of barracks. That will help a bit.

Friday—Kinyo-bi, 18 Sept 1942

Showery all day. Dug up and transplanted some white lillies into my flower bed. Again we waited in vain all day for tobacco, but they promptly delivered today the Vitamin B tablets that the Jap medical student first mentioned only yesterday! It all depends on who wants the stuff! Meanwhile I have heard nothing about my dental repairs, requested 10 days ago! This P.M. as Callahan and I were playing pinochle and everybody else in the room but Chase had his mask off, a Jap sentry came up on the porch and bawled us out ferociously—whether for not saluting or for being without our masks, we never knew. In spite of my saying "Wakarimasen" (I don't understand) he barked more Jap at us, but finally left. Boning corporal by showing off, we judged. Borrowed Johnny Pugh's book on Spanish and studied an hour or so this morning, topping off with a short session with Bill Braly—all for something to prevent my rusting out. My pinochle score with Callahan is .450 and +Y1.52. Started marking our squad members positions with flat white pebbles, but rain drove me inside. Got 300 Vitamin B pills, made in Tokyo, and I started taking 2 before each meal. It is called Wakamoto. Got a haircut.

Saturday—Doyo-bi, 19 Sept 1942

Fair in A.M.; showery in P.M. We have to get out on general policing of barracks and grounds every Saturday morning: picking up twigs and leaves, sweeping out gutters. Our orderlies mopped our floor and cleaned our windows yesterday, so we didn't do that. In fact, we have had to mop the floors only that first time. After we finished police, Berry and I went snail hunting and collected a washbasin full including many big ones, 4–5 inches long. After lunch I got my shower while waiting for the snails to boil. Then Berry and I took them outside the kitchen and cleaned them—a messy, slimy job because they hadn't boiled long enough. Various Jap soldiers gathered to watch us and showed varying degrees of nausea over the idea of eating these "hata tsu mari." They tasted like chicken gizzards and are not *my* idea of a delicacy but they are edible and, I hope, serve to change one's metabolism—and furnish a welcome change from the eternal rice. We ate several and then took the remainder to our rooms, including the yellow broth. This time many more of my room mates partook. Brezina said they were excellent. It is funny to see the change of mind, of our officers as regards eating these snails: at first they laughed contemptuously at our prize glutton (Richards) for eating them raw (and that is a bit thick) and asked me if they are really edible. I being the only conchologist here. They openly scoffed my opinion that the snails really *are* edible, and I remember how I struggled in vain to get that first big snail cooked. Now, however, all is changed: gangs of officers are continually (snooping along the hedges and around the trees with eyes on the ground), looking for these formerly despised snails, and hardly a day goes by without at least one batch of snails being boiled in our kitchen, in spite of the opposition of our enlisted cooks, who are less helpful than the Japanese themselves. Everybody seems now obsessed with a craze for eating them and braising them.

Transplanted remainder of Brezina's sultanas, also a few more white lillies to my flower bed. Today our exchange came back to life, thanks to the return of the Jap sergt. A ration of salt arrived for everybody (1 cupful for a month), then tea for everybody (and I let Callahan have my share); also a package of Japanese toilet paper, large and precarious sheets which must be doubled for safety's sake. (We slit each sheet lengthwise and fold it in halves, which brings it to about the surface size we are *used* to.) It is another commentary on the poverty of Japan in general and this place in particular that the Jap lieutenant is issuing paper for our use in making our wills, said that he can get no paper for use with ink! So I must economise on *this* paper to the utmost!

Sunday—Nitiyo-bi, 20 Sept 1942

Reveille is now before daylight: days are shorter. The difference between summer and winter sunrise time is much more evident here than in Manila. This morning there was unusual air activity: a flight of 9 fighters flew about us and 1 did good stunts; later 7 bombers flew around. We received the rest of our month's salt ration and (mirabile dictu!) three bananas! Balsam, etc. went snail hunting. I got some old basket bamboo at the kitchen and put it to soak, for weaving a shelf. A banana on my noonday rice helped get it down. Barely enough rice to cover the bottom of our bowls. Many gangs out hunting snails early with surprising success. Snails must be a terrible garden pest around here, judging from the way the supply keeps up.

Monday—Getuyo-bi, 21 Sept 1942

Autumnal equinox. Worked in sun preparing splints for my bamboo shelf and weaving them. I find it very troublesome and slow, due to my inexperience. This P.M. Balsam and Brezina served up a few snails and they were unusually good— the few morsels helped a lot, since we rec'd but a few grains of rice (about a teacupful) for supper. These scanty rations are alarming.

One for the book: this P.M. I interviewed the interpreter ("Et Cetera") about my dental work and he explained that my request had gone forward for decision, that higher authority tells them to "borrow tools from local dentists and do the work here in camp ourselves"! that the local dentists have no spare equipment! Evidently the local commander takes this as a reason for ignoring the whole thing! I explained that I was due for the work the day we left Tarlac and asked to go to town, under guard, and have the work done here. He said he would ask the Jap camp commander. Such disregard of prisoners' health is typical of the treatment we get. And yet, only today, the White Rabbit said that their internees were being treated not so well by the British but "very well" by the Americans. On our side of the medal: Sgt. Cavanaugh was on a burying detail at Balanga, during that terrible march, and one Filipino soldier was still breathing when the

Japs made them bury him. Col. Callahan, on another detail of 4 who dug a grave, declares that one Filipino soldier, thrown into the grave tried to climb out, but was bayonetted to death by the Japs. Col. Snell II Corps was also on this detail and saw it. He fainted. Callahan *saw* 4 Filipino soldiers shot for being unable to keep up!

Tuesday—Kayo-bi, 22 Sept 1942

Last night I slept cosily under two blankets. Went on vigilant guard this A.M. from 1:00–2:00 and woke Callahan. Cool and bracing this morning, much more invigorating than Manila climate. *Very* skimpy rice for breakfast. Today sugar came in for the British. In P.M. we got the welcome news that we no longer need wear those damnable diphtheria masks and we all rejoice! Today I started afresh as a "tea-granny" and I used my new tea ball (made from surgical bandage) for lunch and 3:00 P.M. and the same spoonful of Formosa tea gave good results. May be able to use it 3 times? Our tea is usually sad, because we have been unable to get really *hot* water. While at the bath-house this P.M. I "acquired" a brass cleat and 2 brass screw-eyes for use at my window and for suspending our mosquito bar, thus doing away with dangerous nails. Continued work on weaving my shelf. Lawrence slapped twice today for complaint on food.

Wednesday—Suiyo-bi, 23 Sept 1942

Tea is sure a diuretic—had to visit latrine twice last night. Hell of a life when remarks like that are noteworthy; it just shows how empty our lives are. Used the "visiting card" method of registering and it was a great success. Others are copying it. We have to buy a new bango registry book or the Japs will put their own guards on, to check up on those going to the rear between 9:00 P.M. and 6:00 A.M.!

Started out right after breakfast and collected snails with fair success. Cordero, Brezina and Balsam did also. Cordero dug a storage pit for our snails. I squared up my flower bed and then finished installing markers for front rank of Squad 4. Got some more splints and worked on my shelf. It is very troublesome; wish I'd never started it. About ⅔ completed, if the abaca whippings hold.

They say Lawrence was beaten again this morning; others say that the Japs later apologized to him. It seems that an official written complaint will be made to higher Jap authority, for the complaint of skimpy food was justified. It appears that the Japs love to slap faces; with them it takes the place of oral reprimands. They were unusually active today in barking at everybody who didn't see them from afar; jump to attention and bow. The Jap mess sergeant came to look at our supper.

Thursday—Mokuyo-bi, 24 Sept 1942 (Japanese holiday)

Bad night; 4 trips, but my ankles are down a bit. Am losing the nail from my left big toe, due to the bad infection I had there at Bilibid and Tarlac. Roasted a snail in its shell but probably not long enough, for it was not very good. Full of yellow eggs the size of peas.

Today was a Jap holiday; big flag at main gate, but the coolies worked all day at building the brick wall. Neck high and only 1 brick thick, and very poorly laid. The Japs "heard we are out of cigarettes," so they sent over 1000 scags = 100 boxes, "to be divided equally among officers and men." The British say "of course" they'll give more to their men. This gives us 3⅓ cigarettes per person. Net results: Pat owes me 5 scags. On our pinochle I am 102 points ahead. Eschewed tea today. They say our tobacco order will arrive day after tomorrow. Our starvation rations continue—decreasing, if anything. Today Ted Chase and I begin our week's detail as food disher-outers.

Quite a sizable earthquake at 12:45 P.M.; the vibration was first in one direction and later at right angles. We all hoped it hit Tokyo hard. Many of our officers are getting themselves slapped these last few days.

Friday—Kinyo-bi, 25 Sept 1942

Today Gen. Wainwright and Sir Percival asked for a conference "x" who sent his underlings but would not come himself. The object was to find out exactly what the Japs want and tell them of our eagerness to cooperate: to iron out apparent misunderstandings, etc. I asked the interpreter (whom Campbell has named "Mortimer Snerd") for the decision about my teeth and he said the camp commander had given him no decision. It looks bad for me, judging from what has just happened to an enlisted man; he had a bad toothache for 4 days and his jaw was badly swollen. Dr. Glatly begged the Japs to send the man to a dentist in Karenkou, but what they did was to borrow some tools from somewhere and make Glatly (who is not a dentist) gouge out the man's filling and pack the tooth with something to stop the ache! Now the man has a badly ulcerated tooth. I wonder if they call that humane treatment! This afternoon we got another typhoid shot, but Glatly injected it into the deltoid muscle, so most of it was forced out!

This P.M. those of us who had bedding rolls received them back and turned in our Japanese straw mattresses. We cooked up a mess of snails this P.M. and mixed them with our evening rice with gratifying results. British did not get paid today, in spite of advance notice.

Last night the guards raised hell with people going to latrine: objected to the noise of our getas, yet their yelled commands make twice as much racket. At one time they had 20 officers lined up out there. They insist on entry at end, exit via centre and there wash our hands, wearing getas only from our steps to latrine and return. They made us a speech about it at reveille. My waist now measures only 32 inches. If Landon and Priscilla could only see me now!

The upshot of the conference this morning is that the Japs said that our joint request proved that Wainwright and Percival had patently violated the orders which prohibit conferences except when a Jap officer is present and that no more such letters would be written by us, and that hereafter anybody who has a complaint must present it in person to the Jap OD.

Saturday—Doyo-bi, 26 Sept 1942

Duck! . . . The soup last night consisted of plenty of water: full bowls for all. Today arrived 72 smoked ducks and put the whole camp in a dither. We'll have 36 in our evening soup and 36 tomorrow. To cap the climax, 18 kg. of *meat* also arrived, which is said to be for breakfast. We don't know what to make of this sudden munificence. Of course we pay for the ducks at Y3.50 apiece but the meat is said to be a free issue. This afternoon we redeemed our stored (extra) shoes, to clean them. Soup at night was rich in oil and tasted plainly of smoke, but everybody was up in arms over the scarcity of duck meat in the said soup and the chorus is "who ate the duck meat?" All I got was 3 neck vertebrae with their attached shreds of meat and 1 piece of skin. Installed white pebble markers for 6th squad. The guards were very quiet last night and comparatively subdued today.

Sunday—Nitiyo-bi, 27 Sept 1942

Heavy shower at 1:30 A.M. but reveille clear. Don Hilton had got 6 good snails by end of bango. Meat! . . . Today was a red letter day: meat in soup at all three meals,—duck bones (and meat) plus some suspicion of beef at night. It had a fine effect on morale of everybody and, I hope, answers the duck meat question by indicating that *all* the duckmeat went into the soup. It is hard to get exactly the same crumbs of meat into each bowl, yet tonight Col. Bonham had the nerve and bad taste to complain (not to my face) that somebody got more of something than he. Most of the day was routine: shave, laundry, plaiting twine, installing markers, etc. Still no delivery of tobacco, which is said to have finally arrived in Karenko and is now being distributed to merchants. We *may* get ours tomorrow.

It is said that 24 officers and 16 men, war prisoners, will join us tonight—probably Americans from Mindanao. Listened to Gen. Keyes, Indian Army, talking about that service.

Monday—Getuyo-bi, 28 Sept 1942

New arrivals. Sure enough, our friends from Mindanao and Cabanatuan came in at about 10:45 last night in a rain storm, wetting them through. Marched to the small Barracks B where they exchanged their shoes for clogs and then came to our big barracks and occupied the two rooms reserved for them. There is now a Cholera at Takau, which town they passed through, and hence they will be quarantined from us for 5 days. However, we got chances to talk to some of them and so got budgets of news. I was overjoyed to find my former assistant, Col. Dorsey Rutherford because he told me about my son-in-law, Brooke Maury, FA whom he had as his adjutant at Camp 3, Cabanatuan. Brooke is well, cheerful and in good flesh. Rutherford has gained lots of weight. Evidently the prisoners at Cabanatuan fed lots better than we are doing. Col. Nap Boudreau, CO of that camp also arrived but I did not see him, though they say he has my bedding roll and Bible which must be mistakes. Also saw Col. Jack Cook, QMC who was in charge of our supply base in Cebu. When the Japs came, he burned the supplies and, accidentally, the city of Cebu (for which the Japs kept him in jail when they finally caught him).

The list of newcomers includes 16 enlisted men, 24 officers, and the British governor of Malaya.[23] Will know more about them later; the 4 generals are— Sharp,[24] Chynowith,[25] Vachon,[26] Grandma Seals[27] the ex-adjutant general and. ... At reveille this morning Berry asked me to lead the calisthenics for a week. It was cloudy and sprinkled but cleared up by mid-forenoon. I tried in vain to melt lids off some milk cans to make me some containers. Stretched my lash ropes again. Transplanted a few papaya seedlings.

We learn from the newcomers that Sam McCullough died, after we left him at Bilibid, probably of cancer of the prostate. He was terribly thin when we left him but they tell us that, when he died, he weighed only *40* pounds. Unbelievable!

Tuesday—Kayo-bi, 29 Sept 1942

Rained hard last night, sprinkled at reveille and showery all day. Starting yesterday P.M. guards ran amok with their petty persecution, centering on supersensitiveness to saluting. The sergeant came up on front porch and dragged Bowler, Bronner and Berry and a Limey from upstairs over to the guard house for not saluting him though he was outside on the porch and they were inside their rooms with windows closed and did not see him! There was lots of yelling by sentries at the benjo all night. I saw Menzie get slapped, with frantic yells. Another sentry made a man kneel on the concrete, for some fault in saluting. They raised hell all over the lot. Today they have calmed down much. Rain at reveille drove us indoors, so no calisthenics. Gathered a cupful of berries from the tree near the kitchen and put them in my noon rice. Don't know what they are but others copied me and gathered them later. The berries are well liked by the flies which flock to them. Our tobacco still has not arrived! Gathered more berries and enjoyed them in evening rice.

Pay day! We were paid this P.M. Pay = 310 yen; Deductions were Y248 deposited in postal bank, Y7.60 for food for August, 10% = Y31.00 to start the pig farm, 1% = 3.10 for enlisted orderlies' services; received in cash Y20.30. Gave Y10.00 as deposit to our post exchange, making a total of 15 + 7 + 10 = Y32 paid in. Jack Vance says my credit balance at PX is now Y11.04 but I make it 11.54.

Our scale of pay is : Lt. Gen Y483.33, Maj. Gen. and BG Y416.66, Cols. Y310, Lt. Col. Y220, Major Y170. As to the 80% of our pay which they claim is deposited to our credit with the postal bank: we sign the book that we "have received" this money but they give us no receipt, so we have nothing to show that the Jap government owes us a sen!

Wednesday—Suiyo-bi, 30 Sept 1942

Still raining and continued, off and on, all morning, but it stopped about noon and remained overcast the remainder of the day. Started making cans into receptacles. Went upstairs and saw Gen Sharpe, ex-CO in Mindanao, who was in organized reserve work in Calif. He gave me a scag and a cigar. Also saw Nap Boudreau, who says that the Japs broke open my boxes in Btry. Cheney and threw my books and records down the dump. He has my Bible (probably Paul's). Went out after lunch gathered more berries. Started a new type of plaited watch job. Transplanted more papaya seedlings. Rain again in P.M. and kept up.

During the Bataan Campaign, Filipino Supply officers with divisions gave much to Filipino troops and witheld them from the American troops which were fighting for the Filipinos. Generals Lim and Bapinpin (Filipinos) always ran swell messes at all times; they are now in Manila helping the Japs organize the new Constabulary.

This P.M. the long-delayed delivery of tobacco occurred and what a disappointment. We needed over 6000 packs of scags plus lots of cigars and leaf tobacco. They gave us 2000 and the blessed interpreter said, "That's all you get." This gives us only 90 cigarettes for a whole month! This is the latest proof that this camp has become a punitive camp and how. We are evidently reduced to 1 scag after each meal. Meanwhile we hear that Sharp's camp in Mindanao was humanely run: they had an unlimited purchase facilities and were practically unhampered. Wish I had space for recording the petty and major annoyances they pile onto us.

Thursday—Mokuyo-bi, 1 Oct 1942

Rainy reveille indoors. Usual routine. (Gathered more berries for evening rice last night.) This A.M. Campbell and Brezina started their weeks tour of chow disher-outers, relieving Chase and me. They used the long-advocated scheme of measuring the rice out into tea cups. Our allowance just fills the cup and the meal is completed by about twice that amount of hot water containing more or less vegetables and greens.

Usual morning routine. Rain stopped in mid morning. We cooked snails this P.M. and I ate mine with evening rice. Brezina used a clove of garlic in cooking them, making them the best batch we've had. The camp is still agog over our gypping on the tobacco deal; some are kicking because everybody (including non-smokers) got the same amount.

More excitement over the detailed rules for us to follow in case of air raids here. The main point is that *we must remain inside our rooms!* And they call *that* giving us a chance for our lives! There will be a drill next week. Either Wood or Hoffman must now sleep in the OD room—so the Japs are really apprehensive. Some of our more sanguine officers see evidence in this that our Gen. Drum, in Australia, is already in action and moving northward! I foresee that, if and when he does, the Japs will move us to Japan for safekeeping—and we all dread that prospect. [Here he draws a detailed map of Taiwan in margin.]

Friday—Kinyo-bi, 2 Oct 1942

Fair today. The Japs gave us a schedule showing when we can put in requests for tobacco, toilet articles, etc. Details later. They also got very busy with air raid measures: placed outside each door some poles with rope cat-o-9 tails at ends, with 6 coir mats for fire bombs; the hall and benjo lights shaded with cloth. Extra sentry at each door. They've also put lysol trays with mats at benjo doors, for disinfecting our clogs. Cordero made a new snail safe. The "berries" are all gone now. Tonight Baggy Pants (Lt. Wakasuti) came by this evening, and explained Jap names for day of week—"Sun-day," "Moon-day," etc.

We are now told we can *ask* for tobacco thrice weekly, so we are asking for 20 scags per officer per day. Made 2 small garden rakes.

Saturday—Doyo-bi, 3 Oct 1942

Rained a bit last night but I led calisthenics at reveille and cut it short because it started to sprinkle. Looked like rain all day, but cleared away in forenoon. Managed to cut a strip of tin for making a razorblade knife. Pat Callahan beat me 4–1 pinochle. Rakes work fine.

Yesterday they asked (1) who has farming experience! (2) who is willing to work in garden? Gardens will be run by squads, which is bad news for our squad. We all fear that it will result in our working under a bayonet. We had part of an air alert tonight and had to close our curtains.

This P.M. the Japs delivered 1490 packs of cigarettes for *free* distribution to enlisted men on a basis of 20 per NCO and 10 per Pvt. Yet they let us buy only 9 packs—or really 12, but made us give up 3 each to the enlisted men! This was only last Wednesday. Our newest lieutenant demanded a new requisition for Sharps' men for tobacco, but produced nothing.

Sunday—Nitiyo-bi, 4 Oct 1942

Went on vigilance guard last night, from 1:00 to 2:00. Sentry made an officer crawl from our *benjo* (which is temporarily out of use) to the other, because he attempted to use the wrong one. Day dawned beautiful and continued so. I completed my razor-blade knife, made from part of a milk can. Got a short sunbath in A.M. but was so annoyed with Nelson's roseate picture of our future that I left and cleaned rust off my old salt tin. Better rice ration at noon, though Alec got most of the camotes therein. This morning Louis Bowler showed intrepidity by swapping soup bowls with Brezina, the disher-outer, under the assumption of unfairness of distribution. I had previously announced, when I had that job, that anybody could always exchange with me—but nobody did. This evening Cordero divided up a papaya, given him by a Jap.

The days—and weeks pass swiftly—too swiftly when I think how Landon and I could be enjoying them together. Dammit. Still no sign of our being allowed to write home. But they do say they will try to get the services of a dentist, one who is said to believe in *pulling* teeth, not filling them!

Another air raid alarm at 7:45 P.M. We closed our curtains and then lit our light again.

Monday—Getuyo-bi, 5 Oct 1942

Another fine day, just like yesterday. At breakfast, Berry accused Brezina of partiality in dishing out the soup and Brezina, as usual, acted like a sulky child, told him he was quitting the job. Brezina claims to be Czechoslovakian, but he sure has German characteristics, notably in his table manners. To hear him inhaling his soup is worth travelling miles.

Air raid practices in mid-forenoon, both for town and out here. Gen. Pierce was slow to run into our quarters, so a Jap chased him, throwing rocks at him, causing Pierce to run, shedding his clogs en route. Tea as usual about 10:30 A.M. Air alert continued until after 12:00, but Baggy Pants let me out and I gathered some "berries" from a tree on our parade ground. While doing this, 5 Jap bombers flew over us headed north. Berries quite tasteless. Our enlisted men were all out on parade ground all day, cleaning the gravelled roads of grass, and hoeing the edges in preparation for the inspection, by the "commander of the Taiwan army and the boss of all the Taiwan prison camps"—this latter probably being the sourpuss lieutenant colonel who was so angry the day we arrived.

Our rice and vegetables for lunch were universally held to be our all-time nadir in quantity. All of us have long ago lost all our fat and, for some time, our muscles have been wasting.

Wakasuti

The Japs are all steamed up over air raids: they have a fine, deep-throated siren in town, much better than our shrill one at Corregidor, and they sprang several alarms with it today. The all clear is one long blast. They pulled one alarm just after 7:00 P.M. and it lasted until after 10:00. They had already taken away our white incandescent and installed a blackout bulb of about 15 watts, which leaves our room so dark that we can do practically nothing, except play cribbage in the small spot of light directly below the lamp. So we lay on our beds and listened to the numerous Jap guards scurrying around our porch and grounds, screaming and yelling and snarling commands around. At bango we were lucky: when they finally called our roll they dismissed us to let another squad use our hall space. Gen. Sharp's squad got mixed up with our 3d Squad and wound up by standing in ranks for an hour.

Tuesday—Kayo-bi (Fire day), 6 Oct 1942

Slept poorly, if at all, from 4:00 A.M. on Fire day. I am still leading calisthenics. This morning I earned the gratitude of my room by opening one of my 3 cans of corned beef and dividing it among the 10 officers in our room. It was a wonderful treat. Worked an hour, cleaning the can for use as a container and then when I got it cleaned, he swapped me a Nestle can for it! I had been carefully saving my beef for the time when the starvation program *must* be jolted defensively for me. In view of the short rice rations recently, I believed the time was *now*. The change for the better in the feelings and outlook of all of us was most marked.

Worked on the markers on parade and concluded not to shift the line into parallelism to barracks. Air raid alarms kept up rapidly all morning but were not for us. Our guards were evidently training the children at the school, just across the river, using 2 pistol shots to simulate the explosion of bombs—at which signal the children all hit the dirt in most approved style.

While I was taking our legally authorized shower-bath and sunbath, the Japs made us a delivery of bananas and cigars. We get 5 bananas only and 18 instead of 25 cigars, but no scags.

Lt. Wakasuti dropped into our room and chewed the rag with us for a while. I tried to get the Japanese for turning out and on our blackout lamp, but the more he talked the more confusing it was. The cigars are all dried out, but better than nothing.

More air alerts, off and on, all day, including the usual one at evening roll call. The blackout lights are sure a pest. Received word of impending inspections Thursday and Friday by comdrs of Taiwan prison camps and Taiwan army.

Wednesday—Suiyo-bi (Water day), 7 Oct 1942

Fine day but turned cloudy at 3:30 P.M. Our enlisted men are busy, scalping roads, so we all turned to and mopped up our floors and washed our shelves and woodwork. Then I went outside and installed the markers for Nos. 1 of all remaining squads before lunch. Rice! At noon we were astounded to find out rice ration increased to almost double. Baggy Pants was in the kitchen, supervising the dishing out of chow! We wonder if this is sporadic, just because of the approaching inspection, or whether the increase will be permanent. Anyway, it was gratefully received.

We were to have a rehearsal parade—first at 2:00 P.M. then at 4:00 P.M.—then called off!

Thursday—Mokuyo-bi (Tree day), 8 Oct 1942

Fine cool night for sleeping. Air alarms minimized today. Spent all our time rehearsing for tomorrow's inspection: turned us out at 8:30 and rearranged us with generals and brigadiers together. Then we waited 30 minutes for the officers to arrive. After rehearsal they pulled a new ceremony: Reading the rescript of the emperor's declaration of war, 10 months ago. This will be repeated every month and they "will let us participate with them." After our camp commander had made his usual political speech, a soldier came down from HQ bearing ceremoniously at the height of his forehead two long white boxes which our CC saluted and received and handed with equal ceremony to the interpreter who also saluted and then read this official exposition of Japan's reasons for war. Afterwards it was returned with similar ceremony. We followed the commands of a Jap sergeant all of whose orders sounded exactly alike and we could only guess at what was wanted—a fact which old "Sourpuss" caught, but to save "face" for the sergeant, they kept him in office. Released at 10:10.

Formed again at 12:50 for more rehearsing and were sent back to get our shoes. "Sourpuss" who is the lieutenant colonel in charge of all Taiwan prison camps, officiated and we stood around and rehearsed (tried to guess the sergeant's orders) for 1½ hours so our day was pretty well shot and all for nothing.

Our increased rice ration continues. Used 1 banana at each meal, to give a taste to it. But the rice fell off again for night, because Wakasuti "was so busy he forgot to tell the kitchen crew to continue the increased ration." This sounds bad; I predict we'll return to our starvation rations when tomorrow's inspection is over, and that he holds the helm—and hence is the one who has been responsible.

During the air alarms, the rumor was rampant that 4 Taiwan cities had just been bombed, and our wishful thinkers were all steamed up. Me, sceptical me, I branded it a damn lie.[28]

Authentic report from Cabanatuan: One of the Jap guards, had 6 Americans out in town, on the loose. They were detected and *all* were shot for being out of camp without authority.

This evening they removed our blackout lights and re-installed our white lights. The improvement was wonderful, so much so that I sat up, after bango, and read *Cellina* until 8:50. The Japs say "No more air alarms for a while" and this seems effectually to disprove the 4 cities being bombed, and makes our rumormongers sick.

Friday—Kinyo-bi (Gourd day), 9 Oct 1942

Fine day. Our guard changed today and a new bunch takes over. Great bustle everywhere over the inspection: we did last minute sweeping, etc. and then turned out at 8:35. The CO of the Taiwan army arrived on dot of 9:00 A.M. He was a chunky, moon-faced man with wide-spread luxuriant mustache. He received our "eyes right" and we had to follow him with our eyes as he crossed our front and took post in front of our center. Wainwright and Sir Percival ran out in front of him and Wood read their speech. The CO brought in a small package (cigarettes, etc.) to them, also some small, cheap books for us. Then he went up to HQ for tea and later came back and walked through our barracks, wherein we were lined up.

Pork! For 2 days we've been excited over the Jap promise that we would get a pig to eat today. But it develops that the pig is a present from the Jap general, and when it reached our kitchen, the local Japs cut off both hams, to include the loins! Now, when our enlisted cooks steal what *they* want, if we get more than a *flavor* we'll be lucky.

With Carter's help, I started surveying a new line of markers for our assembly formation. For evening meal we had more rice than usual and real soup with rich pork flavor—and even a crumb or two of the pork in it. Universally hailed as the best meal that we've had here at this camp. Everybody more cheerful, as a result. Gosh, how little it takes to please us now! We repaired our electric lighter this P.M. A couple of Jap newspapers (in English were given to us: "Japan Times and Advertiser"—Practically nothing but propaganda.)

The new guard is less savage than the old. No racket at benjo tonight or in posting guards.

Saturday—Doyo-bi (Ass day), 10 Oct 1942

Cool and breezy. Worked most all A.M. on rectifying assembly lines. The British finally got their heavy baggage this morning and as it had been well soaked by rain, they spread most of it on the parade grass to dry. The new American prisoners got their heavy baggage at 1:00 P.M. and most of them sure had lots of it. Gen. Vachon, from Mindanao, had *8* trunks! Boudreau gave me Landon's Bible, the only salvaged article of mine from Corregidor. Sharp gave me 2 cigars; Rutherford gave me a pack of Filipino cigarettes and a piece of laundry soap. Boudreau gave me a small notebook, good for Jap language study notes.

Pork in the soup at noon and it was luscious, though the rice was gummy. My ankles are now swelling up toward my calves. Consulted Glatly but with no results toward getting eggs or other foods.

Sunday—Nichio-bi (Sunday), 11 Oct 1942

Overcast dawn but soon turned sunny, though that poisonous ass, Balsam, insisted on sealing up our room air tight. Just after lunch (wherein the "soup" had a trace of fat) we cooked up our last (?) batch of snails and I put the refuse into my flower bed. But I haven't used feces, as have some of us—with odoriferous results. Lined up front rank of Squad 5 on my new orientation, which corrects the Jap error of some 10. Col. Cook lent Campbell 2 books of poetry but, as I was sunning my wafer-thin mattress, I couldn't lie down and read. Am copying my Japanese notes into the new notebook that Boudreau gave me. We were due for a delivery of fruit yesterday but, *of course,* the Japs failed to deliver.

Monday—Getsuyo-bi (Moon day), 12 Oct 1942

Just another day. The rations are now scantier than ever! There are 42 Japs in camp and 317 of us prisoners, and, yet, when the vegetables arrived this morning, the Japs took *half* and the best half of course! They are deliberately starving us.

I went to sick call this morning because my ankle swelling is extending up to my calves. The Jap medical student assumed charge—told me to increase dose of Vitamin B pills to 18 a day and entered me as a "bed patient"—for which I got a red circular card, and am supposed to stay in bed most of the time. Yet I spent most of the afternoon installing stone markers for our assemblies. In evening: they unlocked the other door in our room: Cordero and Boatwright fought.

The Japs gave us some pamphlets a few days ago and last night our room fell heir to 3: American Traditions (3 essays), etc. (2) Religion and Literature (3) Courtship of Miles Standish. Enjoyed essays by John Muir and Walt Whitman. These booklets evidently Jap school texts.

This evening Jap lieutenant told us we'll get 52 ducks tomorrow and thus cheered us up. Queer that we can buy smoked duck (a luxury) but not pork, which costs much less. Perhaps because all food is rationed under Army control. Am now reading "British Poets."

Tuesday—Kayo-bi (Fire day), 13 Oct 1942

Dawn clear and cool. Filled out another questionnaire, on tissue paper, on such items as family worries, intimate friends, acquaintances, status of relatives, etc. plus many questions that we've previously answered many times over. This A.M. I started working on my markers but the Jap med student caught sight of me and made me quit; prescribed barefoot strolls in the grass morning and evening if I *must* walk—otherwise lie down as much as possible.

Masks! This P.M. another case of diphtheria developed among the British and so, dammit, we must wear those damnable masks again! Donned them about 4:00 P.M. Permanganate gargle also now on tap and our selfish souls—such as Gen. Brougher—are filling ketchup bottles with it. "I've got mine; to hell with *you.*"

Duck! The duck at evening in the soup was fine! There were only about 27 in the soup and we fed 40 more people than before, yet there was more meat than before. More ducks—or geese—tomorrow, the rest of the 52. Our long-awaited issue of cigarettes arrived and was an insult. I put in for 100 packs and got (swagger sticks) exactly 4 packs = 40 scags = about 1 day's supply in peace time! The sergeant says this was all of the tobacco on hand in the warehouse—i.e., 1000 packs on our requisition of 5680 packs! This is another example of Japanese persecution, and this hits us right where we live. Everybody furious.

Wednesday—Suiyo-bi (Water day), 14 Oct 1942

Went to reveille, though marked as a bed patient, in order to get the calisthenics. Knife! Yesterday P.M. they returned my boy scout knife—but not my lighter! Sharpened it today. Stuck around the room most all day, though I took time to dig a trench in my flower bed for fertilizer. Breakfast and lunch were lowest yet in quantity and our prospects of slow starvation are now actualities. My muscles are largely absorbed now and I am very weak.

Jap dentist appeared this afternoon, but most of the officers lied and said their teeth are *now* aching, so he took them first and I was left out. He promised to return—but I don't know. Fiddled around, doing little but odd jobs: bamboo ruler, splicing string, reading.

Tonight we had 2d half of the ducks and it was fit for a king! The rice was scanty but, like last night, must have been cooked with a bit of grease, for it was most delicious and needed nothing else. We could have eaten thrice the amount. Too bad we seem to be restricted to one such feed a month—our last one was on the day the Mindanao crowd joined us.

We have a few newspapers now: "Japan Times and Advertiser" printed in English in Tokyo—mostly propaganda. We get bitter amusement from 2 articles on the atrocities committed by Americans on Jap repatriotes and by Dutch on war prisoners, for these very "atrocities" against which the Japs scream are but a small part of the things they have done and are doing to us! Hardly a one of us has been able to keep a watch or ring or a fountain pen—or a bit of money. I have noted these reports in my notebook, in the hope of using them some day. Callahan got 2 notebooks—but none for me.

Just as we were going to bed tonight, they brought back to me the straw Jap mattress that I turned in when I got my own wafer-thin mattress. It prevents the iron slat-work of my bunk from marking me. That little Jap tech sergeant is good. They all laughed heartily when I thanked them with "Doome arigate."

Thursday—Mokuyo-bi (Tree day), 15 Oct 1942

Sugar is supposed to be rationed out to us today—after gypping us out of our allowance since the 5th but nobody really expected it. Our food still skimpier, if possible. The projected farm has been approved and may start any year now, though we are all so weak that I doubt our capacity to do much physical work. I omitted reveille this morning and BP came to inquire about my health. Got a long joint of bamboo for a ruler. Wish I could continue working on my markers—managed to do front of 8th Squad this P.M. My ankles are now swollen alarmingly up into my calves.

Got my cigarette lighter back this P.M. but the Japs had carefully removed the flint!

Friday—Kinyo-bi (Gourd day), 16 Oct 1942

Japs say—no sugar nor salt has arrived. Opened a can of corned beef (I have 1 more left) and mixed a little with the little rice they gave us for breakfast, and am hoping it will keep until I have used it for 4 meals. My conscience hurts not to share the beef with all in our room, but my health demands it. It took me a couple of hours to clean and polish the can. Our orderlies scrubbed our floor this morning. Our month's issue of salt today; about 1½ milk cans. Plenty for me but insufficient for Callahan. Bad luck: could not find my spare flints for my lighter: guess the Japs got them.

Wainwright (and possibly Percival) was allowed to write a letter home today—but nobody else. To show the censorship rules: He wrote "With me are all of the generals and most of the colonels" and they made him take that out! When the rest of us will be allowed to write is unknown. After bango, am reading a P.I. text book on English literature before turning in. Found my old favorites, Ulysses and Kubla Khan.

Saturday—Doyo-bi (Ass day), 17 Oct 1942

Overcast, windy. This is the middle of a 3-day holiday—said to be a Harvest Festival. We were turned out at 9:50 A.M. for a parade, but my red circular card excused me, so I snuck some fertilizer onto my flower bed while nobody was looking.

Had a good night last night, going only once to benjo. My ankles are down appreciably this A.M. For breakfast I used the last of the can of corned beef, which leaves me one for final reserve.

The following officers of 59th CA were sent from Cabanatuan back to Corregidor, ostensibly for questioning but they actually did heavy handling of ammunition and stores. Those underscored had returned to Cabanatuan about 3 September, meeting Rutherford et als during the latter's 20-day stay in Bilibid before coming here: Lt. Cols. N. B. *Simmonds,* D. D. *Edison,* Maj. *Stennis,* Capts. F. J. *Gerlich,* Cooper, Major H. *Julian,* Lt. Col. L. S. Kirkpatrick, Capt. H. H. Hauck. (This list is from Rutherford.) They say that those who returned after their sojourn at Corregidor were (comparatively) as fat as pigs, showing that they got good and plentiful chow there. As to my boxes of books, etc., which I had stored in my Btry. Cheney: the Japs made the fatique details open the boxes with fire axes; the Japs took what they wanted and had the remainder thrown over the cliff onto the Cheney Dump! What a crime! Our men tried to throw some of my stuff up on top of the Cheney magazines, inside the battery—but I don't know what it amounted to—and anyway, one rainy season would ruin the stuff. Rained slightly tonight.

Sunday, Nichio-bi (Sun day), 18 Oct 1942

Cold overcast day. The Japs today started removing the iron manhole covers to our benjo and substituting wooden covers! No better proof can be had of Japan's desperate need of iron. Right after breakfast I chased out to the north wall and got a good batch of snails. We cleaned and boiled them right after our skimpy lunch and they tasted good. Mixed them with my evening rice.

Yesterday we closed one door and opened the one by Chase's bunk, thus giving us more room between our bunks on our side of our room. Campbell, as usual, selfishly fought for most room, but anyway the situation is slightly improved for us —but those on the other side of the room, now experiencing the conditions under which *we* had existed for exactly two months, are screaming bitterly about drafts.

Last night I was on vigilant guard, leaving the cinch trick from 5:00–6:00 A.M. 78 men went out during my tour. Deadbeated reveille. No calisthenics. During the morning I installed markers for 12th Squad and a few black markers for our calisthenics formation. I sure like to stay outdoors every possible minute, the weather is so bracing.

The rumor is that our rice ration is to increase by 2 oz. a day, but I'll believe it when I see it. Now we are getting about a coffee-cupful for every meal.

Monday—Getsuyo-bi (Moon day), 19 Oct 1942

Overcast all day. Shave and laundry. Today they took my all red card away and gave me, in its place a red and white circular card which permits me to lie on my bed when I wish, but does not excuse me from roll calls, but does allow me to go out and work. So I went out and put in the front rank markers for Squads 6 and 7. Dentist! This P.M. the Jap dentist showed up again and at last I got an audience and he roughly and hurriedly drilled out my broken filling and put in a rubber one that splayed out annoyingly before I'd finished supper. Why he didn't put in a permanent filling, I don't know, unless he is simply after a larger bill. He brings his foot-power drill and a very old and cheap chair and spreads his stuff out on one of our tables in the hospital room. A big crowd of patients, and I have seen more elaborate dentures among our officers than I knew existed!

Visited Rutherford upstairs this P.M. and gleaned a scag and a cigar. He broke my heart by telling of a man at Cabanatuan who bought a silver clarinet for only 5 pesos! Two other wooden ones for sale for P20 and P30! Also a $200 Grafley camera for only a few pesos! Sugar due for issue today, but of course nothing doing—they're only 4 days late already! Tried to get a pair of British shorts from Robinson but in vain, he "had only *3* pairs"! Rice continues at its all-time low and the "soup" is miserably thin.

Tonight they broke out wooden clogs, so we guess that the 51 new prisoners will arrive tonight and occupy the barracks across the parade ground. Nationality and precise number unknown but according to precedent, there go our hopes of getting *any* supplies for at least 10 days—if not for good. No! New prisoners did not arrive, but a new guard *did.*

Tuesday—Kayo-bi (Fire day), 20 Oct 1942

Cool, slightly overcast. We were weighed again today, using a counterbeam scales. On them I weighed 73.5 kilos, but I went to kitchen and, on the spring scales that were used on 15 Sept, I weighed 75.5 kg. which is a net loss of 1 kg. As we were weighed, bananas came in and we got only 5 apiece, and not very good quality. In forenoon we got a package of green Formosa tea, just like 1 issue, costing 82 sen. Coffee! We also got about a tablespoonful of raw peanuts. The sugar also arrived but they short-changed us shamefully, giving us only about ½ bag for 317 persons. I got a teacupful—to last me a month. Our allowance is 399 lbs. for 317 men and we actually got 145.5 lbs.!

Wednesday—Suiyo-bi (Water day), 21 Oct 1942

Smoked my last Jap cigarette yesterday—and at least 8 days to go before we get more! The new Jap guards seem young and even less savage than the old gang. Have asked to buy some manuals on Jap language, and am toying with the idea of trying to buy a Patek-Philippe watch and a clarinet.

Thursday—Mokuyo-bi (Tree day), 22 Oct 1942

In Japan *Times–Advertiser* of 10 October, page 1, the Japs scream "Inhuman Treatment accorded Jap Internees in New Caledonia—Interned on Neuville Island in 100-year-old church—brick floors *strewn with hay* for sleeping quarters—roofing tiles for dishes—1 blanket (why was *that* needed?)—compelled to work, wearing torn and ragged clothing—shoes were so shabby we might as well have been barefoot." All this is bounteous treatment compared with the way the Japs treated us. Even now they are systematically starving us and will not even let us buy food with our own money. (I forgot to note, Tuesday, the swell cup of real coffee that Rutherford gave me in Bowlers' room. He brought the coffee from Manila.)

Yesterday at 1:00 P.M. we had our first Spanish lesson: Cordero, instructor (he speaks Spig Spanish) Brigadier Duke was master of ceremonies. We are handicapped by lack of paper.

Friday—Kinyo-bi (Gourd day), 23 Oct 1942

A cold, overcast, windy day but a big one. Chynoweth gave me a can of sardines, some thiamine tablets and a fine red med corps coat that will be *good* in colder weather. As a surprise, a big box of bananas came in, 7 apiece—but all small ones. I got an extra one. Finished installing markers for all front ranks, but bastids kick them out of the ground, so I foresee constant repair work. Cordero got 26 snails *outside* the wall, thanks to a good humored sentry and Brezina cooked them with garlic and "gobbi" (a potato-like vegetable). Sharp lent me "Reading I have liked." Sgt. Whitehurst bought the watch I wanted: Sweep 2d hand and illuminated dial, damn him! Papers dated 14 Oct., received today, show Stalingrad not yet captured by the Germans in spite of many previous and premature reports—which encourages us all greatly. We all hope the Soviets hurl them back.[29] Dentist came again today; he put a 3d temporary rubber filling in my big cavity but an amalgam in the smaller—so that much is finished. In P.M. a high wind arose and by evening it was cold as hell. But H.H. made us doff our jackets for bango. This barracks has no outer doors, so the gales blow right down the halls. Made up my bed with 2 blankets and hung another across the lower half of my window. Turned in promptly to keep warm, instead of reading, after bango.

For British shorts, write Gieves, Ltd., 21 Old Bond St., London—W. England, and ask Mr. West to make them "with back straps and (automatic) side buckles, with *no* front fastenings (and no? front fly?). Recommended by Air Commodore C.O.F. Modin RAF.

Saturday—Doyo-bi (Ass day), 24 Oct 1942

Still cold as hell this morning, especially inside the barracks. The lieutenant made us doff jackets for reveille—especially razzing Gen. Brougher—who then caused comment by indicating that if sick Gen. Parker could keep one on, *he* could! (Parker's was uniform). Brougher was the one who against orders, kept a 30-passenger bus parked at his CP in Bataan; ostensibly so as to make his CP mobile, but actually to house his servants, mess and personal establishment.

"What, then, are the situations; from the representation of which, though accurate, no poetical enjoyment can be derived? They are those in which the suffering finds no vent in action; in which a continuous state of mental distress is prolonged, unrelieved by incident, hope, or resistance; in which there is everything to be endured, nothing to be done. In such situations there is inevitably something morbid, in the description of them something monotonous. When they occur in actual life they are painful, not tragic; the representation of them in poetry is painful also."—*The Choice of Subjects in Poetry,* by Matthew Arnold.

Held our Spanish class at 1:00, featuring Braly, who done noble. Then I went over to bath-house and made the mistake of getting into the warm tub. By this time the wind was blowing a gale and it was "colder than a harlot's kiss." I commenced donning all my clothes, but had violent chill, in spite of 3 blankets, lasting until after supper. So I broke down and put some of my precious sugar on my scanty rice, in an effort to get some heat into me. Made up my bed with 3 blankets, including a felt one, rigged another (plus both curtains) as wind brakes at window.

Sunday—Nichio-bi (Sun day), 25 Oct 1942

Thank heaven, the wind ceased during the night and, having slept warm all night with only 2 breaks, was able to stand reveille without suffering. Wind started up again and blows worst in our hall. Warmer outdoors. Am working on a bamboo ruler. Glad I was on vigilant guard a few nights ago, as the rest of our room were on duty last night in the cold. Campbell had acquired a big topcoat. Chase has got a sweater and part of a blanket (from Chynoweth) from which to make a "slip-on." Wish I could get some woolen cloth for lining my MD red jacket. Meanwhile, I hope the S.O.B. who stole my West Point sweater dies the death of a dog!

Some Jap Red Cross agents are inspecting this camp today and, as a result, we are getting lots more rice for lunch (so rumor saith) we are also told that our "farm" starts tomorrow: Officers over 55 will care for our stock: the others to work in the garden in 30-minute shifts. Squad leaders in charge "assisted by 2 strong NCOs." List of "weak" officers and those over 55 was turned into Japs last night.

Much griping because British brigadiers are excused from OD and vigilant guard duty, same as our boy generals. I am older than any of our generals, yet I find no trouble in doing my tours of these easy duties, with the other colonels. Our generals asked to be excused "because it was customary, in the U.S. service, and they would lose prestige" by doing such duty! If they only knew how much more prestige they are losing by their lazy deadbeating!

This P.M. I bummed from Brigadier Curtis a pair of British shorts which fit fine and lack only two small buckles at the waist. Also borrowed his Spanish grammar by Hugo. Meaty. Reviewed Lessons 1–4 in evening. Weather turned milder by evening, boding a fair tomorrow. My ankles are back to normal, which I attribute to the can of corned beef that I ate. Last night, at bango, BP was comfortably lit up, said "This is a good squad—always a good squad" and mixed with the squads later.

Monday—Getsuyo-bi (Moon day), 26 Oct 1942

Slept under 3 light blankets, with only 1 break for the benjo. Overcast but warmer this morning with but little wind. Chase sick. At the Han Chos' conference this A.M. important developments. Work! (1) We start work this P.M. (2) Bigger rations start tonight (3) Our OD hereafter to preside at kitchen and prevent our enlisted men from hogging our chow. (4) Everybody but civil governors to do OD duty. (5) All but major generals and those over 60 to do vigilant guard. (6) Tobacco to arrive tomorrow and toilet paper this P.M.

At 1:00 P.M. everybody turned out. After the usual 20′ delay waiting for "L.P."
[Long Pants] the men got tools (mattocks, hoes, rakes, shovels and a few sickles)
and we marched out the gate in column of twos to a space inside the new wall
near the hospital buildings—overgrown with grass. 1st 5 squads worked 30′ hoeing and spading up the ground for a "seed bed" or "experiment garden." Relieved
for 30′ and then did another trick. Wore my British shorts. We got a basinful of
snails out of the grass. Quit at 4:00. Learned that the Japs had tied it up as usual
and although they say extra rice was issued, our cooks deny it! Anyway, the exercise will do us good.

My guess was right! We got our "increased" ration—but how the Japs must
have laughed at us! It works out like this for our complement of 317 prisoners:
Old ration 64 kg.: new ration 76 kg. = increase of 4 kg. per meal which means
12.6 grams or 4/10 ounce per person! And you can send a full half-ounce for one
airmail stamp. There was great bitterness expressed in camp tonight over the disappointment. According to best available dope, the foregoing weights of rice for
all of us costs a total of $6.68 a day and, for each one of us, almost exactly 2
cents a day. And I doubt that our vegetables cost as much as that! Our old ration
was 7.1 ounces of rice per man, the new one = 8.44 oz. The cold spell is over and
we got some nice sunning while at work this P.M. Even rickety Gen. Wainwright
was weakly wielding a hoe, just like everybody else. Japs failed to issue toilet
paper (as promised).

Who is this that darkeneth counsel by words without knowledge? Job 38:2

Tuesday—Kayo-bi (Fire day), 27 Oct 1942

A fine day. We formed for work at 8:40 and continued our labors in the "seed
garden" working two 30′-shifts in the nice warm sun—mostly working the
ground over and taking out the grass roots, plus a little spading. We turned in at
11:30, when they told us we would have 2 hours off, but to be ready to turn out at
2:00 P.M. which gave us a chance to get our semi-weekly shower. Our rice at noon
was just perceptibly more than at breakfast. Upon being turned out at 2:00 P.M.
for work, a light mist was falling so they excused us for the day. Welcome news
to all of us, not because of the work, but because it let us do laundry, tailoring
and the other work. (One soldier was hunting around here during the cold spell,
looking for the officer who (he claims) had offered him 100 pesos for his pea-
jacket! Another wants $50 gold for an Arlington watch, gold filled case with only
11 jewels! Some of our soldiers are looking for suckers—and finding (?) them.
Sgt. Whitehurst, the worst crook of all, says he has won 850 pesos and 2 watches
at poker. Damn him, he has already sold the watch I want to Pvt. Kindriewicz.)
We drew a cupful of salt this P.M. Gave some to "Pat."

Last night occurred some more looting by our Jap guards: Foster lost a watch,
Lothrop some money at about 3:00 A.M. They promptly reported it "within 3 min-

utes" and the Jap OD got right on the job investigating. What a contrast to our valiant leader (?) Wainwright, who was robbed of a watch sometime ago, but told me himself this morning, that he did not even report the loss "because it would only be the start of another Lawrence episode"—in other words, he was afraid the Japs might slap him! What a leader to protect our interests! Gen. King is just as bad. Both of them have simply folded up and quit!

Fish! This noon we had some fish in our soup, and some more at night. Supper was a great meal: much more rice than usual and the fish-flavored soup was plentiful and full of solid vegetables, not just onion tops. No telling what the fish was: guesses included shark, manta, tuna. To cap the climax, we got our long-delayed cigarettes: 20 packs allowance (10 in each) plus 12 extra. Our "Akabono" brand, in blue box cost 13 sen; the "Minam" in brown boxes cost 20 sen (I got 8) and the black box 28 sen. The enlisted men's (red and white box) cost them only 4 sen, but officers can't get 'em!

A great improvement in our morale tonight, due to more chow, and to tobacco.

Wednesday—Suiyo-bi (Water day), 28 Oct 1942

Fine day. Started a new laundry scheme: soaking dirty clothes in basin overnight instead of washing them out in 1 operation. Object: to save soap, which is still unprocurable. Balsam and Cordero had fresh "Chinese cabbage" from their garden. *Looked* nice. Today is a holiday—Karenko Shrine day, so we did not turn out for work. With water, I puddled back into place, the markers for Squad 1 and for calisthenics. Brig. Curtis lent me 2 buckles for my shorts. Held our Spanish class at 1:00 P.M. with Pappy Sellick[30] as feature.

Beef! Our rations now are much better: more rice and much more "soup." (When I mention "soup." I mean green vegetables, mostly onion *tops,* in water.) Tonight however, it was the best we've had, for it was rich meat soup—carabao. Highly enjoyed by everybody—but Gen. Bluemel[31] incurred wrath of his colleagues by calling it "hog slop". He also seems to have "quit."

Tonight the Jap OD (BP) [Baggy Pants] changed the system of checking out to the latrine. At 9:00 P.M. he told the vigilant guard about using prisoners' numbers instead of names. You do it." He's the best Jap around here. When he is on duty he goes to our kitchen, takes off his coat, and adjusts equitably the food that our kitchen crew has dished out.

Thursday—Mokuyo-bi (Tree day), 29 Oct 1942

Fine day. Laundry. Shaved. We all went out and worked this morning and had dried minnows in our soup for lunch. Had a date with the dentist this P.M. so I did not turn out and enjoyed the privilege of deadbeating hugely. This P.M. they gave us 9 little lady fingers made of rice flour and they were a grand treat. BP visited our squad room and chinned quite awhile, mentioning that he was stuffed full of rice cakes! Dried minnows in the soup tonight. Made lots of new benjo cards.

Friday—Kinyo-bi (Gourd day), 30 Oct 1942
Fine day but threatened rain in A.M. so we didn't go out to work but, instead held pay day. We colonels drew 20 yen in cash, out of 310 earned. 3.10 for orderlies and 15.90 for our food for September and 271 added to our deposits. Majors had less deposits and so drew a few sen more than colonels.

Turned out at 2:00 P.M. and spaded. 21 airmail and other letters arrived and were delivered to us. I received none and so won a pack of cigarettes from Brezina. Weather turned windy and I fear is brewing up another typhoon and cold spell. The minnows were dried out leftovers in storeroom. This morning I completed reinstalling markers for Squad 2 and puddled them in. Also worked on my Spanish discourse for Saturday.

Saturday—Doyo-bi (Ass day), 31 Oct 1942
Breezy but a fine warm day. Our "detention" building where the solitaries may be confined is finished; some of our men cleaned out the carpenters' rubbish this P.M. Hope I never get put in there! No farm work today; we scrubbed our quarters instead. In P.M. had date with the dentist and, I hope, this finishes my worst tooth. At 1:00 P.M. we held our Spanish class and I was the lecturer. We were supposed to get smoked ducks today, in place of the pig that Gen. King requested for Halloween. When Callahan asked "Mortimer" why they had not arrived, he phoned HQ and with much hearty laughter said "they are out of stock." Now I am betting they will double-cross us on 3 November also, they promise us pig for that day. Gen. Pierce was shooting off his face about our claims for lost property, today, and excoriating officers—"Why some of these sons-of-bitches are even listing cuff buttons!" (And they selected this half-baked loud-mouthed nit-wit for a general officer.) He had shipped all of *his* property to the U.S. but had just bought some Chinese rugs which were in the Army bonded storehouse in Manila. Its records were probably destroyed and it would be interesting to see the claim Pierce will submit.

"There is something not altogether unpleasing in the misfortunes of our friends."
The camp is buzzing over those 21 U.S. letters which arrived yesterday: we wonder how our relatives learned our status, and if all have been actually informed that we are living and prisoners. We are still baulked in our requests to write home—even a post card.

Sunday—Nichio-bi (Sun day), 1 Nov 1942
Started blowing, yesterday and continues today, overcast (and chilly inside). At

reveille LP lectured us against catching cold by getting in drafts. Yet they neglect installing doors of our main halls and he keeps us standing in our drafty hallways waiting 15′ for him to come for bango. Same for reveille: keeps us waiting for him, and then also afterwards while he debates without OD.

The Jap clocks must be terrible, the time of calls varies so much from day to day. Last night bango was 9′ early. Today, reveille was slated to change from 6:00 to 6:30 A.M. so they sounded it at 6:15! Capt. Hoeffel has a ship's chronometer with him which he evidently "acquired" from some Navy ship so we can check on these babies.

Col. Callahan vouches for another bit of scandal reflecting upon the integrity of one of our "officers and gentlemen": this chap (whose only identification to me is that he was a post exchange officer probably in or near Manila—but he is known to Callahan) bought at Estrella del Norte (a Manila Jewellers) a P750 wrist watch "for his exchange stock" and yet, later in Bataan, this officer was wearing this watch! He claimed to have locked up expensive cameras, watches, etc. in the vault at Ft. Santiago but that somebody looted the property!

Monday—Getsuyo-bi (Moon day), 2 Nov 1942

No garden work today and very little rice again. This A.M. work was called off because of "inspection" but, after we had cleaned up carefully, a party walked through barracks. Callahan gave us each a sliver of the papaya which BP gave him, and it was the sweetest I ever tasted. In P.M. great excitement over rumor that we were going for a walk outside. Actually, they took Wainwright, the 2 British squad leaders, the civilian governors and 4 enlisted squad leaders, all under guard into town where they posed Wainwright et al at a cafe table (but no food) for movies. Other shots were taken of prisoners strolling about, etc. All evidently to show how well American prisoners are treated and the great privileges accorded them! What lying evidence! This is the first time any of us has been allowed outside the wall and ignores our starvation rations. This A.M. they took movies of Gens. King and Wainwright in their rooms, chatting, going to bed in their pajamas, etc. This was under the same Jap be-ribboned officer who supervised those pictures taken of us in the hold of the *Otara? Maru.* Times of calls are now very ragged. Today turned warmer towards evening. Having finally rec'd a lousy "notebook," I started compiling a list of war prisoners here with pertinent data for all of the 208 officers and 7 civilians. Got 4 lousy bananas today—but nothing on last "fruit day."

Tuesday—Kayo-bi (Fire day), 3 Nov 1942

Holiday: for birth of Emperor Meijiwho ruled for 40 years preceding present emperor; one of the most important of Jap holidays. We formed at 8:15; camp commander officiated at a short, snappy ceremony. Overcast day but not cold. Later they took movies of our squad waking and rising in the morning—and blew out our fuses. Fat! In evening our soup was enriched by boiling therein about 30 lbs. of pork fat. I guess the Japs got all the lean meat.

Wednesday—Suiyo-bi (Water day), 4 Nov 1942

Our squad on benjo guard last night but, being over 60, I was excused. Day dawned beautifully, with sun on the mountains. No work in A.M. In P.M. squads 1–7 turned out; bath day for 8, 9, 13. As the dentist was expected, Glatly had Callahan and me remain in. Acquired a better piece of bamboo for a ruler. We were *issued* 3 more lousy bananas this noon. Balsam furious because the Japs took all the good and big bananas. Waited in rain all P.M. for dentist.

Thursday—Mokuyo-bi (Tree day), 5 Nov 1942

Beautiful day. In P.M. Squads 9–14 turned out for work at 1:30 P.M. Browne and I are on chow detail for 7 days, starting at breakfast this morning. Nothing unusual today. My hopes of getting a watch from stingy skinny Wainwright have gone glimmering. The Japs brought back his ordnance watch repaired (a beauty) that he was going to give me when the Japs bought him a new one for the Y50 that he got—but he cancelled the purchase! when I would have been glad to buy either one! Drat him! Waited all P.M. on dentist and had him grind down the big filling a bit—and am now through with him! Worked today on my data-sheets of prisoners.

Friday—Kiny-bi (Gourd day), 6 Nov 1942

Day dawned beautiful. No work on farm in A.M. We all wish the Japs would get busy and buy the pigs, etc. for our farm and also fill a few of our back requisitions. No work in P.M. Routine day.

Saturday—Doy-bi (Ass day), 7 Nov 1942

Drizzled last night, overcast day. Had our pictures taken in groups of 15 with placards hung from our necks showing our names and prison numbers. Jap *Times* of Oct 26 (p. 3) says that captured U.S. Airmen "who raided Japan on April 18 . . . and bombed schools and killing non-combatants have been severly punished in accordance with military law."[32] Rumor here says they were *beheaded!* Front page story in *Times* of Oct 20th—"Death penalty will be given future raiders . . ." But they admit that 10–20 planes bombed Tokyo—"merely showed bestiality." Same paper says Frances Long returns to America and says the Japs treat their prisoners fine! Phooey! Page 3 has illustrated story of U.S. inhumane treatment of internees, etc.—which was more humane than their treatment of *us*.

Borrowed 2 books from British. Get Pete Masallo a DSC. We were issued 2 more bananas today. BP drew out Jap Catacona alphabet for Balsam and took hold of our overdue tobacco requests, indicating thereby that the LP threw them away, perhaps. Worked on my roster of officers.

Sunday—Nichio-bi (Sun day), 8 Nov 1942
Beautiful day. Received 2 more bananas. Nothing unusual today.

Monday—Getsuyo-bi (Moon day), 9 Nov 1942
Cold and rainy—received 3 bananas. Radio! Great excitement at noon because about 4 officers in each squad (including ME) are allowed to send a 100 word radiogram home! Spent the afternoon composing a radio to Landon—and hope she gets it. Later we were told that tomorrow we'll be allowed to write home. Radio will be on a broadcast—probably mixed up with propaganda.

Tuesday—Kayo-bi (Tree day), 10 Nov 1942
Fine day. Collected data on officers list. They started spading up the parade ground for squad gardens this morning. We thought that the gardens were to be over the hill. Received another banana. In P.M. I turned out and worked in our squad garden until 4:00 P.M. Camp commander served us camotes at 3:45 which were delicious. Enlisted men rushed the basket and grabbed lion's share. Also, though it was announced that only those of us who were working were entitled thereto yet officers (and men) came running from barracks. Our rice, all day, has been at high water mark.

My radio to Landon was approximately "All safe and sound and proud of my hundred and seventy pounds. Yearning for you and Priscilla so keep the home fires burning and prepare two fatted calves. Would appreciate handout concentrated foods now. No Red Cross here. All belongings at Corregidor lost so prepare partial claim your part. Consult officer. Also pay interest two insurance loans. Advise selling apartment. Work for job for me at soldiers' home or archives or shall we adopt California? Will reform upon return scorning my desk so we can concentrate upon gracious living and how. Am probably writing tomorrow. Chins up, believe."

Wednesday—Suiyo-bi (Water day), 11 Nov 1942
Received 3 bananas today. No garden work. Maj. Gen. Beckwith-Smith[33] died this morning, after being rushed to the "hospital" at about 4:00 A.M. Had been ailing for a few days, but was up and around. Japs report death due to heart failure and admit that if he had been better fed he would have survived. Gen. Key says he had same ailment as the other Limey had a short time ago—a sort of diphtheria. My guess is streptococcus. They gave him an injection, which did no

good, and a tracheotomy. He was jovial, a prince. Services at 3:30 this P.M. followed by cremation. We all go into our nose masks for another week. Chow detail ends!

Thursday—Mokuyo-bi (Tree day), 12 Nov 1942

Rainy but cleared by 11:00 A.M. In P.M. the first 8 squads turned out for work: we were marched *outside the wall* (for the first time since we've been here!) to the river bank and given a plot of ground to spade up and clear the grass and prepare for planting. Plain signs that it had been a garden before. We assaulted a papaya tree and stripped it. I got 5 and gave 2 to Chase who is sick in quarters and does not work. Worked two 30-minute shifts and turned in. We are all very weak. When the interpreter turned us out at 1:00 P.M. they say he was mad as hell—and that it was because the Dimei Party (which has been quizzing us officers for the past few days) were told especially by the British in no uncertain terms, that we need more food! Perhaps that is the reason why we get such punitively short rations tonight—both rice and soup are the lowest yet! The presence of Domei is also probably the reason why the camp commander gave us those camotes on Tuesday! Smoked my last cigar tonight.

Friday—Doyo-bi (Gourd day), 13 Nov 1942

Fine day. Put 2″ tuck in waist of my British shorts to fit my 32″ waist. Better rations today. A physical exam of sorts this morning: marked me "nutrition poor; edema, severe, both legs" but that won't get me a gram of protein. 2 bananas. Turned out 1–4 at 1 P.M. to work in garden but, on discovering that we were the ones who worked yesterday, they excused us and turned out Squads 9–14. I worked in our squad garden, hoeing, in A.M. and set out about 50 onion roots and 5 cloves of garlic in my flower bed. Got time in P.M. to shave and launder. It was? also significant that today the Japs sent out a work party of 2 officers and 20 men, who hiked 6 kilometers through town and to a big cemetery, where they prepared a plot about 50 ft. sq. for our burials! Our tobacco order finally came in, this P.M. and amounted to 67 packs (of 10 each) for me—but no more scags this month!

Saturday—Doyo-bi (Ass day), 14 Nov 1942

Clear in A.M. but started misting at 11:00, as we finished working in our squad garden and rained off and on all rest of day, so had to go for my shower in a drizzle. Highlights today were that British and some American generals went to cemetery to inter the ashes of Gen. Beckwith-Smith in our new plot in the cemetery. They carried a wooden cross about 4′ high, on which was his name, etc. He was 52 years 4 days old. Our men who went to the cemetery yesterday, brought into our room a basinful of fine camotes from the cemetery and we tipped them cigarettes.

Thanks to Brezina ordering cigars for me, I got a full box of 25 plus 9 (Cost Y9.52). Tonight it was so cold and windy that we formed for bango in the barber shop. Good.

Gen. Keith Simmons today gave me a pr of shorts, Fox puttees! and a shirt belonging to Gen. Beckwith-Smith, who was quite small. The shorts fit fine, but the shirt was so small I returned it. Shorts rather smaller in thighs than my other pair.

Cross cut Jap sardines.

Sunday—Nichio-bi (Sun day), 15 Nov 1942

Today I made a wall receptacle for our benjo cards. At breakfast I opened and ate ¼ of the can of sardines Gen. Chynoweth. My conscience hurt me and made me feel like a dog, not to share it with the rest of the room. Sardines, but my edema is the only in the squad and I need it far worse than they. Besides, they have had plenty of stuff that they didn't cut me in on. Received 2 good bananas, part of the mess gratis! Turned cold and windy but moderated at night.

Monday—Getsuyo-bi (Moon day), 16 Nov 1942

Showery in A.M. but turned out at 1:00 P.M. for work in new garden outside the wall. Drizzling, so I wore getas instead of my shoes. Turned in early because of rain; turned warm last night, but overcast and drizzly all today. Were given Y10.00 from our deposits, leaving mine now at a total of Y629. This P.M. Collier and Campbell changed berths, as we decided to use the door on our side of the room as the permanent egress, so there was a great to-do and I lost 1 shelf in the rearrangement. The Sultana's that I transplanted from Ives' place are blooming bravely and my papaya plants have started growing.

It is fine to feel on Easy St.—if only temporarily—on smokes. The other day, our profiteering enlisted men were offering for sale these 10-scag packages of Akerbono cigarettes for *one peso* a pack!

Great anxiety now about our letter writing: in spite of the Japs telling us we must use *their* paper, they yesterday accepted letters written on *our* paper, and BP wondered why our squad had written none! So now we don't know *what* to do. Cold tonight, so used 3 blankets.

Tuesday—Kayo-bi (Fire day), 17 Nov 1942

In spite of being cold and showery, this was a Red Letter Day—in our childlike estimation: Braly lent me a wristwatch and I gave it with Y10 to interpreter to get repaired, also asked him to get me some index cards and notebooks. Conferred with BP about front storm doors to help prevent hurricanes blowing through our halls but he only laughed and asked if I would build them.

We got 2 ripe bananas today, plus salt (of which we have plenty) plus 75 cubes of *sugar,* tea, and mirabile dictu! pencils and a few notebooks of the cheapest tablet form—but I got 1 and shall transfer to it my dope about claim for property lost by enemy action. To complete the day we had a few fragments of fish in our evening soup. Gave interpreter Braly's watch for repair and Y10.

Wednesday—Suiyo-bi (Water day), 18 Nov 1942

Overcast. Yesterday P.M. BP was coaxed into relieving the congestion in our room by ordering 1 officer to move into each of the rooms across the hall. Berry doesn't like it and so the move has not been made. Callahan and Collier are the 2 who have been invited to join the lodges across the hall. It is a prize bunch of mad dogs left—forever snarling and snapping at anybody who opens his head. No work in garden today; cold and rainy all day. Rained at night.

Thursday—Mokuyo-bi (Tree day), 19 Nov 1942

Partially overcast all day but we worked on river bank garden in P.M. When we returned Berry capitulated and ordered the 2 officers to move. They did, but Berry immediately demanded ⅓ of our total locker space! This created a furore. Berry appointed Boatwright as room corporal. Glad I argued him out of appointing me.

Friday—Kinyo-bi (Gourd day), 20 Nov 1942

Clear day for a change. Squads 9–14 worked this morning, extending our river plot towards the town. Meanwhile I worked at rearranging my cupboards. It is very hard to condense my junk into only 2 of them, so I started adding intermediate shelves and here's where my wattled woven shelf comes in fine. Got a few pieces of board near kitchen and sawed them with a queer native saw—it cuts on the pull stroke and not the push! In P.M. our squad turned out and continued the garden work. Finished a Gissing book while resting. Pomelo! Rice ration tonight was the best ever. At noon we got fresh fruit: one big Pomelo for each 4 officers. Tasted fine.

Saturday—Doyo-bi (Ass day), 21 Nov 1942

Rained most of the night but fine sleeping. Overcast in A.M. The Japs admitted to us yesterday that in a battle in the Solomons, Nov. 12–14, they had lost many ships, including 1 or 2 battleships, etc.—more than we lost!! Osak Manichi reports (1) U.S. elections: House = 221 D, 209 R, 5 misc., (2) Conscripts to get 1 year training in U.S. prior to overseas duty, (3) Many Japs in Hawaii to be sent to U.S., (4) 80% of our shipments to Europe and Africa sunk en route, (5) From late July to late Oct. Japs say they sank 21 American subs., (6) On p. 2 is text of Jap protest to U.S. over mistreatment of internees, every "atrocity" of which is more than matched by our experiences as Jap prisoners. Today we got fine big rations of rice. The British wrote letter claiming that Beckwith-Smith would have lived had he been decently fed. One rumor: Japs have asked higher-ups for 10% increase in our ration. But LP is quoted as saying that if complaints of short food do not cease, our ration will be cut! Sounds just like him. The British turned out for work in garden this P.M. Spent all day making shelves and rearranging cupboards. It now develops that Berry's gang needs only about half of the 8 cupboards he demands!

Sunday—Nichio-bi (Sun day), 22 Nov 1942

Slightly overcast. Calisthenics, for 1st time on Sunday. Yesterday in weighing I managed to jiggle the faulty scales up to 72 kg. which, if accurate, means that I have lost about 60 lbs. and now weigh only 158.4 lbs.! which is what I weighed when I was in grammar school at about 14 yrs. Weighed 180 or so when I entered West Point! Posted my big presentation benjo card on my cupboard door. We have now had 6 consecutive meals with increased rice. Watch! Today I gave BP my written request to buy a watch (Patek-Philippe).

Monday—Getsuyo-bi (Moon day), 23 Nov 1942

Beautiful day. BP visited us at breakfast and asked me about my football career. Gen. Pierce had posted him last night on benjo guard. Today is a Jap holiday, celebrating Harvest. In spite of this, LP turned out Squads 1–8 for farm work, but camp commander happened along and cancelled the order! Guard. Although officers over 60 are excused, I went on benjo guard tonight from 11:30–12:30, between Browne and Callahan. My benjo cards are still a great help, though now we have to record only prison numbers. A beautiful full moon tonight. I wonder if Landon notices it and if so, what she is thinking? Fish! Got 2 green bananas today—and at noon fish in the soup!

Tuesday—Kayo-bi (Fire day), 24 Nov 1942

Turned out for work this morning, extending our ground preparing operations along the river bank. Killed a snake about 2′ long: evidently venomous for it had a triangular head like a rattlesnake and 2 long fangs. Beautiful warm brown background with deep brown marks on back like a python, each loop being underscored on each side with a horizontal dash of the same dark brown. Finished Wells' *Time Machine* while resting. Got a bath and did laundry before lunch. For 11 straight meals now, we've had our increased rice ration but the soup continues skimpy of vegetables—principally scallion tops in warm water. Anyway, it is a beautiful day! Hirsch lent me a pair of low shoes as both of mine are worn through in the soles and the Japs are so short of leather that we can't get shoes repaired.

Wednesday—Suiyo-bi (Water day), 25 Nov 1942

Unexpectedly they turned us out for farm work this morning though it was cold and threatening. We are sure breaking out a lot of ground and the Jap soldiers are right on our heels with their planting. We have also planted carrots and turnips in our squad garden. PX officer bought up all "chirigami" (toilet paper) in town and issued 3 packages to each of us. It is very treacherous flimsy tissue. We also got 2 bananas today. British excused from work in P.M. I worked on my data list for officers. Learned at 4:00 P.M. that more letters from us to the States are being accepted, so wrote my draft to Landon but could not finish it. The interpreter returned to me Braly's watch which he had taken to town for repairs at cost of 4 yen, but the damn thing stops, as before! About 17 watches were sent to him for repair 3 weeks or more ago and only 7 have come back!

Thanksgiving, Thursday—Mokuyo-bi (Tree day), 26 Nov 1942
Overcast but nice and warm. LP created furore at reveille by announcing that today is *not* a holiday for the British and Dutch, so they will work on the farm! 29 rabbits received yesterday were in our soup this noon, giving us (to our surprise) the most meat we've ever had in 1 meal. It was delicious. And the rice is keeping up, too! Finished my 2-page letter to Landon and now the only question is when will it be mailed? Enjoyed our holiday. In evening, we couldn't tell whether the rumored 15 fresh ducks were in our soup or not. The British worked both A.M. and P.M. today. We received today Jap newspapers dated Nov. 15 which are pure propaganda, they minimize the import of U.S. landings in Africa (Algiers, etc.) say that there have been 81 air duels in the Aleutians, that the German subs have sunk a half million tons of shipping in the 1st 10 days of November and lots more tripe. Warm night.

Friday—Kinyo-bi (Gourd day), 27 Nov 1942
Wind rose suddenly about 3:00 A.M. from the east and it was cold as hell all day. But we turned out and worked on the farm both morning and afternoon, finishing the river bank strip up to the property line. The Jap provost marshall general of the Taiwan army looked over the hundred of us, picked me out and said, "Very old, but looks very brave." Got colder at night and we nearly froze. Piled all my blankets on my bed. Had to visit Benjo 4 times, worse luck. This east wind is bad! From China?

Saturday—Doyo-bi (Ass day), 28 Nov 1942
Wind dropped about 5:00 A.M., so it became more livable and, by noon, the sun was shining and felt grateful indeed. Our usual Sat. clean-up was intensified this morning preparatory for an inspection which was held at 1:15 P.M. by camp commander. We gathered in our rooms, and they even came into our room; camp commander made long job of it. Weather turned cold again in P.M. Brezina is on chow detail now and he is lousy. Campbell riled him on the soup and Brezina fussed on his first rice job. They say that the ruler of this camp will be

"changed" shortly and our wishful thinkers like Callahan, claim the new ruler will be beneficent. However, if it is true as rumored, that we are to come under the provost marshall and his secret police, I believe the future is dark. For instance, on Friday, when he inspected barracks, he found some of the British sleeping—which our present rules permit between 1:00–3:00 P.M. That evening we received notice that hereafter, no sleeping is permitted in daytime. Weather moderated 1:00 P.M.

Sunday—Nichiyo-bi (Sun day), 29 Nov 42
Fine sunny day, for a change and nobody objected to opening our windows. Papers say MacArthur has moved his HQ to New Guinea,[34] and Americans here visualize his driving north, toward us. They are also elated over U.S. landing in North Africa.[35]

Monday—Getsuyo-bi (Moon day), 30 Nov 1942
Puttered around all morning while the British turned out for work. We turned out in P.M. and continued the clearing operations. Everybody agrees that the British squads accomplish very little work. The interpreter came in and delivered a wristlet for Braly's watch. Cost Y2.43. As usual, they make only 1 size and this strap is very tight. Showed him a sample of the duplicating notebook I want. Today the Japs turned back many of our letters and issued new rules: Letters must not exceed 300 words (and, at first, they allowed 2 pages); envelopes must be prepared in a new way. Having used up our paper and envelopes, how are we to get more for the revised forms? My letter to Landon is written almost as finely as this and I *can't* condense it into 300 words. Turned it over to Col. Gillen, the OD, for submission to the interpreter. Clothes! As we went out to work, many bales of clothing arrived, and they were issued after dinner. Much hilarity ensued, over the funny fits that resulted! The "work" clothes come in only 2 sizes, small and very small; the winter clothes (blue) came "large" size only! The cheapest shoddy materials made by snide cheap methods. The "work" clothes consist of shirt and shorts; rough, scratchy cloth defectively woven, natural tan color, said to be like the "encenita" cloth of southern Calif. Of blue, porous clothes, we got a "jumper," plenty big, with tight wrists, buttoned down front; also a blue coat and trousers to match, thick but porous ribbed material like jute sacking. Ted Chase could cut out the trouser pockets, thrust his arms through the holes and have a suit of coveralls. Upon turning in tonight, the usual squabble about ventilation occurred, Balsam insisting on hermetically sealing the room.

Tuesday—Kayo-bi (Tree day), 1 Dec 1942
Another fine day. Got a diphtheria shot at 10:00 A.M. Turned over my work suit to Cordero for credit because it is skintight, even in my present emaciated state.

Have adjusted Braly's watch so that now it gains only 7 minutes a day. Prices of our new clothing: Shorts Y5.58; Work suits large Y14.50; Blue suits Y29.68; Jumper Y18.03. Received pay this P.M.—only 15 yen cash.

Wednesday—Suiyo-bi (Water day), 2 Dec 1942

Overcast but warm. Squads 1–8 turned out for farm work this morning, and we turned out in P.M. in our squad garden. Got in my semi-daily shave. Callahan visited dentist in town this P.M.! The cost, to prisoners of *all* this jute clothing which has just been sold to us is 13,600 yen! And we all agree that its actual value cannot be more than ⅕ of that! We wonder who is getting the rake-off? Similarly with this Jap dentist: my bill is 47.00 which, BP informs me, is equal to $23.50! And the only work he did was to fill 2 teeth, one of which was a refill of a broken filling. To be sure, he inserted 6 temporary rubber fillings before he put in the permanent filling but that, I believe, was only to fortify his robbery and not as a necessity. It gripes us to be thus played for suckers.

Thursday—Mokuyo-bi (Tree day), 3 Dec 1942

This A.M. worked on squad garden. In P.M. I excused from farm work and watched our rooms. Heavy rain about 3:00 P.M. drove everybody home, and I was late in getting the hot water for everybody's tea. Berry published a lot of new orders about our regulations and more are issuing tomorrow. They place *only* squad chiefs on the OD roster, and fat Gen. King leads off today. Many other duties are changed. Tonight it blew up cold again.

Friday—Kinyo-bi (Gourd day), 4 Dec 1942

Day opened cold and rainy and we held bango inside, after waiting long for LP. No hot water for tea until 9:00 because fires extinguished for lack of coal! Cold as hell all day—no outside work and we all huddled in our rooms all day, shivering. We each got a little camote bun, and was it good! Today also saw the big administrative shake-up: Berry is relieved as squad chief in favor of Braly (a fine move) and all British squad leaders are changed. I am squad librarian, relieving Cordero. Also a lot of new rules were issued. Set watch exactly with chronometer at 2:00 P.M.

Meat! I had 3 pieces of ½ inch cube, tough meat in noon soup, which was quite flavorless. Bitterly cold and windy tonight; wind whistled through the hall, and of course there is no heat. Got into a squabble with Collier about smoking in our room since we have only one ashtray. Very cold even in bed and couldn't get my feet warm. A soldier swapped a pair of wool socks to an officer tonight for *30* cigars! Finished copying from Gen. Pierce's Jap book.

Saturday—Doyo-bi (Ass day), 5 Dec 1942

A bit of sun at breakfast but soon clouded over and got cold again. But shaved anyway. Worked in squad garden in P.M. Continued cold as hell all day—still colder at night. Today our big tobacco order arrived and I got 150 packs of cigarettes, which now fixes me up with a reserve. Tonight at about 10:00 P.M. arrived Lt. Gen. Heath[36] and Maj. Gen. (?) Maxwell from Singapore with 2 batmen. One good feature is that it ran our generals' 4 orderlies out of Room 7 and our OD went in there. Donned trousers and 2 coats to go out tonight.

Sunday—Nichio-bi (Sun day), 6 Dec 1942

All day it has been colder than a harlot's kiss. But Sgt. Hundley brought me in a hot brick at 7:00 P.M.! Spent lots of time handling newspapers and books on my new job as librarian for the squad. All books to be turned in tomorrow. Today's papers tell us the shameful dope in the Roberts Report re: Pearl Harbor! Gosh but that hot brick felt good at my feet. It was the first night I've been able to keep my feet warm. And I didn't have to "go" until 4:30 A.M.!

Monday—Getsuyo-bi (Moon day), 7 Dec 1942

Thank Gawd it turned warmer, along toward morning and the wind dropped. Sun came out; bids fair to be a fine day. But there was snow in the ravines at top of mountains to the west of us this A.M.! Squads 1–8 turned out for farm work at 9:00 but I decided to take advantage of the exemption they've given to men over 60, so I deadbeated the formation with a clear conscience, because the Japs will probably grab the best and the most of whatever is raised in the gardens anyway; hence our labor will bring us nothing. Grand feeling to have the squabblers out of the room, and be able to do what I want. Turned cold again tonight and I am using 4 blankets.

Tuesday—Kayo-bi (Fire day), 8 Dec 1942

First anniversary of the start of this war; I have been a prisoner 7 months two days ago. Rescript day! Turned out at 9:30 for the ceremony of listening to the reading of the emperor's "Rescript." They omitted the Jap version and a concensus of our officers declares that the Japs at this ceremony were lots less cocky than at the same ceremony 2 or 3 months ago—i.e.—they realize the U.S. is now "coming back." I spoke to the Interpreter about getting for me some of the 2 commemorative Jap stamps that are being issued today 2 and 5 sen values plus tax 3 sen. He promised to get them, but I doubt him. I specially want them as they show the attacks at Pearl Harbor and Corregidor? LP told me, through Wood, that the Japs consider it very laudable that I should voluntarily turn out for work with the others, but that they wish me to cease. I said I want some exercise, so they told me to see the doctor. Spent most of the afternoon copying Jap lesson No. 5. It is a holiday, today, for the Japs (they now insist on being called "Nipponese") but they turned the British out for work in the afternoon. Tonight, for the 3d night in a row, Sgt. Hundley brought me a hot brick before bedtime and it is a Godsend for warming up my icy feet. Makes a whale of a difference in my nights—they are now comfortable. Fish! Trace of fish in soup at noon!

Wednesday—Suiyo-bi (Water Day), 9 Dec 1942

A cold and watery sun appeared, lacking in warmth. Worked in our squad garden all morning. Our gang worked on farm in p.m. but it was too cold for me to get anything done on my own hook. We are all glad to see Berry's tour as soup server draw to a close.

Thursday—Mokuyo-bi (Tree day), 10 Dec 1942

Fine day after 10:00 A.M. Shaved in hot water in my room. Worked in garden levelling beds and helping plant carrots. Bathed and laundered in warm sun at 12:45. Our squad worked on farm in P.M. and I got hot water for their tea. It is great, to deadbeat that farm work and have the whole room to myself—except for invalid Ted Chase. Planted a row of carrots in my flower bed. Salvaged a big batch of newspapers from the hospital and cut out many clippings.

Big day for our PX, as BP got some action on our back orders: pens, ink, notebooks, razors and blades.

Friday—Kinyo-bi (Gourd day), 11 Dec 1942

Today we get another diphtheria shot. Chilly, forbidding day. Our PX representative monkeyed around all day over the shipment and finally distributed our stuff in evening. Quite like Christmas. My bill was Y12.06, including a fountain pen 4.95, tablets, tooth powder, etc. Am now busy trying to adjust Braly's watch by Hoeffel's chronometer. Rumor now is that, somewhere on this island there are 4 tons of Red Cross Christmas boxes (11 lbs. each) for us!

Saturday—Doyo-bi (Ass day), 12 Dec 1942

I can't nail the interpreter to get the special postage stamps or the duplicating notebook I want—or my change! This last big PX order put me in the red, but Moore says he will lend me 10 yen. Today we were weighed again—I am down to 71.5 kilograms or 157.3 pounds an all-time low. Most of us are continuing to lose weight on our starvation rations. It is humiliating to see the pot bellies on our enlisted men who work in our kitchen, and know their fat is due to the food they steal from us! Gen. Sharp was OD tonight and used Chastaine to help apportion the food at night meal. Yet the men robbed the soup of Squads 1 and 2 and gave most of the beans to other squads, specially 7 and 8, their own squads. Our squad was ripe for mutiny. I am now spreading newspapers between my blankets and it helps a lot.

Sunday—Nichio-bi (Sun day), 13 Dec 1942

Yesterday BP came into our room—chatted; he was full of war news, all favorable to Axis. I asked him what he was going to do when he became *our* war prisoner, at which he laughed and asked when that would be. When I said "soon," he retorted that it would not be until after I was dead. Japan had lost but few ships, USA many, etc.

This A.M. they started an air raid alarm about 5:00 A.M., so we held reveille and bango in the dark. All clear about 7:45. Put my blue clothes to soak, to leach out the weak dye and shrink them and while getting the hot water, the kitchen detail told me that American planes, perhaps from China, had bombed Takau this morning. It is probably a lie, merely to explain this morning's alert.

Monday—Getsuyo-bi (Moon day), 14 Dec 1942
Fine weather all morning with a nice warm sun, while our gang worked on the farm. I puttered about, with this and that; hung out the blue suit to dry and got my hands indelibly stained. The suit, I learn, is ersatz—being made of wood fibre! They are falling apart already. We got an issue of 2 native oranges this P.M. and I was shocked to see 2 fine big oranges on Brawner's bed—he having evidently drawn his ahead of time. I thought our squad was above such practices, but evidently we are all alike! (This is written with my new pen.)

Weather became overcast by noon. I was one of the 4 who worked on squad garden in P.M.

Tuesday—Kayo-bi (Fire day), 15 Dec 1942
Second fine day in a row! Witnessed a fire drill at 10:00 by the local firemen assisted by our gang, and it was like an old county fair, with hand pumping engine etc. We sure would be out of luck if our barracks burned, for they have no other place to put us. So, when a fire occurs we must grab a blanket and our clothes and rush barefoot out of the building.

Today our long-wished for issue of *soap* arrived, and we each got one cake 1″ x 2″ x 4″ of imitation castile soap, and this must last us God-knows how long—3 months, they tell us, adding that the Jap army is *without* soap. Asked to buy the November "Contemporary Japan" featuring Hiroshige's block prints. Have had no action about buying stamps and watch.

Wednesday—Suiyo-bi (Water day), 16 Dec 1942
Warm last night but my blood is so thin that I slept under 4 blankets plus newspaper interlining. Bowler got slapped for not saluting at 11:30. This morning there was great ado over an inspection of this camp by a medical general, so we cleaned more carefully than usual. We hoped we might bring to his attention our dire need of food—and soap but, as they always do, he walked past all rooms (including the hospital) and barely looked in! Yet they keep harping at us to "take care of your health." At the hospital this P.M. I could not get even a square inch of

adhesive tape! The doctor (Glatly) says we have run our hospital here all this while on merely the lousy little batch of supplies that we brought with us from Tarlac, that the Japs have furnished us nothing!

This P.M. a tobacco order came in and I drew 50 packs of Akerbono cigarettes, though I am 9 yen overdrawn. Borrowed 10 yen from Gen. Moore but Vance says I don't have to pay it in. Washed a sheet and my best shorts and had a wipe shower-bath, the weather was so warm.

Thursday—Getsuyo-bi (Tree day), 17 Dec 1942

Fourth nice day in a row! A new work scheme started: only Squads 1 and 2 went out and worked on the farm, but opened no new ground, but did weeding instead. I got the tea-water for our gang. 20 pigs for our farm were delivered here today half grown—*10* boars, which leads to hope that butchering will commence shortly. Worked today on sewing up a moccasin which I have cut from the bottom of a barrack bag. The highlight of the day was the arrival of our monthly ration of sugar—1 pound or 72 cubes! We feared it would be omitted this month. Somebody said the pigs cost us Y100 each. They are skimping down on our rations again. When we finish our meals all of us are ready to start right in all over again. Always actively hungry!

Friday—Kinyo-bi (Gourd day), 18 Dec 1942

Cold, overcast day, with spits of rain; bum growing weather, but many personal gardens seem thriving. The new lieutenant visited us this morning and was much interested in my Jap notebook. The interpreter also came in, talked with Boatwright about seeds. Everybody hopped him about the paper razor strops recently sold to us. Again I asked him about the stamps and notebook he owes me. Pay! This P.M. we received Y15: five that they owed us from pay day plus 10 from deposited funds. I added Y3 to it and deposited it in PX. Brigadier Simson offered to trade me his snappy overseas cap (scarlet top) for a $29 aviator's windbreaker! Started raining at 4:00 P.M. and turned colder.

Saturday—Doyo-bi (Ass day), 19 Dec 1942

Cold and rainy all day and turned still colder in P.M. Pay. Received our December pay today—but only 20 yen in cash, of which I turned Y15 in to PX. Worked on my mocassins, but mostly on remodeling Beckwith-Smith's shorts, enlarging the legs. No outside work of any kind today. Received a third diphtheria shot this morning. Will surely sleep under all my covers tonight.

Sunday—Nichio-bi (Sun (like hell!) day), 20 Dec 1942

Turned warmer last night, so it wasn't so bad, but today was cold and rainy up to 2:00 P.M. when the sun came out and it was delightful. Sewed on moccasins and shorts all day. Nothing else accomplished. Most everybody in our room is coughing with a cold. This distribution of papers keeps me running.

Monday—Getsuyo-bi (Moon day), 21 Dec 42

Have had reveille diarrhea for 3 days and this morning it caused me the unspeakable accident. Luckily it was long enough before reveille so that I could bathe and wash out the drawers before reveille—and also lucky that the weather had turned warmer. We had a bit of sun this forenoon so I washed a sheet and towel but it soon turned overcast. Installed again the markers for front rank of Squad 7 this P.M. This noon our rice and soup rations were back at the all-time low. I wish I knew the reasons for this starvation diet! They are slowly but inexorably starving us to death.

Tuesday—Kayo-bi (Fire day), 22 Dec 1942

Just another day—nothing happened of note. Got some diarrhea medicine from Glatly and hope for a better night.

Fine day all day. Bowels under better control. Another cursory inspection at 1:00 P.M. James repaired the hinge of Braly's watch, so it doesn't stop when the back is opened. The first of the "repaired" shoes are back, and such repairs! A hole in a sole has a small piece of thin flexible leather nailed over it! Our cigars now 3 days overdue and I still lack my stamps and notebook! Am checking Jap verbs against Wood's dictionary. Beautiful moon rose tonight.

Wednesday—Suiyo-bi (Water day), 23 Dec 1942

Sun started to show at reveille but had no chance—day was overcast and not too warm. Our cigars arrived; 44% of our order. Luckily, I had arranged with Hoeffel to sell me his allowance—12 cigars! The "Moko" cigars cost Y0.28 each and are made of clippings in a wrapper. Also got 2 packs of "Daiton" cigars. 10-entract size in a paper box for Y2.00. Too expensive! Also arrived some Shirinaga cigarettes, our most expensive brand. Y0.28 for package of 10 in purple box with white stork on it. Having plenty of Arenoko's on hand, I cut my order from 30 to 20 packs. Brezina is sick with a bad cold.

4 American officers arrived. Tonight there arrived from Manila 4 more American officers, prisoners of war: Gen. Stevens, who was at Tarlac with us, Col. Horan[37] from Baguio, and Cols. Mitchell[38] and Tarkington[39] from Mindanao. Maybe they will join our squad. My moccasins help greatly in changing to getas at night. My diarrhoea continues.

Christmas Eve, Thursday, 24 Dec 1942

Mostly overcast but not too cold for my "sponge" bath and laundry. Interviewed the Jap medical student about getting some burnt rice for my diarrhea and surprising! he agreed and gave the order to Sgt. Provost at the kitchen, so I got my 1st handout after dinner tonight. Very busy all day, puttering around. Cornered the interpreter and gave him another yen with which to buy my notebook— He already had Y2.50 which he has forgotten to return to me, drat him!

Tonight our choir, by special permission, is touring our barracks, singing Christmas carols and it wrings my heart strings to remember how Landon and I and the children used to sing them—and somehow "Little Town of Bethlehem" seems to bring Paul, especially, back to me. This is the 2d Christmas that Landon and I have spent apart—and I hope it is the last. "Merry Christmas" is a hollow mockery.

Our new arrivals brought me welcome news of Brooke: He is still at Cabanatuan where they have combined their two camps at Camp No. 1. He commands Group No. 1 has even gained weight, and seems to be getting along in fine shape. How welcome to learn the good news about him! Wish Priscilla could know about it.

This damn Ersatz pen leaks onto my fingers!

Christmas, Friday, 25 Dec 1942

Wonderfully beautiful night last night; equally beautiful day: best we've had in months. Aired my bedding. For lunch we had meat for the first time in weeks. It was pork: they cooked it in the soup and then finished cooking it in the rice. I got 1 piece, about the size of a filbert, but the soup had a wonderful flavor. We also got 1 orange, 3 bananas, and (at last!) a half "loaf" of bread. Hirsch came in and we divided the tiny can of oleo that we bought jointly at Bilibid 7 months ago! We had agreed to save it for *bread* only. I took great delight in cutting 3 thin slices off, buttering them heavily and Fletcherizing them. This used up half the loaf.

To show that we are in a punitive camp: *After* lunch (at which many ate all their bread) the Japs sent notice that there would be *NO* rice served tonight—that we should save our bread, to take its place! (Am going to have my peanuts roasted.) But, thanks to Col. Hoffman talking to the Japs right away, the edict was cancelled and we got our rice OK. The cut was made by "Bandy-legs Henry" the jejune snot of a Jap mess sergeant We also got duck in our soup at night, so that the night meal was better, even than lunch. We also got 1 camote cake in the P.M. which I ate immediately. But a highlight was the nibbling I did on bread, thickly spread with oleo; I sure did enjoy it. But I got no burnt rice tonight.

All in all, this was a wonderful day: one which all of us will remember all our lives.

Saturday—Doyo-bi (Ass day), 26 Dec 1942

Cold overcast day. LP gave us 2 poinsettia blooms yesterday which the gang insisted on hanging up. So they wilted, but this morning, after I clipped them last night and put them in bottles of water, they revived perfectly. I also salvaged 3 more blooms from the garbage. Set out some turnip plants, also some poinsettia joints.

Aftermath of yesterday's rice episode: the Japs relieved Sgt. Provost from the kitchen for not meeting the emergency and now in charge is the English Sgt. Brown—who brought us all those recipes from London's Savoy Hotel. We all hope for better results. He is putting the duck giblets in tonight's soup: a good start.

Sunday/Monday (Monday), 27—28 Dec 1942

Nothing noteworthy except that I borrowed 10 yen from Gen. McBride[40] and the interpreter at last brought me the "expensive" (73 sen) notebook that I've been teasing him about for over a month. BP says I can't buy the Patek-Philippe watch I want, because they can't handle "difficult conditions." We got some peanuts and Braly kindly roasted mine for me. Also, I broke down and opened my next to last can of milk mixed up a batch of that moldy cocoa and cooked it in the kitchen, and drank it all myself. Dumplings formed in cooking, showing the adulteration. Sunday night we held our first "Sing-song" and terrible to relate a British soldier recited "Gunga Din" (also terribly) and our Cornell[41] butchered "Casey at the Bat." I stuck it out until they started singing "Old Black Joe" and then I quit. The Jap officers all attended and the camp commander presented the performers with 5 bottles of sake!

Tuesday—Kayo-bi (Fire day), 29 Dec 1942

At every meal I doled out to myself 2 tablespoons of milk, weakened by 6 spoons of water. My ankles are terribly swollen again. Last night I had to trot 6 times, my record! It was a beautiful day all day. As we hear that 25 more men and 50 officers are coming, I spent the afternoon laying out the key markers for their roll call formation, and so forgot to cook some more cocoa. But I got a good batch of burnt rice, and ate that for my diarrhoea. Our poinsettias are beautiful, including the 3 that I salvaged from the garbage. Newspapers arrived tonight, the latest date of which is Dec 22d.

Wednesday—Suiyo-bi (Water day), 30 Dec 1942

Just another day. I manage to keep busy during all waking hours, and this damn librarian job sure takes up a lot of time, keeping our newspapers in circulation properly.

Thursday—Getsuyo-bi (Tree day), 31 Dec 1942

Dark, dreary dismal day. Brown and I started our week's tour as chow handlers and for our supper we had a thick soup that defied my serving efforts. I have insisted on my dishes being mixed among the others, so I can't know whose bowls I am filling—for some of our officers crab over imagining they are getting 2 grains less rice than somebody else. Childish, but a lot of earthy psychology is coming to the surface because of our starvation rations. I didn't think that men in general and officers in particular could sink so low.

We spent this morning on orderlies work, cleaning our windows and scrubbing our floor. Then the dyspeptic camp commander gave us his "annual" inspection at 1:30 and so ended his day's duties.

This is sure a hell of a way to end a year. I happened to hit the benjo at exactly midnight tonight, and so exchanged sardonic "Happy New Years" with a couple of Limey's there.

When we get our evening rice at 5:30 or 6:00 P.M. I feel that the day is over: it is dark by the time we finish our chow. Chow detail! Then we wash our dishes while an orderly wipes off table. Then Boatwright and Carter usurp the center of the table for their cribbage game; I use one end for writing (damage claim now) until bango time; meanwhile brushing my teeth and making up my bed. After bango I read the papers, letting the others read them during the day. Then a defensive visit to the benjo, and douse the light and climb into bed just before the "lights out" at 9:30.

Here ends 1942.

Notes

1. Falk, 113. Brig. Gen. William E. Brougher: Wainwright, 53, 161, 270. General Brougher had commanded the 11th Division under Wainwright's I Corp. According to Wainwright, he was one of the truly great combat soldiers of Bataan. He, too, had been a prisoner at Cabanatuan.

2. Morton, *Philippines,* 131, 133–35, 138, 171, 174, 218, 305, 310, 314–17, 320, 328, 407. Brig. Gen. Clinton A. Pierce had commanded the 26th Cavalry. A large number of his men and horses had been caught in the open on 9 December by Japanese bombers. He lost a great number. Later, on 24 December, his reduced unit of 450 men fought one of the truly great cavalry delaying actions of the war. For this action he had been promoted to brigadier general.

3. Falk, 86–87, 104–5, 157. Col. Virgil N. Cordero had commanded the 72nd Infantry on Bataan and later had undergone the "Death March."

4. *Register,* 29. Unfortunately, Bunker actually predicted what was to happen aboard numerous POW ships during the war. Some were torpedoed. Others were bombed, and hundreds of prisoners were caught below deck and drowned.

5. Chunn, 9. This is probably Col. H. M. Peck, who had been on the "Death March" and imprisoned in Cabanatuan.

6. *Register,* 20. Col. Harrison Henry Cocke Richards had been the CO of an infantry regiment on Bataan; he had undergone the hardships of the "Death March." He lived to retire from the army in 1947.

7. Takao: seaport on southwest coast of Taiwan.

8. Morton, *Philippines,* 286, 425–27. Col. Malcolm V. Fortier had been the senior instructor to the 41st Infantry Division of the Philippine army.

9. Cow-towing: low Oriental bow, a sign of subservience.

10. *Register,* 338. Col. Alexander Hunkins Campbell had been the commanding officer of the Air Warning Service for the Philippines. He had partaken in the "Death March," during which he was bayoneted in the back. He was repatriated in 1945 and retired in 1952.

11. Falk, 247. Col. James V. Collier had been General King's G3 for the Luzon Force. He had done most of the negotiating with Homma.

12. Morton, *Philippines.* Col. Kearie L. Berry had commanded the 3rd and 1st Infantry on Bataan; later he commanded the entire 1st Division, which took part in the battle of the pockets on Bataan. He lived through the imprisonment and was repatriated in 1945. He later retired as a brigadier general.

13. Wainwright, 14. Lt. Col. Alfred Balsam had been Wainwright's Philippine Division quartermaster. *Register,* 331. He had taken part in the "Death March," survived prison, and was repatriated in 1945.

14. Morton, 195–98. Col. John R. Boatwright commanded the 53rd Infantry Regiment, which had been on the slope of Mt. Natib during Bataan's first battle.

15. Dupuy, *Chronology,* 35. This was obviously referring to two separate actions. First, the Marine landing on Guadalcanal on 7, 8, 9 August, during which time the Japanese won a naval victory and control of the waters around Guadalcanal in the Solomons. On 17 August the Second Marine Raider Battalion raided Makin Island in the Gilberts. They had landed by rubber boat. The Marines on Guadalcanal held out until reinforced and the Raiders were successful.

16. *Register,* 352. Lt. Col. John R. Vance had been the finance officer on Corregidor who had cut up two million pesos on the day of the surrender. He lived through the imprisonment and retired in 1954.

17. Falk, 196–97. Colonel Lawrence had been the Luzon Force quartermaster. He had been at Camp O'Donnell.

18. *United States Naval Chronology, World War II* (Office of the Chief of Naval Operations, 1955), 30–32. From 1 August to 28 August the United States had lost or damaged in the Solomons area eight destroyers, two transports, four heavy cruisers, and one carrier.

19. Morton, *Philippines,* 327, 406. Col. Irvin E. Doane had been with the U.S. 31st Infantry on Bataan.

20. *Register,* 425. Maj. John Ramsey Pugh had been the G2 of I Corps on Bataan; later, he became G2 on Corregidor. He endured the war and retired from active duty as a major general in 1966.

21. Wainwright, 181–82. Lt. Gen. A. F. Percival had been the commander and chief of the British forces in Malaya. He had been captured there by General Yamashita. He survived the imprisonment and was later invited by General MacArthur to attend the formal Japanese surrender.

22. Ibid., 81. Sir Mark Young, the former governor of Hong Kong.

23. Ibid. Sir Shenton Thomas was the former governor of Malaya.

24. Ibid., 143–45. Maj. Gen. William F. Sharp, Jr., had been the last general to surrender. He had been in command of Mindanao, which had to surrender at the fall of Corregidor.

25. *Register,* 322. Maj. Gen. Bradford G. Chynoweth had been the commanding general of the Visayan Force. He retired in 1947.

26. Morton, *Philippines,* 512–13. Brig. Gen. Joseph P. Vachon had been in command of the Cotabato–Davao sector in the southern islands.

27. Wainwright, 102, 107. Brig. Gen. Carl H. Seals. He and his wife had been captured in the PBY escaping from Corregidor, which had crashed in Mindanao.

28. None were bombed during October.

29. Dupuy, *Chronology,* 36. On 1 November the Russians halted the Germans "in the heart of Stalingrad."

30. Wainwright, 38. Brig. Gen. Clyde Andrew Selleck had commanded the

71st Division PA on Bataan. *Register,* 318. He had participated in the "Death March." He returned to the States in 1945 and retired as a colonel.

    31. Falk, 81. Brig. Gen. Clifford Bluemel had commanded about 1,300 Americans and Philippine Scouts, remnants of the 31st Division PA, northeast of Cabcaben. On 9 April, his unit was the last to surrender, having fought well right up to the last. He took part in the "Death March" and was handled brutally on several occasions. *Register,* 317. He returned to the States in 1945 and subsequently retired in 1947.

    32. Dupuy, *Chronology,* 31. This refers to the Doolittle raid against Tokyo launched from the carrier USS *Hornet.* The captured pilots and crews were beheaded.

    33. Wainwright, 182–84, 188. Maj. Gen. Merton Beckwith-Smith. He had been the British commander of the 18th British Division in Malaya and had been commander of the "Crack Coldstream Guards."

    34. Dupuy, *Chronology,* 37. MacArthur had moved his headquarters to Port Moresby on 6 November.

    35. Ibid., 36. This had taken place on 8 November.

    36. Wainwright, 182, 195, 201–02. Lt. Gen. Sir Lewis Maclesfield Heath had been commander of the Indian III Corps in Malaya. He had been badly wounded in World War I: "About three inches of bone had been removed from his left arm between the elbow and shoulder. His left arm simply hung by its flesh and muscle. To relieve the drag upon this tissue . . . [he] had a small loop sewn on the left lower pocket of his blouse. He would fit his fingers into the loops to support his arm."

    37. Ibid., 140, 143–44, 146–47, 149. Col. John P. Horan had commanded small units in northern Luzon; they surrendered after much coaxing by Gen. Sharp on 14 May. Many of the detachments refused to surrender and were the core of later guerrilla units.

    38. Morton, *Philippines,* 513, 514. Col. Eugene H. Mitchell had commanded the 61st Infantry (PA) in the southern islands. He was literally captured when his CP was overrun. His unit had been nearly decimated.

    39. Ibid., 503, 508, 516. Col. Hiram W. Tarkington had commanded the 61st Field Artillery in the Cagayan sector on Mindanao.

    40. Wainwright, 227–28. Brig. Gen. Allan Clay McBride had been chief of staff of the Philippine Department. He later died of starvation.

    41. Morton, 502, 577, 581. Col. Theodore M. Cornell had commanded the hastily organized Leyte and Samar force of about 2,500 men. On 10 May he received General Sharp's orders to surrender; initially he refused to accept the message, and he continued to carry out his plans to break his unit up into guerrilla bands. On the twentieth, one of General Sharp's personal couriers arrived, and he subsequently surrendered.

Notes: by Colonel Paul D. Bunker, 59th CA

Friday—Kinyo-bi, 1 Jan 1943
Starting this year as a Prisoner of War at Nipponese Prison Camp No. 4 at Karenko Taiwan (Formosa) Japan, at which I am No. 29.

Today the sun shone for a while in the morning but in the afternoon the cold breeze sprang up and sky became overcast. At 8:30 we all formed for the New Year's ceremony of concerted yelling of "Banzai" thrice at the flagpole. Camp Commander was our cheerleader and we all had to be in uniform. Holiday for the rest of the day. For breakfast we had a heavy doughy dumpling in the soup; at noon we had a few filbert-size pieces of pork and Boy, didn't it taste wonderful! The soup, too was very thick. In evening there was a little pork fat cooked in the soup which added to the soybeans, made it tasteful. We also got a small camote cake which was delicious. In evening we had our 2d "Sing Song."

I copied Rutherford's dope about the American prisoners at Cabanatuan's Camp!

Saturday—Doyo-bi, 2 Jan 1943
The wind dropped at about 2:00 A.M. and today, the overcast was warm and I went about in my British shorts. Last night occurred the 2d of our Sing-Songs; much better than the 1st. Our double quartet was good, but Giblin in his recitation about hating women, was super excellent. Nothing doing today, it being a continuation of the Jap holidays. For breakfast we had the same gluey soup as yesterday morning; too thick to strain the liquor out! In P.M. I cooked up the last of my Bilibid cocoa, but didn't have enough sugar for it. Glommed it all myself, a bowlful. At least it fills my stomach. My ankles get slowly worse. There was burnt rice available this noon, but that "fairy" Sgt. Provost is back in the kitchen and he distributed it to all squads and saved me none. They say that our total rations of beans for supper are to be reduced by 5 kilograms, and this P.M. the beans boiling in the cauldren were certainly much less than usual. There is also a rumor that shortage of Jap shipping prevents sending all the local sugar to Japan and hence we *may* get more sugar. Would to Gawd it's so but, to quote the slogan taught us by bitter experience "We'll believe it when it's on our plates."

To think that it is impossible to buy paper like this—or any paper for use with ink!

Sunday—Nichio-bi, 3 Jan 1943
Pretty good day—Had some pork in the soup today. Finished my can of milk at last.

Monday—Getsuyo-bi, 4 Jan 1943
Windy as hell all day, getting steadily worse until night. Colder than a harlot's heart. Got hot bath in A.M. before it got too cold. Then they hurriedly turned out *all* squads for work, clearing a new big farm plot, up on the hill, where the wintry blast whistled through everybody. They also turned out in P.M. and suffered some more. Glad my 61 years excuses me from that work. Thick soup every breakfast for Jan 1–5, inclusive. They delivered 22 goats tonight, for our stock farm, but everybody says they are small and not large mountain kind. Sgt. Hundley fixed me a hot brick and I went to bed with all my clothes on and hence managed to keep warm and cosy, what with newspapers between my blankets.

Tuesday—Kayo-bi, 5 Jan 1943
Wind dropped before reveille. A kid was born to our goats last night. Ducks! Thick soup for breakfast; very short rice and watery soup for noon, and 30 ducks in soup tonight.

Yesterday I gave the interpreter 20 more sen, to cover "shortage" for my Jap dictionary and he said I'd have to wait a week "they are coming." Absolutely nothing seems obtainable locally: I have permission to buy 2 copies of "Contemporary Japan" containing reproductions of Hiroshige's prints and when I tried to pay him the Y2.00 for them, he said "Oh, we have to order them by mail, it will take 2 months!" And Sunday, after a long wait, LP brought Gen. Wainwright the "expensive" watch he asked for. It is a nickel-cased, 7-jewel Elgin, with traces of rust on the works, and will probably cost Wainwright 50 yen. He turned it over to me, instead of the good engineer watch which James wangled out of him. When I tried to swap, James became violent and almost abusive. He sure is crazy as hell.

They are tethering our goats on the front parade and the place looks quite pastoral. Spent the P.M. with the Mindanao gang, getting data. If you ask them a simple question they start telling you the history of their part in the war.

Wednesday—Suiyo-bi, 6 Jan 1942
Clear at dawn; beautiful sunny morning but wind sprang up about 1:00 and it turned cold. Laundry and basin bath in A.M. and, in P.M. installed markers for a prospective 3d Squad. Yesterday the interpreter gave me 2 sheets of paper and told me to write up my "Thoughts on the New Year." Many other officers required to write "compositions" on similar subjects. I fear I stuck my neck out by saying that my fundamental thought is that the USA would eventually win, and what would then be our relations to our captors? Also that I begrudged spending my few remaining days here instead of with my family.

Tonight we elected permanent food servers: Cordero and Carter for rice and Campbell and Carter for soup.

Balsam is sick with diarrhoea and makes a great fuss. I gave him part of the charred rice I got at the kitchen, this morning, on doctor's orders. But I don't get it very often, so it is lucky my diarrhoea is about cured.

Thursday—Mokuyo-bi, 7 Jan 1943

Our work detail was well chilled this P.M. but L.P. wanted to work them another shift, from 4:00–4:30 and, when Penrose remonstrated saying that our officers had worked all morning, were tired, and were over 50, to which LP retorted that we had fought the emperor's soldiers and now we would work like soldiers. He told Crews that the big field which is now being prepared will be planted to camotes *for the pigs*!!! And here *we* are just yearning for camotes! And the 200 kilograms of camotes which we bought are being doled out to the gang working on this "farm" building, but we never get any of them. For Christmas we bought and paid for 3 cases of apples, but they all went to Jap HQ and, while Jap soldiers were munching apples all over the Post, again we never got a smell. This same procedure holds whenever edibles are bought for the mess, and even when smokes come in. They've just let 3 baskets of oranges rot instead of delivering them to us.

Tonight as usual put a lot of newspapers in between my blankets. These Jap blankets are so short that I have to wear my Ersatz jumper at night. Have at last finished my tentative list of property destroyed by enemy action and it practically fills one of my notebooks. I need Landon's help, especially on linen.

Rescript day, Friday—Kinyo-bi, 8 Jan 1943

They turned us out this morning for some kind of a ceremony involving a salaam toward the emperor's palace, but they refrained from reading the "Rescript" declaration of war. Holiday for remainder of the day but it was so cold and dreary that nobody enjoyed it much.

Yesterday, much to our surprise, arrived our monthly ration of sugar a week ahead of schedule, 1 pound of cubes. Enlisted men receive a pound of granulated (much better) and the other half of the sack went gratis to the Jap officers' mess. Cigarettes also arrived, giving me a reserve, now, of 200 packs of 10 scags each.

Yesterday also, the Jap doctor looked me over as to my swollen ankles, cussed me out and told me to stay in my room and spend as much time as possible in bed until the swelling goes down. I could hardly refrain from yelling "If you know anything, you know as well as I do, that what I need is PROTEINS and not inactivity." Beat Horan 2 games of cribbage after dinner. He is notoriously mouthy, it seems.

Saturday—Doyo-bi, 9 Jan 1943

Much to our surprise, instead of cleaning up this morning, they turned everybody out for work in the big new garden. Overcast, chilly. Those newspapers between my blankets are sure a fine thing these cold nights. Hunted other squads for extra papers and Curtis gave me a 2d copy of the Japan *Times* containing the description of the taking of Corregidor.

My pen came back this P.M. presumably repaired, but time alone will tell. I hate to use ink on this record because it is so vulnerable to water; a pencil mark (unless rubbed) is so much more nearly permanent (See Nausen's Farthest North).

Everybody turned out for work this morning and we cleaned up in P.M. for tomorrow's inspection. We were paid 15 yen from savings this P.M., 5 of which was for Victrola records, thus bringing on more talk, kicking because it gives non-subscribers 5 yen clear! Traded a carton of my Akebono cigarettes for a carton of the enlisted men's kind, to give them a good try-out.

Every night I make up my bed with newspapers in a different way, striving for the optimum arrangement. All of the recent ones, though laborious, are cozy.

The tentative total amount of my property loss at Corregidor is $10,726.06[1] and I wonder how much, if any of it, I'll ever get back from our government!

Sunday—Nichio-bi, 10 Jan 1943

Fine day until supper, when rain started. Got in my laundry and open air bath. Rumor is that half of the enlisted men (prisoners) will leave here for parts unknown, since "there are too many here." There are 106 enlisted men of all nationalities and 220 officers and civilians. LP made the inspection this morning, came into the room, but said nothing. Tonight the sentry walks the porch to avoid the rain and stops to watch the cribbage game at every passage. I went to kitchen in rain and got a speck of burnt rice; gave some to Braly and Balsam. Also tried out some onion roots (refuse from our kitchen) as flavoring but it was not so good. Whereas one little frond from a garlic plant gives a hearty fine flavor to a full ration of rice. This P.M. I coughed up *25 whole pesos* for a grey flannel shirt, which will be fine for night wear.

Monday—Getsuyo-bi, 11 Jan 1943

The coldest, most miserable day we've had: a high wind and right off the icebergs! Bought a wool undershirt for 10 pesos and put it right on, with most every other garment I own and was still cold! Squads 1–6 turned out to pull weeds in P.M. but stayed only until 2:30 P.M. and I had not yet gone for the tea water but, instead, was preparing 4 newspapers for issue. Our Excep. articles requisition showed up plus some sweaters that BP gathered up on his own. 30 sweaters for 320 men! Last night Pvt .Werst accidentally clipped me with his clogs and we wakened Glatly to swab the bloody hand. A crumb of brown rice tonight after a swell chow—beans cooked in Soy sauce and sugar and served separately! Made great difference!

Had a row with Carter over Brezina giving me a frond of garlic. He is a gutter-snipe if there ever was one! My flannel (nite) shirt was swell last night.

Tuesday—Kayo-bi, 12 Jan 1943

The wind dropped about 3:00 this morning and reveille was bearable. Had a good night's rest, warm and cosy under my newspapers. Sun was out, off and on, all day, the actual temperature however continued cold. All hands turned out for work on the new farm, both A.M. and P.M. sessions, the P.M. one being quite uncomfortable. Got a haircut in p.m. and paid Sgt. Cavanaugh 8 cigarettes. Went to kitchen at 3:45 and got a bucket of hot water for our workers tea when they marched in at 4:00 P.M. Maj. Browne,[2] in charge of the stock farm, now has as assistants the 3 lieutenant generals, the 3 governors and all officers over 60 years of age. We herd the goats on 1-hour shifts, and feed the chickens: the cleaning of same is done by our enlisted men. However, we do not go outside the wall we only stand around and watch these goats while they are grazing inside the wall, on our parade ground. And I am excused from even that, so long as I am on sick report and have this red and white round sicktag. Brezina came back from hospital this P.M.

More articles on our "exceptional articles" requisition kept coming in, off and on, all day, but very little progress was made in issuing them out to us consumers. No fruit for a long time, though the Jap cartmen said they were bringing in bananas. Yesterday we were issued 10 rice cookies, the size of a half-dollar. Only 36 sets came in, and we were all disappointed that the issue was not of sugar-coated peanuts. BP brought in, as samples, some cotton sweaters that appeal to me; we are now trying to get more of them. I first thought they were wool sweaters but I should have known better: there is no wool.

However, the bum looking winter uniforms which they issued to our enlisted men, being lined with corduroy, are much warmer than the wood-fibre jute blue clothes they sold to us officers at such outrageous prices. The underwear issued to enlisted men, also, seems to be of a sort of canton flannel and is fine and warm. Wish we officers could get both!

Wednesday—Suiyo-bi, 13 Jan 1943

Fine weather in P.M. so I got a bath at the laundry tubs. Washed out my new flannel shirt and undershirt that have been soaking since yesterday to save soap. Everybody went out to work both for A.M. and P.M. sessions, leaving Brezina and me in blessed solitude. Our "exceptional articles" were delivered and a poor one it was: I got some "face cream" for use on my hair, 1 notebook instead of 3 asked for, a few pins, rice mucilage, pencil and eraser! Cost Y2.01.

Our poinsettia blooms, we got at Christmas which have just about gone. I have been keeping them going, in joints of bamboo that I cut. Campbell's snarling about newspapers at last becomes unendurable, so tonight I asked Braly to appoint somebody else as "librarian."

Starting today, charred rice from the kitchen goes to the hospital and is dispensed from there, but of course Glatly didn't know about it until later. Our cigars, due on the 9th, have not yet arrived. Am now making up a card index diary of the Jap reports of the war.

Thursday—Mokuyo-bi, 14 Jan 1943

Last night was beautifully warm, clear and starry, and dawn promised a fine day, but it clouded up after noon and got cold again—but I got my bath and laundry done. Jap soap is no good; it will not lather. For breakfast "soup" we had, by actual measurement, one heaping tablespoonful of onion tops and other "green vegetables" boiled in plain water, plus a cupful of boiled rice. Usually we have a bit more vegetables.

This afternoon gave us another example of the Japanese policy of humiliating us wherever possible: here was Lt Gen. Wainwright, late highest commander of U.S. troops and Lt. Gen. Heath, late supreme British commander—and what were they doing? Herding our 22 goats on the parade ground! If they ever claim to be sick, they report (as we do) to our hospital, and although we have plenty of high ranking doctors here, who decides whether they are sick or not, and who "prescribes" for them? A Nipponese buck private—or he may not be even that— all we can find out about him is that he once started a medical course, skipped the middle of it, and is now, instead of getting a diploma, is or has worked on a correspondence course which he is supplementing by actually "practicing"—on *us*! Our doctors are entirely subordinate to him.

Our men turned out for work both A.M. and P.M. again and LP came around to check up on the excused and absentees. I traced some maps of war areas. Went to bed without newspapers in it as the evening and night were unusually mild.

Friday—Kinyo-bi, 15 Jan 1943

Day mostly good but breezed up cold in evening. However, I got my bath in. Yesterday LP caught about 20 deadbeating work, so the immediate decision was to cut out our precious beans from *everybody's* ration—which we learned about today. Furthermore, at reveille, LP made the announcement, through *his* interpreter and Col. Corkhill, the OD, that many had been absent and that, "while the work is voluntary everybody would turn out"! Several people laughed and then the trouble started! LP asked why the laughter? Wood talked long but without results. Modin came out and said some people *couldn't* work because they are starved and he was ordered back into ranks. Again LP wanted to know why anybody laughed. Then said that if anybody laughed, when the Japs have given us *extra* food [*sic!*] for working on the farm and are to give us extra meat (we've had none since New Year's) from our stock farm, they would drop both projects, for they mean only extra work for themselves. They also ordered that squad leaders immediately list those who do not wish to do this "voluntary" work. Several people put in their names, including Hirsch and Hammond, and we are wondering what will happen to them. To straighten out the laughter thing, Hoffman explained that it was caused by the incongruity of Corkhill's announcement and no ridicule of anything Nipponese was intended. Also, we hear that letters of apology were sent the Japs. As a result LP was doling out candy to our workers this afternoon and our beans went back into the ration! Horan relieved me tonight as squad librarian—thank Gawd!

A peculiarity of the Nipponese is their abhorrence of individual punishment in such cases; all they know is collective punishment.

Saturday—Doyo-bi, 16 Jan 1943

Last night I made up my bed for a cold session, but it turned warm and I had a cosy, unbroken snooze until 2:30 A.M. Sprinkle at reveille drove us inside for bango, but all hands turned out for work at 9:00 A.M. Windy but not cold. At 11:00 I used the last of the ¼ pound of Lipton's tea that I bought over 5 months ago at Bilibid. Copied another cartoon of Fortier's. Decorated 2 empty cigar boxes with covers from cigarette boxes. Turned cold and windy in P.M. Drank lots of tea while pasting clippings into one of my notebooks. The interpreter came in this P.M. and said I probably would not be allowed to buy an expensive watch in Tokyo. Several officers in the room asked him to get them any kind of watch. From what he let fall, it is likely that the letters we wrote a month 1½ months ago have not left here yet! Poor Landon! I hope she is not worrying over not getting the letter I promised in my radio.

We have 72 white Leghorn chickens now—and they are a scrubby lot—not laying and evidently incapable of laying. The fools seem to think that a White Leghorn is a *meat* fowl!

Sunday—Nichio-bi, 17 Jan 1943

A fairly cold and nasty day, but the wind died down about 4:00 P.M. They took my red and white sick card away from yesterday on Glatly's report that my swollen ankles had subsided—which is only partially true: my feet are still so puffy that I can barely force them into my largest shoes. We got a bath from 12:40–1:00 for 20 of us. Wound up with a *cold* shower and the reaction was pleasant. I am on chicken-feeding detail today—postponed the A.M. feeding to daylight!

Another commentary on our humiliating status occurred today: At our stock farm, BP mentioned that extensive butchering of beef is now occurring near here, to can beef for the Nipponese army and that the offal thereof (hearts, livers, etc.)

were being acquired to feed to our *pigs!* though they've steadily refused to give us humans meat of any kind except on the rarest occasions. Col. Wood immediately told him that we prisoners would like to have the "offal" to *eat,* and would be thankful to get hold of it! As a swell result, they say we will tonight get some 30 kg of hearts, liver, etc. in our soup—and everybody is all excited over the prospect. But I never, in the old days, would have thought it possible for me to be thankful (or to accept) the offal from the Nipponese slaughterings.

Monday—Getsuyo-bi, 18 Jan 1943

Beautiful day. Workers out both A.M. and P.M. and sore over the new work rules: instead of working half the crew for 30 minutes while the other half rests they now work everybody for 30 minutes and allow them only 10 minutes rest—not enough for a smoke. So they were all fagged out when they turned in this P.M. I changed our marigold window flowers, since Brezina refused to be "bossed." I also watered our Squad Garden No. 2. Spent all morning copying Nippon Lesson No. 9 and P.M. Lesson 10.

Our cigar order finally arrived and, to our horror, the government has boosted the price of a box of 25 Noko cigars from Y7.00 to Y16.00! and, for 10 opera cigars, from Y2.00 to Y4.00! We cancelled our order and they say the town merchants are doing the same because they cannot find buyers at the exorbitant price. Y16.00 a month—for only 25 bum cigars would practically exhaust our allowance of Y20.00. Rations were much better all day, and at evening the beans were cooked separately. Somebody has brought in some roots of (I think) sarsaparilla—anyway, it smells like root beer. We shave the bark off the roots, leach it with hot water and the decoction adds an agreeable flavor to our insipid rice.

Tuesday—Kayo-bi, 19 Jan 1943

Last night was one of the finest I ever saw: bright moonlight, no clouds, and not too cold. I *had* to stop out back and admire the stars. Old Scorpio is beginning to rise in early morning so spring cannot be far behind. Some of our chickens dead with diphtheria. I did my first goat guard from 10:30–11:30 this morning. The goats are all small and all black. Started re-sewing my left moccasin. 2d night with a furled mosquito net: much better!

Wednesday—Suiyo-bi, 20 Jan 1943

An overcast and breezy work day. Tripe in noon soup; liver in evening. Yesterday, with a hot wire, I broke tops off some bottles and made salt containers that will not rust. Got 3 tiny tangerines this noon—very few vegetables in the soup, to pay for it. Herd guard from 3:00 to 4:00. Tonight, in our "soup" we had liver and heart of 2 beeves for 320 people—but it was *good!* Tomorrow we'll have the corresponding tripe for noon and liver, etc. for night. In that way, we get a suspicion of meat, 2 meals out of 3. It is a Godsend, and will be sorry when it stops in a week or so. My swollen ankles are much improved by the diet.

Thursday—Mokuto-bi, 21 Jan 1943

Fine, clear day. To show how childish grown men can become: Col. Brezina brought a kettle of hot water at 11:00 A.M. for the workers' tea when they should come in from work. And he hid it in his locker and guarded it so I should get none—all because we had a tiff yesterday. I am more than ever convinced that he is no Czech but a German of the most poisonous kind—probably a Hessian or Prussian.

Supper was gorgeous, simply because they cooked the beans and liver separately and served it separately, it was delicious and the soup was unusually good. Too bad to be hurried by a physical check of bedding. We are also cheered by announcement that our kitchen will hereafter get double our old allowance of sugar, plus an allowance of flour for thickening soup and more midzu—a curd for soup. Another wild rumor is that there will be no more work after 1 Feb. and then "the rank basis will take effect" whatever that means.

Friday—Kinyo-bi, 22 Jan 1943

Last night Boatwright whimpered that he was tired and wanted to put out our light right after bango, so I omitted my evening reading and spent an extra hour in bed, dammit, and had a bad time getting through the night. Today dawned fine. Herd guard 9:30–10:30, plus Sledge, Bluemel and 1 other who are on duty all day. 5 officers herding 23 goats!! The snails have all disappeared; hibernating, I suppose. Made a seasoning from chopped orange peel and sugar for my rice. Had quite a lot of tripe in the soup tonight, and cooked more tender than usual. Turned in right after bango to avoid discussion about burning the light, which annoys Boatwright—he "needing" his 10½ hours sleep!

Saturday—Doyo-bi, 23 Jan 1943

Just another day—overcast but not windy. No bathing. Herd guard 2:00 to 3:15 because old fluff Rawitzer was late coming out! Carried water for our squad garden. Gang worked this A.M. and Pvt. Hill scrubbed floor in P.M. Continued copying Fortier's cartoons and card index diary of War. Made a cover for one of my cut-off bottles. Tried a new way of cutting the bottles yesterday, but it was a flat failure. This P.M. O'Day[3] got his letter home, written *1 Dec back* unread, because it was on Jap army paper! I believe that they have forwarded *none* of our letters! A lot of tripe in the soup tonight.

Sunday—Nichio-bi, 24 Jan 1943

Good day all day. Last night Col. James, Sig. Corps and Pvt. Walker got orders they will leave for Taihoku and probably Tokyo—perhaps, for radio work. If the

Japs expect to get any code dope out of him, they'll be disappointed. I made tentative arrangements with him to buy me a Patek-Philippe or Rolex Oyster watch in Tokyo. Pay! We were paid, this noon and by kicking, I caused the paymaster to give me Y90 in cash instead of the Y47 I expected! Hooray! Paid Moore and McBride each the Y10 I borrowed from them. On herd guard with Garfinkel from 4:00–5:00 and got 1 can of manure, plus a pocketful of "locust" reeds. Last night one of our good pigs died. Ostensibly of pneumonia—but they had fed it a chicken that had died of diphtheria (?). Tripe in the soup tonight but skimpy rations otherwise. Later: the pig died of pierced intestine—due to chicken bone, dammit! If they had killed and bled him right away we could have eaten him, as it is, we lose two good meals, all through LP's worthlessness! Tough luck.

Monday—Getsuyo-bi, 25 Jan 1943

A swell day all day; this warm spell has kept up for well over a week now and we're all praying it may continue indefinitely.

Col. James left this morning in a new civilian suit the Japs let him have (for Y132.00) and he says they gave him a fine breakfast, with Fish! Also allowed him to draw Y1000 from his deposited money and told him he'll have a room of his own in a hotel! Had liver and heart meat in breakfast soup. Everybody worked this morning but this P.M. nobody worked: the British for pay and the rest of us for weighing. I weighed 68.5 kg. (checked with 68.7 on the other scales). This is 150.7 pounds which is the lowest I've ever weighed since I was 16 years old or so! It also shows a loss of 6.7 pounds since Dec 12th and 11 pounds since Oct 20th. And I sure am weak as a cat! The fine sun compelled me into my usual swab-bath and laundry. We are now making flavoring extracts from "tumilao," sasafras, orange peel, etc. for our rice. Gawd but we'd like to have a square meal for once—just one meal where we'd leave the table feeling well fed instead of still starving. Copied more of Fortier's drawings.

Tuesday—Kayo-bi, 26 Jan 1943

Nothing special today. Fair, and workers were out A.M. and P.M. Hirsch et als, who refused to "volunteer" for farm work have had no punishment visited upon them as yet. Today we received a bunch of sweaters—all the same size, of course, and I feared mine would be too small, but it fits well on my wasted-away body. Cost Y6.27 and is only cotton knit, so I use it as an undershirt, next to my skin. Grey color. Our village wits call them our varsity sweaters and wonder what class numerals to put on them. Rained quite heavily this evening. Herd guard 10:30–11:30.

Wednesday—Suiyo-bi, 27 Jan 1943

Overcast, but workers turned out in A.M. "House slippers" arrived; felt soles.

Made tray for my card index War diary. Interpreter says my dictionary won't be here for 2 months! Takes longer than between P.I. and U.S. On P.M. they formed us on the parade and made an entirely new assignment to squads. Our No. 2 squad now has 30 men. All American generals in Squad 1. First assignment to rooms was arbitrarily by Prison No. and I was slated to move across the hall into Room 5. *Squads rearranged.* Went out on herd guard with that horrid future ahead, but Braly got permission to "make minor changes within the squad" and so, luckily, I am to remain in my present place, where I have at least a small space in which to hang my clothes—though I am losing over 35% of my wall locker space to Col. Amis who, with Aldrich, has been crammed into our room making 10 in here. Worked frantically the rest of the day, compressing my junk into the remaining space. Beautiful day all day.

Thursday—Mokuyo-bi, 28 Jan 1943

In moving about, yesterday, the watch that Skinny Wainwright gave me fell on the floor and broke the balance pinion pivot, dammit. Beautiful day and workers went out, both A.M. and P.M. So busy making my shelving and rearranging my stuff that I omitted shaving. Hernia! While bathing, discovered I have suddenly developed a hernia on left side—could see its bulge there. Guess my wasted belly muscles have simply given way! What a rotten break at my age!

It now appears that there are 51 officers and 24 enlisted men coming, and that is why they are crowding us to make room. Americans, British, Dutch, Australians, etc. Gawd help us then, for how they are going to cook, with their present kettles, for that many more people, is beyond us! They can install a cauldron for our pigs, but although there is plenty of room in the kitchen, they evidently won't install more cauldrons there.

No herd guard today and tonight we had a Red Letter Meal. Not only was there a suspicion of tripe in the soup, but the beans were cooked separately with a nice sauce of soy and carrots and sugar, but also the soup was hot with *curry!* To cap it, I had 1 garlic leaf cut fine into my rice. Sorry to come to the end of it and as usual, felt all ready to start eating a *regular* meal.

Today they cleaned out our overflowing dust bin and also the benjo.

Friday—Kinyo-bi, 29 Jan 1943

Last night was breezeless and our room was very stuffy—because of the demands of our "draft dodgers"—so I got a headache. But it cooled off today; overcast. Post was visited by another domei delegation of about 15 newsmen and photographers. Among others, they interviewed Gen. Percival and asked him about our food. Rumor has it that he answered them without mincing words. The British have lots more guts in that way than do our own (alleged) "leaders."

Saw our doctor about my hernia. He says it's an incipient hernia, all right, and says "come back in 10 days and we'll see if it's any worse"! A great help *he* is! He also says he cannot get me a truss, but kindly suggests that I try to get permanent pressure on the break!

We are dishing out our food in the conference room since our squad expanded but today we had to serve the soup in our room and rice in Crews, because domei took chow room for their lunch—which I wish we had for ourselves. This P.M. I pruned my radishes and made a salad—but 2 or 3 others did the same, so mine was superfluous.

Saturday—Doyo-bi, 30 Jan 1943

Gang went out to work this morning, opening up an extension of the farm. Herd guard in P.M. We continue getting a modicum of tripe in evening (more than usual tonight) and a trace of heart and liver either in morning or at noon. Fair weather continues, much to our delight. The Domei gang still here and Percival treats 'em rough: stuck out his tongue when photographed and refused to give interview "because you misquoted me so badly last time." A whale of a new list of taxes goes into effect for Japs: Sake 100%; sugar 70%; geishas 200%, etc.

Sunday—Nichio-bi, 31 Jan 1943

Overcast all day but not cold. Another "reign of terror" started last night, with sentries getting very hostile, and barking at us all day. Bath at 3:15–3:45 for our 30 men, so I deadbeated 3:00 P.M. herd guard. Have washed some of the dirt out of my cotton "sweater" Domei gang still here. Gosh but Aldrich does love to talk! Autocrat. He even blate on symphonies. Our phonograph concerts continue nightly but we contribute no more for records. The Jap government has proscribed all American swing records, specially in the Philippines.

Monday—Getsuya-bi, 1 Feb 1943

Yes, the heat is sure turned onto us. Even BP, when he came in from the A.M. work session, looked sour as hell. I dug up pits for 7 tomato plants, and goat manured 4 of them. We have 6 "cripples" in our room, so it is still crowded at the table even when the others are working. Beautiful sunny day, so I got my open-air bath (and laundry). Aldrich frantically collects recipes for eats and many in our room copy them. Made a good job of cutting the top off a Sake bottle this P.M. 75 new arrivals tonight: 24 enlisted and 51 officers (mostly Dutch).

Tuesday—Kayo-bi, 2 Feb 1943

Beautiful day. New arrivals had baggage overhaul this A.M. Mostly from Batavia, and some have been en route as long as a month or more! They will strain our cooking resources. Camp went into mourning tonight when we received the *last* of the "offal" issue, as tripe in our soup. Gosh how we wish the "meat" issue would continue!

The newcomers brought us news (?) which has our wishful thinkers all excited viz: (1) Germans have been forced out of Africa. (2) U.S. now holds *all* of Solomons and New Guinea. (3) In Caucasus, Russians are pinching out 500,000 Germans and are going great guns on other fronts to the north. (4) That the newspaper accounts which we get have a mess of tripe.[4] Only 1 American arrived: one Col. Searle, field artillery. No work.

Wednesday—Suiyo-bi, 3 Feb 1943

Started raining hard last night and continued drizzling and raining all day. No work and hence skimpy rations again. And the heat is still on, with sentries yelling about; Gen. Vachon was among those who were slapped this morning. But none of us cried when Pvt. Smith, our grafting tailor (?) got bopped well at reveille. 4 kids born in last 24 hours and, unluckily, 3 of them are nannies hence they bring no meat to our pot. Not much meat on 'em anyway as they are a small breed. Can't see their justification, as LP won't let us milk them.

Thursday—Moku-bi, 4 Feb 1943

Rain all day. This "rainy season" is sure starting in with a bang—It helps our gardens, which have been drying up so much that the Japs have been making the enlisted men carry buckets of water to our "seed bed" garden. All the boys put in a lot of "housework" these last 3 rainy days. Since they are non-work days, our rations are correspondingly skimpy.

Friday and Saturday—

Nothing Special.

Sunday—Nichio-bi, 7 Feb 1943

Still rainy and cold and Aldridge still talking! This seems to be the coldest day that we've had, so far; There are 2 thermometers in camp and their respective owners swear by them—but they do not register alike. Today, the temperature is said to have come down to 49° F which, added to the drizzle, made it seem very cold. Had 101½ beans in my soup tonight, which is about my record. Balsam claimed only 58. Gen. Wainwright was told yesterday that there is mail for us in Jap HQ, including a letter for him—but they have refused to give us said mail! More hazing!

Monday—Getsuyo-bi, 8 Feb 1943

Another cold, dark, disagreeable day. Did my herd guard 3:00–4:00 by aid of Amis' raincoat. Aldridge still talking! He sure has all the answers! Spent most of the day copying recipes on my index cards, though I expect that Landon fortified behind her Fanny Farmer's Cookbook, will *justifiably* laugh me to scorn. But I am trying to get recipes which are not in the Cookbooks. Our 960 bottles of

"Wakamoto" (Vitamin B1) arrived this P.M. and, as usual, the Japs took all the premium coupons out. I got 2 bottles. No work for anybody today.

Tuesday—Kayo-bi, 9 Feb 1943
Overcast but not too cold. Everybody worked A.M. and P.M. Granulated sugar delivered today praise Gawd! but I had 8 cubes left. Brezina and I on herd guard 4:00–5:00 P.M. Corkhill balked on Boatwright in bringing hot water at 4:00 P.M. Generals get granulated sugar and are kicking for brown sugar such as everybody else is getting. 500 grams per person for the whole month! Our whole PX system is now out! Hereafter, we get no cash, but are to get credit of 40 yen a month, out of which we must buy everything except watch and shoe repair and clothing (if any). Nips will do all the buying (giving them additional openings for graft) and deliver in bulk to our PX representatives.

Wednesday—Suiyo-bi, 10 Feb 1943
Rainy in A.M. so no work but they worked this P.M. Received our "cookies" which turned out to be a coupla ounces of sugared "poppy seeds," much more acceptable. Sgt. Cavanaugh, a most estimable major sergeant from Dept. G2 office, died this P.M. of same thing that killed Col. Barry at Tarlac: strep throat or Ludwig's angina. The Japs give our doctors no facilities for diagnosis—indeed, they have robbed our pitiful stock until we now haven't even any adhesive tape. Last night arose another rumor, that 21 German divisions had surrendered in the Caucasus, thereby exciting our wishful thinkers to heights of jubilance. Remade my bed today, to get the newspapers straightened out. We also got a hot bath and, as usual, Gen. Weaver[5] and Brougher, plus Atkinson lingered over into our period. Gawd! what wouldn't I give for a square meal—just one! Now I can encircle my arm above the biceps with my thumb and finger, lacking about ½ inch! Systematic and slow starvation is what the Nips are subjecting us to. A suitable epitaph for Sgt. Cavanaugh would be "Slowly murdered by the Japanese."

Thursday—Mokuyo-bi, 11 Feb 1943
Meat!
Rainy in A.M. so the celebration of this the biggest (?) of all Jap holidays. At 10:00 we gathered in the last squad room upstairs and held burial service for Sgt. Cavanaugh.[6] Crowded. Received one of the usual small potato cakes this P.M., about ⅓ the size of my fist. They are delicious, especially when still warm, at first received. I cut mine into thirds, one portion for 3 successive rice portions.

Tonight gave us the best supper I've had at Karenko: 60 grams (average) pork cooked in each man's rice, and 17 roosters in the total soup! It seemed perfectly wonderful to us. I had saved ½ of my morning and noon rice, mixed it with potato cake, and this addition helped toward a fair imitation of a normal meal. Copied gist of Lawrence's monograph on "Eating our way back to Health," because it is going to be a serious problem, when this starvation era stops, to avoid sickness in getting ourselves back into normal eating habits. They tell us of one batch of English prisoners who had been starved like us and, upon arriving at Mecca where they could get all the food they wanted, 93 of them died that night from excessive (?) eating of meat.

Friday—Kinyo-bi, 12 Feb 1943

Last night was fine and warm, though windy. Went to benjo only once at 3:30! And my ankles have gone down to normal thanks to the little meat I've been getting—but try to tell that to the Jap medical student who handles all medical matters for us! He says to take the old Kniepp cure—walk barefoot in dewey grass! Sun came out at 11:00 A.M. so I did my laundry and took a bath. Everybody worked in P.M. in spite of the wind. Bad news: No more beans! Meat! But to partially offset it, we got some meat in the soup tonight, and *may* continue for 5 suppers. With the curry, it at least gave a fine flavor to tonight's soup. BP has been so glum for the last 24 hours that everybody believed the Jap arms have suffered a reverse.

Saturday—Doyo-bi, 13 Feb 1943

Rained hard all night. This morning a bucket in the open, which was empty last night, was overflowing. Continued raining all day. Our tea arrived and I got a pound of Nittok black tea. The stuff I am using now is NG—skimpy chow both A.M. and noon, but I saved half of rice at each meal and ate it at supper—and was still hungry. No more "saving" like that: the difference at dinner is of no effect. Meat! Got "meat" in the soup again tonight, microscopic in amount. This stuff is gristle and other trimmings at the slaughter house that probably is unfit for canning or sale. But it is a Godsend to us. All of us infested our room most of the day and it was most congested. Turned warmer at night but my bed was already made up with 4 blankets, so let them stay.

Valentine's Day, Sunday—Nichio-bi, 14 Feb 1943

After being deprived of newspapers (the propaganda screeds) for about 2 weeks (last issue received was that of Jan 25th) today we got our Valentine in the 5th February *Times* which tells of the Germans losing the remnants of their 6th Army at Stalingrad—What rejoicing resulted here! The news of the Anglo-Turkish pact was also gratefully received. We doubt that the Japs will let us have some of the intervening papers, which we think may contain news not too favorable to the Japs.

After an overcast morning during which I did a herd guard and pinched a couple radishes, the sun came out and turned it into a beautiful summer day. Got a fine hot bath and sunned the blankets upon which I had spilt my canteen cup of water. Meat! Gristle in the soup again tonight (we hope for 2 days more of that!) and it was delicious! Nice and warm in evening. Tried to send one of the big local snail shells to Tokyo Museum for identification but was refused permission.

Everybody is frantically copying recipes these days. I've even had 2 enlisted men ask to borrow my "recipe book" (mine are on cards, not in a book). Col. Mallonee[7] with his batch of fine New Orleans recipes, pleased my taste even more than Sgts. Drew and Brown, the English chefs. We are all highly pleased with Sgt. Brown's running of our kitchen. Heard a cricket chirping tonight—the first one.

Monday—Getsuyo-bi, 15 Feb 1943

Dawn promised a wonderful day, but how we were fooled. It clouded over by 9:00 A.M. and by midafternoon was blowing a gale. Queer how today the days seem to have become appreciably longer: for the first time, the sun was shining on our mountains while we were still at bango—and we breakfasted with the sun streaming past our windows.

This afternoon our fingerprints were taken by a bunch of Japs and they were really expert! They put the ink on our fingers with a roller instead of rolling our fingers on an inked slab. I believe it is an improvement. Their form of record is identical with ours except that they omit the separate impression of the thumb.

Brawner and Bonham are now dishing out the soup and they are so slow that tonight, everything was stone cold by the time we got it. Meat! Luckily, there was "gristle" in the soup for there were practically no vegetables. This being a non-work day, the chow was light for all meals, dammit. Dutch got their heavy baggage today.

Tuesday—Kayo-bi, 16 Feb 1943

Wind dropped, early this morning; the gang worked this P.M. and didn't get back till 4:45! No herd guard for me today. Sun nice and warm in P.M. so I got a bath and laundered a bit. Spent the rest of P.M. copying Lessons 11 and 12 of Japanese—principally at hospital because Pierce had it wrong. Can't get my lost filling replaced until the new dentist comes! Tonight is probably our last night for meat and it wasn't much. Thought Bonham had skipped me.

Wednesday—Suiyo-bi, 17 Feb 1943

Beautiful day all day: workers turned out A.M. and P.M. Worked furiously at this and that: finished copying Lessons 11 and 12 Japanese; worked on floor plan of barracks. Washed pillowcases. One for the Book: Hereafter "non-workers will get reduced rice and adjustments will be made *within* squads"!! The bastid Jap issue sergeant refused to issue "workers" rice for noon but thanks to having Air

Commodore Modin on as OD he kicked to BP and he promised that tonight we get *both* this noon's and tonight's "workers" rice. Damn the difference!

It seems that little so and so LP and our squad chief held a round table love feast while out at work today. Braly naively told us about it tonight as though it boded better times yet, when analyzed "Boots'" words were self-contradictory and lying. Among other things, he said that: (1) "You've seen that the soldiers get more rice than you, but they are in training and so have to have it." (2) Other camps get more rice but they are "work" camps while this is not (and yet we were told that the primary reason for starting our farm was to get worker's rations for us). (3) That our rations are prescribed from above (from Tokyo, from Taihoku or from this Camp HQ?). (4) That the farm work is about over. (5) That it was fine to get together like this (it was the first time he had tolerated anything like it) and hoped it would lead to more friendly relations, etc. Changed our entrance door today!

Thursday—Getsuyo-bi, 18 Feb 1943
Beautiful day all day. Work A.M. and P.M. I had herd guard 3:00–4:00. Kept furiously busy all day. My feet are still badly swollen. Settlement with PX and deposited Y20 more and we must turn in every single sen in our possession. (Another thing LP said yesterday, when asked if we could buy food from "our own money"—he said "You have no money," "it belongs to the Japan government"! When asked if any of our formal protests had been forwarded he was noncommittal.

Spent much time today correcting my floor plan of barracks.

We are back on straight rations again: no beans nor meat in our evening "soup." but Sgt. Brown does wonders. I doubt if we get any more meat or potatocakes or fruit or anything else from now on. Looks like a hell of a future. The Japs won't let us buy anything but tobacco and now they have the nerve to say there is a shortage of the "Akerbons" cigarettes—the only kind we are allowed to buy!

And now it appears that LP "forgot" to forward our request for holiday rations for Washington's Birthday! And today Pat Callahan is running around giving everybody his alibi for his worthlessness in not following up such an important matter.

Friday—Kinyo-bi, 19 Feb 1943
Was running to the benjo all night long. This morning felt rotten so went to hospital. Had fever and Glatly sent me to bed. Nearly passed out in getting there. After snoozing felt some better and it was fine to get into bed and really rest. Campbell fainted in the benjo this P.M. and fell unconscious in the urinal trough. They put him into the hospital. I find it almost impossible to obey Glatly and

spend 100% of the time flat on my back in bed. I evidently have flu, and there seems to be lots of it in camp.

Saturday—Doyo-bi, 20 Feb 1943

Bleak, cold, windy day. The Jap medical student came around about 1:00 P.M. took my red card away and gave me half-red card: the SOB was mad because I was out of bed. In P.M. recd 25 pk Shirisago scags and 10 Darton little cigars, to reduce my PX balance. Rumor today is that Rostov and Karkov have been taken by Russia.[8] Wonderful if true! Our G2 boys say that the Japs are taking all our Formosa yen because they are going to take us to Japan and want to prevent us buying *anything,* especially food. I dread the idea of going to cold, starving Japan.

Today they gave us a printed postcard to be sent to our wives: "I am interned in *Taiwan*. My health is \ excellent, usual, poor. I am ill in hospital. I am working for pay. I (am, am not) working.\ Please see that *taxes, leans, sell apartment, your health* is taken care of. My love to you *and children*."

We also had to put in another slip, showing our names, numbers, age (62), height 5'11". Rank and Unit, nationality, distinguishing features, "P.C.S." [permanent change of station]. It now appears proved that the five long letters that we wrote to our wives, way back in November have never left here!

15 rabbits and 10 more pigs arrived today so we are hoping that the rumor of "Pork on March 1st" is true. My sugar is fading fast.

Sunday—Nichio-bi, 21 Feb 1943

Last night one of the Jap sentries at the benjo sure raised hell in his hitting officers—Cols. Selleck, Churchill, Dougherty, and another—for real or fancied laxity in saluting! Churchill was hit on the side of the head with the flat side of the fixed bayonet, then smashed on the hand at Churchill's side because the fingers were not stiffly extended and joined; this drew blood and today his face was disfigured and swollen. Dougherty ran foul of the *edge* of the bayonet and got cut. Brezina saw 1 of the British soldiers hit 3 times on the side of the head by this Jap's rifle. There was still another Britisher who got bopped. It was a husky big Jap who committed all these assaults. Col. Hoffman says he is going to report all this to BP.

Yet the Nipponese complain of U.S. "atrocities" and publish that we are well content. No temperature at 4:30 P.M. A lousy cold dismal dark day with nothing to recommend it.

Meat! Today I broke down and opened my last can of corned beef as a desperate remedy for threatened starvation. I can hardly walk without staggering and am weak as a cat. I put one tablespoon of the meat in my bowl of soup and another in my rice and in that way it should last about 6 meals. Need it that way on all 3 today. Last night I slept well until 12:30 and then lay awake until reveille, planning on things I shall do when I see Landon again—and things I want to bring her as presents—including pearls.

Georgie da Wash's Birthday, Monday—Getsuyo-bi, 22 Feb 1943

A swell day but I felt rotten. Slept till 2:30 A.M. and then was awake the rest of the night. Amused myself planning looting trips and procedure, should the occasion present itself in Japan. Used corned beef for breakfast. Sunned myself as well as I could and enjoyed it. For the benefit of the newly arrived Dutch—we had another alleged fire drill this morning and it has the same laughable performance as before. As I was toiling out to attend at 10:00 A.M. the Jap lieutenant whose elbow was shattered in Bataan swung his sword scabbard across my rump—not hard, but this being the first time one of them has touched me, the insult was painful. Feeling rottener and rottener as the day wore on, I borrowed Derham's colored pencils and colored the drawing of my 4″ snail shell as an inclosure to my request for its identification. Then at 2:15 I went to the Hospital and Glatly found I had fever, so gave me some acetamilid or sumpin and sent me to bed and I went willingly enough. Last night I had bad pains in my lungs, but now they were in my belly—as though the corned beef were disagreeing with me.

We had asked for special chow for today but almost nothing came of it: No meat but we heard about lots of extra rice and with camote and sugar in it. They even got so excited they called for extra bucket to tote it in, and extra bowl to serve it in—both of which were found to be unnecessary.

Tuesday—Kayo-bi, 23 Feb 1943

To hospital.

Another done day—no work in A.M. but yes in P.M. I am now sicker than hell. My left foot and ankle are almost bursting through the skin, which, in turn, is so painful to touch, as to be useless. My right torso, lungs and ribs are so painful as to immobilize me. I can't move without incurring devastating and wide flung pains. The medicine that Glatly now gives me is sure the knock-out drops. I can't keep awake! Slept and dozed almost continuously all day and evening. And today they gave me back my all red card. It's a hard job to stare at ceiling from 1:00 to 6:30 A.M. They took me to hospital at 1:30 P.M. and put me in bed and kept me there. In addition to KO drops am taking lots of sulphothyasn, many times a day. [Handwriting deteriorates; many scratchouts.]

Wednesday—Suiyo-bi, 24 Feb 1943

Cold and dreary. The KO drops were so strong I hardly moved all day, but dozed continuously. *Thursday* was the same. We get at least 50% more rice in the hospital and I was foundered, the first meal—but none may be sent to our friends outside the hospital. My bronchitis is bad but pleurisy seems slowly moving in—

Thursday—Getsuyo-bi, 25 Feb 1943
No entry.

Friday—Mokoyo-bi, 26 Feb 1943
Today big news: 60% more vegetables and they *were* in night's soup. Pitched our individ mosquito bars! Gawsh but it's dreary! Too weak to lift the blankets or turn over or sit up in bed. Too weak to cough, yet the compelling urge to cough always tickling and bronchi—and the pleurisy pangs in the ribs. And hour after hour, lying in the wakeful dark awaiting the never-coming dawn!

Saturday—Doyo-bi, 27 Feb 1943
Sunny in A.M. for change. Guess I am a bit better as to pleurisy but getting real beri-beri swelling. Even my hands look like bags of suet. But the worst is my appalling weakness. I can't heave my legs into bed, nor hardly turn over—and every position is painful. Have practically cut out smoking—it's easy when painful results are so prompt.

Sunday—Nichio-bi, 28 Feb 1943
Milk.
Fine day all day so the boys were lucky in having a nice rest day. But the big news for me was the small bottle of *milk* that they gave me toward evening. I had been unable to cram down my rice—even in curry soup so Glatly says "You must eat—and adding this milk made all the difference in the world—not only in the taste but also in the old morale.

Monday—Getsuyo-bi, 1 Mar 1943
Got milk *and* an egg this morning! What a treat! But I squandered it all, at once. My hands and feet now terribly swollen—Japs won't give diuretic. Spent feverish night with much coughing. I feel so filled with phlegm and water that I have no leeway between suffocation if I stop panting to cough a bit. The night is sure a nightmare! It creeps along.[9]

Postscript
For the next fifteen days Bunker struggled on fighting for life. Starvation and infection took their toll. He became too weak to write in his diary any longer. He could no longer hold solid food in his stomach. The pain and infection spread, and his once powerful body began to swell from beri-beri.

General Wainwright was with Bunker when he died. It is only fitting to describe Colonel Bunker's last hours in Wainwright's words: "I sat with him for a part of the last two hours of his life. He had moist beri-beri. His legs, feet, arms, and hand had swollen incredibly from the water with which he had tried to assuage his hunger. He did not know me. Colonel Bunker died and was cremated in the rags in which he had carefully sewn a bit of the American flag he had had to pull down in Corregidor."
16 May 1943*

*There is a conflict as to the exact date Colonel Bunker died. His obituary states, 7 September 1943, but this conflicts with Wainwright's 16 May 1943.

SIGAC-2

UEP-U 728
23 March 1948.

FROM	;	Back
TO	;	Guest for Akin
SVC NR	;	2421 J

PLEASE PASS FOLLOWING MESSAGE TO COLONEL COCHEU FROM GENERAL MACARTHUR. "FROM TOKYO I JOIN MY CLASSMATES IN REVERENT TRIBUTE AS THE MORTAL REMAINS OF OUR GALLANT COMRADE-IN-ARMS PAUL BUNKER ARE COMMITTED TO THEIR FINAL RESTING PLACE ON THE BANKS OF THE BEAUTIFUL HUDSON WHICH HE LOVED SO WELL. IT WAS THERE ON THE GRIDIRON AS A CADET THAT HE FIRST DISPLAYED THAT INDOMITABLE SPIRIT AND INVINCIBLE FIGHTING HEART WHICH NEVER FAILED HIM, REGARD-LESS OF THE TIDE OF BATTLE, AS HE FOUGHT THROUGH OUR PAST TWO WARS. HIS SERVICE WAS CHARACTERIZED BY THE HIGHEST DEVOTION TO THE TRADITION OF OUR ALMA MATER—DUTY, HONOR, COUNTRY. HE KEPT THE SOLDIERS FAITH.

SIGNED MACARTHUR*

*At the time of this publication, Colonel Bunker had just been nominated to the Football Hall of Fame.

Notes

1. Here Bunker listed all his lost property with its estimated worth.
2. Wainwright, 124. Maj. Robert Brown had been General Wainwright's aide. As was the custom of the Japanese, they put a subordinate in charge of superiors in order to cause embarrassment and humiliation.
3. Morton, *Philippines,* 62, 170, 225, 385. Col. Ray M. O'Day had been the 21st Division PA chief of staff and had surrendered on Bataan. Belote and Belote, 285. He had also been a survivor of the "Death March" and was fortunate to live through the imprisonment and be repatriated.
4. Dupuy, *Chronology,* 40, 41. The United States had just about driven the Japanese from Guadalcanal, but it wouldn't be until 9 February that it was completely secured. The Russians had surrounded and accepted the surrender of German General Paulus and the remnants of his Sixth Army. But the Germans had not yet been forced out of North Africa. In fact, Rommel had just defeated the Americans at the Kasserine Pass.
5. *Register,* 321. Brig. Gen. James Roy Newman Weaver had commanded the tank group for the defense of Luzon and Bataan. He had participated in the fierce fighting of the "Battle of the Points." He lived through the war and retired in 1948.
6. Wainwright, 204. Master Sgt. James Cavanaugh had been in headquarters company of II Corps. He died of starvation and a strep throat infection.
7. Morton, *Philippines,* 26. Col. Richard C. Mallonee had been the senior instructor of the 21st Field Artillery (PA). He, too, kept a diary in two volumes. This is on hand in the Office of the Chief of Military History. Falk, 32–33. He, too, had been on the "Death March."
8. Dupuy, *Chronology,* 40. The Russians took Rostov and Kharkov on 14 and 16 February, respectively.
9. The entry on 1 March 1943 was Colonel Bunker's last entry. The remainder of the diary consists of an appendix containing Bunker's compilation of his lost belongings.

Bibliography

Babcock, Lt. Col. C. Stanton. "Philippine Campaign" (Parts I and II). *Cavalry Journal,* March–April, May–June 1943.

Baldwin, Hanson W. "The Fourth Marines at Corregidor" (Parts I, II, III, IV). *Marine Corps Gazette* (November 1946–February 1947).

———. *Great Mistakes of the War.* New York: Harper, 1950.

———. *Battles Lost and Won.* New York: Harper and Row, 1966.

Bank, Maj. Bert. *Back from the Living Dead.* Tuscaloosa, Alabama: Privately printed, 1945.

Belote, James H., and William M. Belote. *Corregidor: The Saga of a Fortress.* New York: Harper and Row, 1967.

Braly, Col. William C. "Corregidor—a Name, a Symbol, a Tradition." *Coast Artillery Journal* 90, no. 4 (July–August 1947).

———. *The Hard Way Home.* Washington: Infantry Journal Press, 1947.

Brereton, Gen. L. H. *The Brereton Diaries.* New York: Morrow, 1946.

Case, Col. Homer. "War Damage to Corregidor." *Coast Artillery Journal* 90, no. 3 (May–June 1947).

Chandler, Lt. Col. William E. "The 26th Cavalry (PS) Battles to Glory." *Armored Cavalry Journal* (March–August 1947).

Chunn, Maj. Calvin Ellsworth, ed. *Of Rice and Men.* Los Angeles: Veterans Publishing Co., 1946.

Conn, Stetson. "Changing Concepts of National Defense in the United States, 1937–1947." *Military Affairs* (Spring 1964).

Cordero, Col. V. N. *My Experiences During the War with Japan.* Nuremberg, Germany: Privately printed, no date.

Craven, W. F., and J. L. Cate, eds. *The Army Air Forces in World War II,* Vol. 1, *Plans and Early Operations, January 1939 to August 1942.* Chicago: University of Chicago Press, 1948.

Dettbarn, Ens. John L. "Gold Ballast: War Patrol of USS *Trout.*" *United States Naval Institute Proceedings* (January 1960).

Dupuy, R. Ernest. *Men of West Point, The First 150 Years of the United States Military Academy.* New York: William Sloane, 1951.

Dupuy, Col. Trevor Nevitt. *Chronological Military History of World War II.* New York: Franklin Watts, 1965.

Dyess, Lt. Col. William E. *The Dyess Story.* New York: G. P. Putnam's Sons, 1944.

Falk, Stanley L. *Bataan: The March of Death.* New York: Norton, 1962.

Futrell, Robert F. "Air Hostilities in the Philippines 8 December, 1941." *Air University Review* (January–February, 1965).

Greenfield, Kent Roberts, ed. *Command Decisions.* New York: Harcourt Brace, 1959.

————. *American Strategy in World War II: A Reconsideration.* Baltimore: Johns Hopkins Press, 1963.

Harkins, Philip. *Blackburn's Headhunters.* New York: Norton, 1955.

Hersey, John. *Men on Bataan.* New York: Knopf, 1942.

Hough, Lt. Col. Frank O., Maj. V. E. Ludwig, and Henry I. Shaw, Jr. *Pearl Harbor to Guadalcanal, History of U.S. Marine Corps Operations in World War II, Vol. 1.* Historical Branch, G-3 Division, Headquarters, U.S. Marine Corps 1958.

Ind, Lt. Col. Allison. *Bataan: The Judgement Seat.* New York: Macmillan, 1944.

Irwin, Col. C. L. "Corregidor in Action." *Coast Artillery Journal* (January–February 1943).

Japanese Land Operations, December 8, 1941, to June 8, 1942 (Campaign Study no. 3). Military Intelligence Service, War Department, Washington, D.C., 1942.

Johnson, Lt. Col. Harold K. "Defense Along the Abucay Line." *Military Review* (February 1949).

Karig, Cmdr. Walter, and Lt. Welbourn Kelley. *Battle Report: Pearl Harbor to Coral Sea.* New York: Farrar and Rinehart, 1944.

Keene, Col. James W. *Some Observations on Morale and Motivation Among Prisoners of War Made from Within.* Thesis for psychology written at George Washington University on 9 May 1963.

Kingman, Brig. Gen. John J. "The Genesis of Fort Drum." *Coast Artillery Journal* (July–August 1945).

Levering, Robert W. *Horror Trek.* Dayton, Ohio: Horstman Printing Company, 1948.

MacArthur, Gen. Douglas. *Reminiscences.* New York: McGraw-Hill, 1964.

McCoy, Cmdr. Melvyn H., and Lt. Col. S. M. Mellnik. *Ten Men Escape from Tojo.* New York: Farrar and Rinehart, 1944.

McGee, Brig. Gen. John Hugh. *Rice and Salt.* San Antonio, Texas: Naylor Company, 1962.

Mellnik, Col. Stephen M. "How the Japs Took Corregidor." *Coast Artillery Journal* (March–April 1945).

————. "The Life and Death of the 200th Coast Artillery." *Coast Artillery Journal* (March–April 1947).

Metcalf, Col. Clyde H., ed. *The Marine Corps Reader.* New York: Putnam, 1944.

Miller, Col. E. B. *Bataan Uncensored.* Long Prairie, Minnesota: Hart Publications, 1949.

Morison, Samuel Eliot. *History of United States Naval Operations in World War II,* Vol. 3, *The Rising Sun in the Pacific.* Boston: Little Brown, 1948.

Morton, Louis. "American and Allied Strategy in the Far East." *Military Review* (December 1949).

————. *The Fall of the Philippines (U.S. Army in World War II)*. Washington, D.C.: Office of the Chief of Military History, Department of the Army, 1953.

————. *Command Decisions*. New York: Harcourt Brace and Company, 1959.

————. *Strategy and Command: The First Two Years of the War in the Pacific*. Subseries of *The U.S. Army in World War II*, ed. K. R. Greenfield (Washington, D.C.: U.S. Government Printing Office, 1962).

————. *The War in the Pacific (U.S. Army in World War II)*. Washington, D.C.: Office of the Chief of Military History, Department of the Army, 1966.

Naval Analysis Division. *U.S. Strategic Bombing Survey (Pacific), Interrogations of Japanese Officials*, Vols. 1 and 2. Washington, D.C.: U.S. Government Printing Office, 1946.

Palmer, Lt. Col. Bruce. "Covering the Withdrawal into Bataan," *Infantry School Quarterly* (July 1950).

Parker Lt. Cmdr. T. C. "The Epic of Corregidor–Batan," *U.S. Naval Institute Proceedings* 69, no. 1 (January 1943).

Potter, John Deane. *The Life and Death of a Japanese General*. New York: New American Library of World Literature, 1962.

Register of Graduates and Former Cadets, 1802–1964. Thayer Memorial Edition, West Point. West Point Alumni Foundation, 1964.

Register of Graduates and Former Cadets, 1964 and 1992. Thayer Memorial Edition, West Point. West Point Alumni Foundation, 1964.

Reports of General MacArthur: The Campaigns of MacArthur in the Pacific, vol. 1. Prepared by his General Staff. Washington, D.C.: U.S. Government Printing Office, 1966.

Romulo, Carlos P. *I Saw the Fall of the Philippines*. Garden City: Doubleday, Dolan and Co., 1942.

Roscoe, Theodore. *United States Submarine Operations in World War II*. Annapolis: U.S. Naval Institute, 1949.

Schultz, Duane. *Hero of Bataan: The Story of General Jonathan M. Wainwright*. New York: St. Martin's Press.

Sherman, Adm. Frederick C. *Combat Command*. New York: Dutton, 1950.

Stimson, Henry L., and McGeorge Bundy. *On Active Service*. New York: Harper, 1948.

Stolley, Fred. "You Only Die Twice." *Leatherneck* (October 1961).

Toland, John. *But Not in Shame*. New York: Random House, 1961.

United States Naval Chronology, World War II. Naval History Division, Office of the Chief of Naval Operations. Navy Department, Washington, D.C.: U.S. Government Printing Office, 1955.

Uno, Kazumaro. *Corregidor: The Isle of Delusion*. Shanghai: Press Bureau of the Imperial Japanese Army Headquarters in China, 1942.

U.S. War Department. *Handbook of Japanese Military Forces,* TM-E-30-F80. Washington, D.C.: U.S. Government Printing Office, September 1944.

Volckmann, Col. R. W. *We Remained.* New York: W. W. Norton, 1954.

Wainwright, Gen. Jonathan. *General Wainwright's Story,* ed. Robert Considine. New York: Doubleday, 1946.

Weinstein, Alfred M. *Barbed-Wire Surgeon.* New York: Macmillan, 1948.

Wheeler, Capt. John. "Rearguard in Luzon." *Cavalry Journal* (March–April 1943).

Wright, John M., Jr. *Captured on Corregidor: Diary of an American POW in World War II.* Jefferson, North Carolina: McFarland & Company, 1989.